THE RECORD OF A

FALLEN VAMPIRE

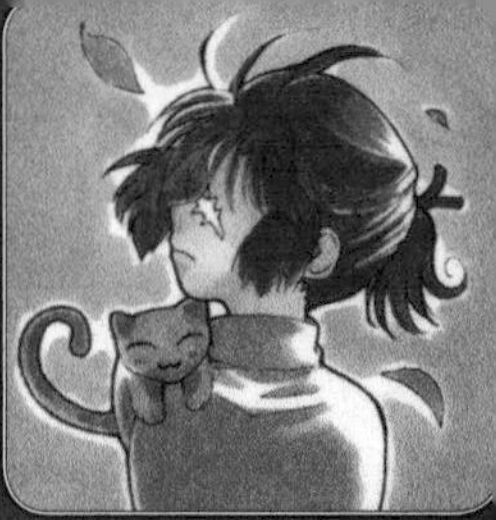

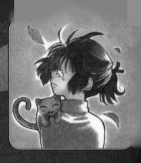

So much happened to while I was drawing second volume. There w things I regret but ca correct and things t brought me great joy. step by step, I'm getting cl to my ideal. *–Yuri Kimura*

Artist Yuri Kimura debuted two s stories in Japan's *Gangan Pow* after winning the Enix Manga Aw Shortly thereafter, she began *Record of a Fallen Vampire*, which serialized in Japan's *Monthly Sho Gangan* through March 2007.

Author Kyo Shirodaira is from N prefecture. In addition to *The Rec of a Fallen Vampire*, Shirodaira scripted the manga *Spiral: The Bo of Reasoning*. Shirodaira's n *Meitantei ni Hana wo* was nomin for the 8th Annual Ayukawa Tets Award in 1997.

THE RECORD OF A

FALLEN VAMPIRE

STORY BY: KYO SHIRODAIRA ART BY: YURI KIMURA

2

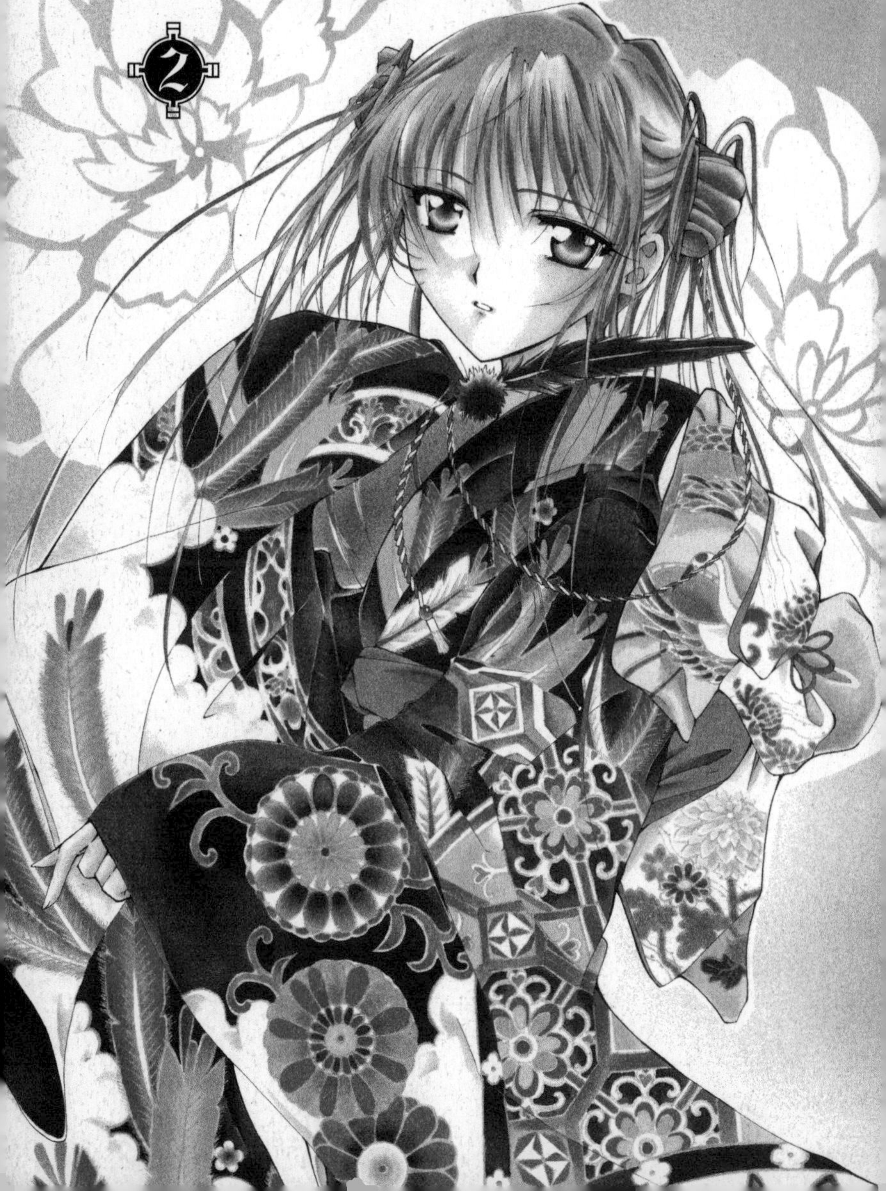

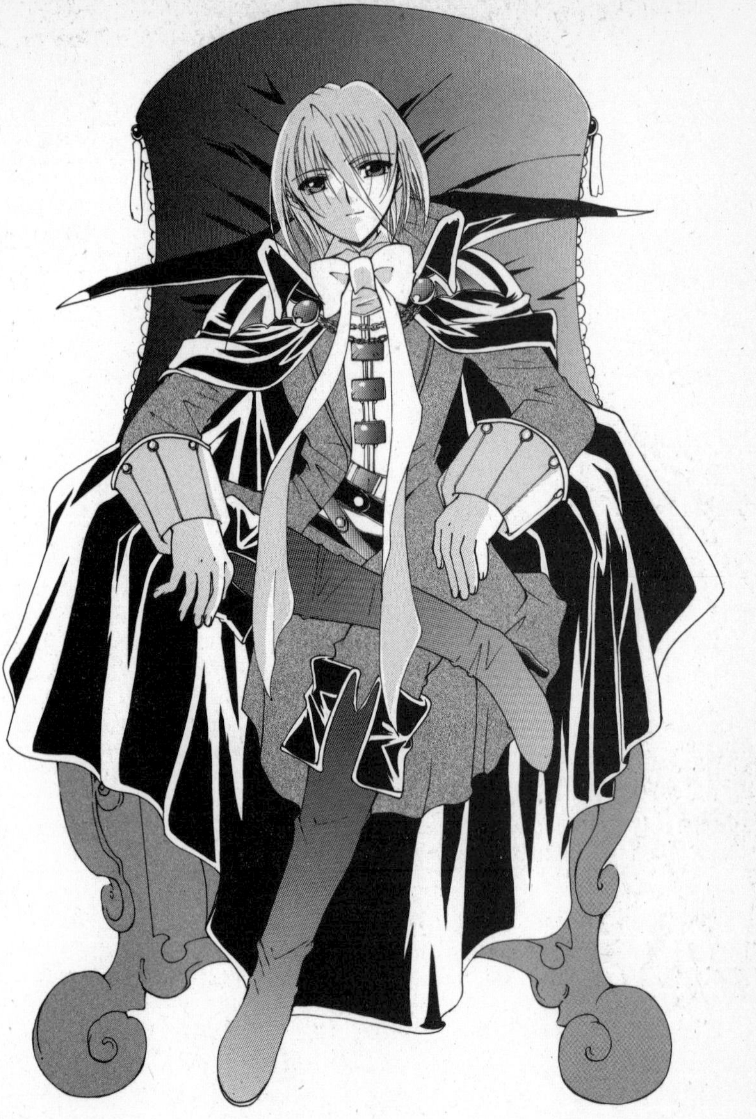

CONTENTS

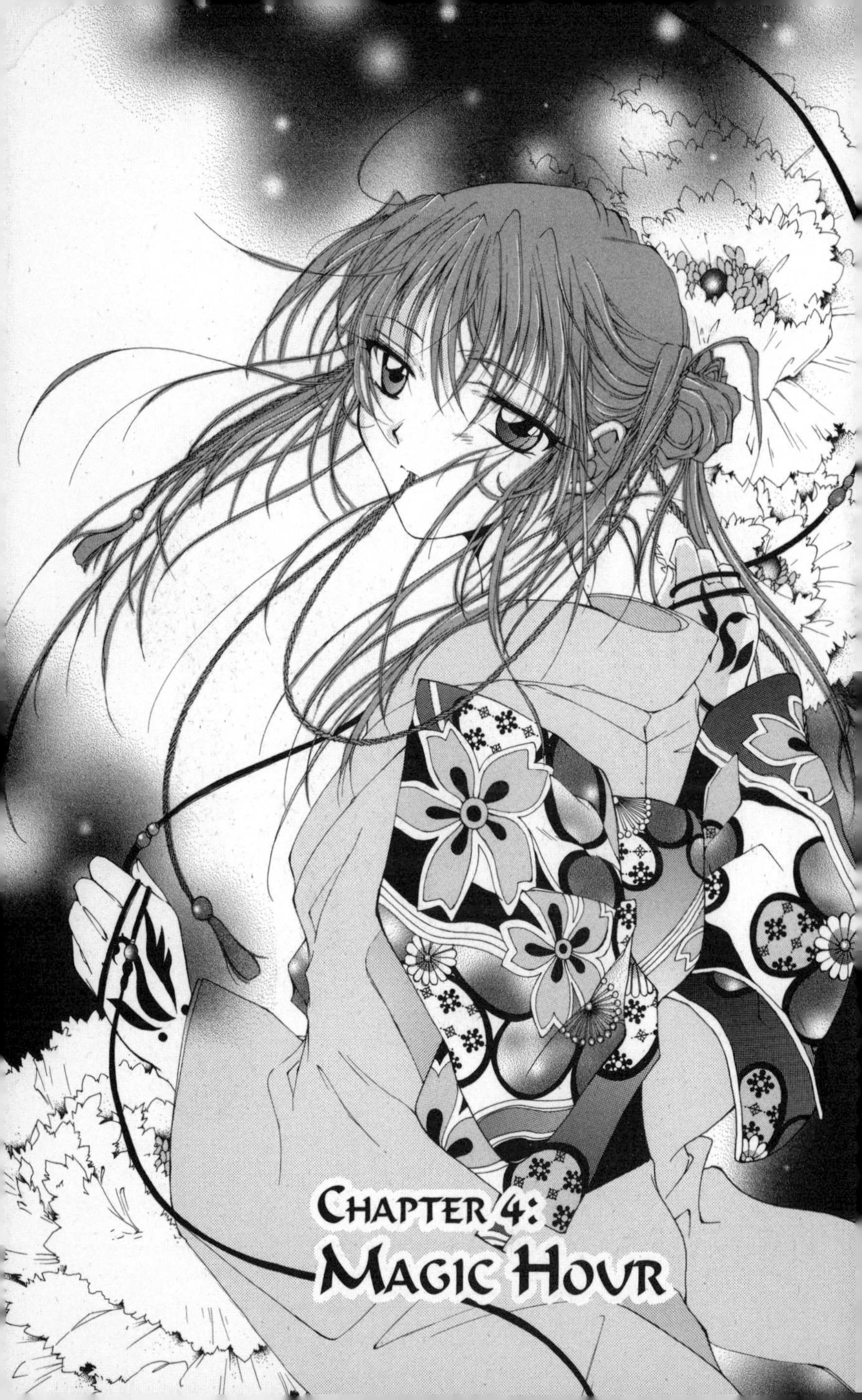
Chapter 4:
Magic Hour

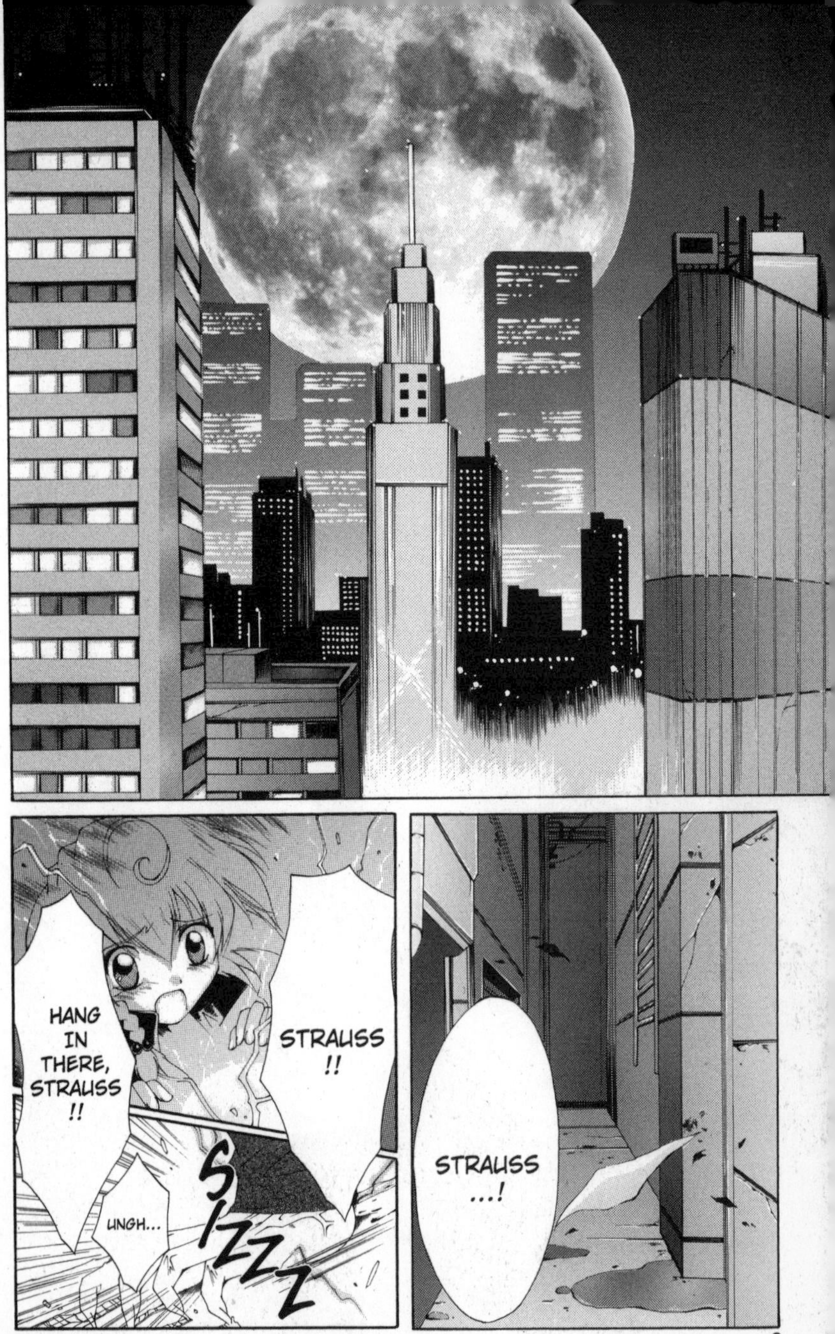
STRAUSS ...!
STRAUSS !!
HANG IN THERE, STRAUSS !!
SIZZZZ
UNGH...

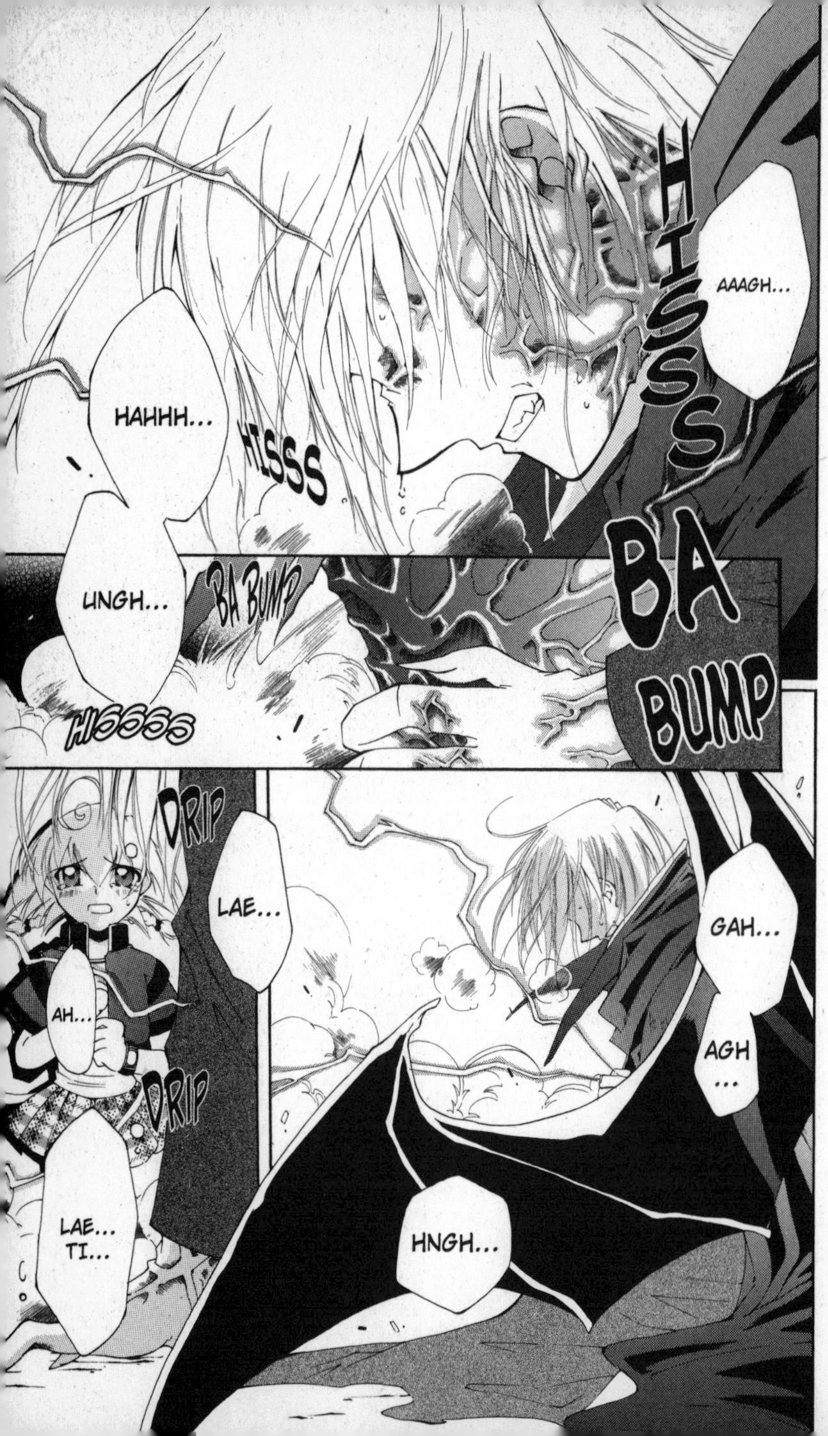
AAAGH...
HISSSS
HAHHH...
HISSS
BA BUMP
BA BUMP
UNGH...
HISSSS
GAH...
AGH...
HNGH...
DRIP
LAE...
AH...
DRIP
LAE... TI...

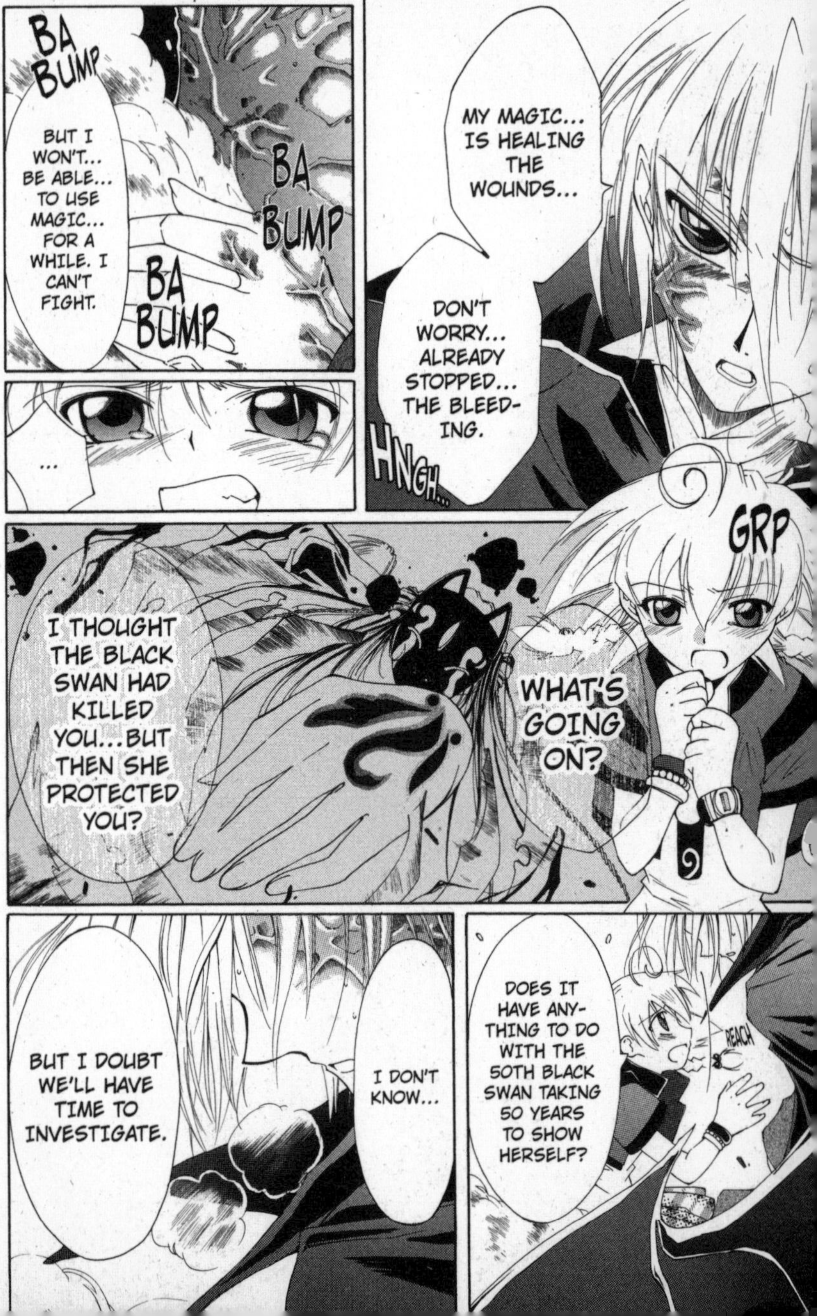

MY MAGIC... IS HEALING THE WOUNDS...
DON'T WORRY... ALREADY STOPPED... THE BLEED-ING.
HNGH...
BA BUMP
BA BUMP
BA BUMP
BUT I WON'T... BE ABLE... TO USE MAGIC... FOR A WHILE. I CAN'T FIGHT.
...
GRP
WHAT'S GOING ON?
I THOUGHT THE BLACK SWAN HAD KILLED YOU...BUT THEN SHE PROTECTED YOU?
DOES IT HAVE ANY-THING TO DO WITH THE 50TH BLACK SWAN TAKING 50 YEARS TO SHOW HERSELF?
REACH
I DON'T KNOW...
BUT I DOUBT WE'LL HAVE TIME TO INVESTIGATE.

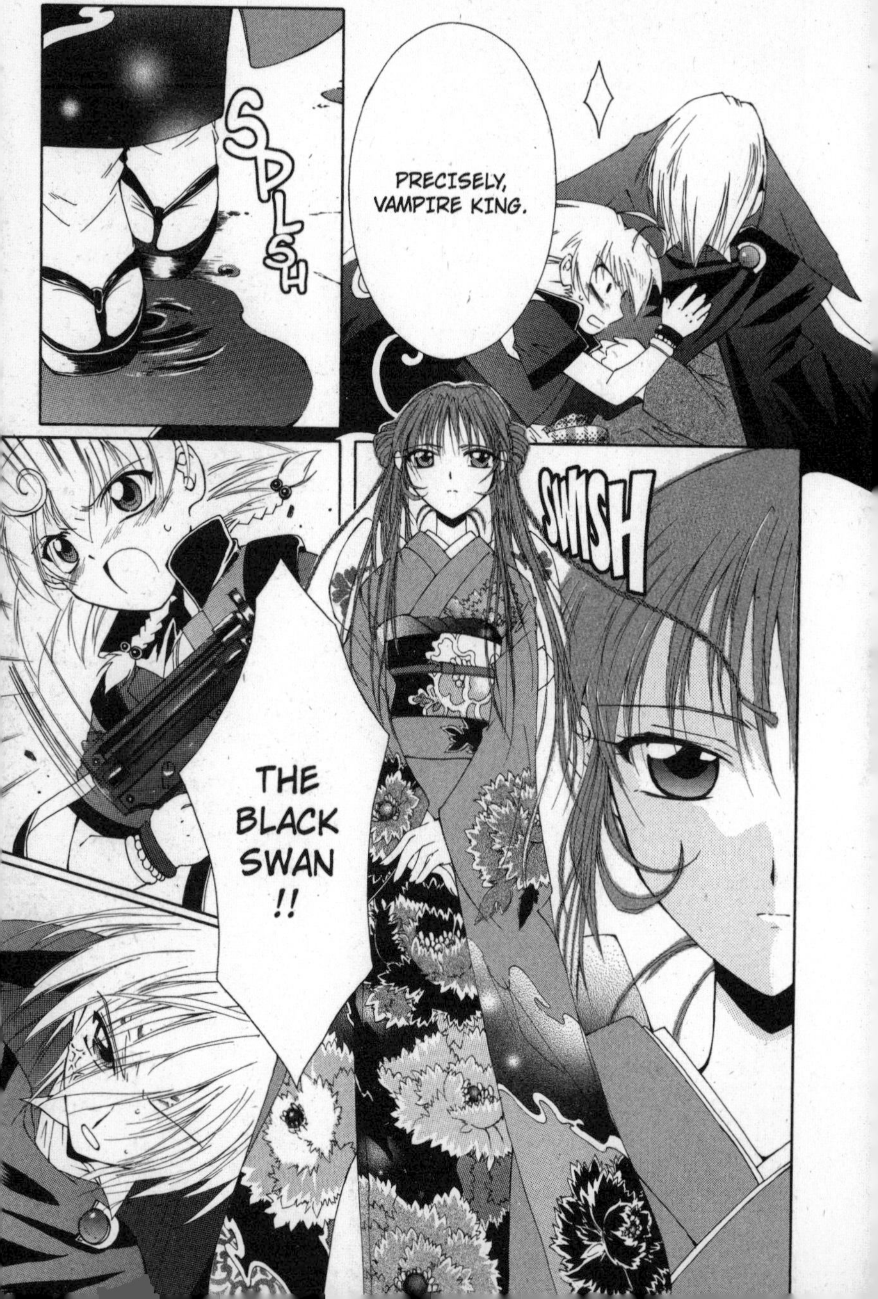
PRECISELY, VAMPIRE KING.
SPLSH
SWISH
THE BLACK SWAN !!

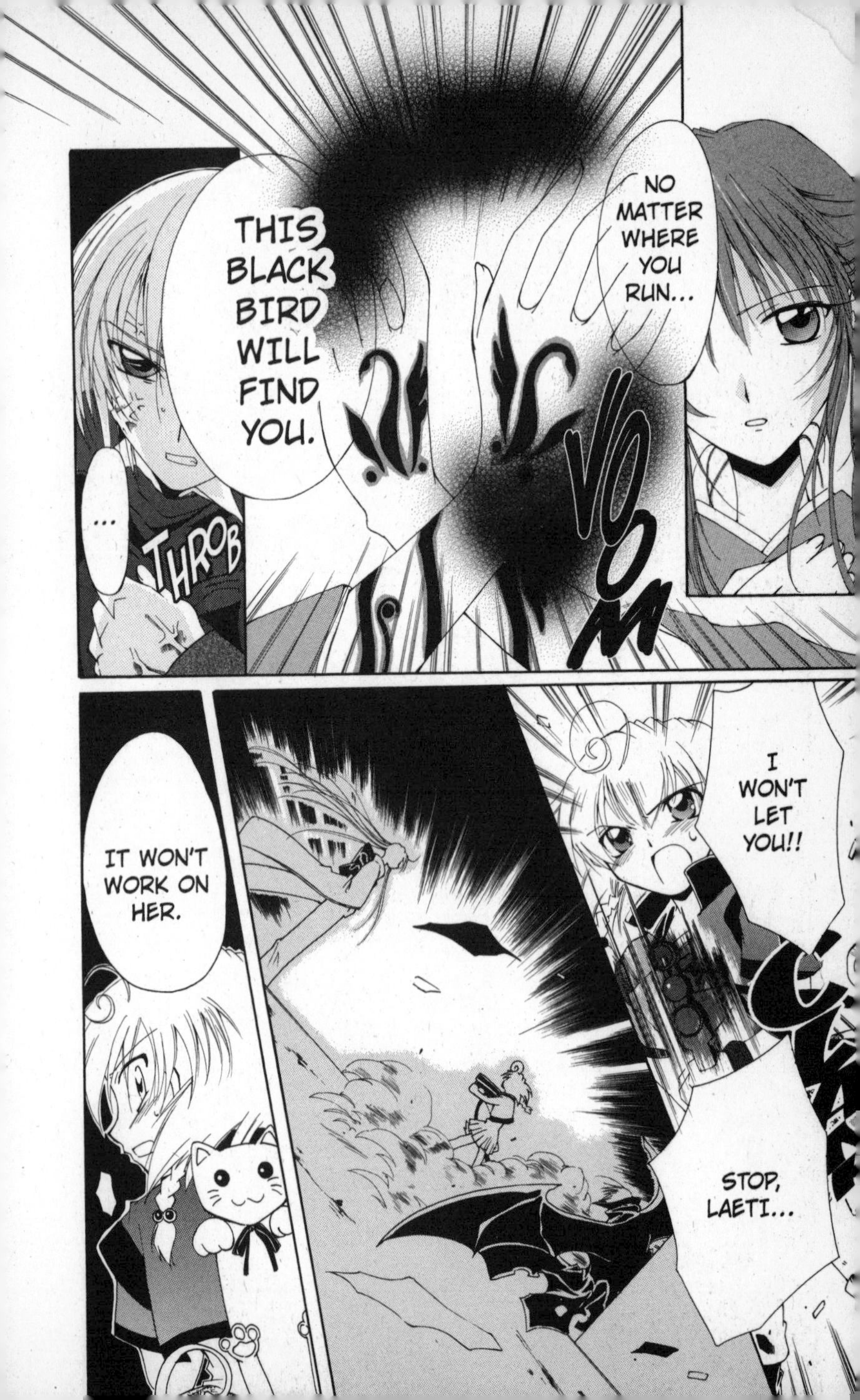
NO MATTER WHERE YOU RUN...
THIS BLACK BIRD WILL FIND YOU.
VOOM
THROB
...
I WON'T LET YOU!!
STOP, LAETI...
IT WON'T WORK ON HER.

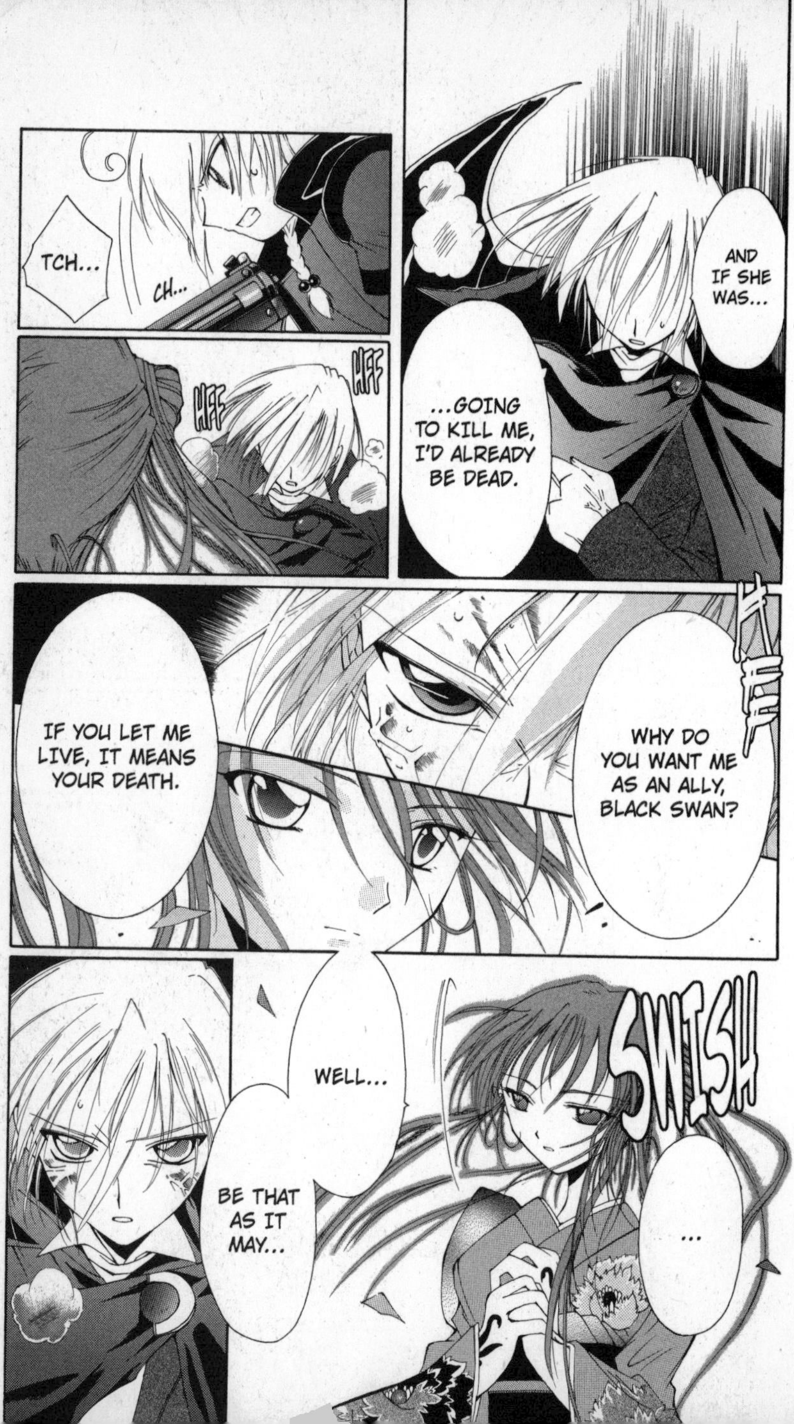
AND IF SHE WAS...
...GOING TO KILL ME, I'D ALREADY BE DEAD.
TCH...
CH...
HFF
HFF
WHY DO YOU WANT ME AS AN ALLY, BLACK SWAN?
IF YOU LET ME LIVE, IT MEANS YOUR DEATH.
SWISH
...
WELL...
BE THAT AS IT MAY...

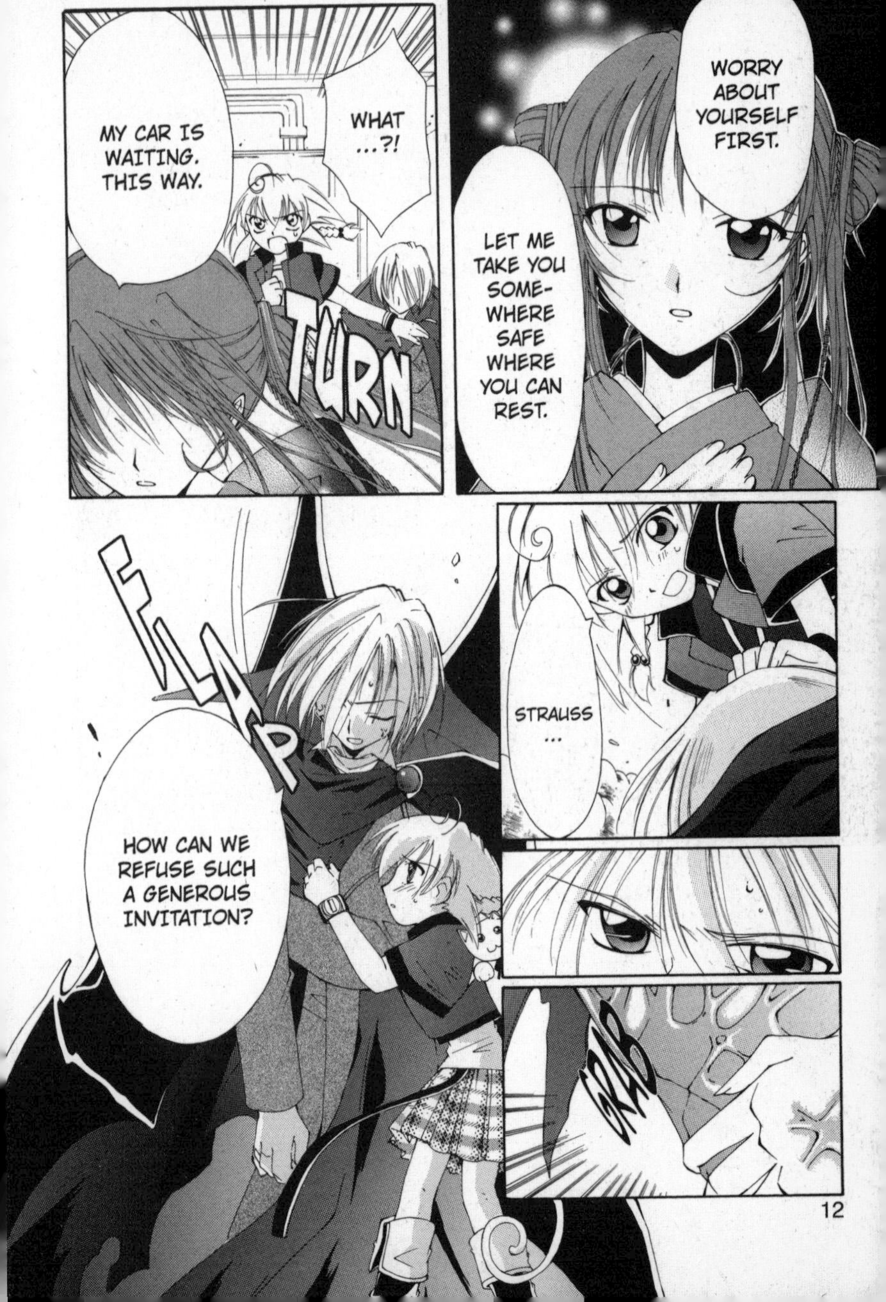
WORRY ABOUT YOURSELF FIRST.
LET ME TAKE YOU SOME-WHERE SAFE WHERE YOU CAN REST.
WHAT ...?!
MY CAR IS WAITING. THIS WAY.
TURN
STRAUSS ...
GRAB
FLAP
HOW CAN WE REFUSE SUCH A GENEROUS INVITATION?

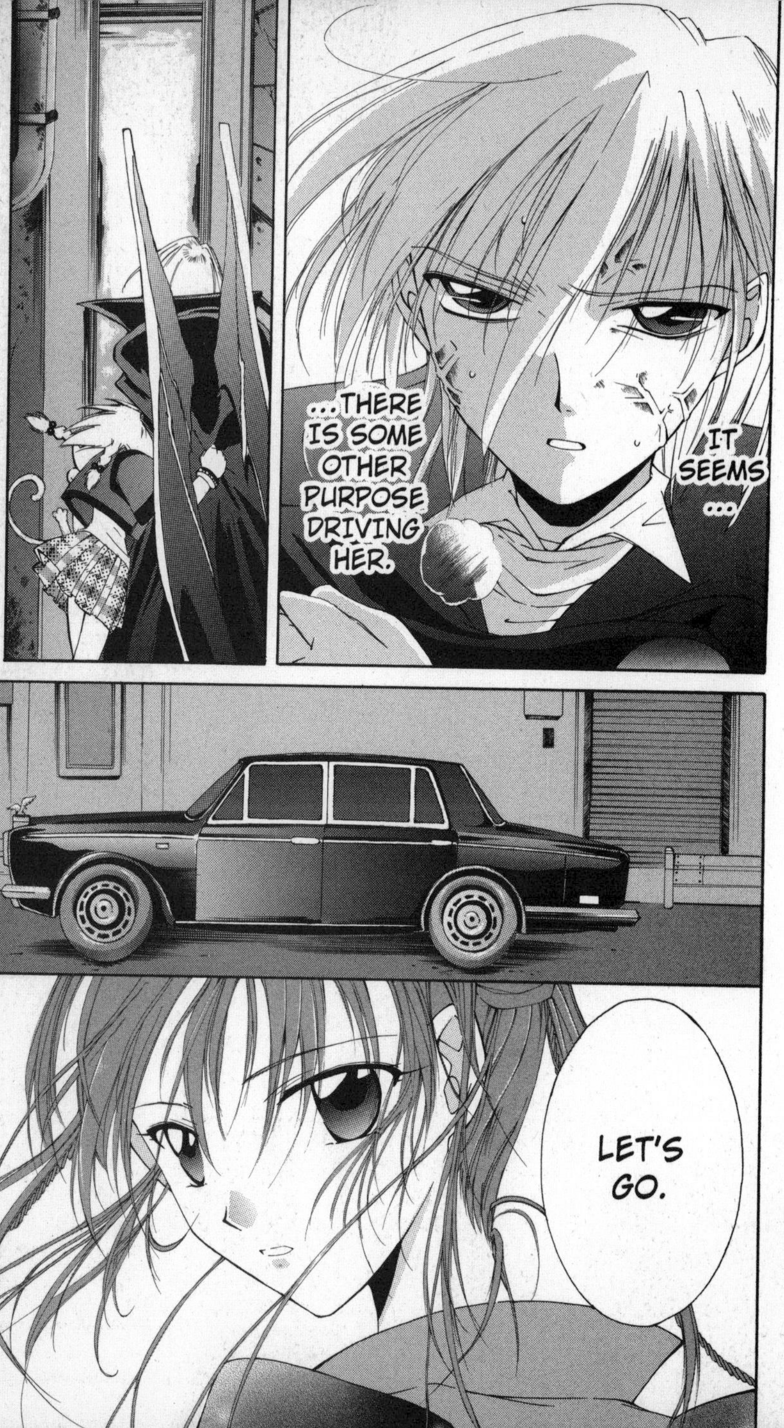
IT SEEMS...
...THERE IS SOME OTHER PURPOSE DRIVING HER.
LET'S GO.

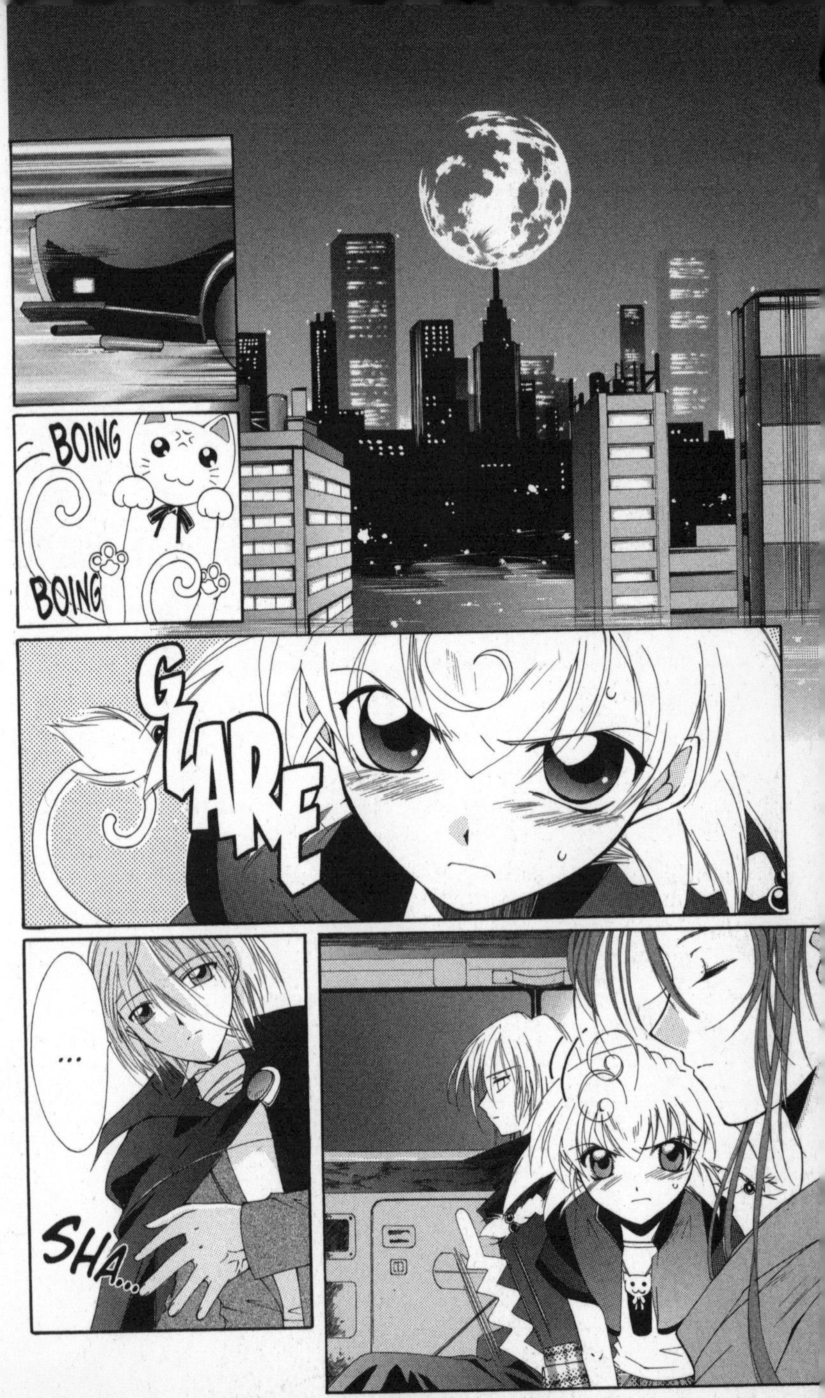
BOING
BOING
GLARE
...
SHA...

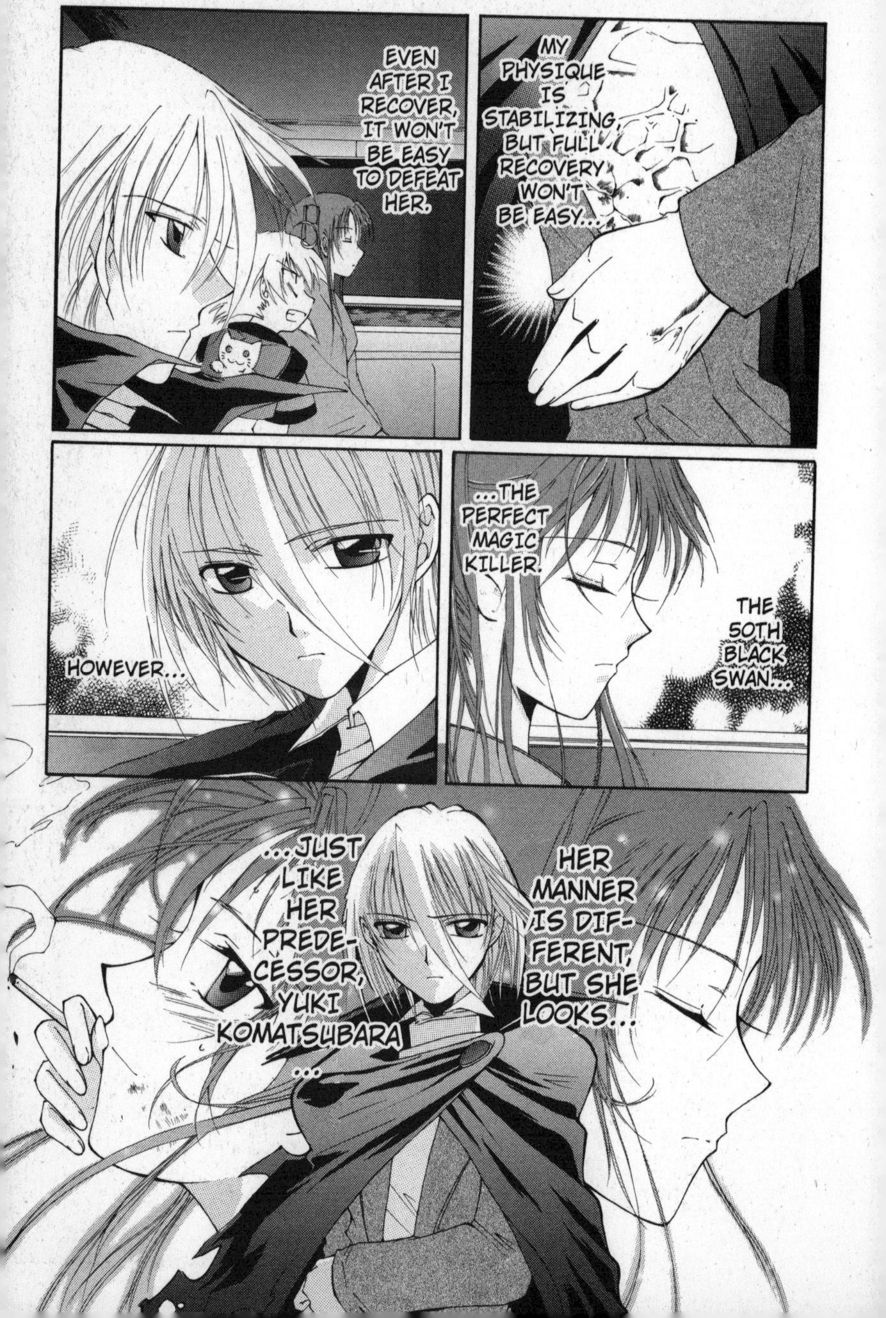
MY PHYSIQUE IS STABILIZING, BUT FULL RECOVERY WON'T BE EASY...
EVEN AFTER I RECOVER, IT WON'T BE EASY TO DEFEAT HER.
...THE PERFECT MAGIC KILLER.
THE 50TH BLACK SWAN...
HOWEVER...
HER MANNER IS DIF-FERENT, BUT SHE LOOKS...
...JUST LIKE HER PREDE-CESSOR, YUKI KOMATSUBARA
...

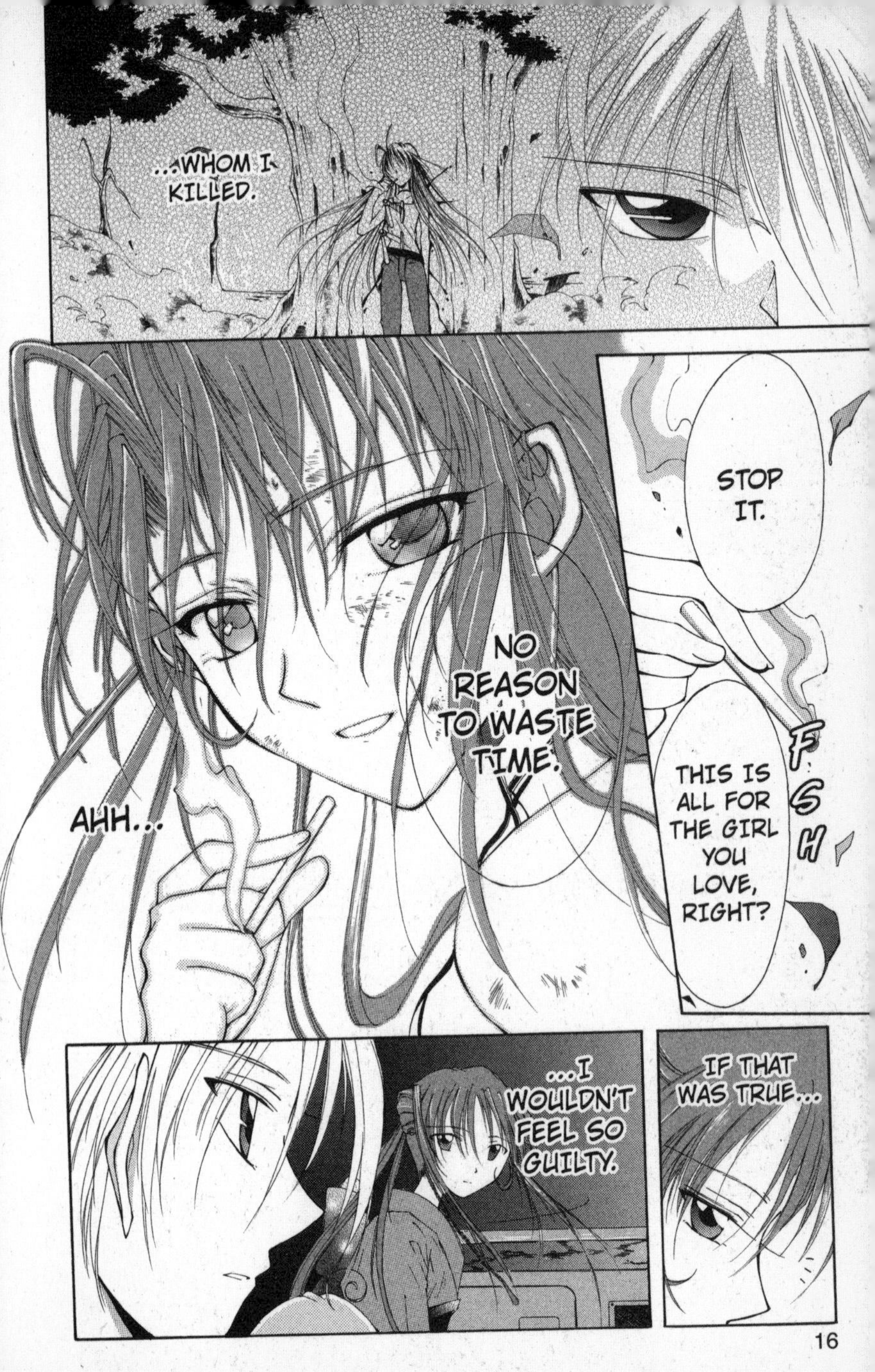
...WHOM I KILLED.
STOP IT.
THIS IS ALL FOR THE GIRL YOU LOVE, RIGHT?
FSH
NO REASON TO WASTE TIME.
AHH...
IF THAT WAS TRUE...
...I WOULDN'T FEEL SO GUILTY.

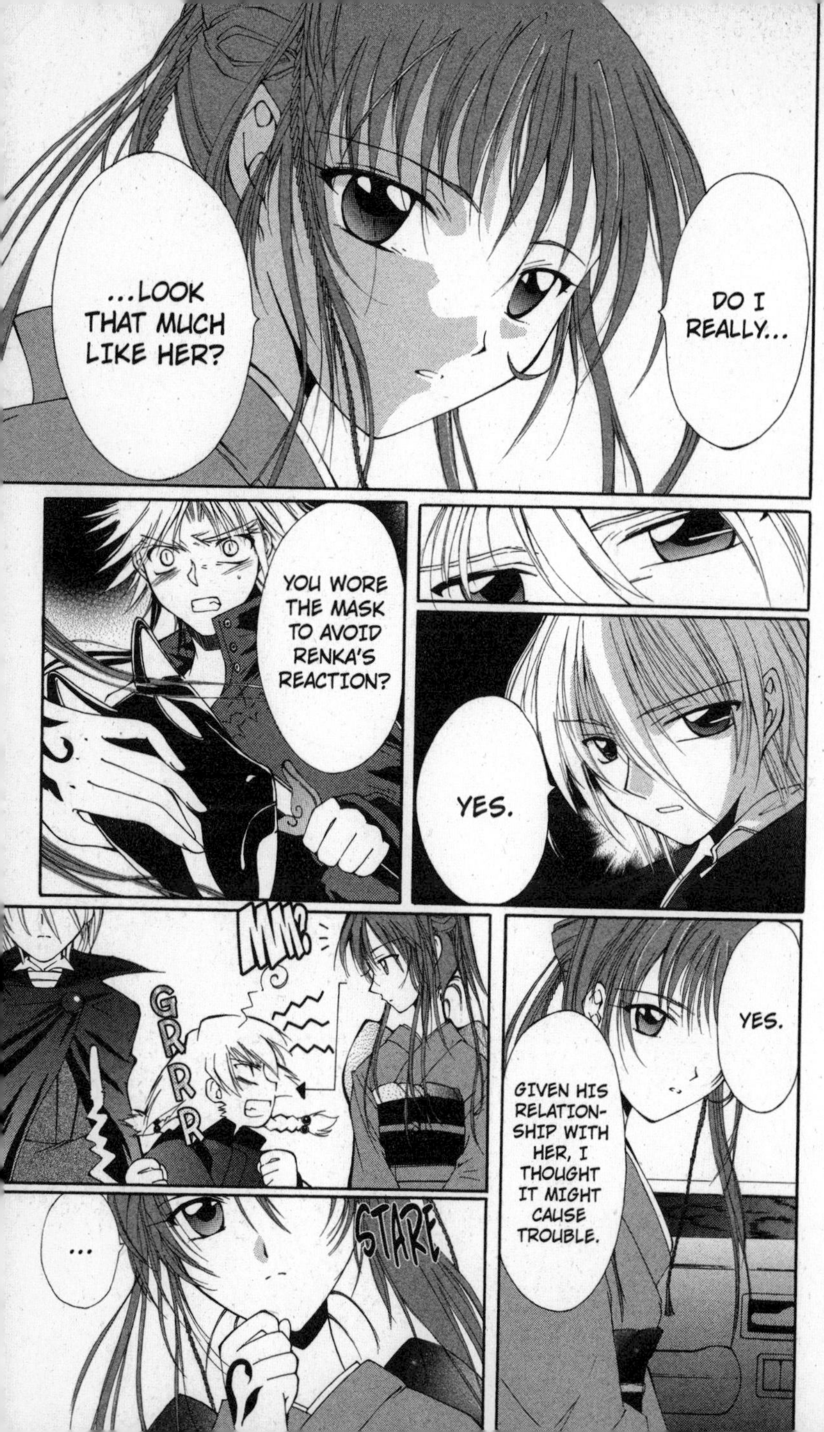
DO I REALLY...
...LOOK THAT MUCH LIKE HER?
YES.
YOU WORE THE MASK TO AVOID RENKA'S REACTION?
YES.
GIVEN HIS RELATION-SHIP WITH HER, I THOUGHT IT MIGHT CAUSE TROUBLE.
MM?
GRRR
...
STARE

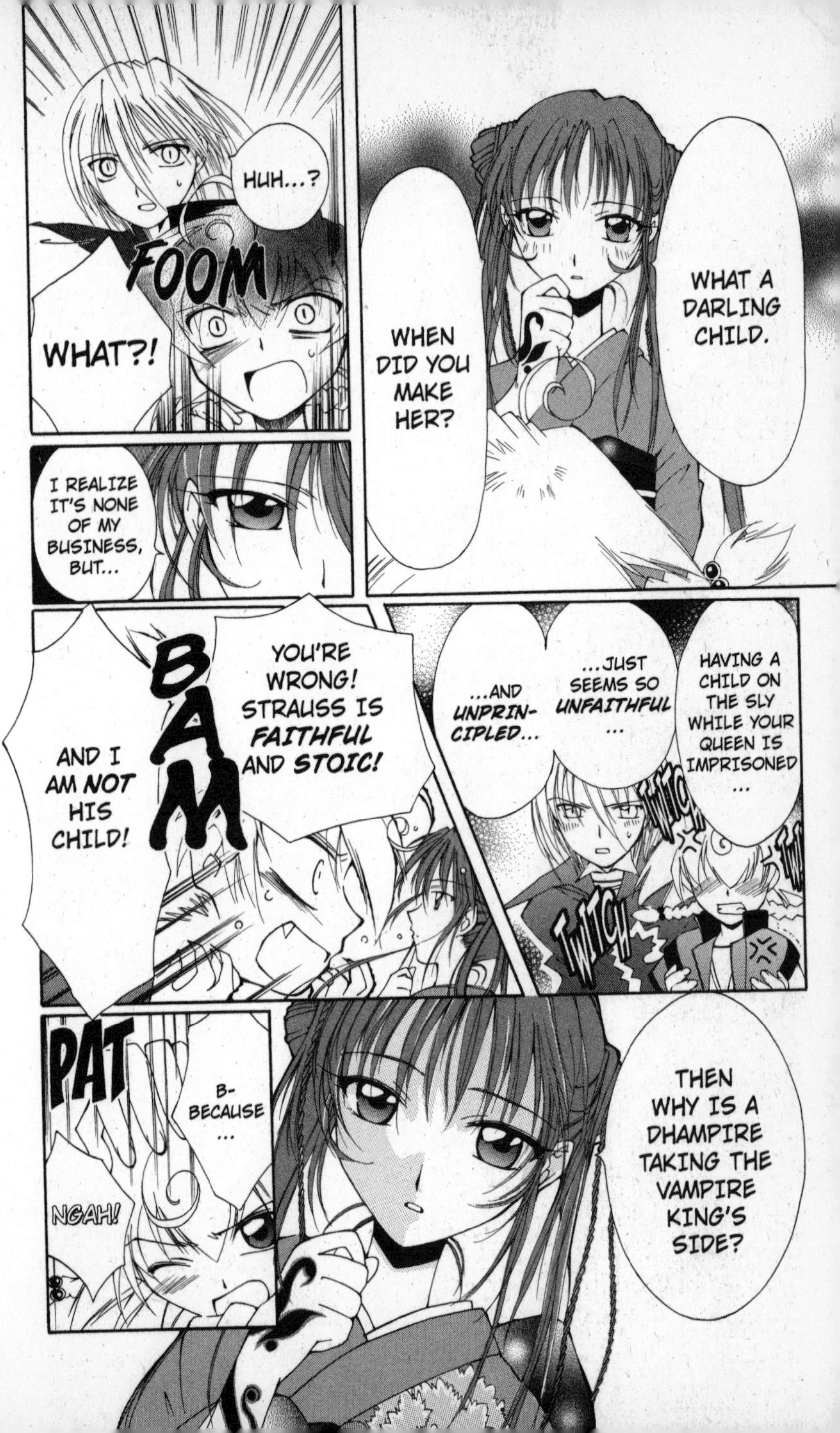
WHAT A DARLING CHILD.
WHEN DID YOU MAKE HER?
HUH...?
FOOM
WHAT?!
I REALIZE IT'S NONE OF MY BUSINESS, BUT...
HAVING A CHILD ON THE SLY WHILE YOUR QUEEN IS IMPRISONED...
...JUST SEEMS SO *UNFAITHFUL*...
...AND *UNPRINCIPLED*...
TWITCH
TWITCH
YOU'RE WRONG! STRAUSS IS *FAITHFUL* AND *STOIC!*
BAM
AND I AM *NOT* HIS CHILD!
THEN WHY IS A DHAMPIRE TAKING THE VAMPIRE KING'S SIDE?
PAT
B-BECAUSE...
NGAH!

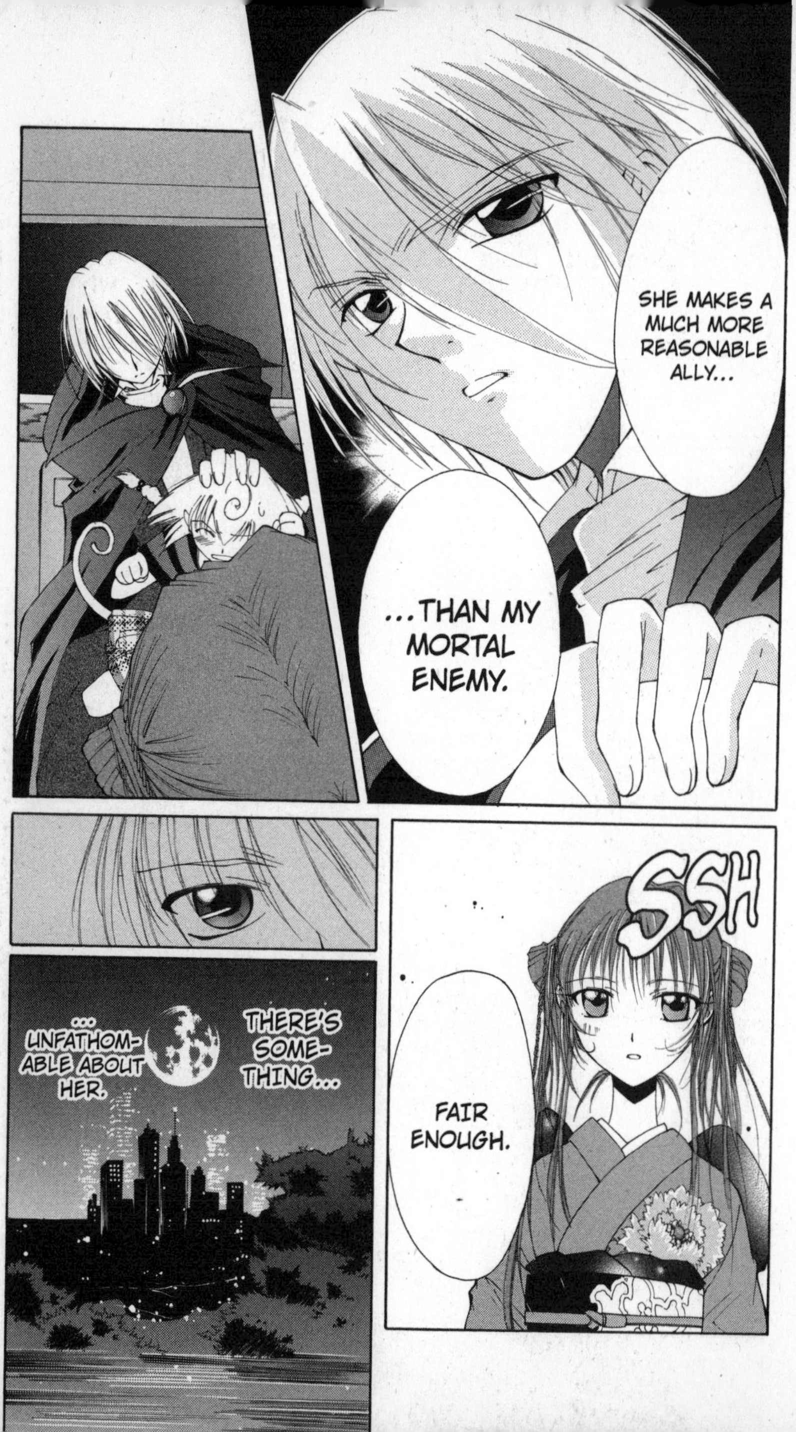
SHE MAKES A MUCH MORE REASONABLE ALLY...
...THAN MY MORTAL ENEMY.
SSH
FAIR ENOUGH.
THERE'S SOME-THING...
...UNFATHOM-ABLE ABOUT HER.

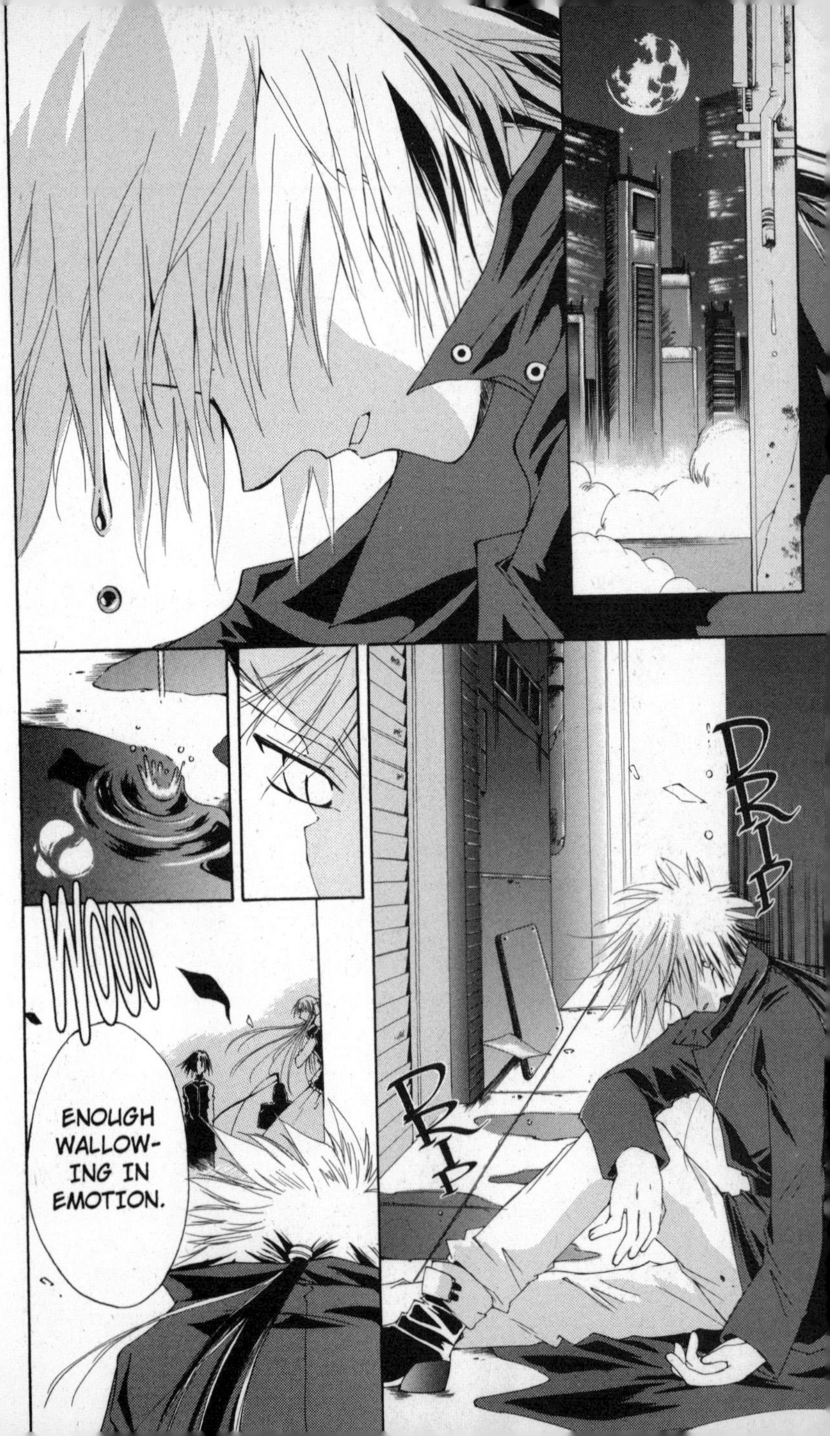
DRIP
DRIP
WOOO
ENOUGH WALLOWING IN EMOTION.

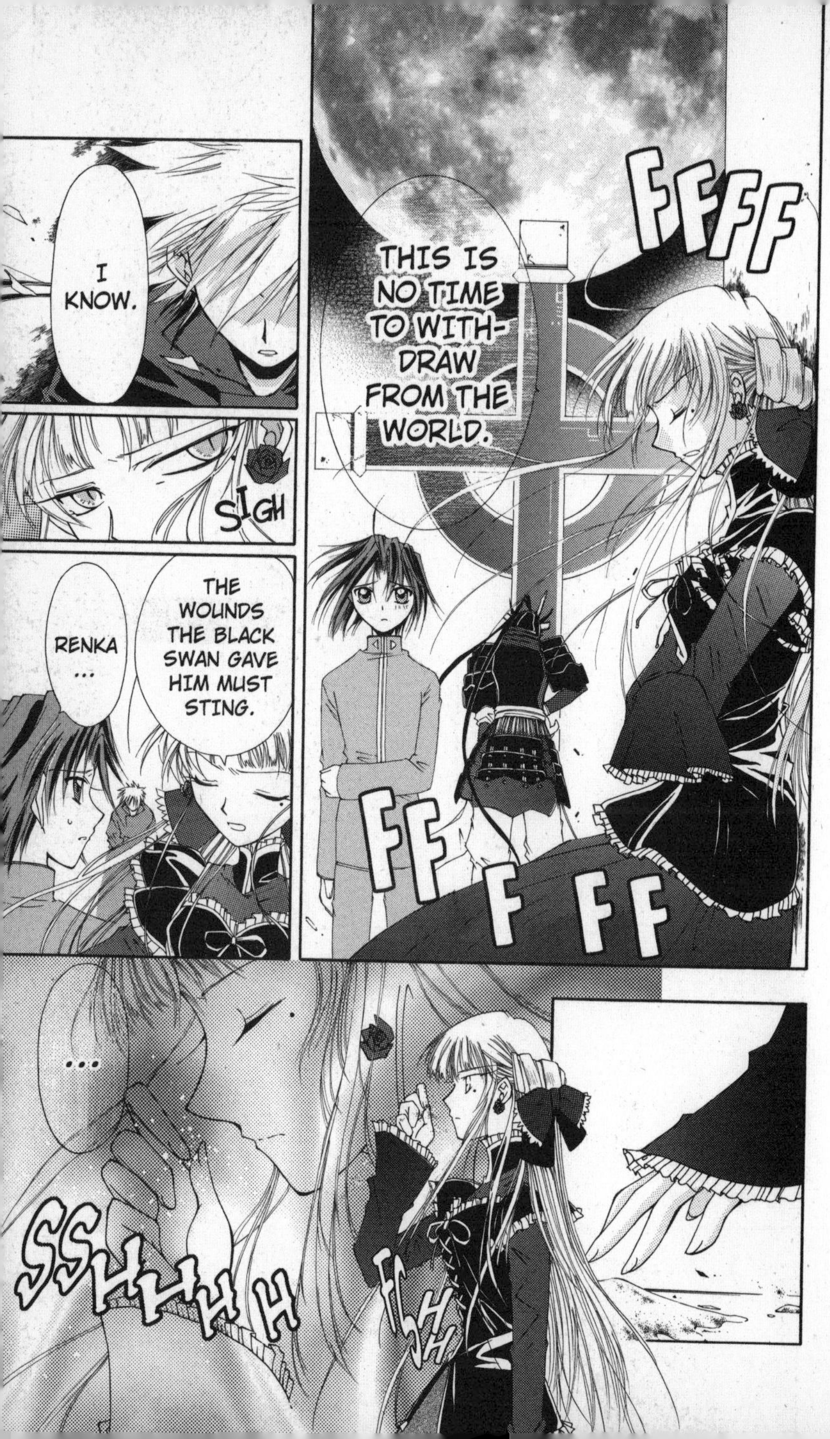
FFFF
THIS IS NO TIME TO WITH-DRAW FROM THE WORLD.
FF F FF
I KNOW.
SIGH
THE WOUNDS THE BLACK SWAN GAVE HIM MUST STING.
RENKA...
...
FSHH
SSHHHHH

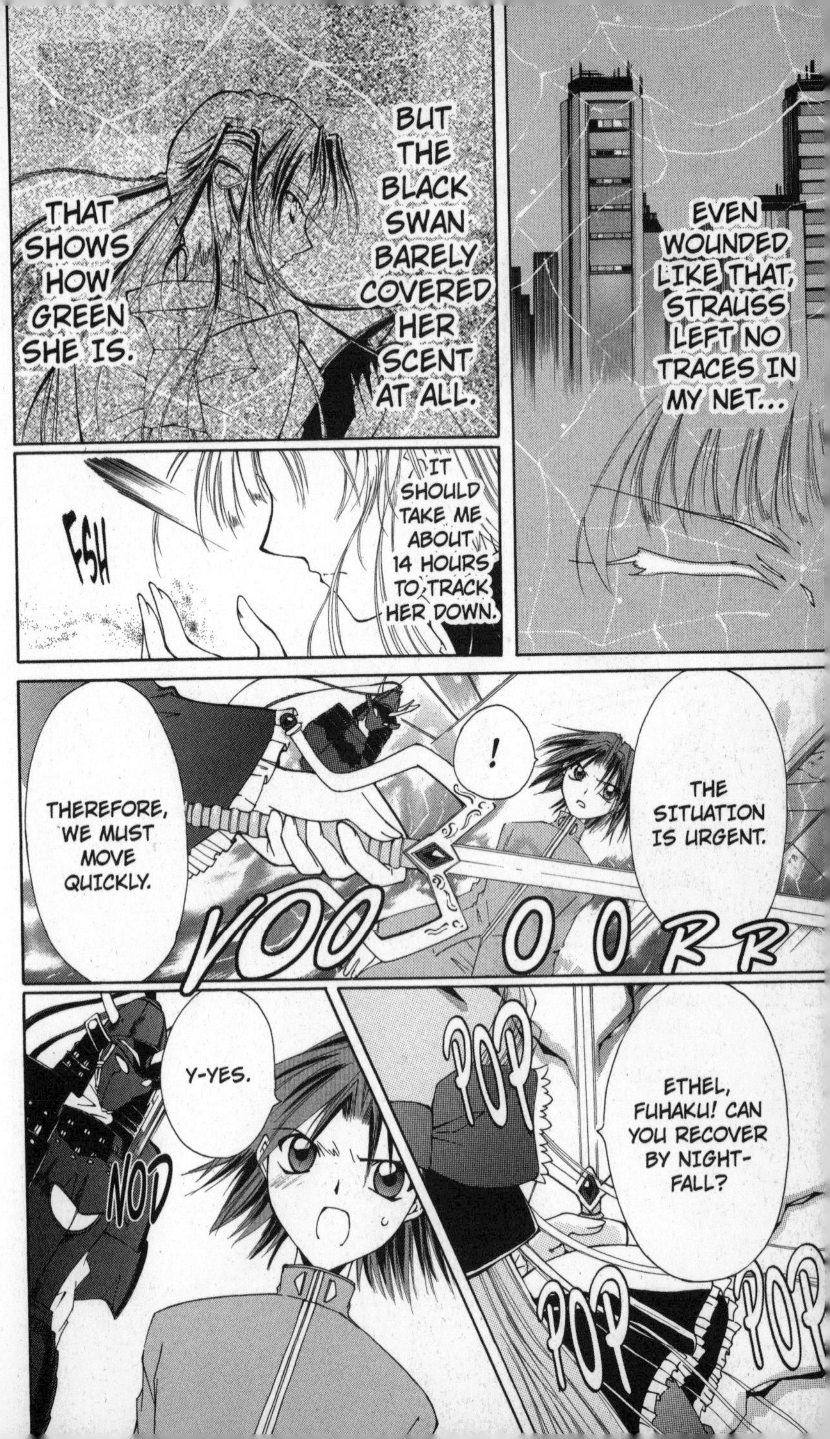
EVEN WOUNDED LIKE THAT, STRAUSS LEFT NO TRACES IN MY NET...
BUT THE BLACK SWAN BARELY COVERED HER SCENT AT ALL.
THAT SHOWS HOW GREEN SHE IS.
IT SHOULD TAKE ME ABOUT 14 HOURS TO TRACK HER DOWN.
FSH
THE SITUATION IS URGENT.
!
THEREFORE, WE MUST MOVE QUICKLY.
VOOOORR
ETHEL, FUHAKU! CAN YOU RECOVER BY NIGHT-FALL?
POP
POP
POP
POP
Y-YES.
NOD

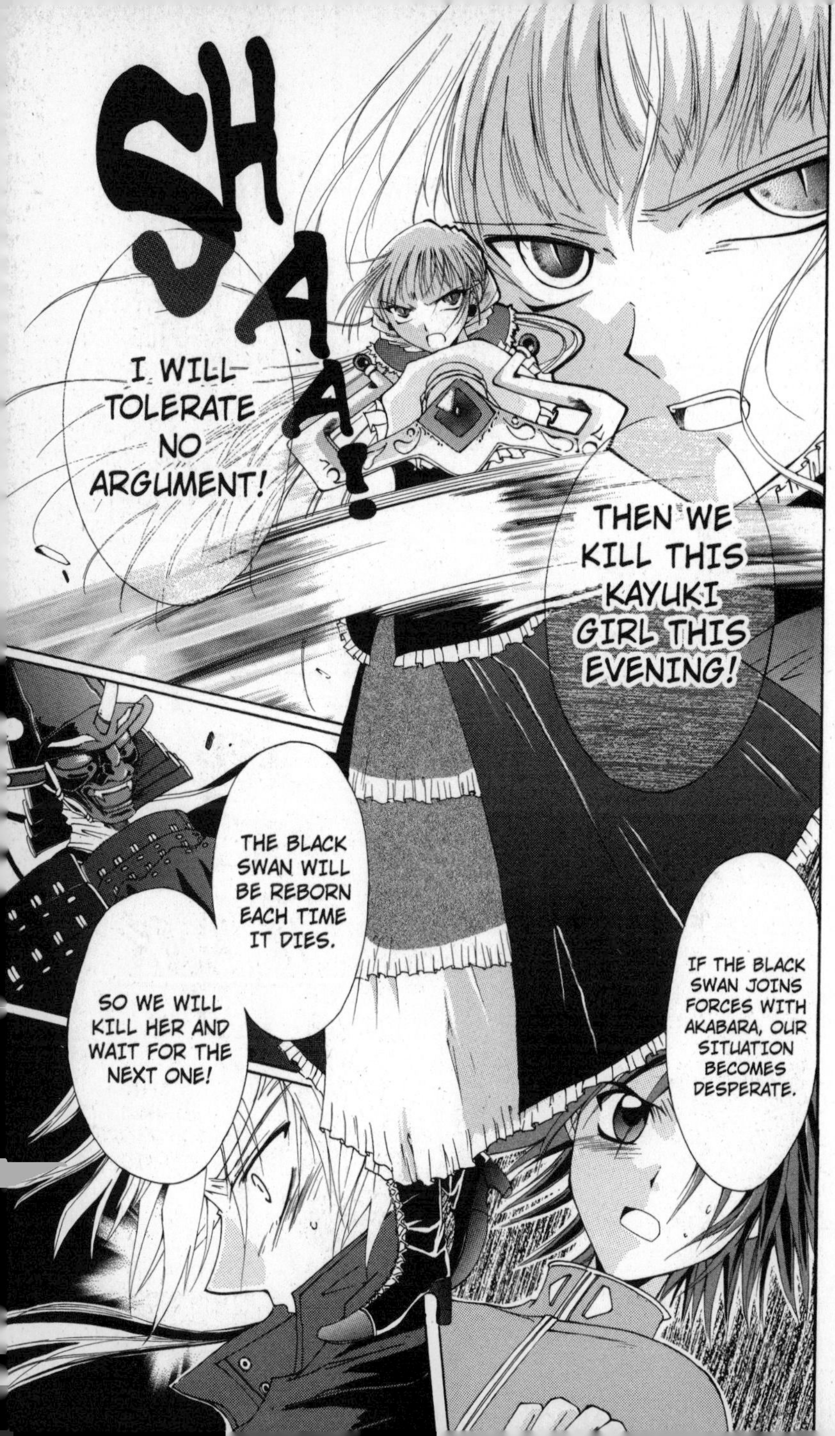
THEN WE KILL THIS KAYUKI GIRL THIS EVENING!
SHAAA!
I WILL TOLERATE NO ARGUMENT!
IF THE BLACK SWAN JOINS FORCES WITH AKABARA, OUR SITUATION BECOMES DESPERATE.
THE BLACK SWAN WILL BE REBORN EACH TIME IT DIES.
SO WE WILL KILL HER AND WAIT FOR THE NEXT ONE!

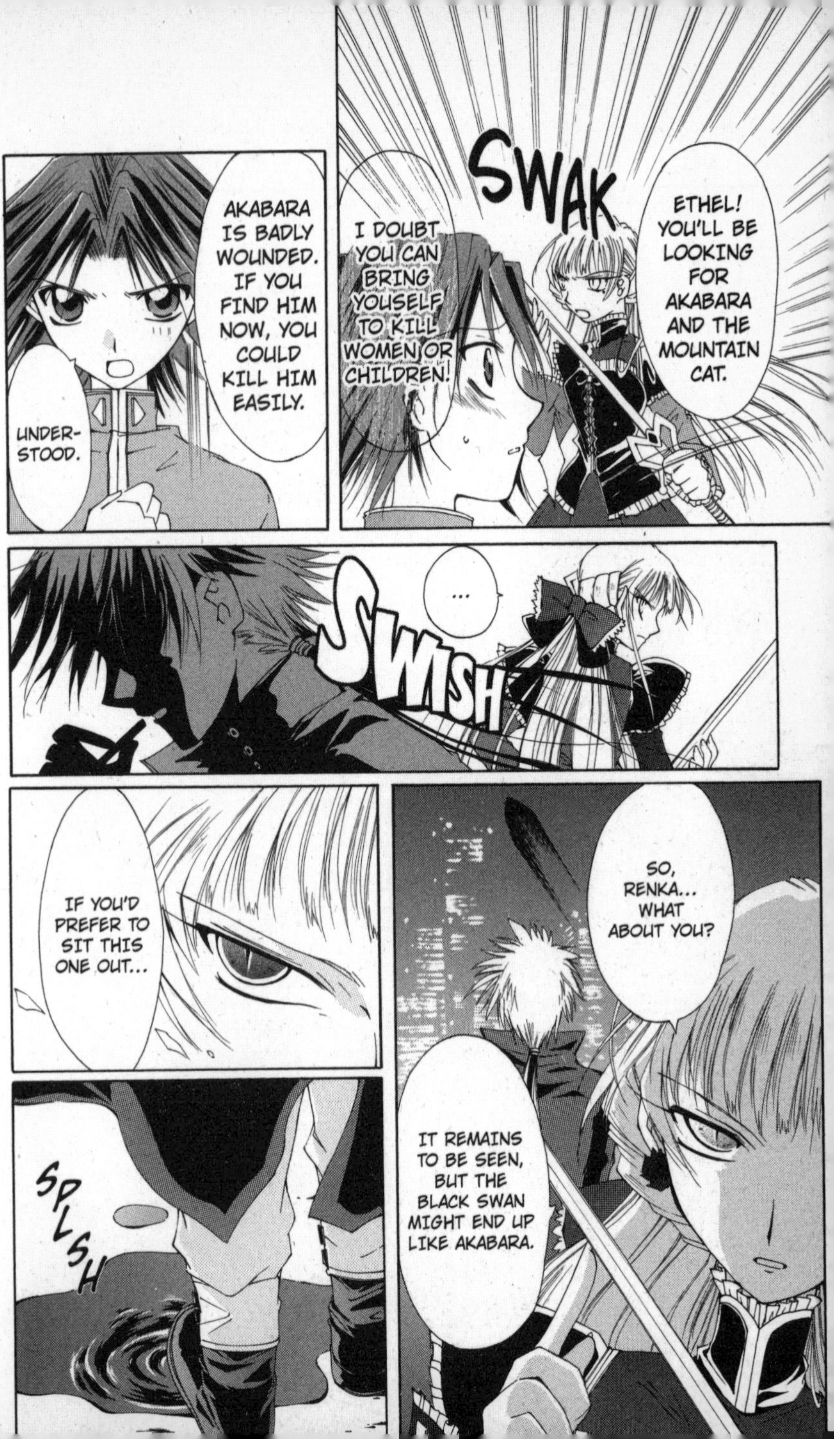
SWAK
ETHEL! YOU'LL BE LOOKING FOR AKABARA AND THE MOUNTAIN CAT.
I DOUBT YOU CAN BRING YOUSELF TO KILL WOMEN OR CHILDREN!
AKABARA IS BADLY WOUNDED. IF YOU FIND HIM NOW, YOU COULD KILL HIM EASILY.
UNDER-STOOD.
...
SWISH
SO, RENKA... WHAT ABOUT YOU?
IT REMAINS TO BE SEEN, BUT THE BLACK SWAN MIGHT END UP LIKE AKABARA.
IF YOU'D PREFER TO SIT THIS ONE OUT...
SPLSH

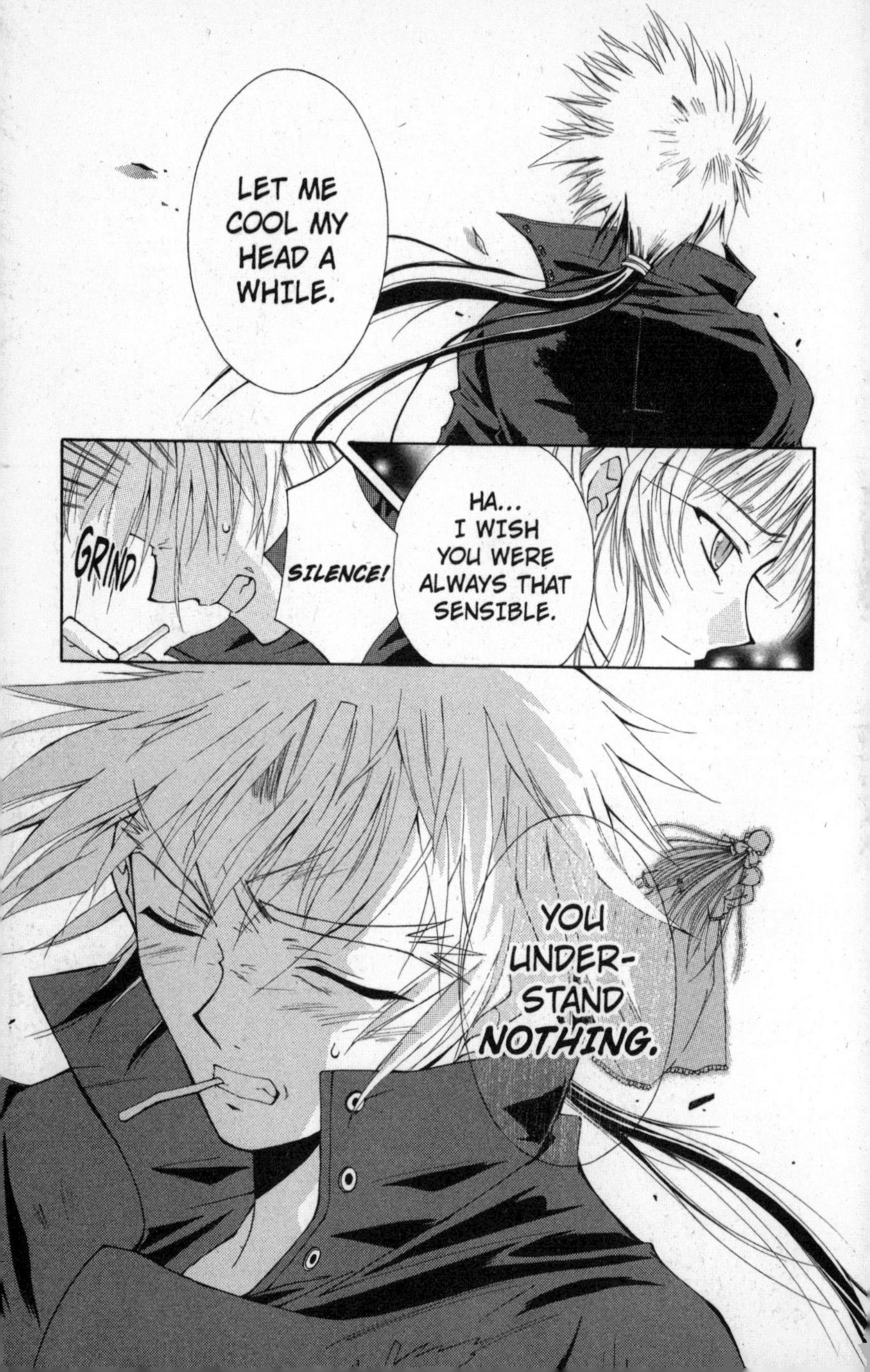
LET ME COOL MY HEAD A WHILE.
HA... I WISH YOU WERE ALWAYS THAT SENSIBLE.
SILENCE!
GRIND
YOU UNDER-STAND NOTHING.

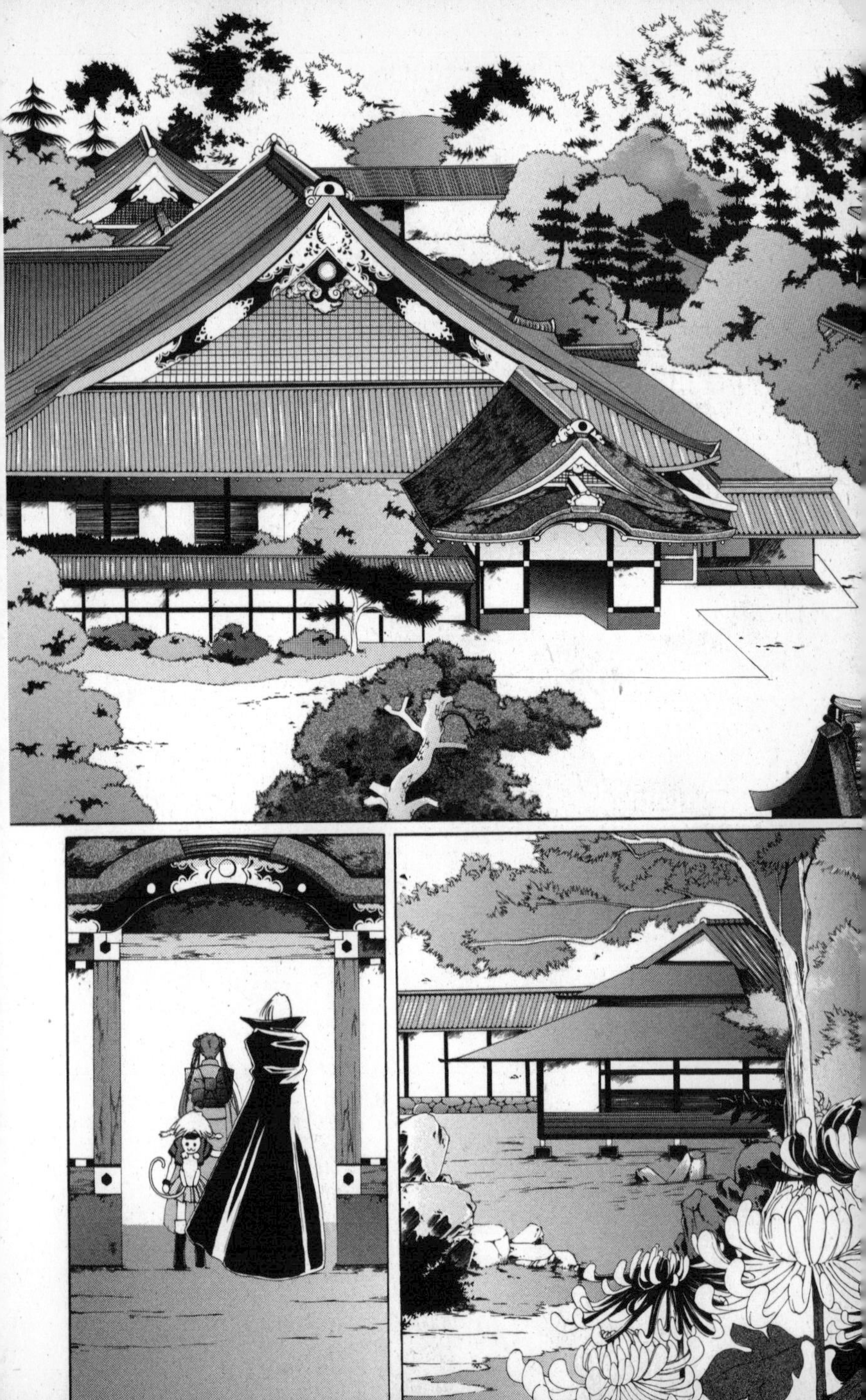

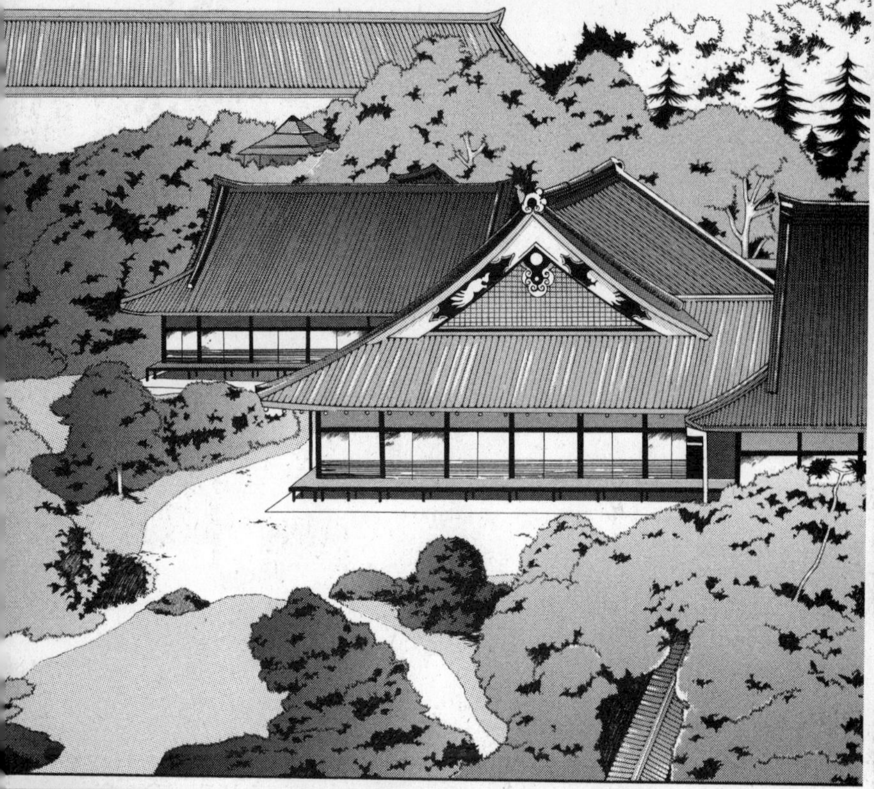

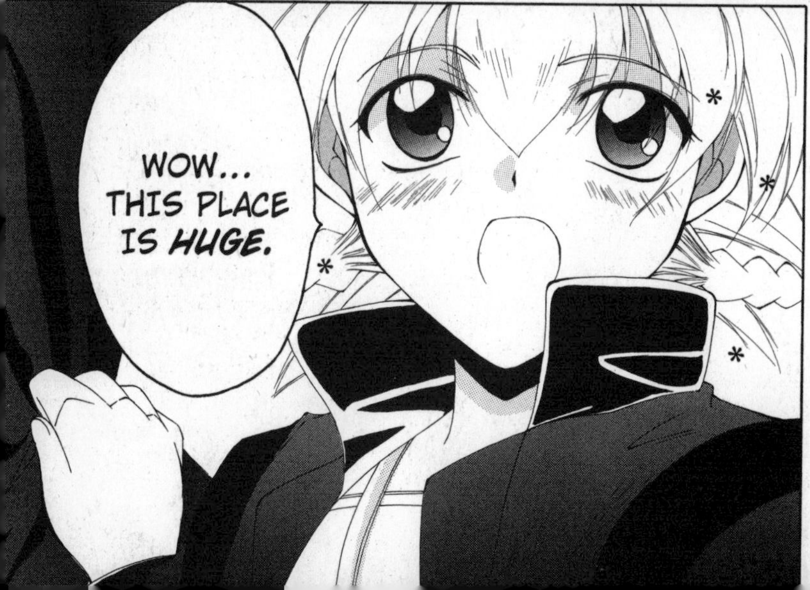
WOW... THIS PLACE IS *HUGE.*

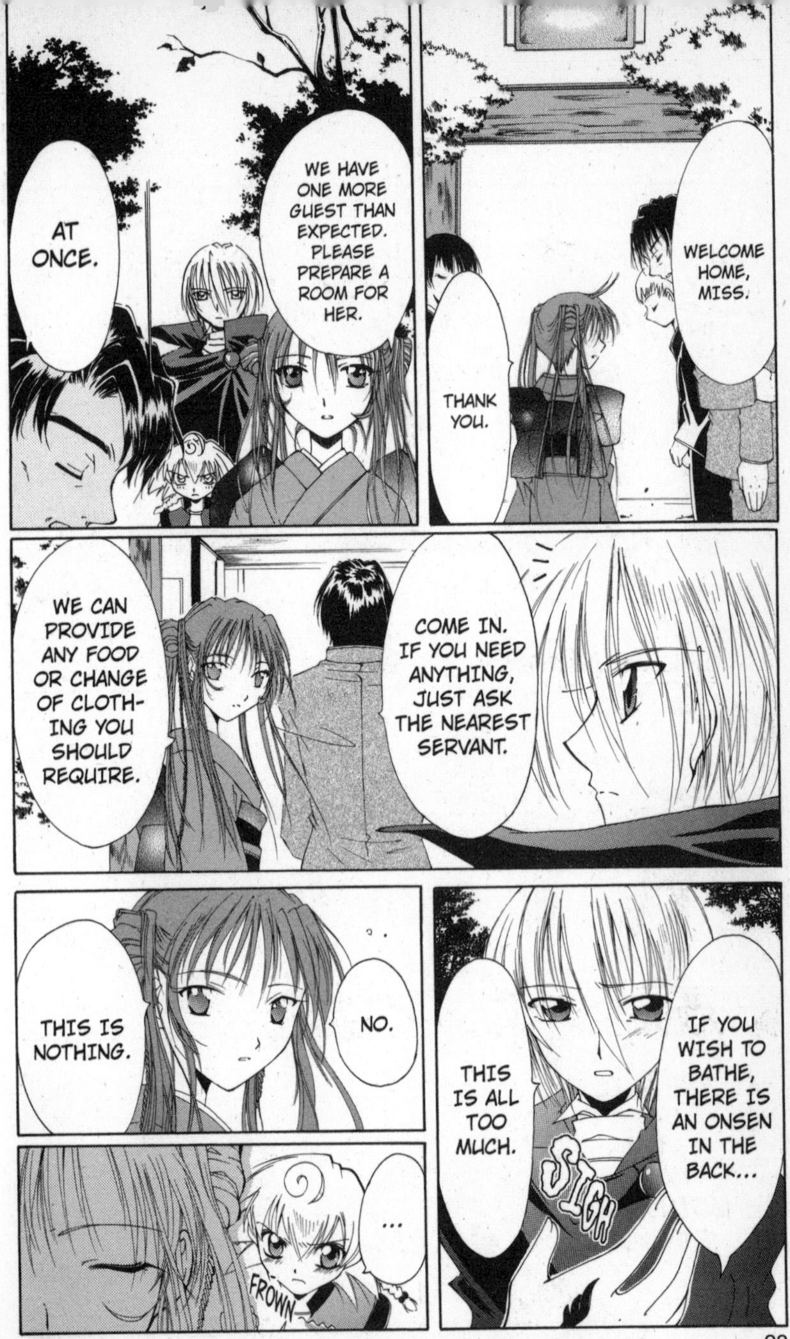
WELCOME HOME, MISS.
THANK YOU.
WE HAVE ONE MORE GUEST THAN EXPECTED. PLEASE PREPARE A ROOM FOR HER.
AT ONCE.
COME IN. IF YOU NEED ANYTHING, JUST ASK THE NEAREST SERVANT.
WE CAN PROVIDE ANY FOOD OR CHANGE OF CLOTH-ING YOU SHOULD REQUIRE.
IF YOU WISH TO BATHE, THERE IS AN ONSEN IN THE BACK...
THIS IS ALL TOO MUCH.
SIGH
NO.
THIS IS NOTHING.
...
FROWN

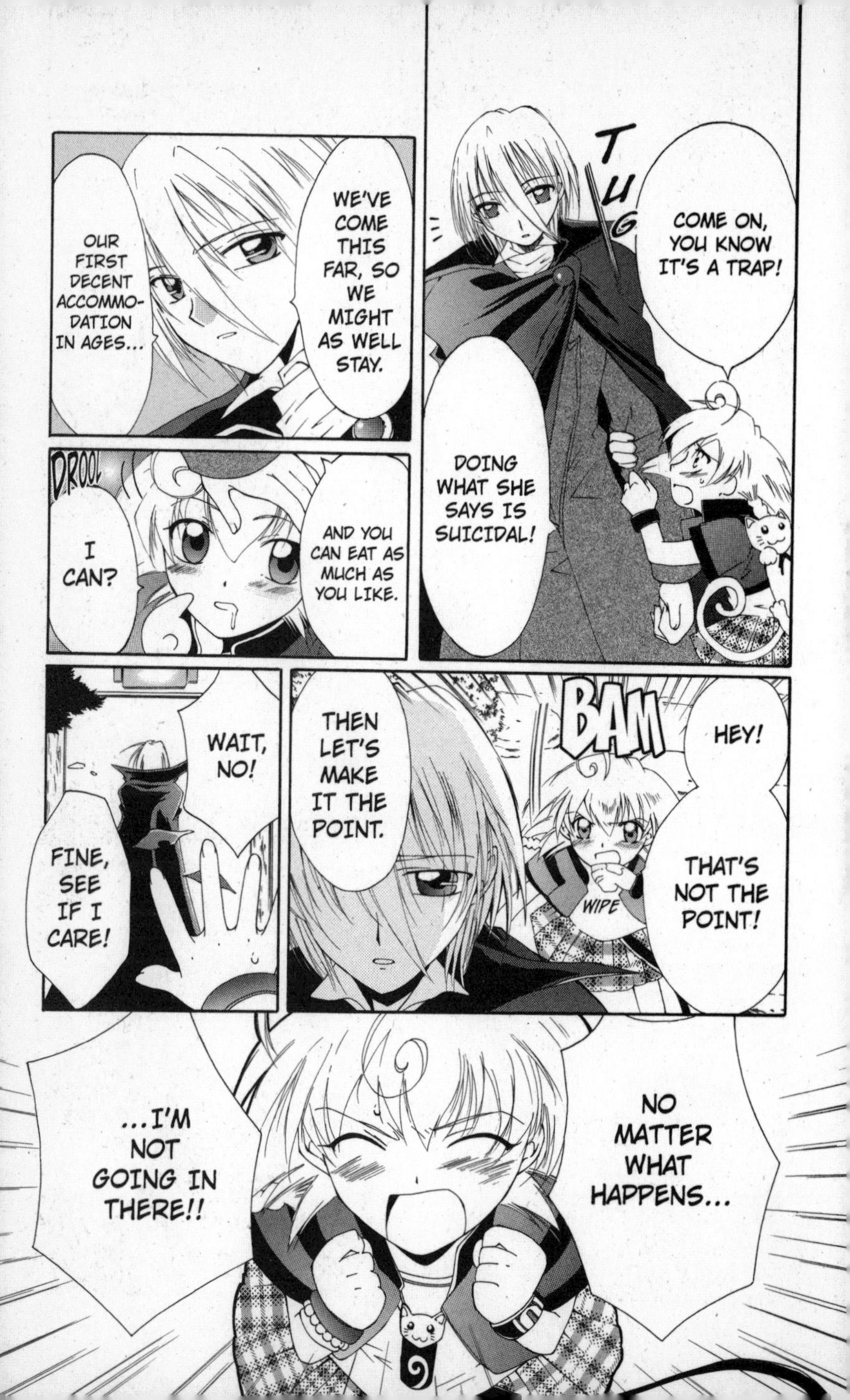
TUG
COME ON, YOU KNOW IT'S A TRAP!
DOING WHAT SHE SAYS IS SUICIDAL!
WE'VE COME THIS FAR, SO WE MIGHT AS WELL STAY.
OUR FIRST DECENT ACCOMMO-DATION IN AGES...
AND YOU CAN EAT AS MUCH AS YOU LIKE.
DROOL
I CAN?
BAM
HEY!
THAT'S NOT THE POINT!
WIPE
THEN LET'S MAKE IT THE POINT.
WAIT, NO!
FINE, SEE IF I CARE!
NO MATTER WHAT HAPPENS...
...I'M NOT GOING IN THERE!!

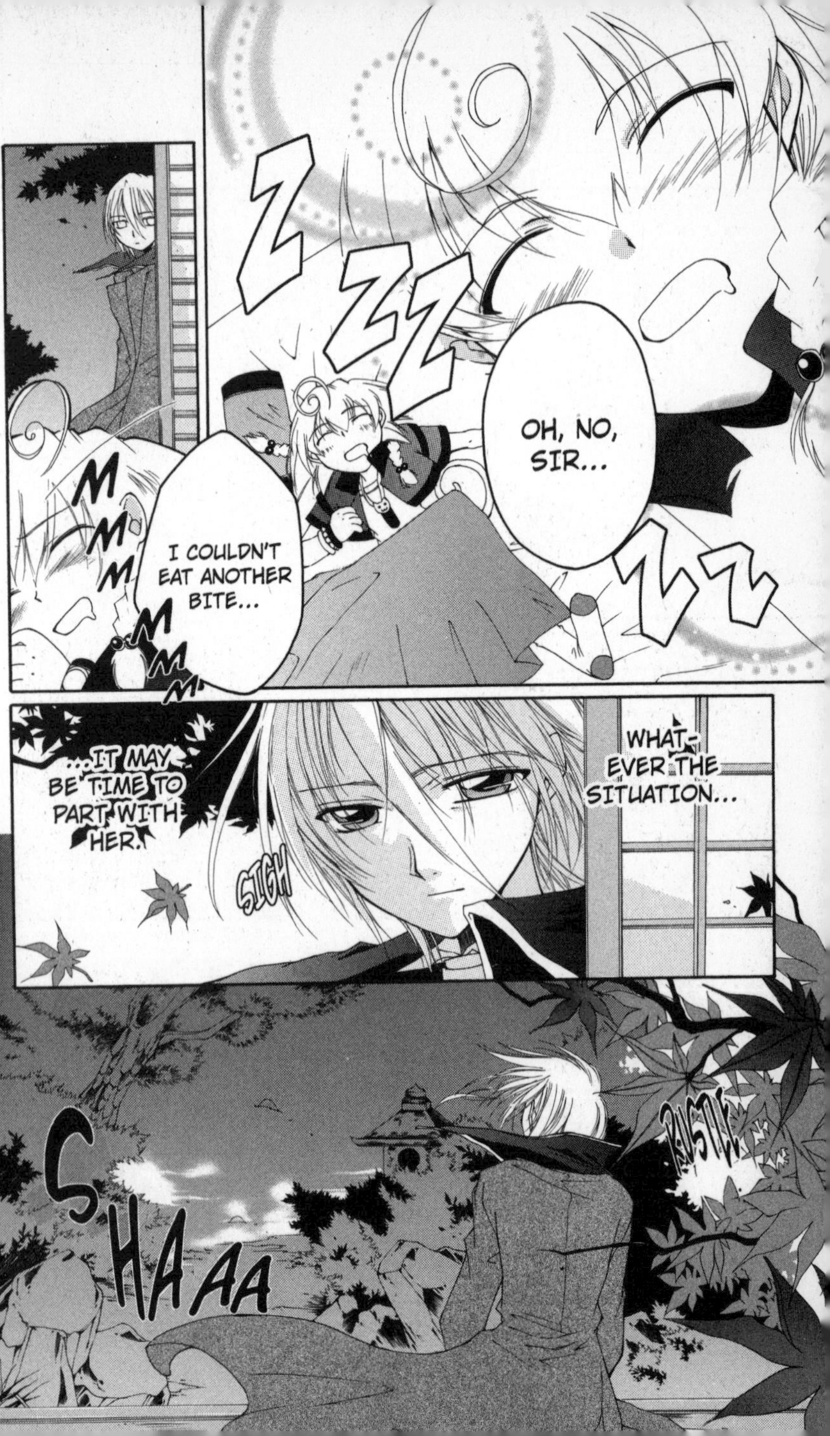
ZZZ
OH, NO, SIR...
ZZZ
I COULDN'T EAT ANOTHER BITE...
MMMMMMM
WHAT-EVER THE SITUATION...
...IT MAY BE TIME TO PART WITH HER.
SIGH
RUSTLE
SHAAA

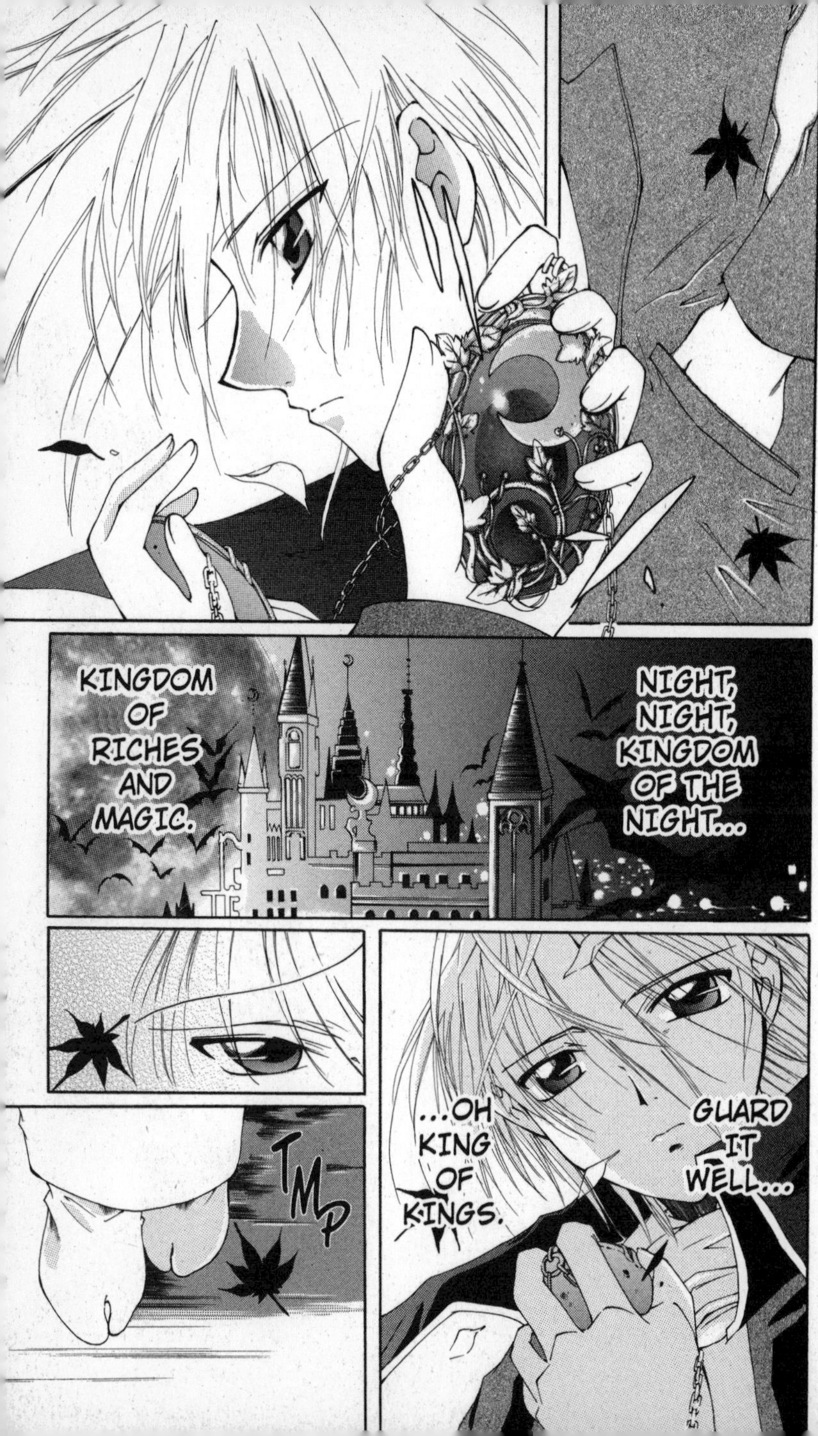
NIGHT, NIGHT, KINGDOM OF THE NIGHT...
KINGDOM OF RICHES AND MAGIC.
GUARD IT WELL...
...OH KING OF KINGS.
TMP

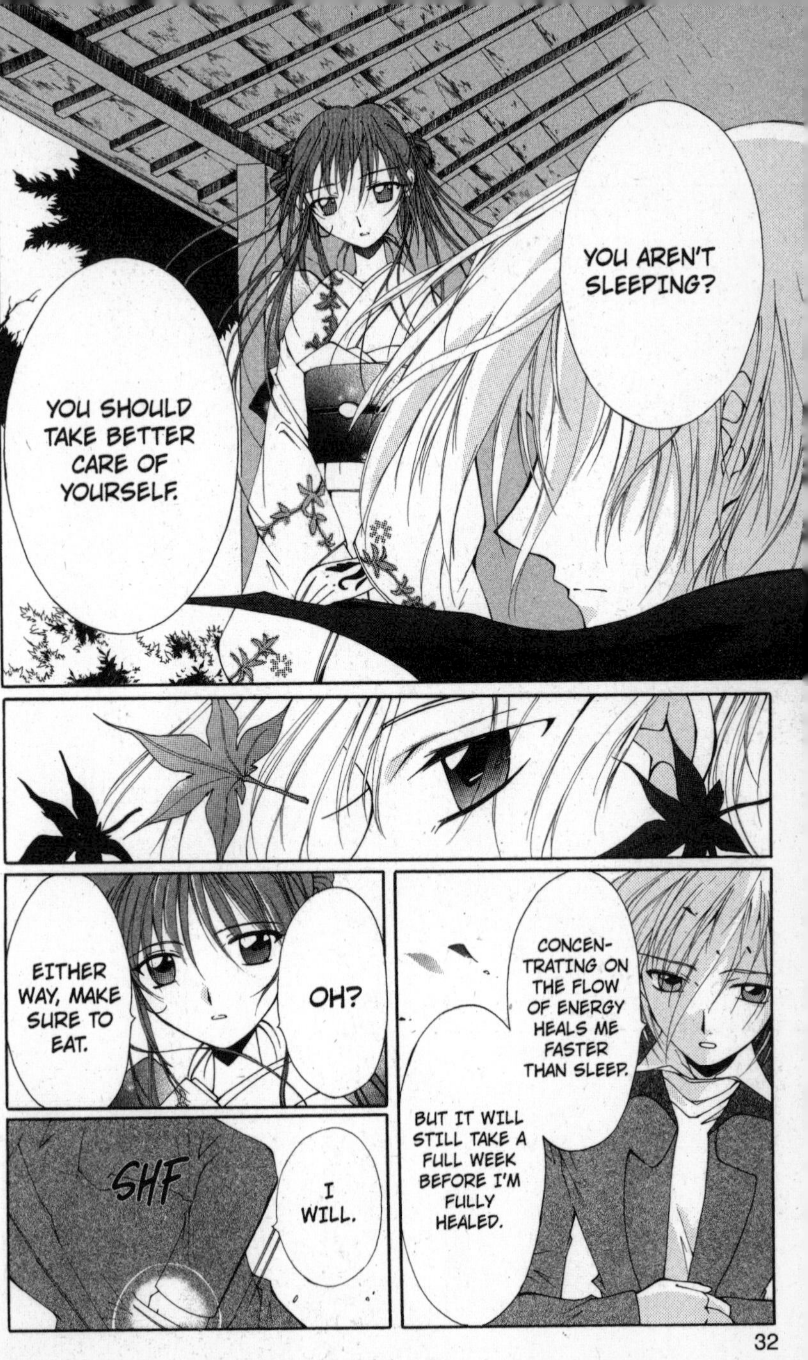
YOU AREN'T SLEEPING?
YOU SHOULD TAKE BETTER CARE OF YOURSELF.
CONCEN-TRATING ON THE FLOW OF ENERGY HEALS ME FASTER THAN SLEEP.
BUT IT WILL STILL TAKE A FULL WEEK BEFORE I'M FULLY HEALED.
OH?
EITHER WAY, MAKE SURE TO EAT.
I WILL.
SHF

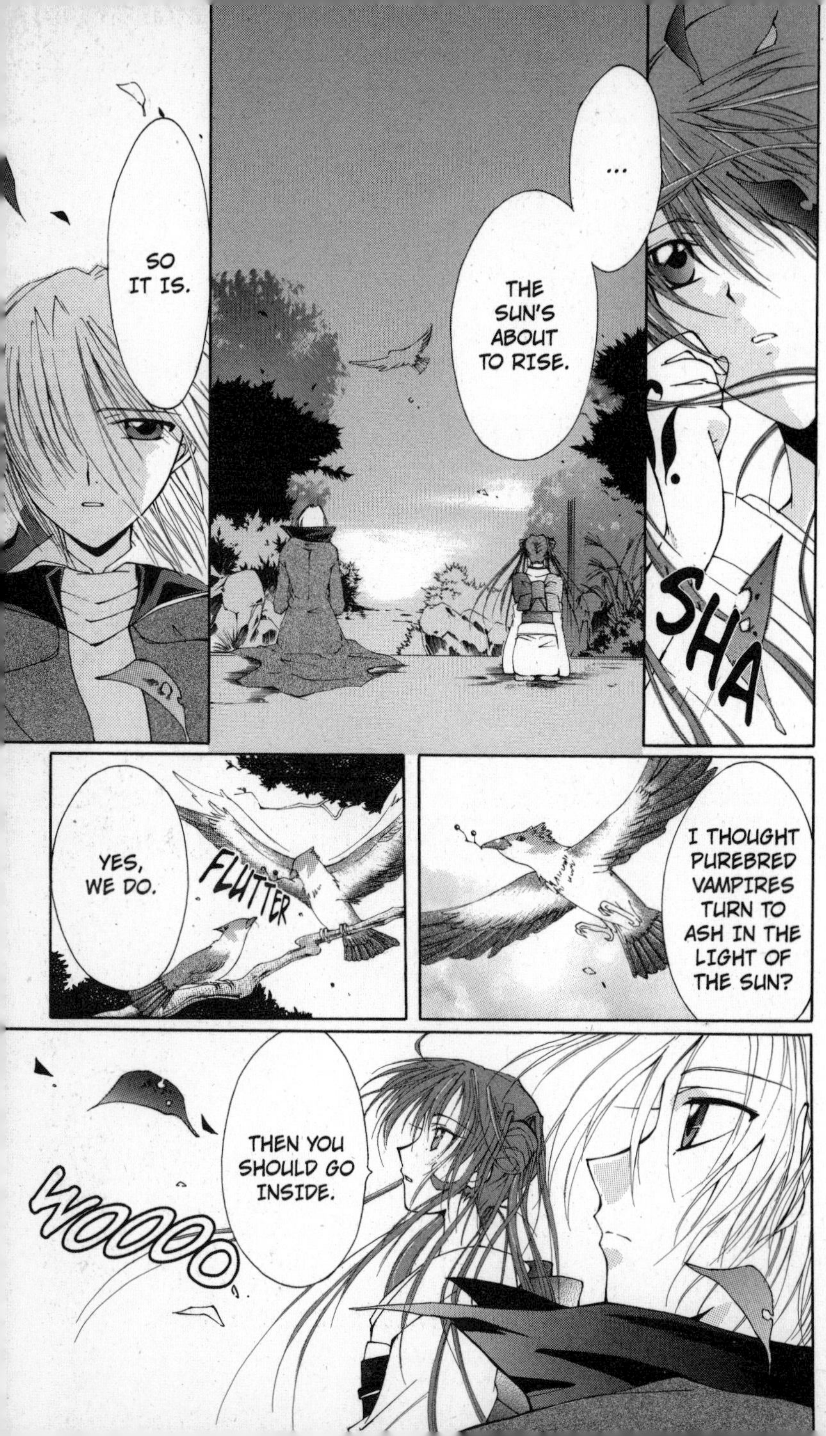
SHA
...
THE SUN'S ABOUT TO RISE.
SO IT IS.
I THOUGHT PUREBRED VAMPIRES TURN TO ASH IN THE LIGHT OF THE SUN?
YES, WE DO.
FLUTTER
THEN YOU SHOULD GO INSIDE.
WOOOO

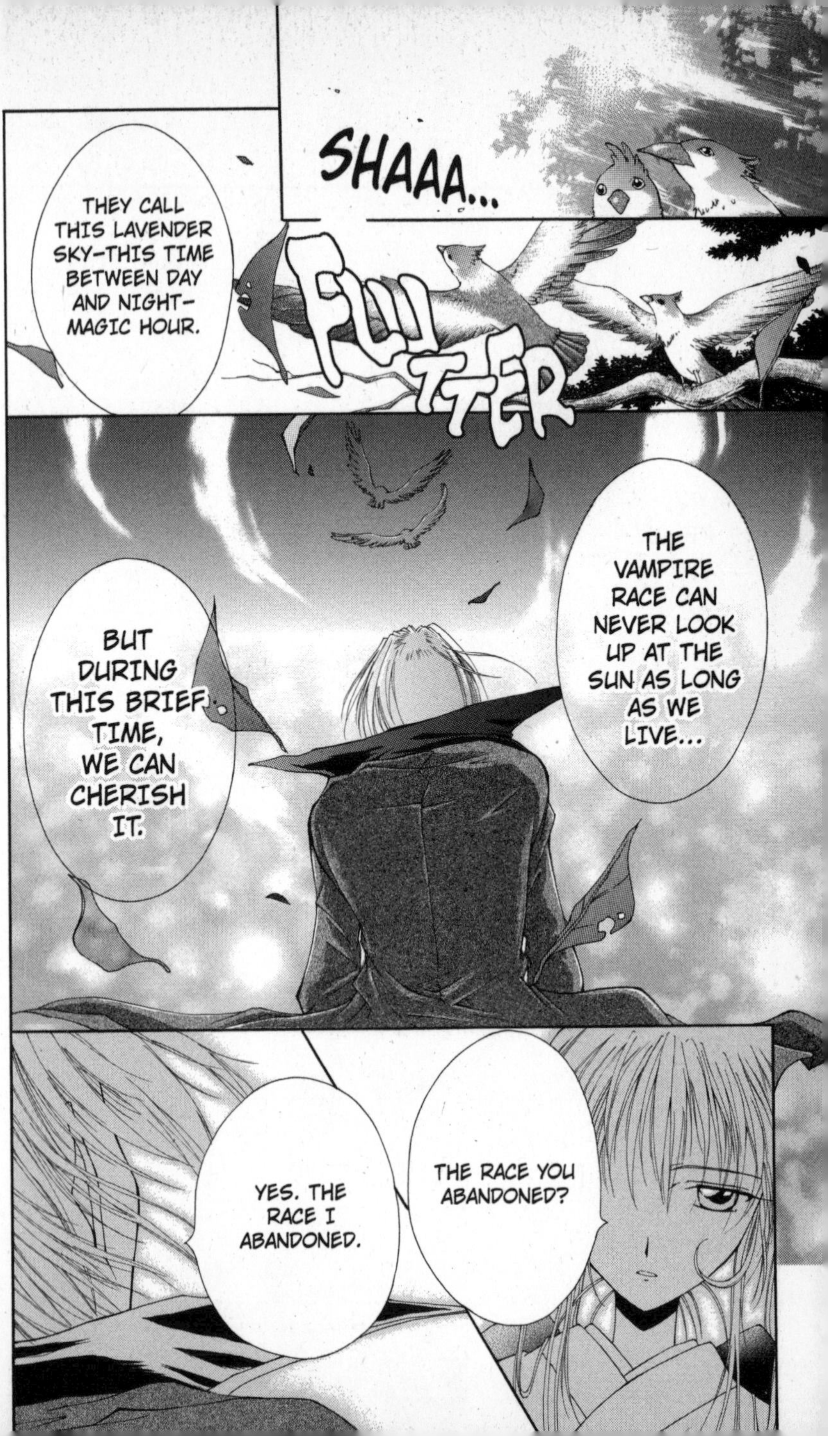
SHAAA...
FLUTTER
THEY CALL THIS LAVENDER SKY—THIS TIME BETWEEN DAY AND NIGHT—MAGIC HOUR.
THE VAMPIRE RACE CAN NEVER LOOK UP AT THE SUN AS LONG AS WE LIVE...
BUT DURING THIS BRIEF TIME, WE CAN CHERISH IT.
THE RACE YOU ABANDONED?
YES. THE RACE I ABANDONED.

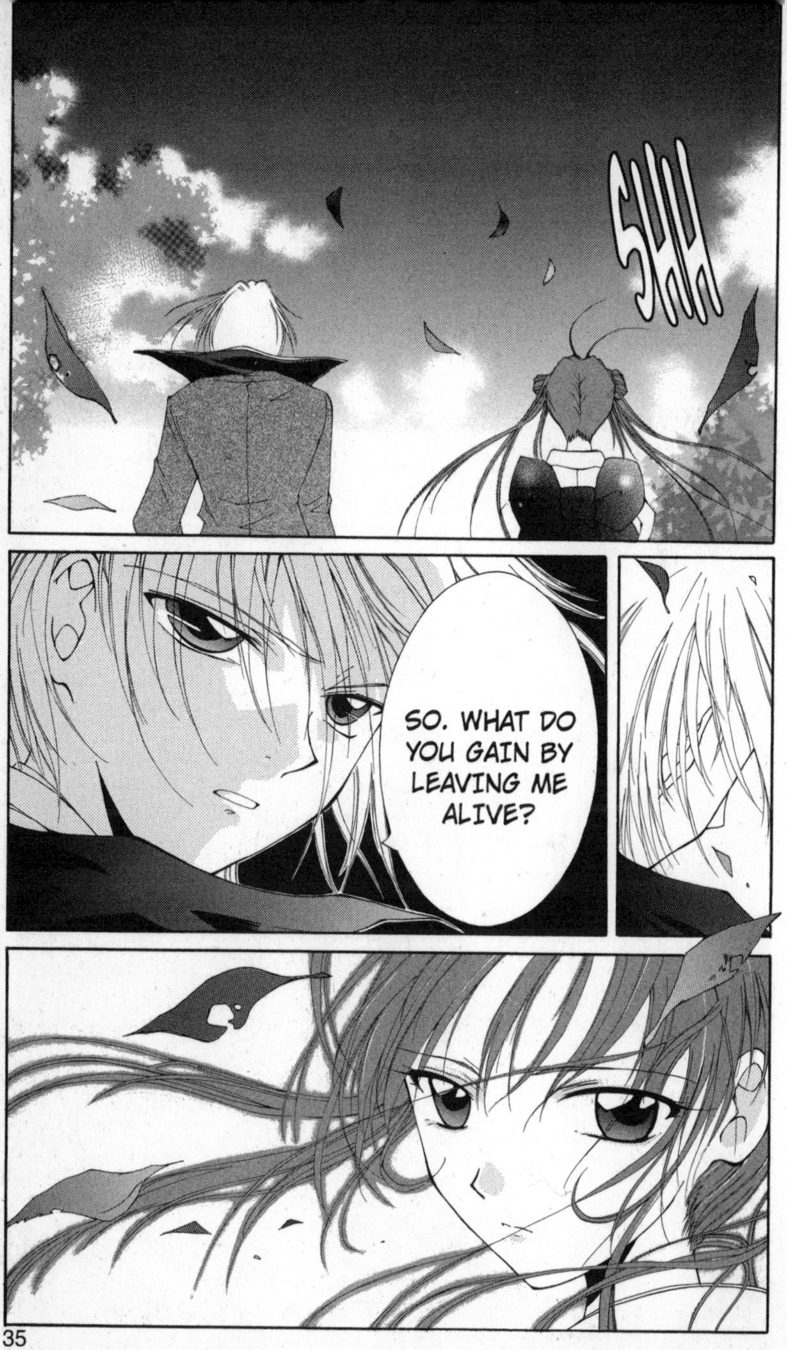
SHH
SO. WHAT DO YOU GAIN BY LEAVING ME ALIVE?

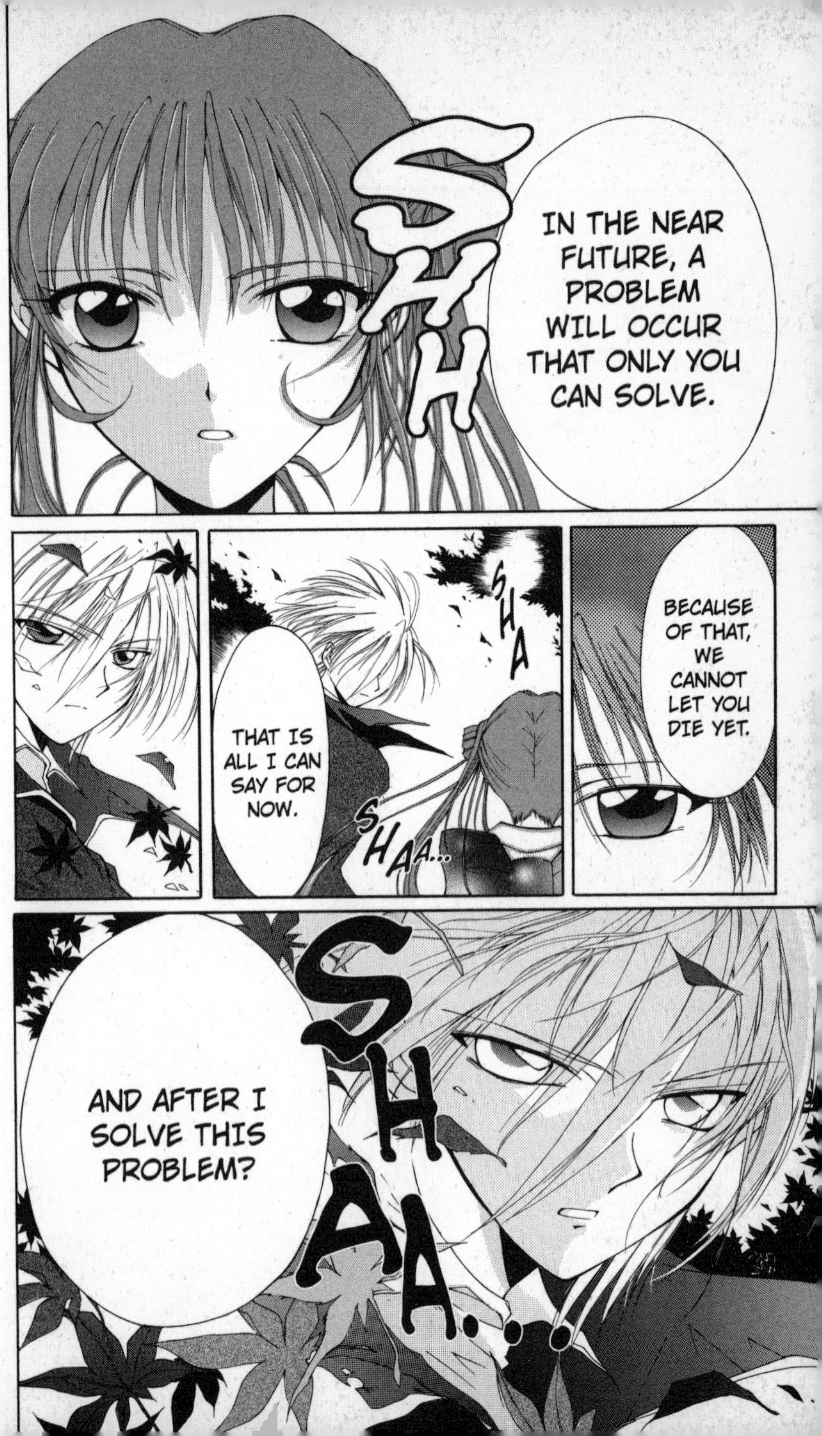
IN THE NEAR FUTURE, A PROBLEM WILL OCCUR THAT ONLY YOU CAN SOLVE.
SHH
BECAUSE OF THAT, WE CANNOT LET YOU DIE YET.
SHA
THAT IS ALL I CAN SAY FOR NOW.
SHAA...
SHAA...
AND AFTER I SOLVE THIS PROBLEM?

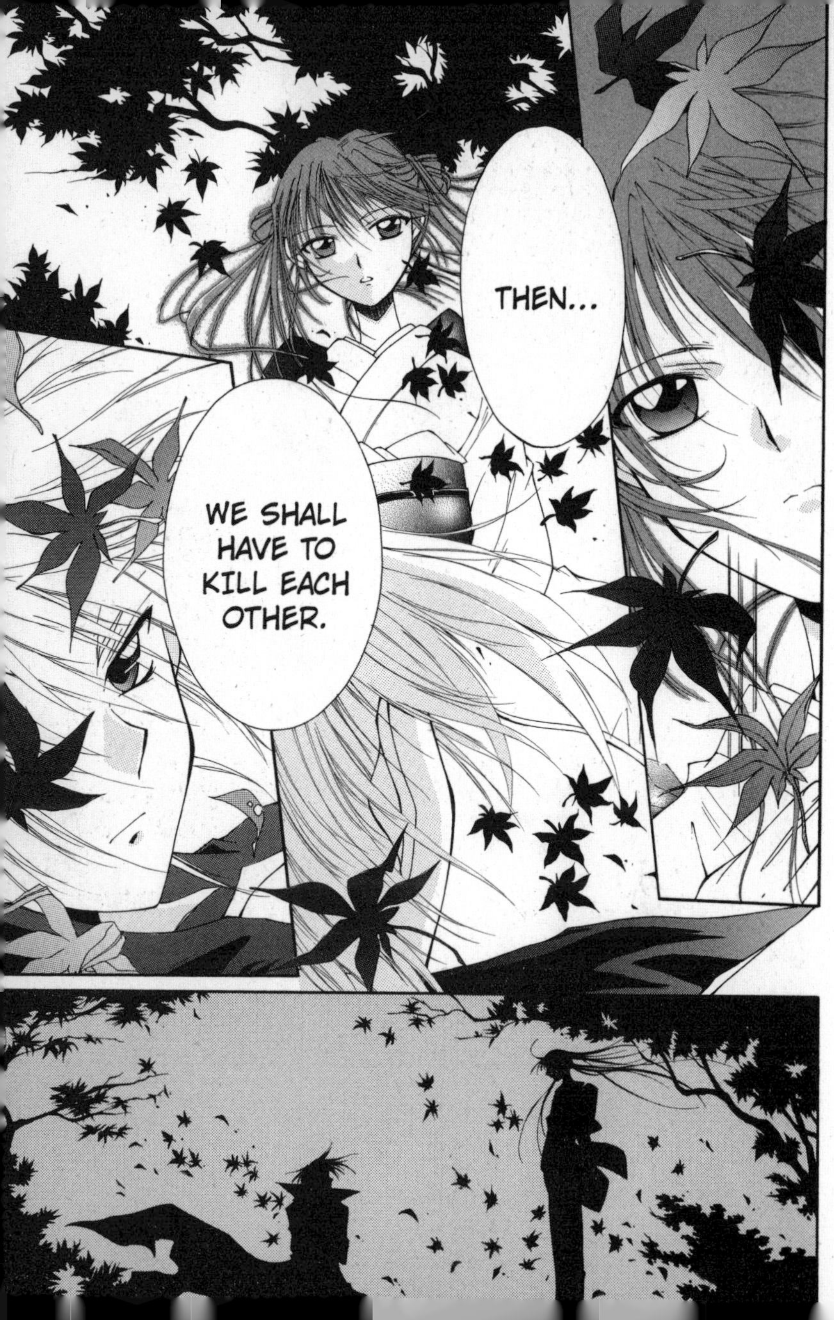
THEN...
WE SHALL HAVE TO KILL EACH OTHER.

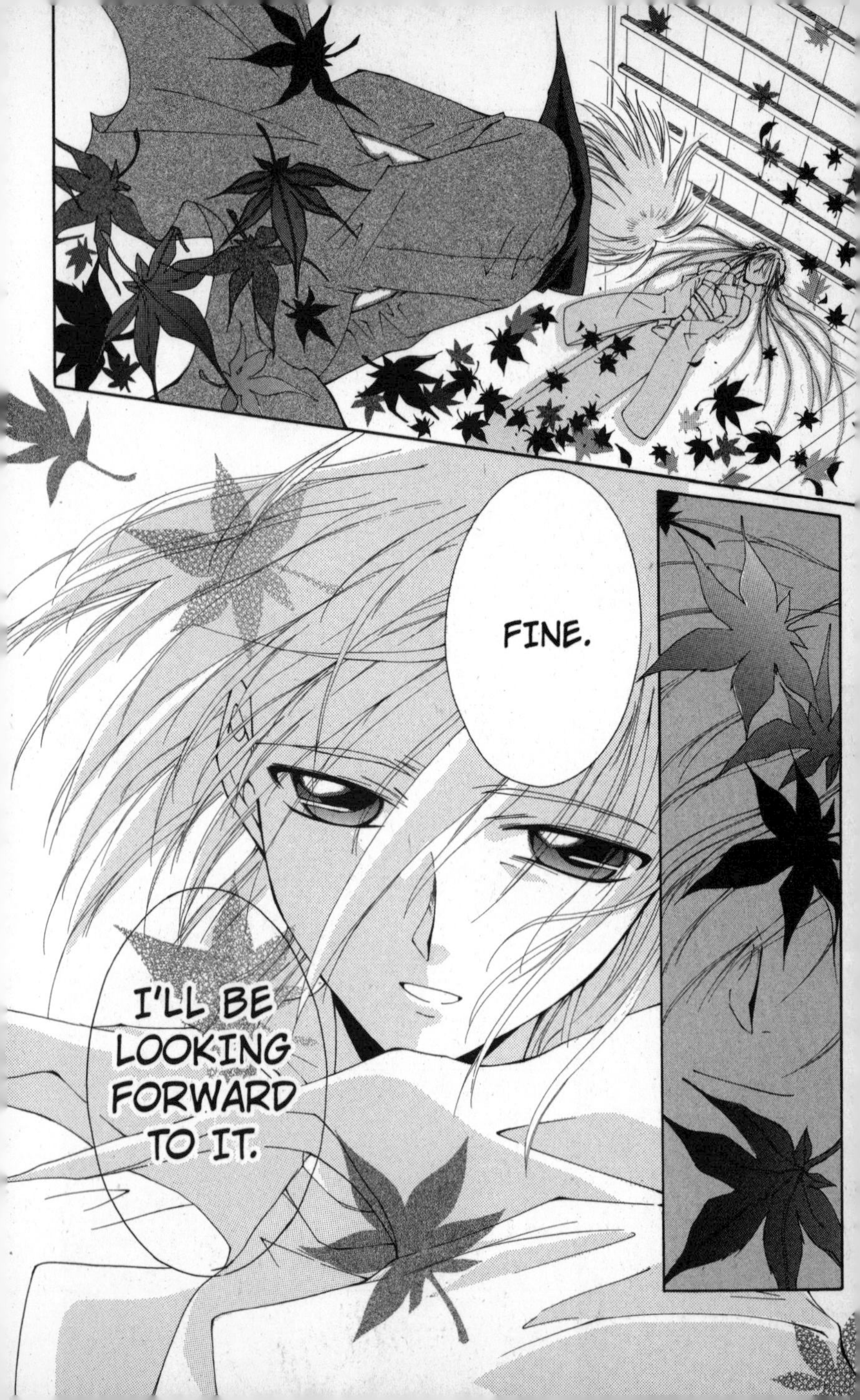
FINE.
I'LL BE LOOKING FORWARD TO IT.

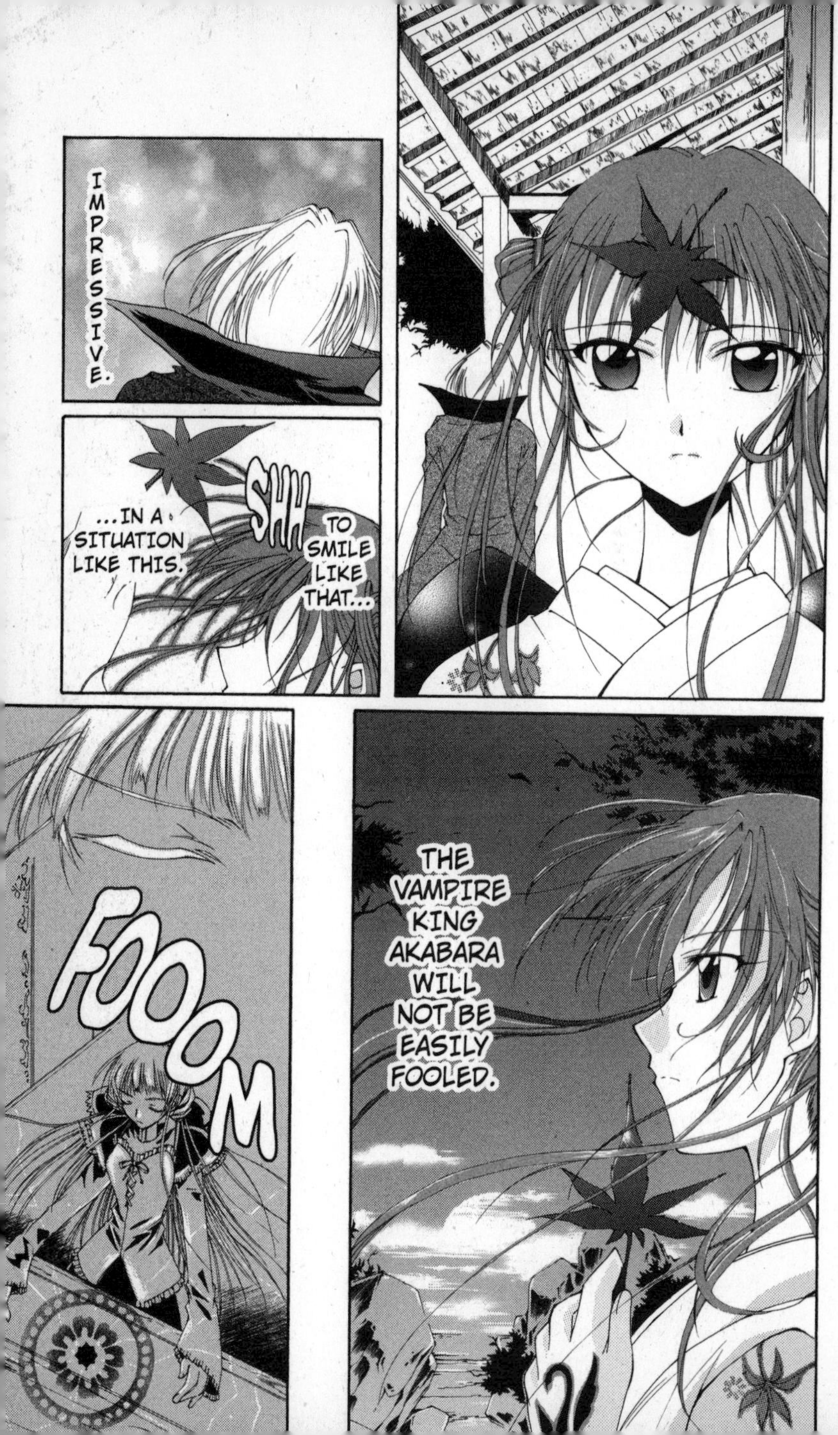
IMPRESSIVE.
TO SMILE LIKE THAT...
SHH
...IN A SITUATION LIKE THIS.
THE VAMPIRE KING AKABARA WILL NOT BE EASILY FOOLED.
FOOOM

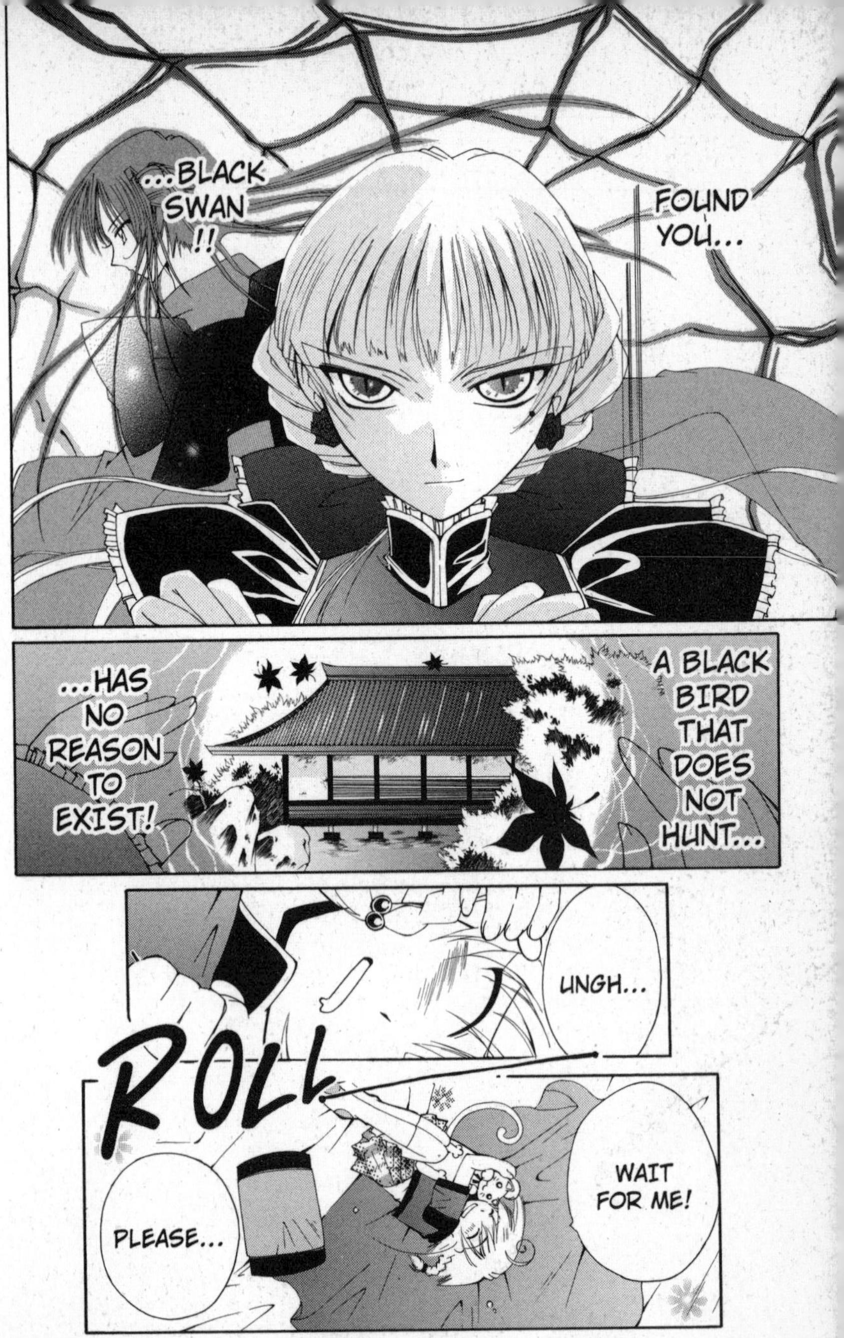
FOUND YOU...
...BLACK SWAN !!
A BLACK BIRD THAT DOES NOT HUNT...
...HAS NO REASON TO EXIST!
UNGH...
ROLL
WAIT FOR ME!
PLEASE...

THE RECORD OF A

FALLEN VAMPIRE

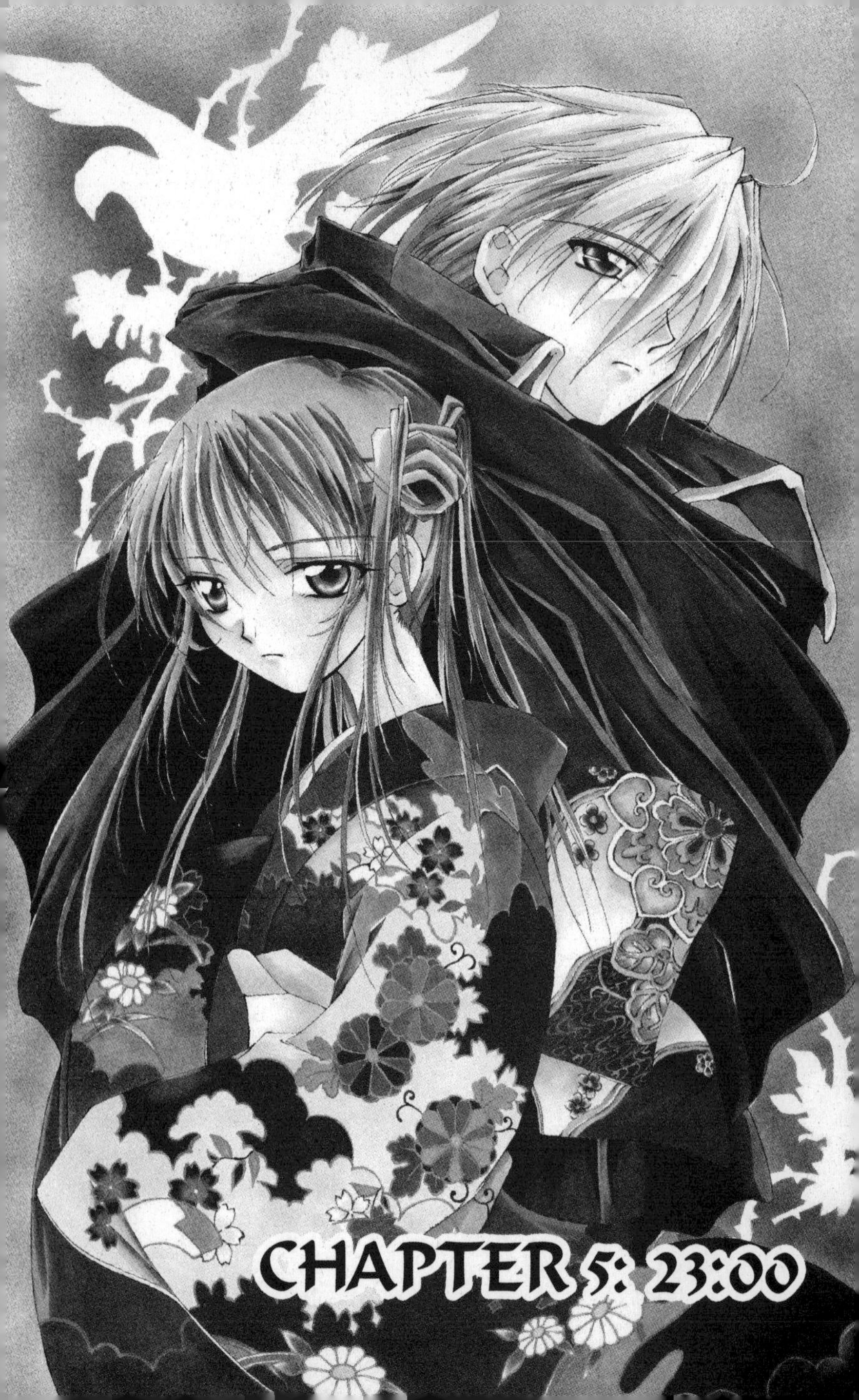
CHAPTER 5: 23:00

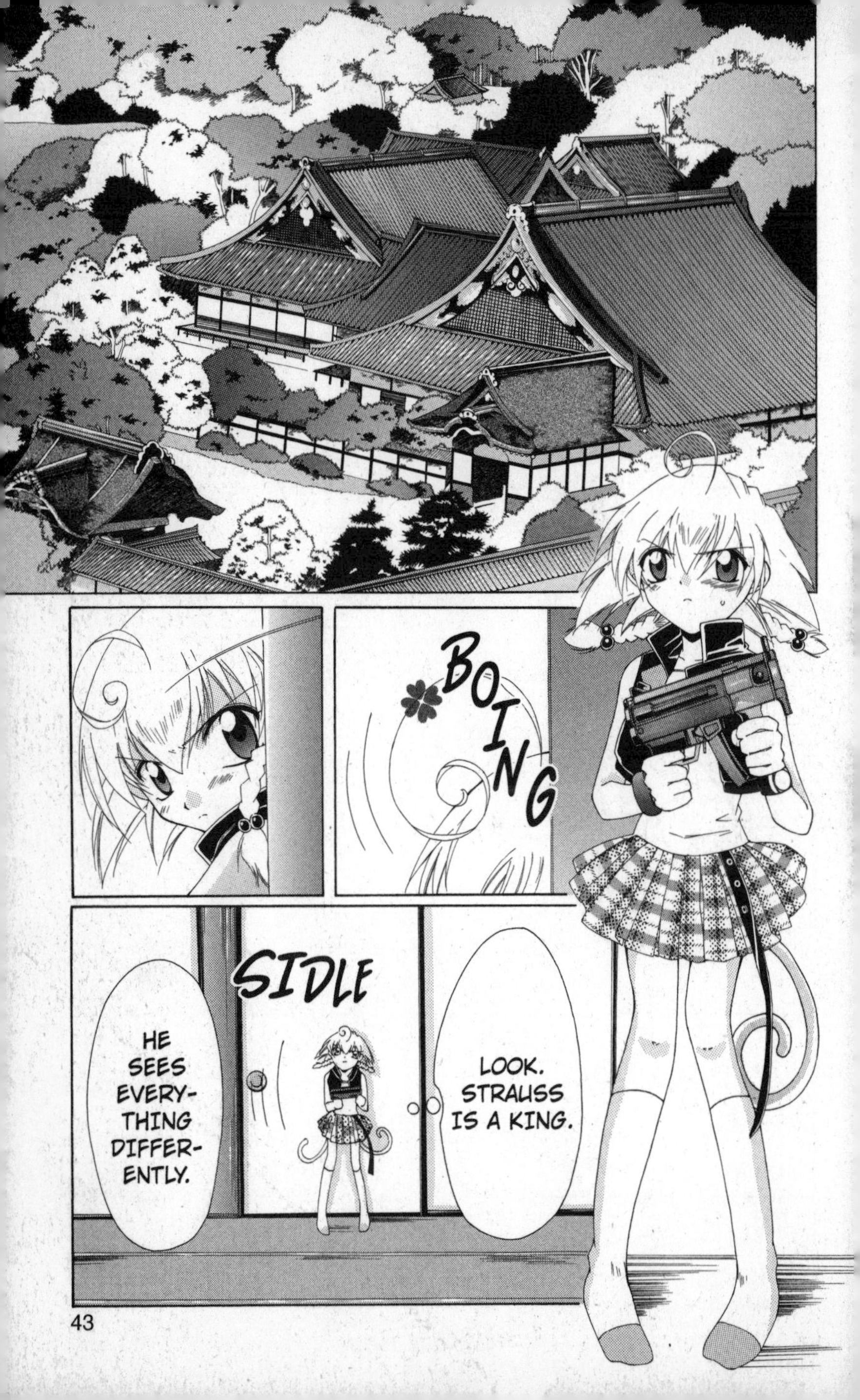
BOING
SIDLE
LOOK. STRAUSS IS A KING.
HE SEES EVERY-THING DIFFER-ENTLY.

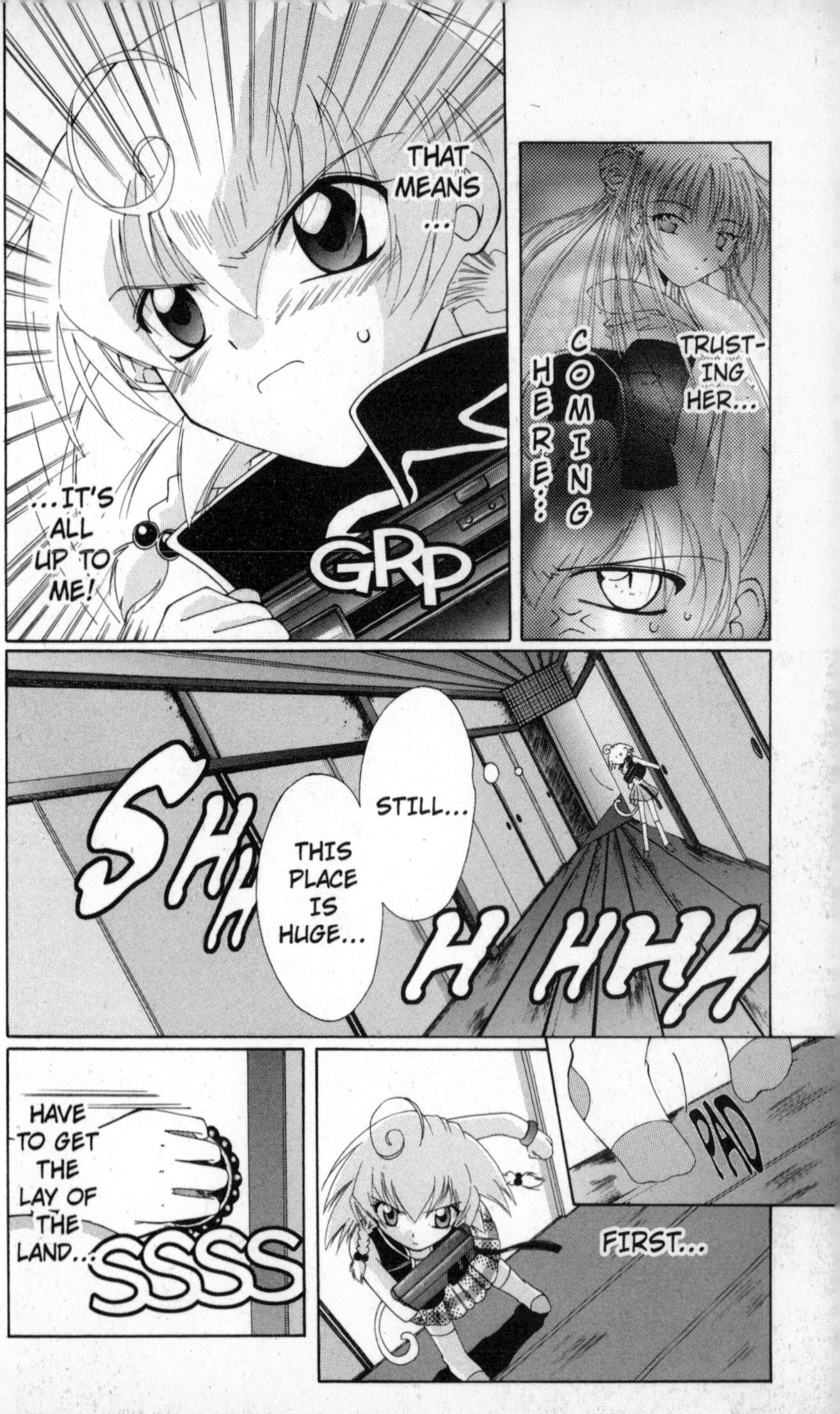
TRUSTING HER...
COMING HERE...
THAT MEANS...
...IT'S ALL UP TO ME!
GRP
SHHHHHH
STILL...
THIS PLACE IS HUGE...
PAD
FIRST...
HAVE TO GET THE LAY OF THE LAND...
SSSS

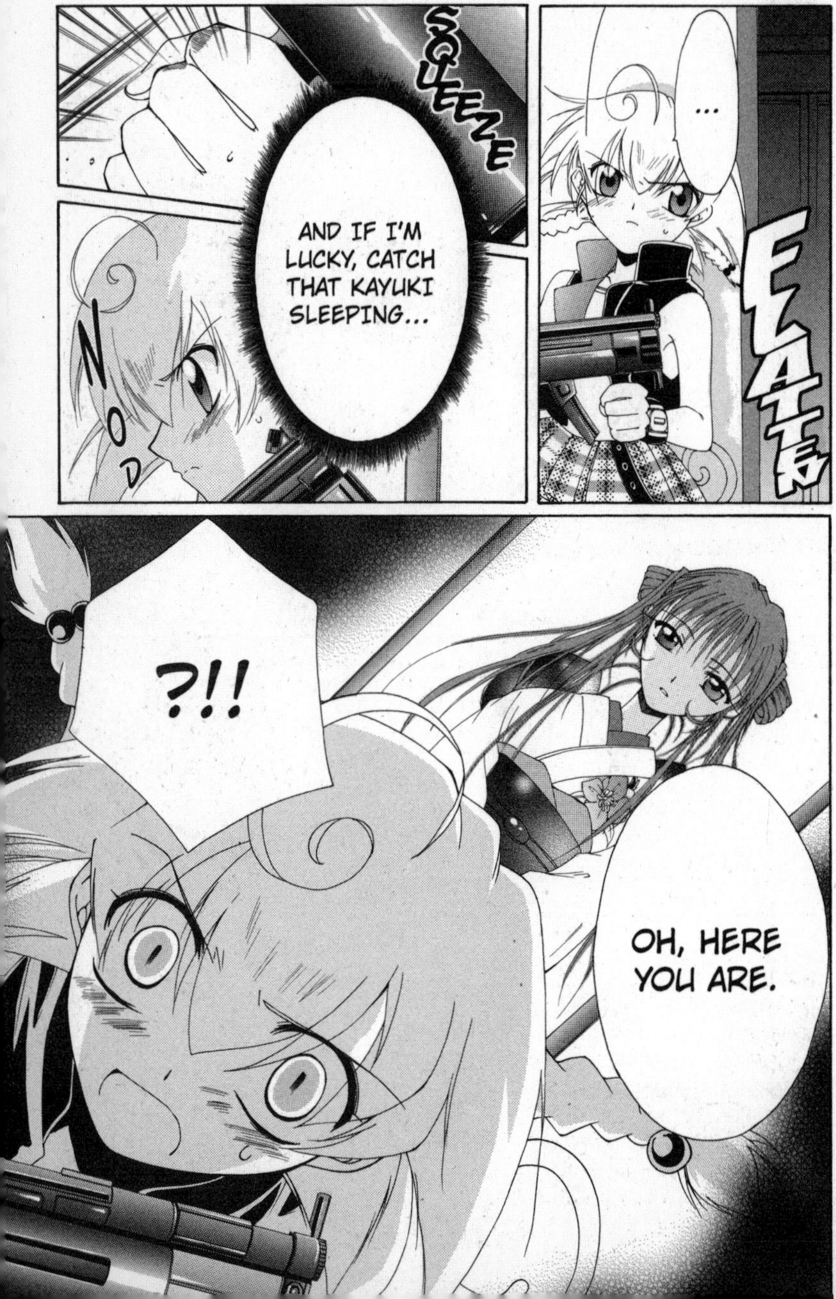
...
FLATTEN
SQUEEZE
AND IF I'M LUCKY, CATCH THAT KAYUKI SLEEPING...
NOD
OH, HERE YOU ARE.
?!!

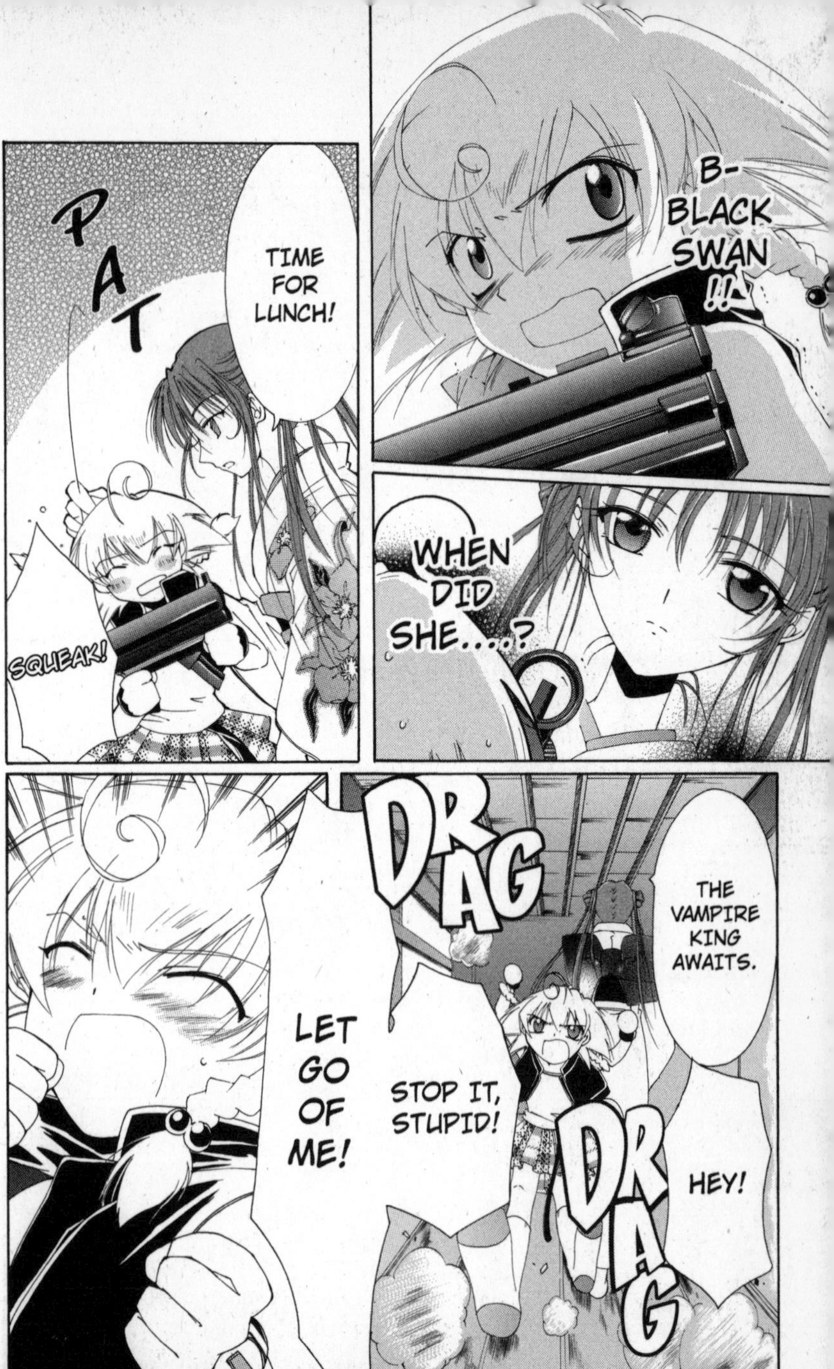
B-BLACK SWAN!!
WHEN DID SHE....?
PAT
TIME FOR LUNCH!
SQUEAK!
DRAG
THE VAMPIRE KING AWAITS.
HEY!
STOP IT, STUPID!
DRAG
LET GO OF ME!

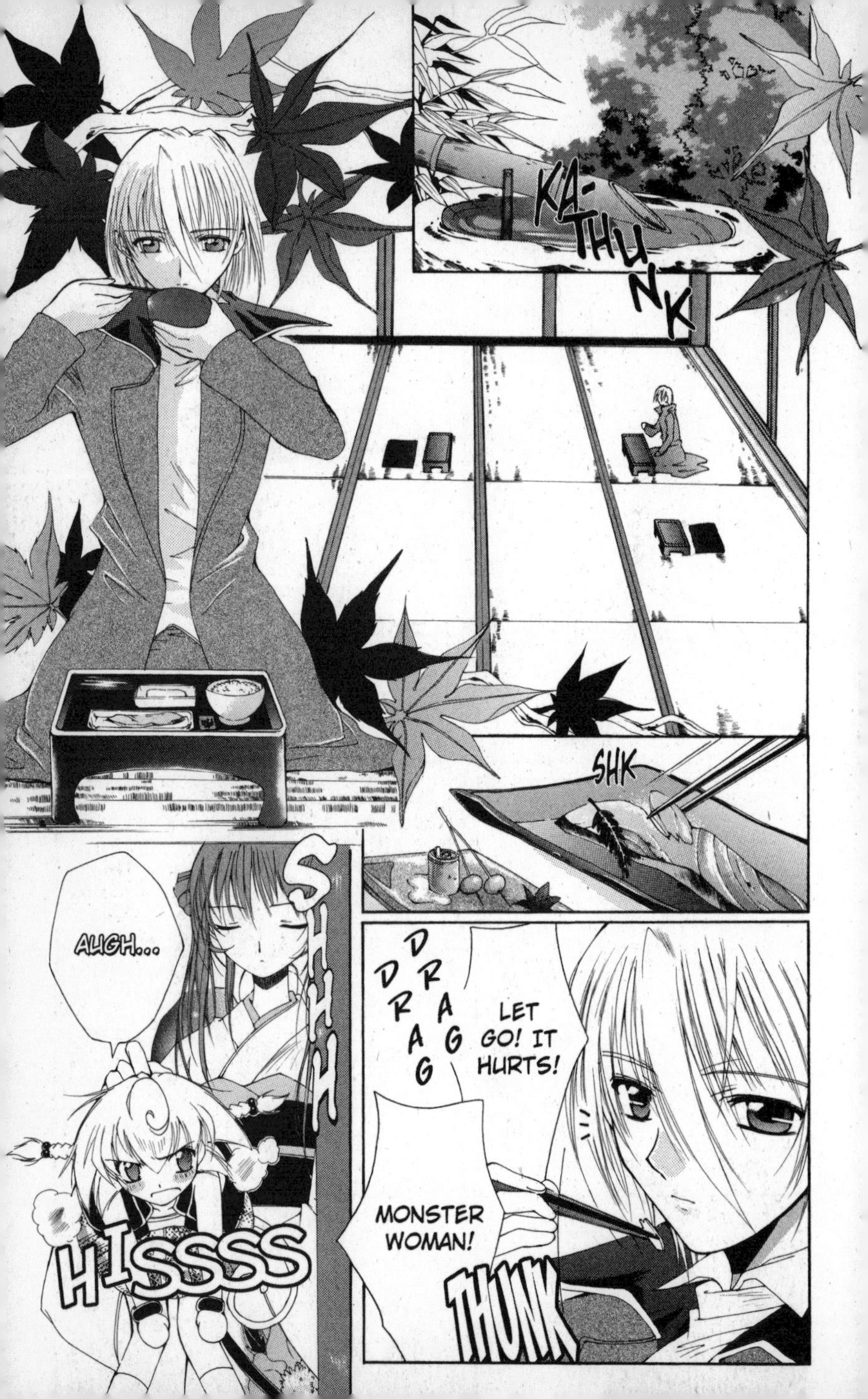
KA-THUNK
SHK
DRAG
DRAG
LET GO! IT HURTS!
MONSTER WOMAN!
THUNK
AUGH...
SHHH
HISSSS

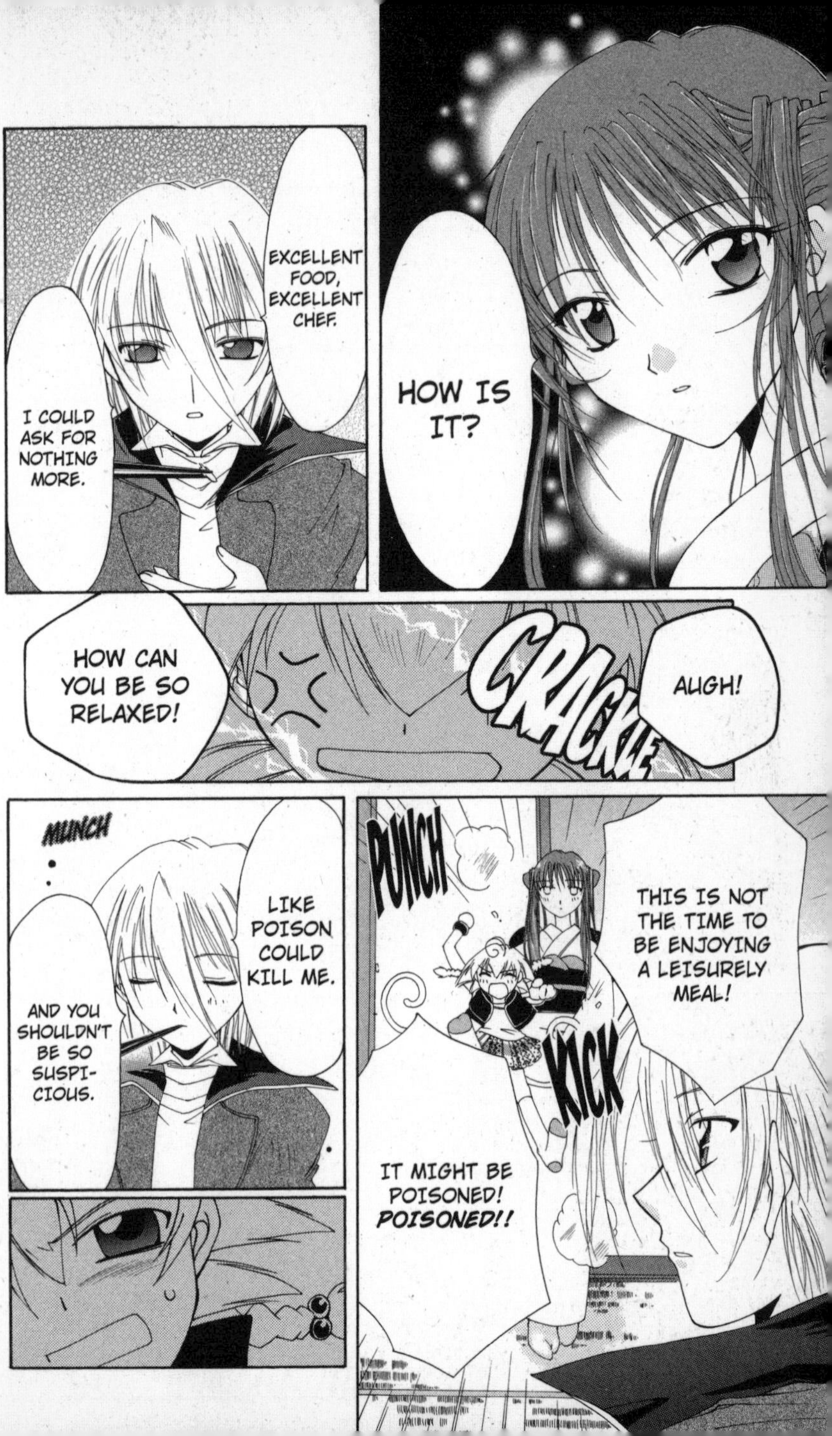
HOW IS IT?
EXCELLENT FOOD, EXCELLENT CHEF.
I COULD ASK FOR NOTHING MORE.
AUGH!
CRACKLE
HOW CAN YOU BE SO RELAXED!
THIS IS NOT THE TIME TO BE ENJOYING A LEISURELY MEAL!
PUNCH
KICK
IT MIGHT BE POISONED! POISONED!!
MUNCH
LIKE POISON COULD KILL ME.
AND YOU SHOULDN'T BE SO SUSPI-CIOUS.

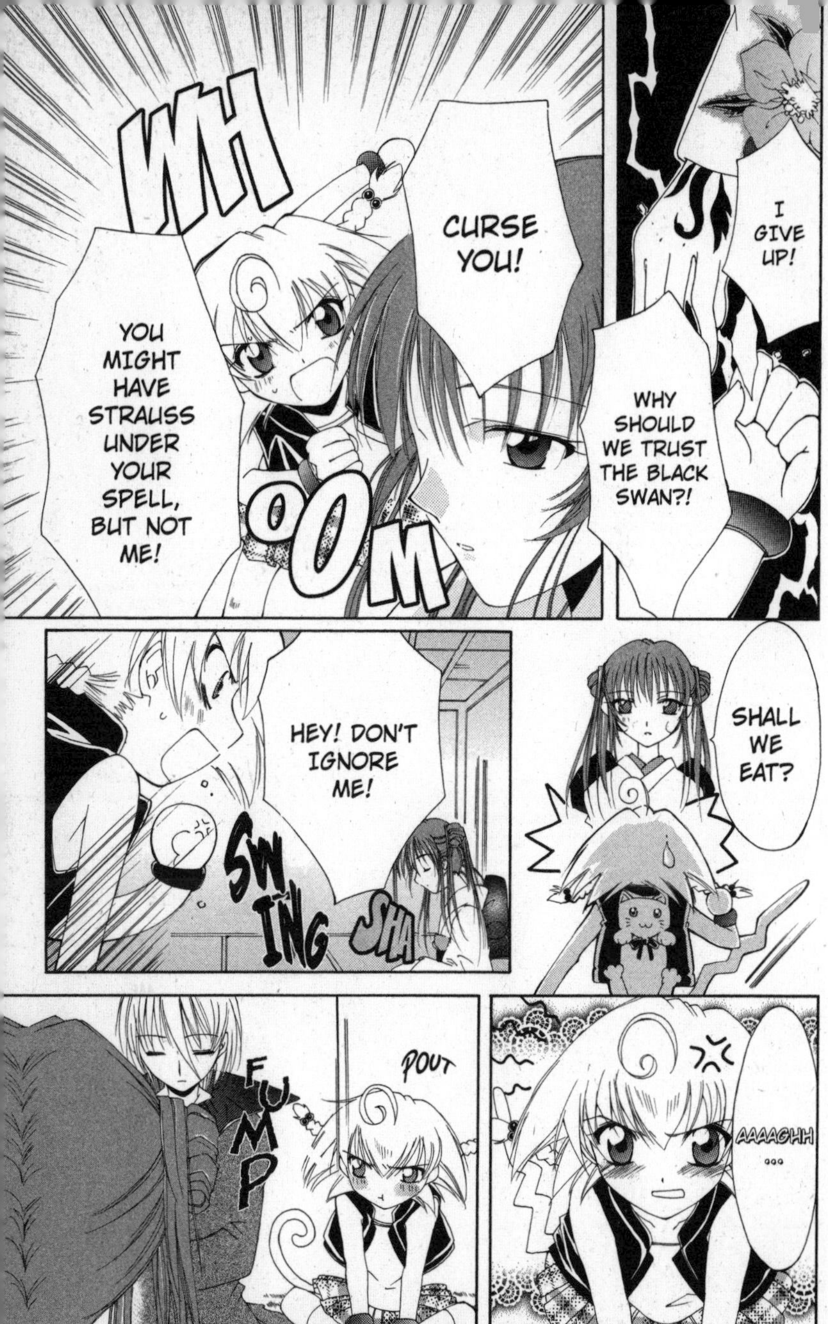
I GIVE UP!
WHY SHOULD WE TRUST THE BLACK SWAN?!
CURSE YOU!
WH
YOU MIGHT HAVE STRAUSS UNDER YOUR SPELL, BUT NOT ME!
OOM
SHALL WE EAT?
HEY! DON'T IGNORE ME!
SWING
SHA
AAAAGHH...
POUT
FUMP

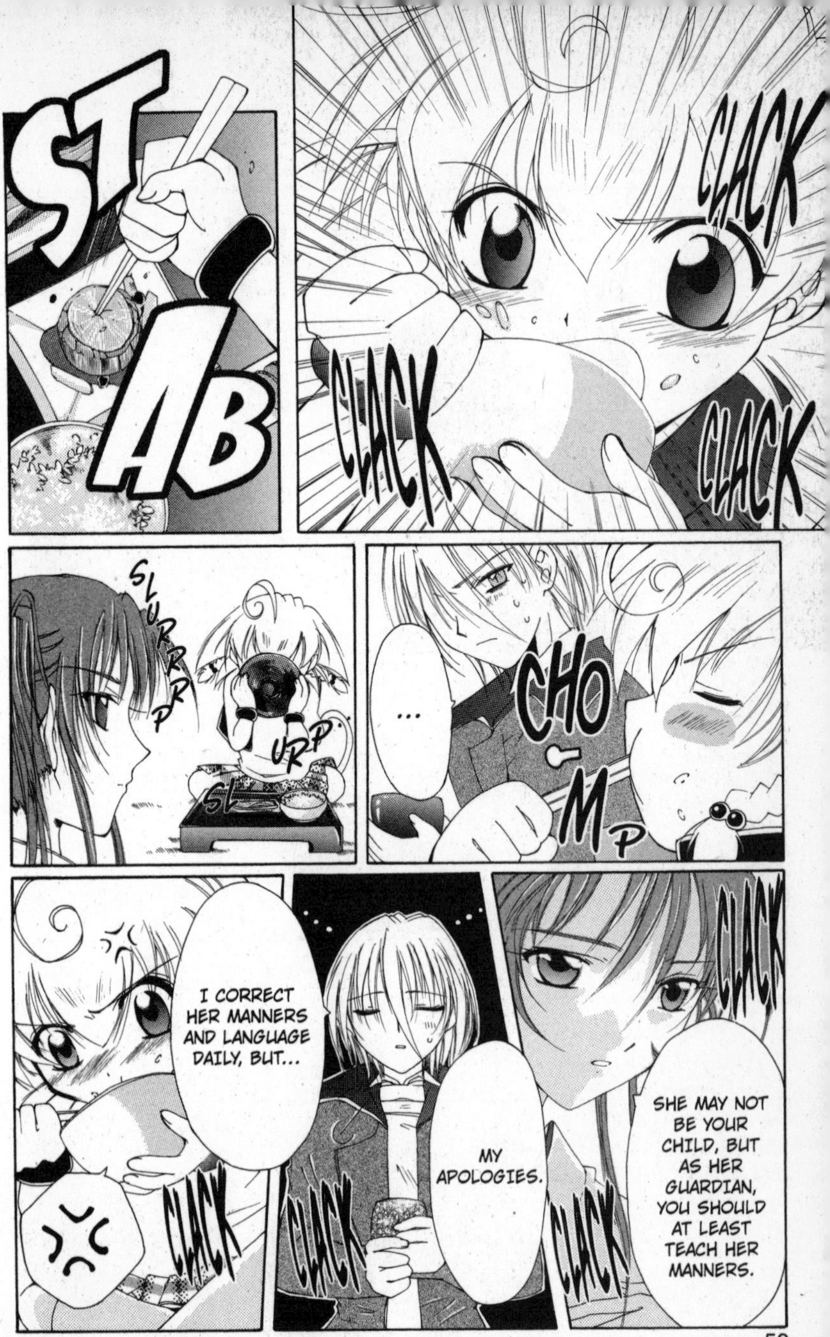
CLACK
CLACK
CLACK
STAB
...
CHOMP
SLURRRP
SLURP
CLACK
CLACK
SHE MAY NOT BE YOUR CHILD, BUT AS HER GUARDIAN, YOU SHOULD AT LEAST TEACH HER MANNERS.
CLACK
MY APOLOGIES.
CLACK
I CORRECT HER MANNERS AND LANGUAGE DAILY, BUT...
CLACK

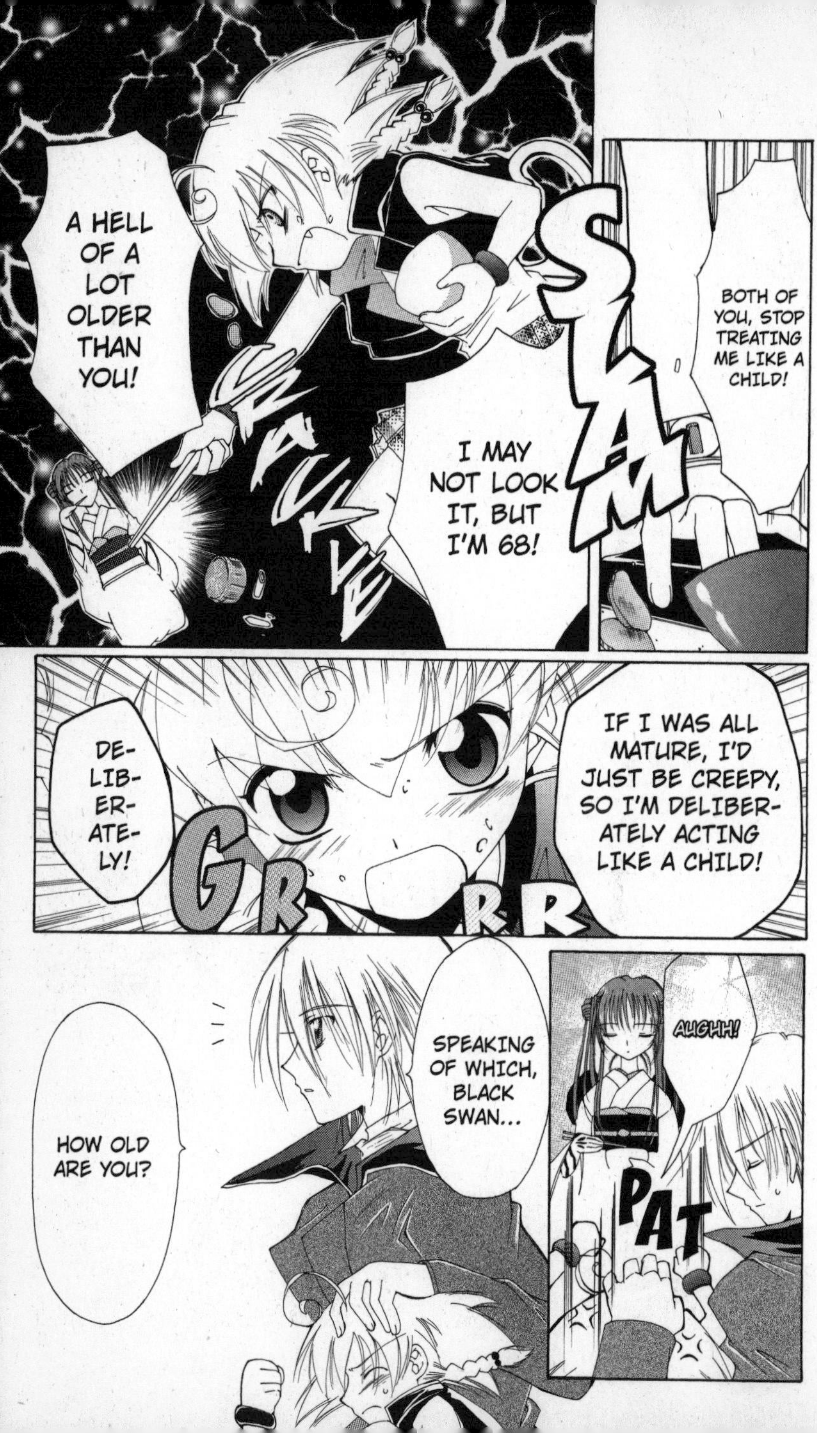
BOTH OF YOU, STOP TREATING ME LIKE A CHILD!
SLAM
I MAY NOT LOOK IT, BUT I'M 68!
A HELL OF A LOT OLDER THAN YOU!
IF I WAS ALL MATURE, I'D JUST BE CREEPY, SO I'M DELIBERATELY ACTING LIKE A CHILD!
DE-LIB-ER-ATE-LY!
GRRR
AUGHH!
PAT
SPEAKING OF WHICH, BLACK SWAN...
HOW OLD ARE YOU?

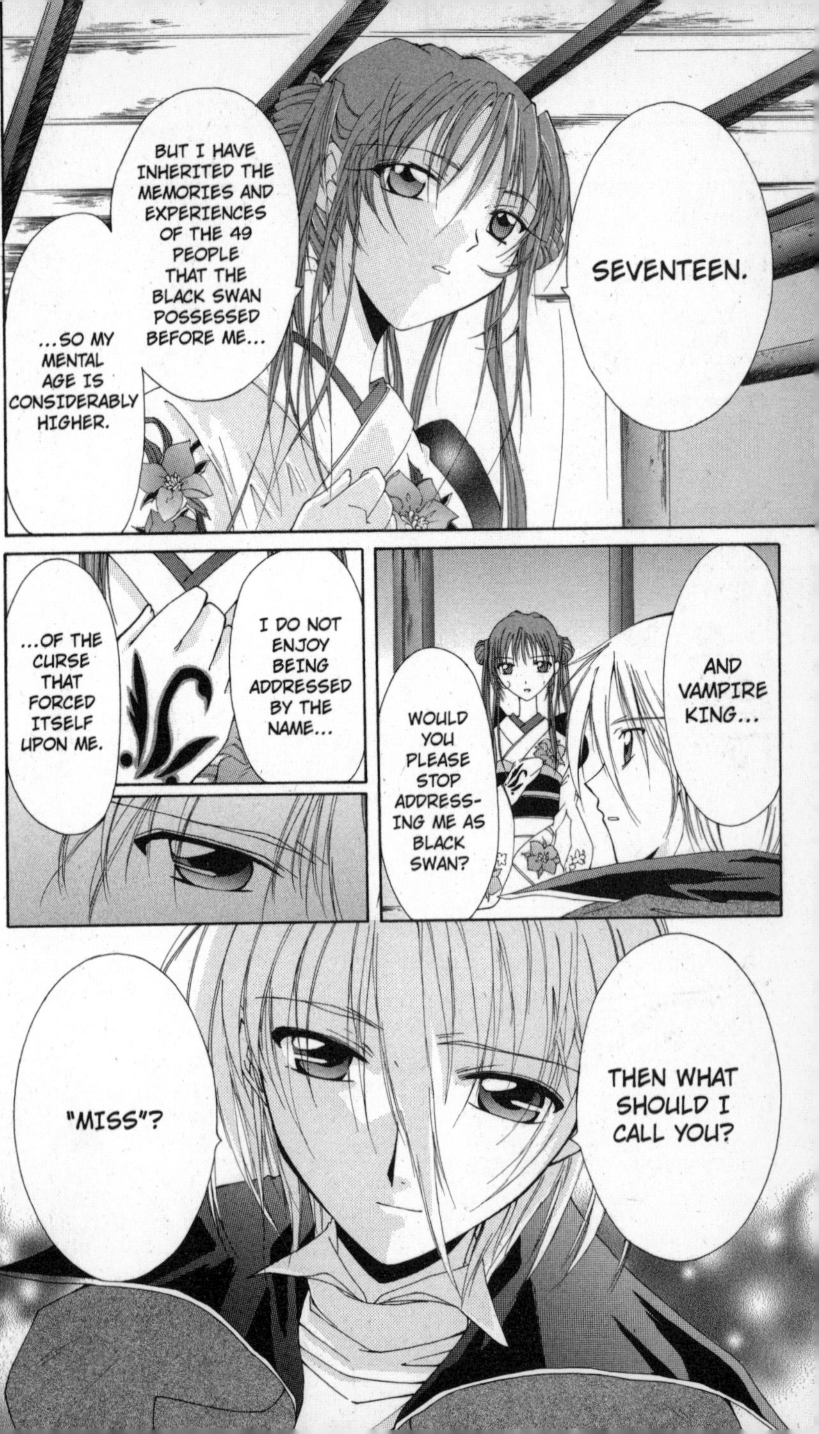
SEVENTEEN.
BUT I HAVE INHERITED THE MEMORIES AND EXPERIENCES OF THE 49 PEOPLE THAT THE BLACK SWAN POSSESSED BEFORE ME...
...SO MY MENTAL AGE IS CONSIDERABLY HIGHER.
AND VAMPIRE KING...
WOULD YOU PLEASE STOP ADDRESSING ME AS BLACK SWAN?
I DO NOT ENJOY BEING ADDRESSED BY THE NAME...
...OF THE CURSE THAT FORCED ITSELF UPON ME.
THEN WHAT SHOULD I CALL YOU?
"MISS"?

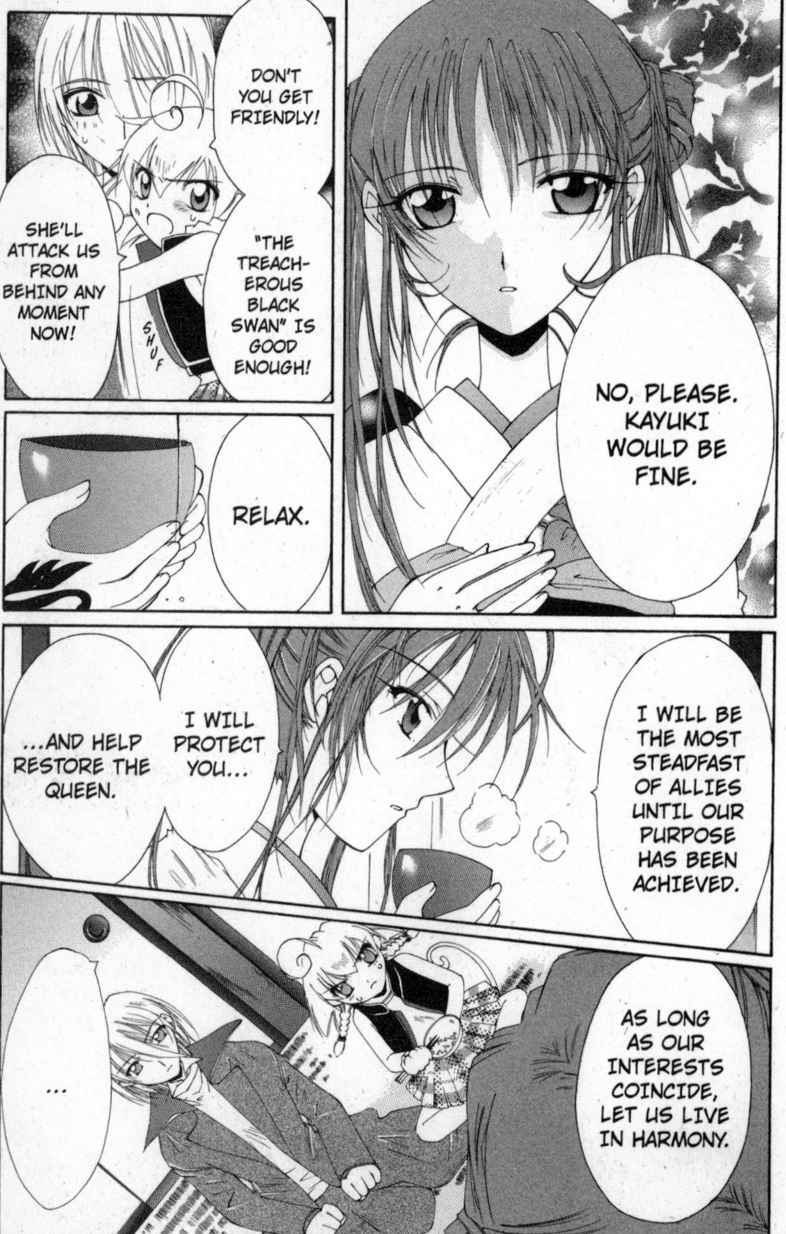
NO, PLEASE. KAYUKI WOULD BE FINE.
DON'T YOU GET FRIENDLY!
"THE TREACH-EROUS BLACK SWAN" IS GOOD ENOUGH!
SHE'LL ATTACK US FROM BEHIND ANY MOMENT NOW!
SHUF
RELAX.
I WILL BE THE MOST STEADFAST OF ALLIES UNTIL OUR PURPOSE HAS BEEN ACHIEVED.
I WILL PROTECT YOU...
...AND HELP RESTORE THE QUEEN.
AS LONG AS OUR INTERESTS COINCIDE, LET US LIVE IN HARMONY.
...

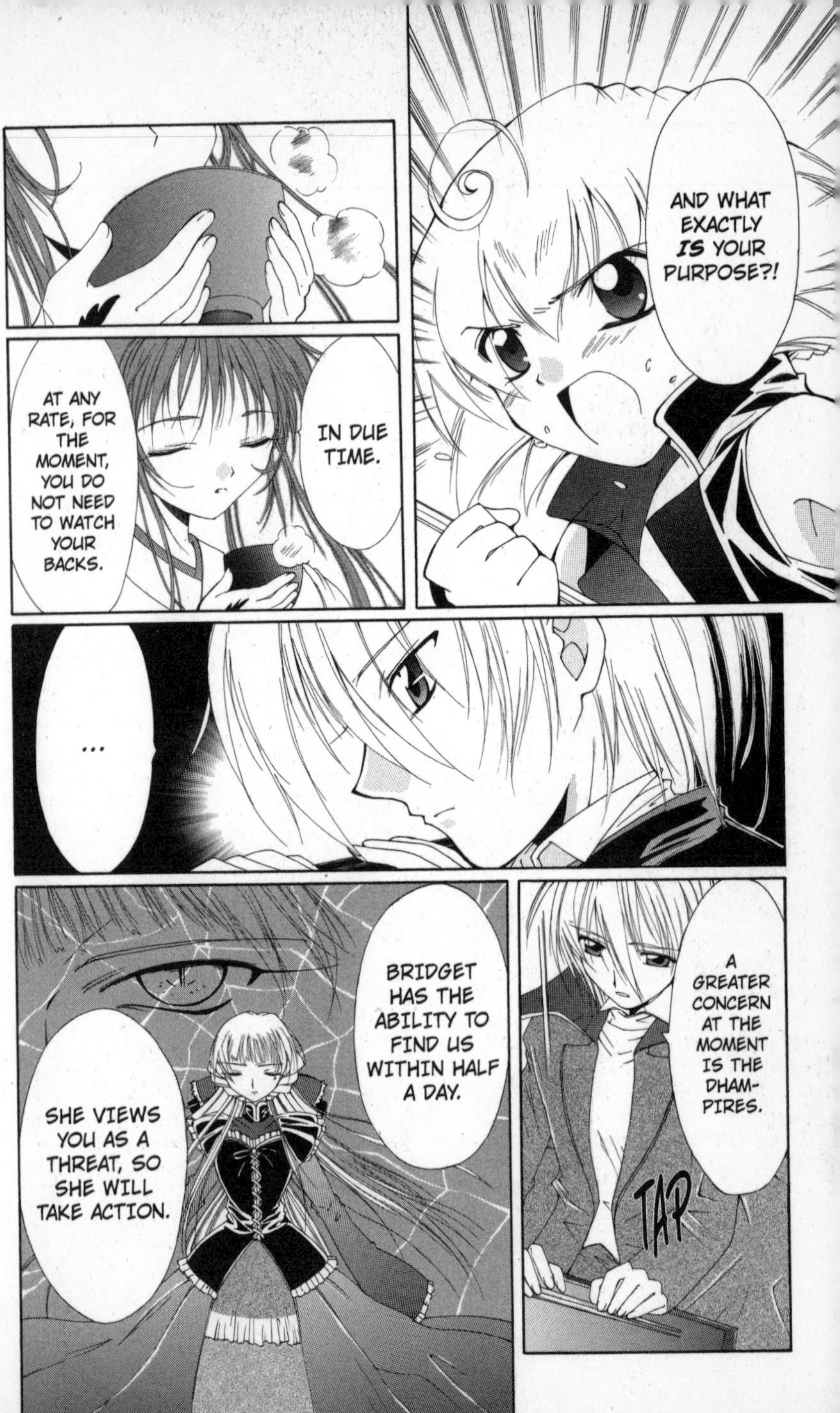
AND WHAT EXACTLY IS YOUR PURPOSE?!
IN DUE TIME.
AT ANY RATE, FOR THE MOMENT, YOU DO NOT NEED TO WATCH YOUR BACKS.
...
A GREATER CONCERN AT THE MOMENT IS THE DHAM-PIRES.
TAP
BRIDGET HAS THE ABILITY TO FIND US WITHIN HALF A DAY.
SHE VIEWS YOU AS A THREAT, SO SHE WILL TAKE ACTION.

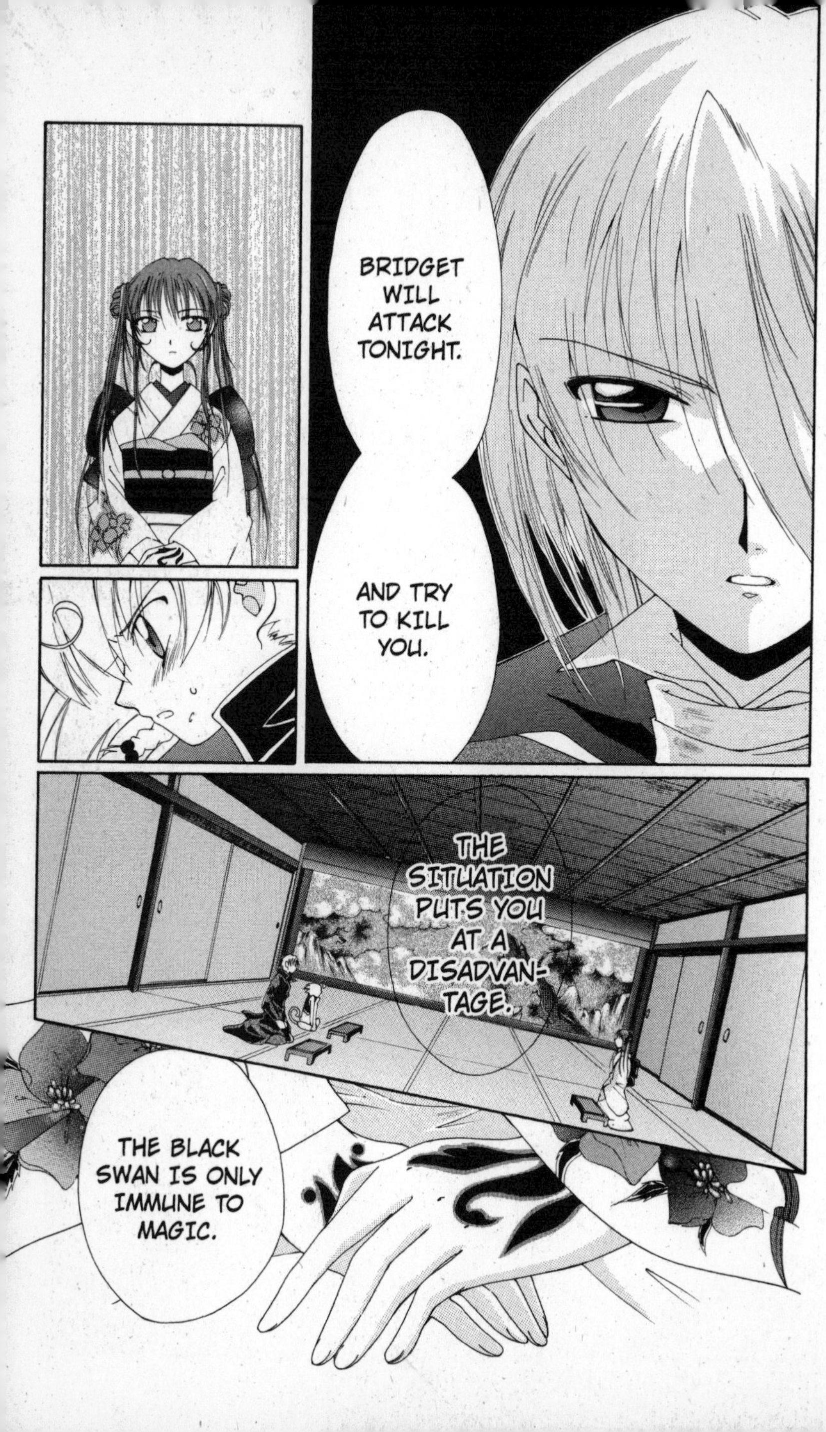
BRIDGET WILL ATTACK TONIGHT.
AND TRY TO KILL YOU.
THE SITUATION PUTS YOU AT A DISADVANTAGE.
THE BLACK SWAN IS ONLY IMMUNE TO MAGIC.

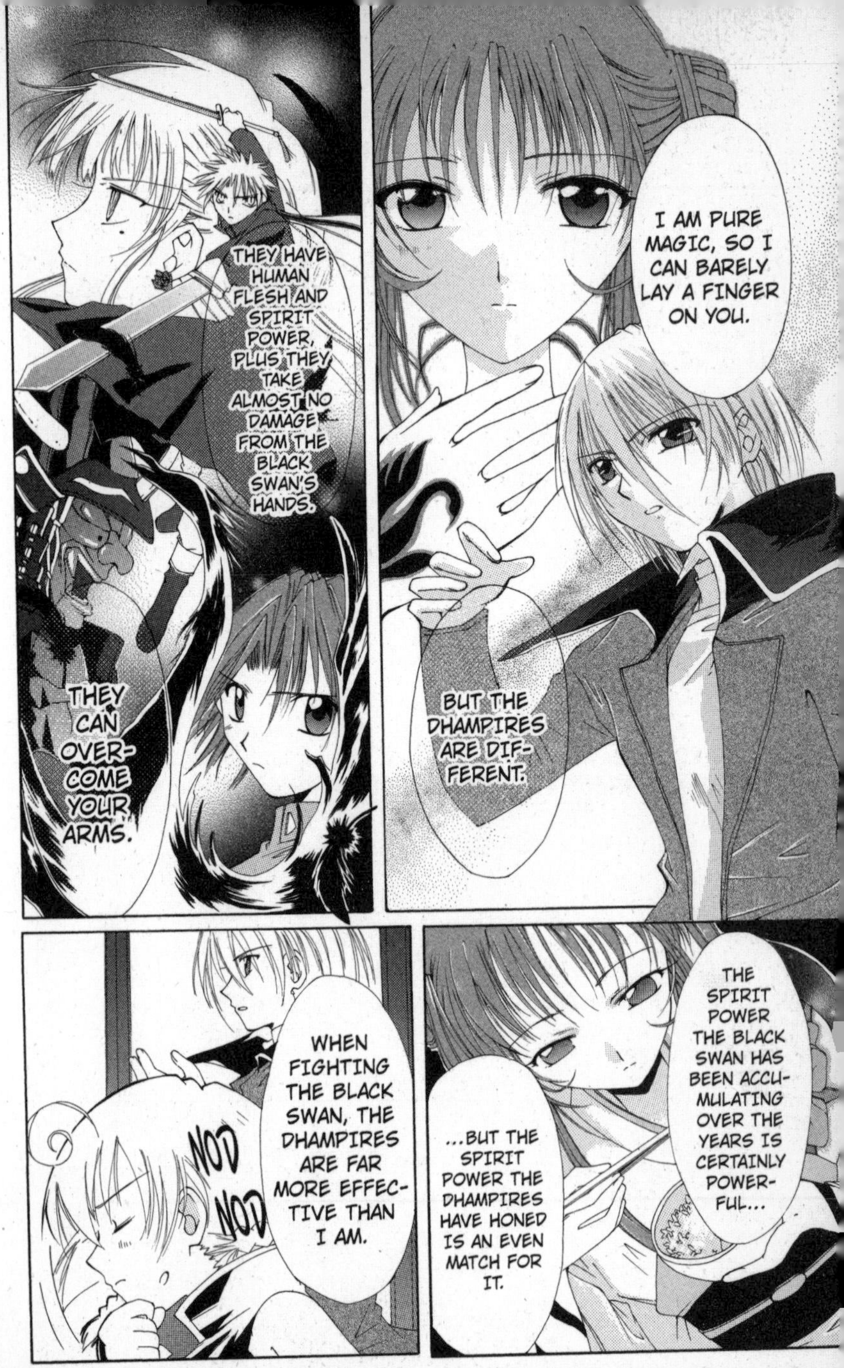
I AM PURE MAGIC, SO I CAN BARELY LAY A FINGER ON YOU.
BUT THE DHAMPIRES ARE DIF-FERENT.
THEY HAVE HUMAN FLESH AND SPIRIT POWER, PLUS THEY TAKE ALMOST NO DAMAGE FROM THE BLACK SWAN'S HANDS.
THEY CAN OVER-COME YOUR ARMS.
THE SPIRIT POWER THE BLACK SWAN HAS BEEN ACCU-MULATING OVER THE YEARS IS CERTAINLY POWER-FUL...
...BUT THE SPIRIT POWER THE DHAMPIRES HAVE HONED IS AN EVEN MATCH FOR IT.
WHEN FIGHTING THE BLACK SWAN, THE DHAMPIRES ARE FAR MORE EFFEC-TIVE THAN I AM.
NOD
NOD

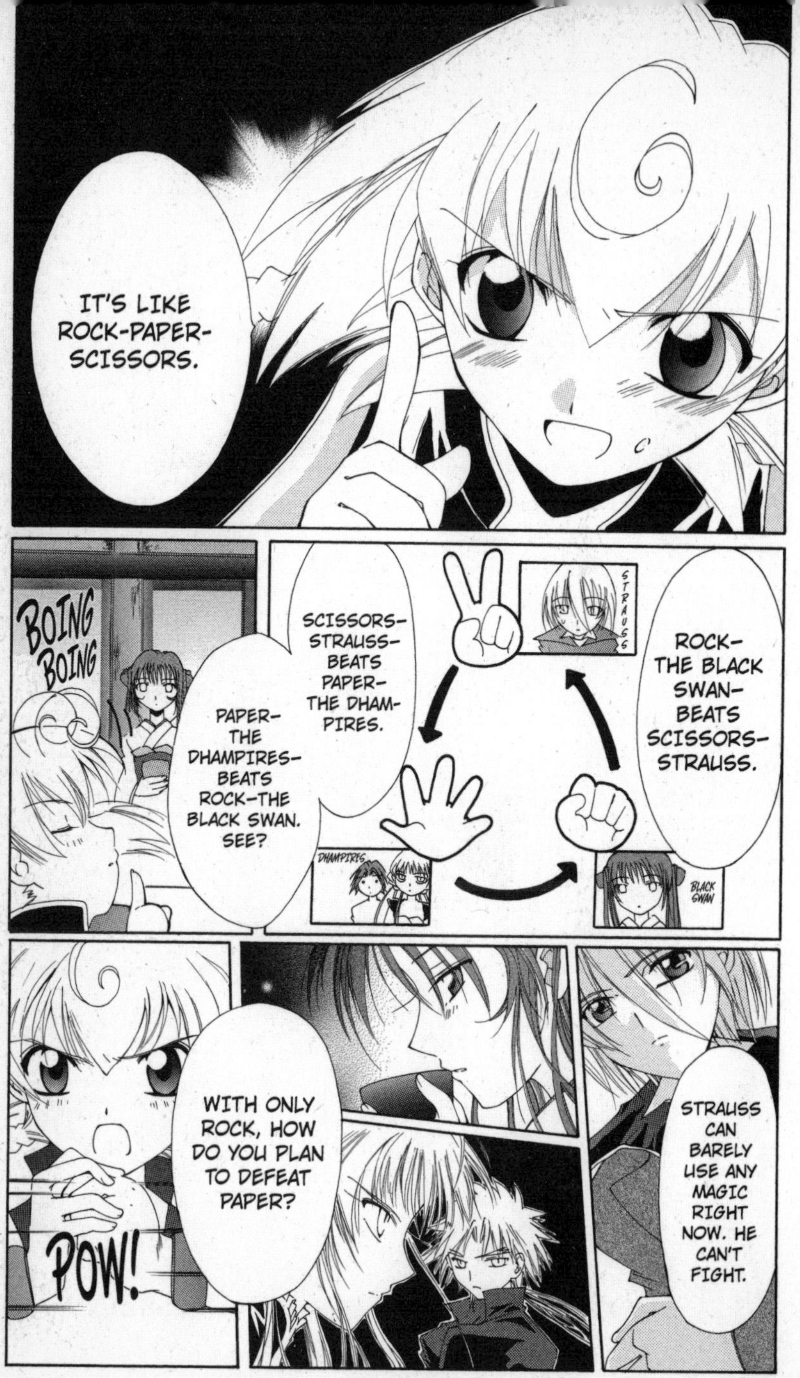
IT'S LIKE ROCK-PAPER-SCISSORS.
ROCK—THE BLACK SWAN—BEATS SCISSORS—STRAUSS.
STRAUSS
SCISSORS—STRAUSS—BEATS PAPER—THE DHAMPIRES.
PAPER—THE DHAMPIRES—BEATS ROCK—THE BLACK SWAN. SEE?
BLACK SWAN
DHAMPIRES
BOING BOING
STRAUSS CAN BARELY USE ANY MAGIC RIGHT NOW. HE CAN'T FIGHT.
WITH ONLY ROCK, HOW DO YOU PLAN TO DEFEAT PAPER?
POW!

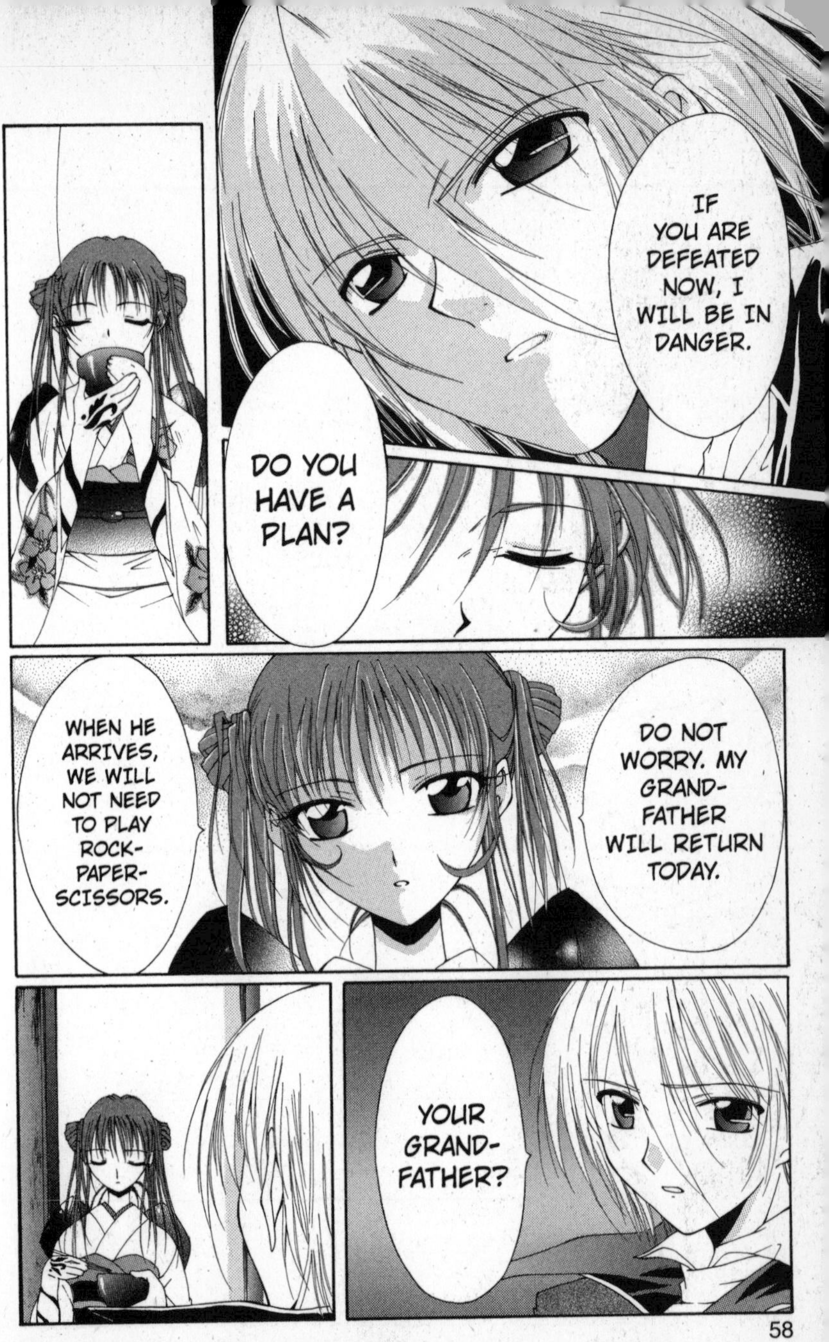
IF YOU ARE DEFEATED NOW, I WILL BE IN DANGER.
DO YOU HAVE A PLAN?
DO NOT WORRY. MY GRAND-FATHER WILL RETURN TODAY.
WHEN HE ARRIVES, WE WILL NOT NEED TO PLAY ROCK-PAPER-SCISSORS.
YOUR GRAND-FATHER?

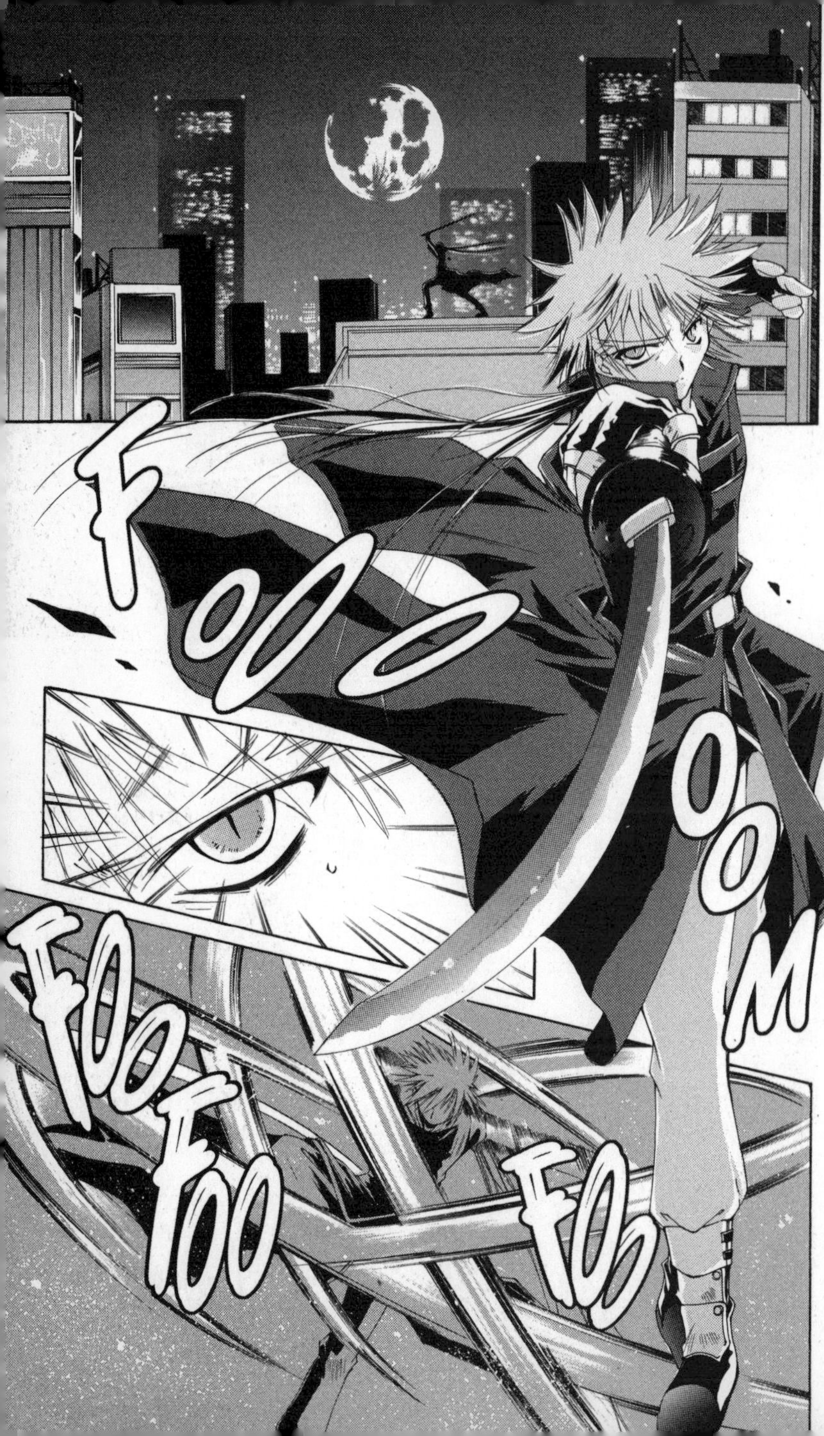
Destiny
FOOO
OOOM
FOO
FOO
FOO
FOO

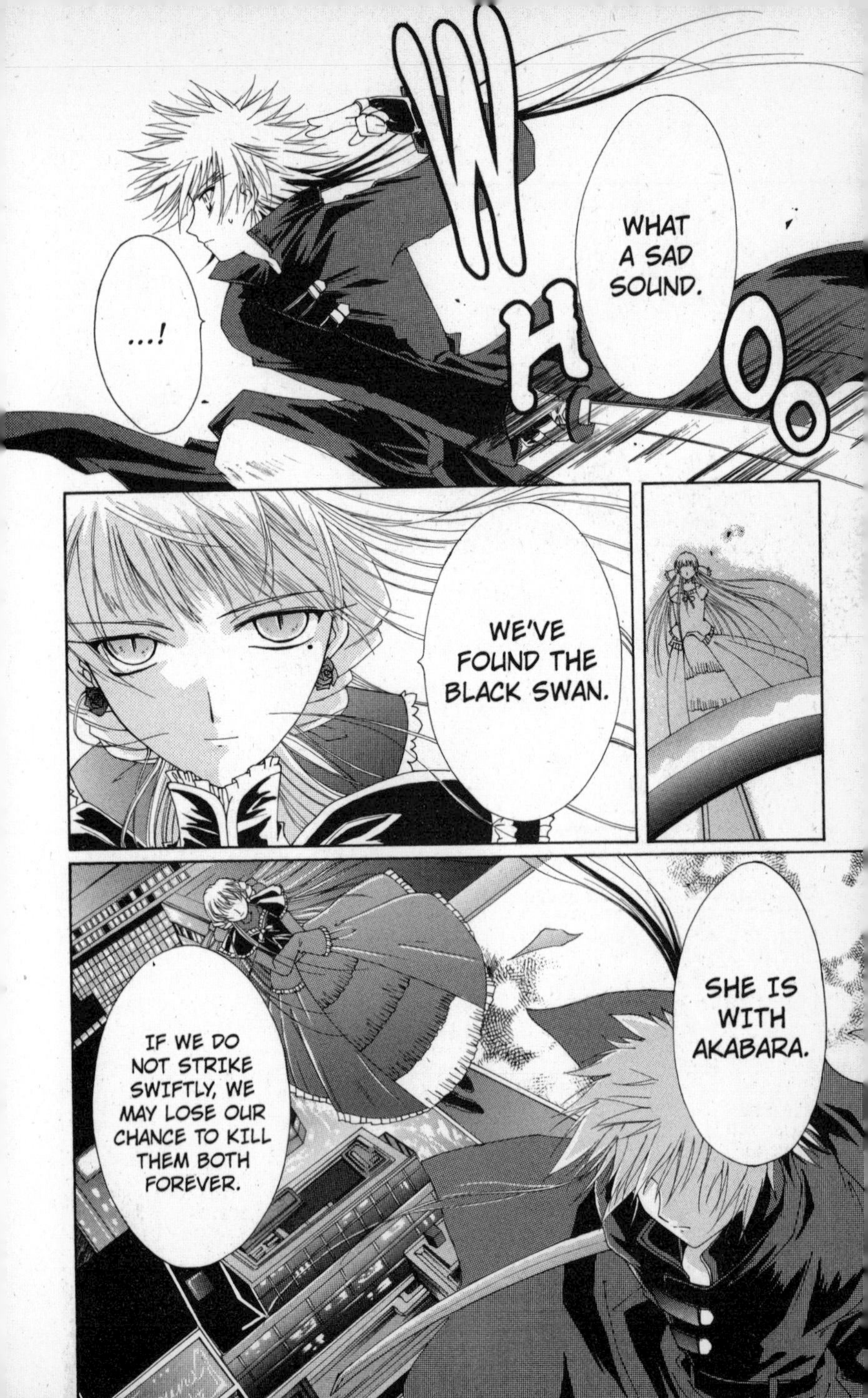
WHOOO
WHAT A SAD SOUND.
...!
WE'VE FOUND THE BLACK SWAN.
SHE IS WITH AKABARA.
IF WE DO NOT STRIKE SWIFTLY, WE MAY LOSE OUR CHANCE TO KILL THEM BOTH FOREVER.

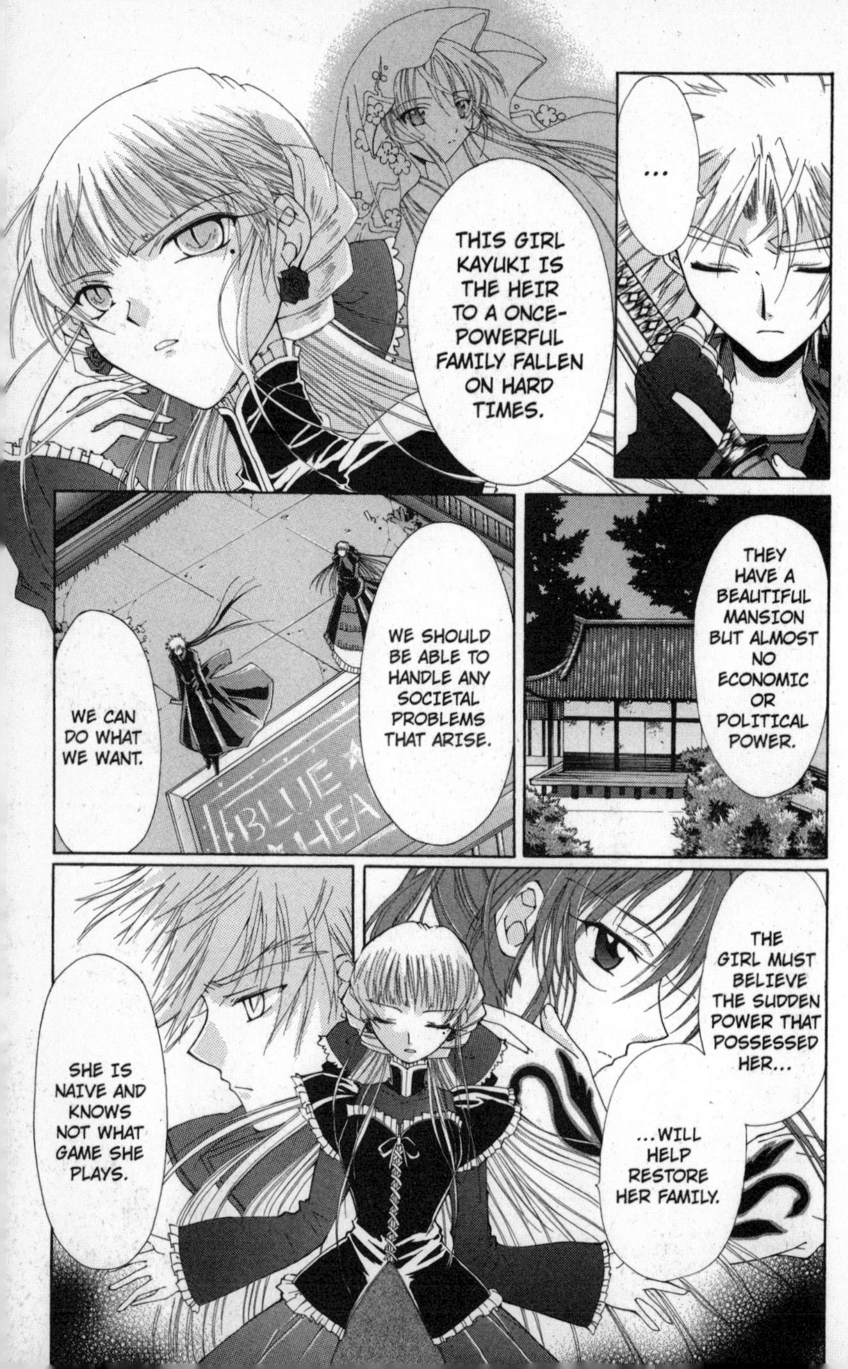
...
THIS GIRL KAYUKI IS THE HEIR TO A ONCE-POWERFUL FAMILY FALLEN ON HARD TIMES.
THEY HAVE A BEAUTIFUL MANSION BUT ALMOST NO ECONOMIC OR POLITICAL POWER.
WE SHOULD BE ABLE TO HANDLE ANY SOCIETAL PROBLEMS THAT ARISE.
WE CAN DO WHAT WE WANT.
THE GIRL MUST BELIEVE THE SUDDEN POWER THAT POSSESSED HER...
...WILL HELP RESTORE HER FAMILY.
SHE IS NAIVE AND KNOWS NOT WHAT GAME SHE PLAYS.

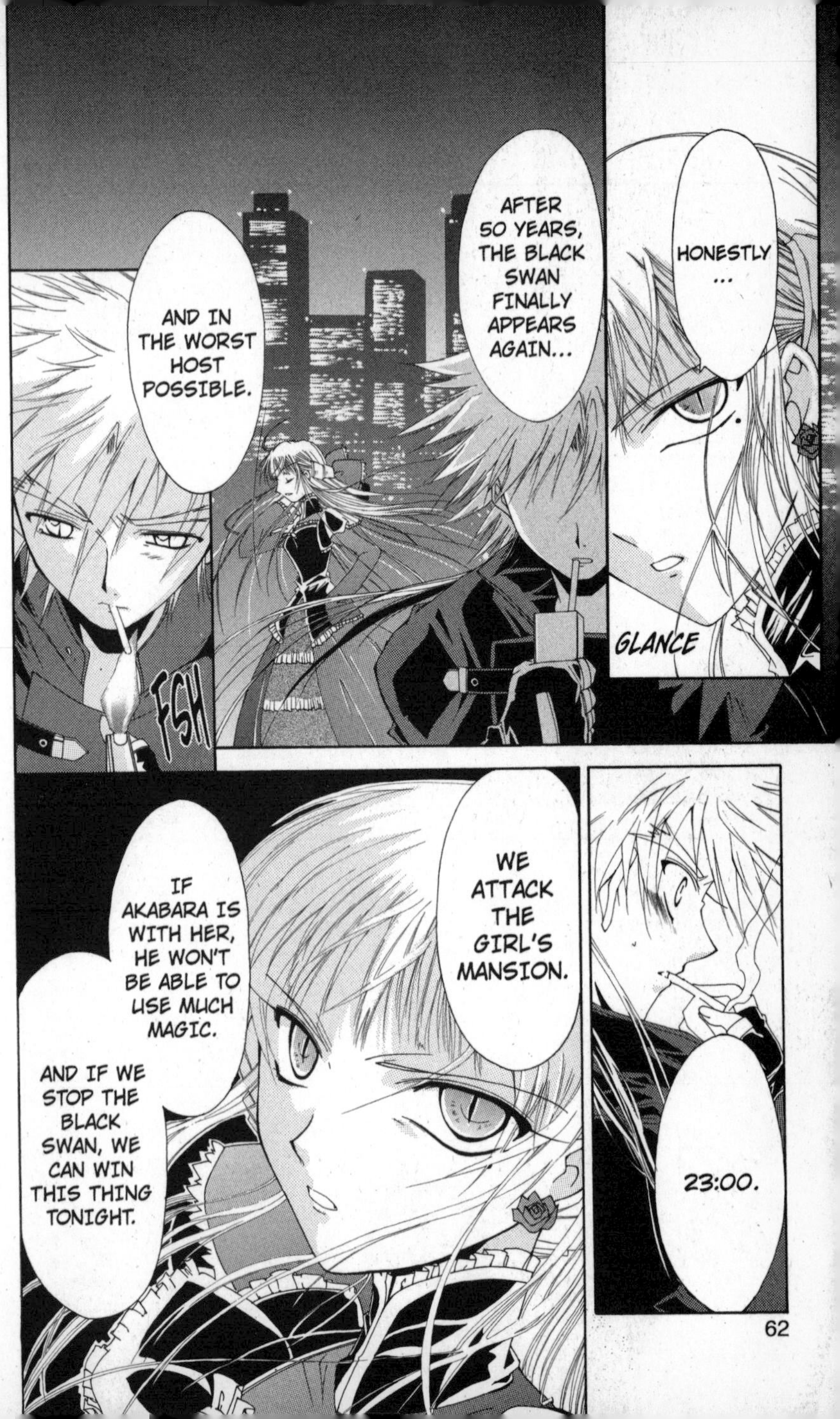
HONESTLY ...
GLANCE
AFTER 50 YEARS, THE BLACK SWAN FINALLY APPEARS AGAIN...
AND IN THE WORST HOST POSSIBLE.
FSH
23:00.
WE ATTACK THE GIRL'S MANSION.
IF AKABARA IS WITH HER, HE WON'T BE ABLE TO USE MUCH MAGIC.
AND IF WE STOP THE BLACK SWAN, WE CAN WIN THIS THING TONIGHT.

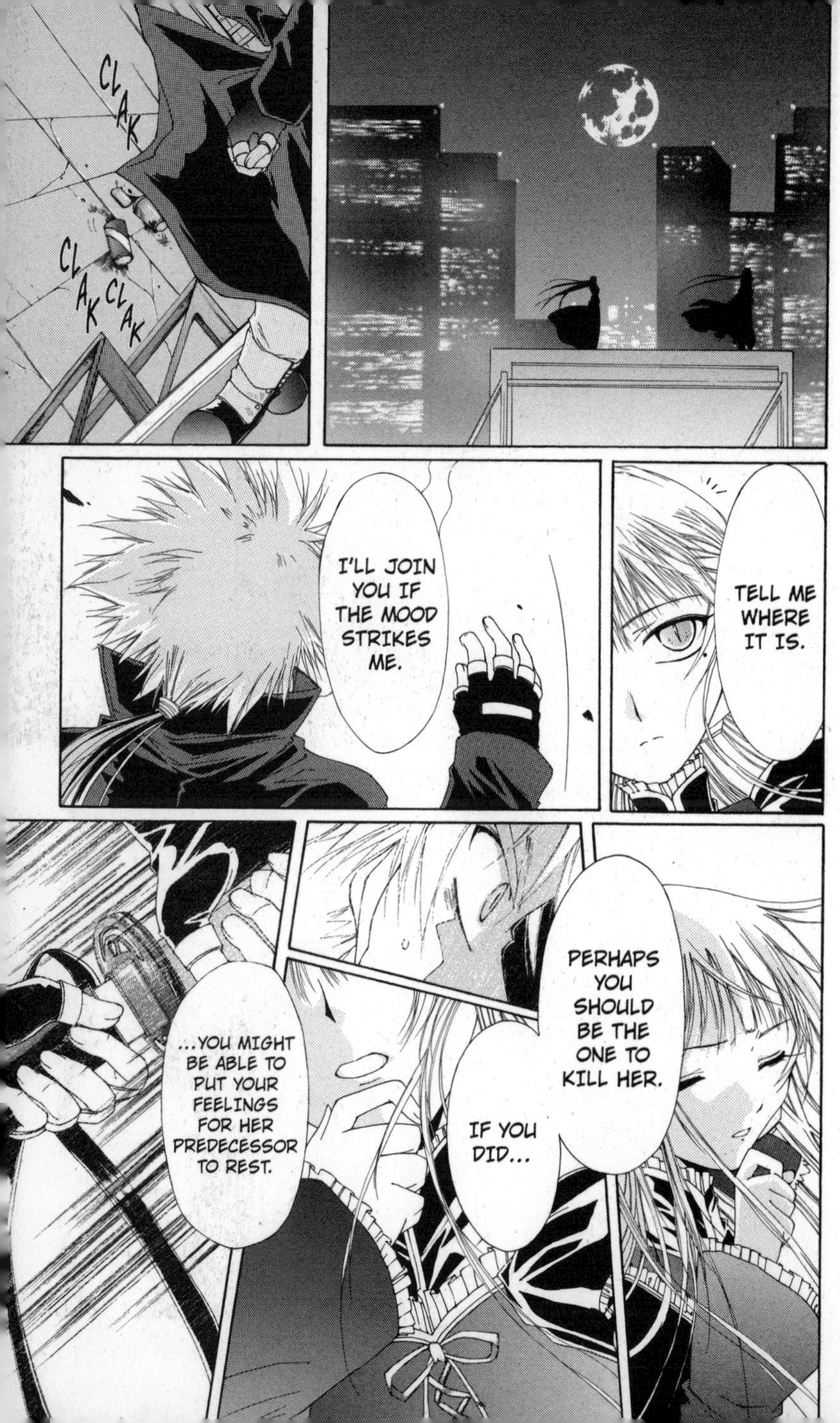
CLAK
CLAK
CLAK
TELL ME WHERE IT IS.
I'LL JOIN YOU IF THE MOOD STRIKES ME.
PERHAPS YOU SHOULD BE THE ONE TO KILL HER.
IF YOU DID...
...YOU MIGHT BE ABLE TO PUT YOUR FEELINGS FOR HER PREDECESSOR TO REST.

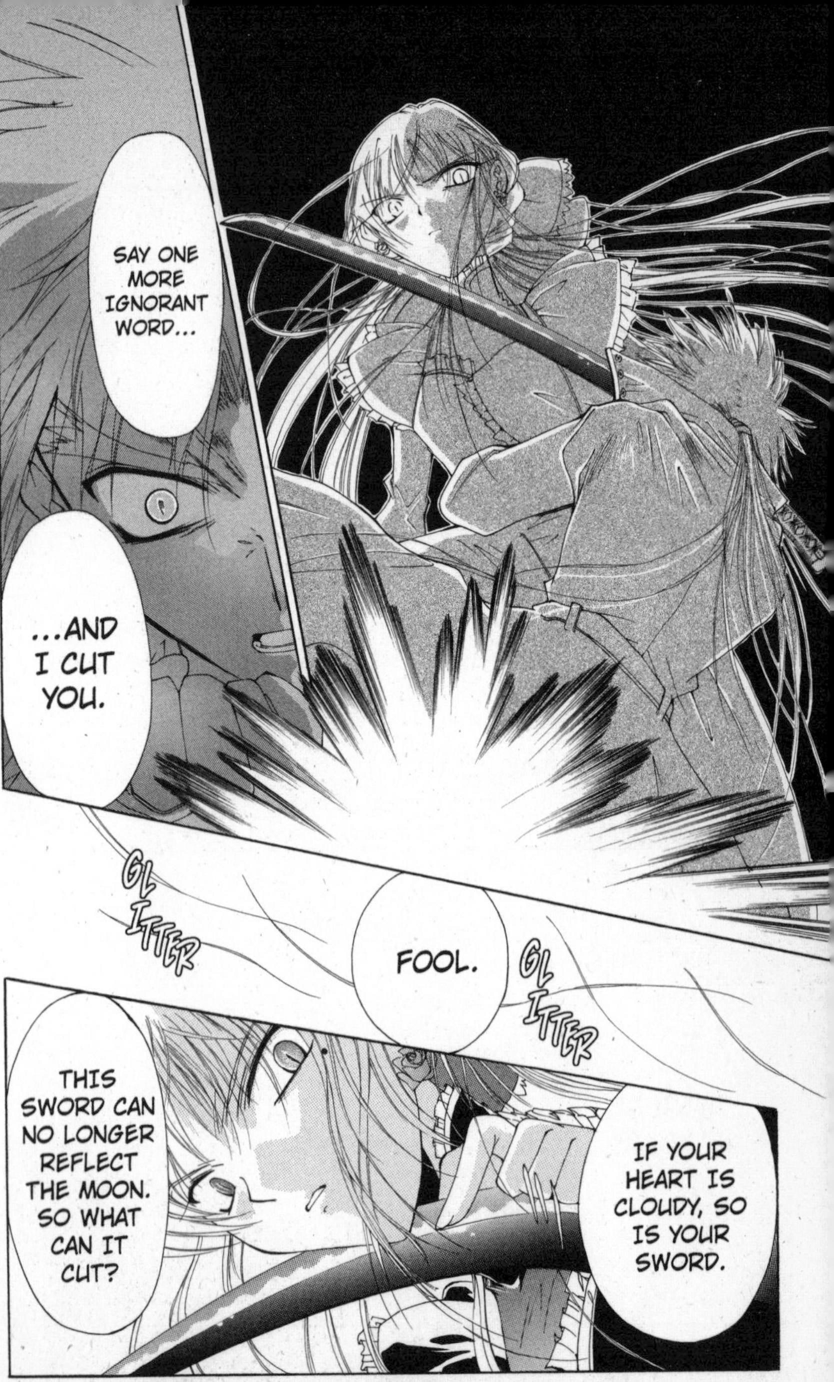
SAY ONE MORE IGNORANT WORD...
...AND I CUT YOU.
GLITTER
FOOL.
GLITTER
IF YOUR HEART IS CLOUDY, SO IS YOUR SWORD.
THIS SWORD CAN NO LONGER REFLECT THE MOON. SO WHAT CAN IT CUT?

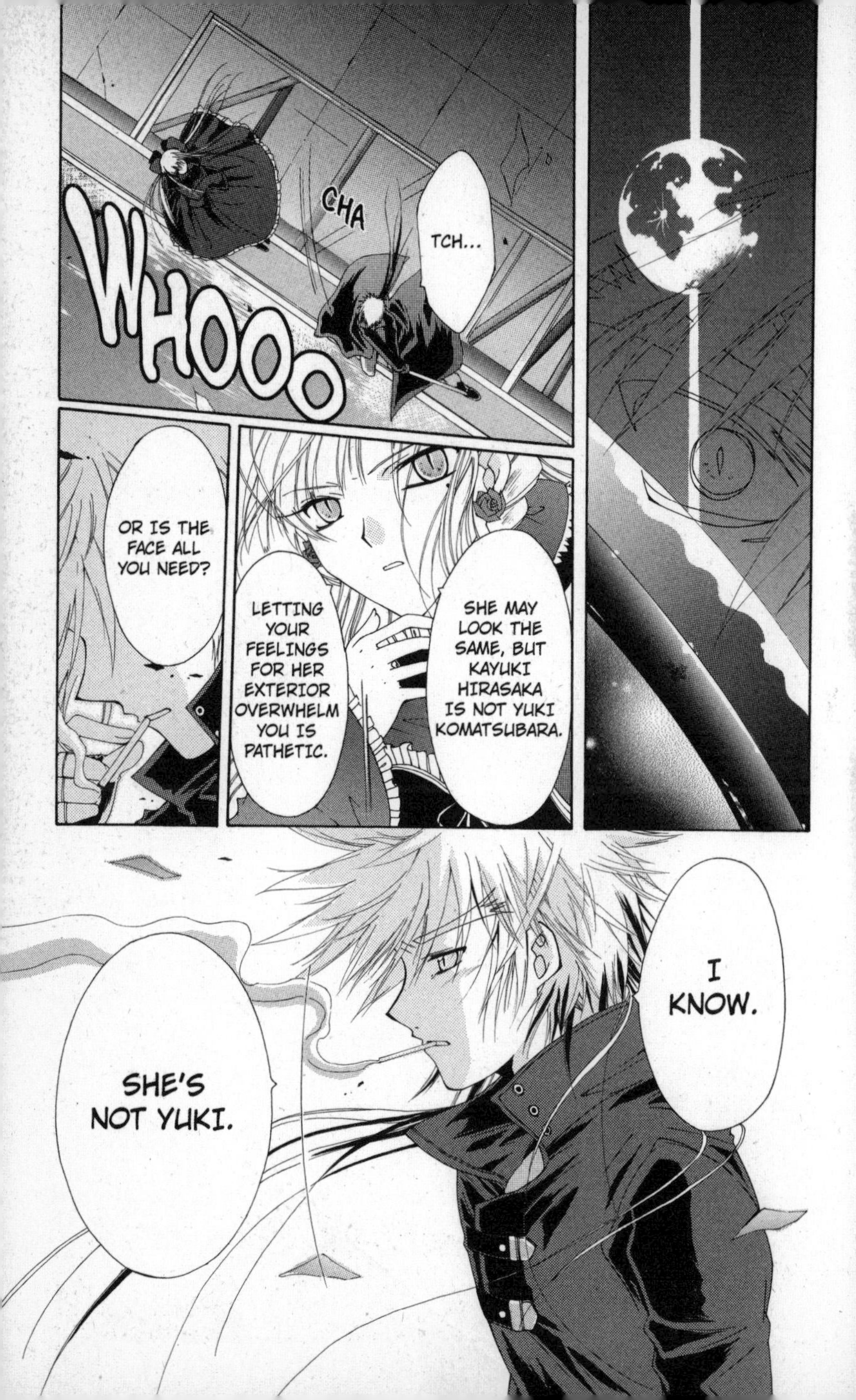
TCH...
CHA
WHOOO
SHE MAY LOOK THE SAME, BUT KAYUKI HIRASAKA IS NOT YUKI KOMATSUBARA.
LETTING YOUR FEELINGS FOR HER EXTERIOR OVERWHELM YOU IS PATHETIC.
OR IS THE FACE ALL YOU NEED?
I KNOW.
SHE'S NOT YUKI.

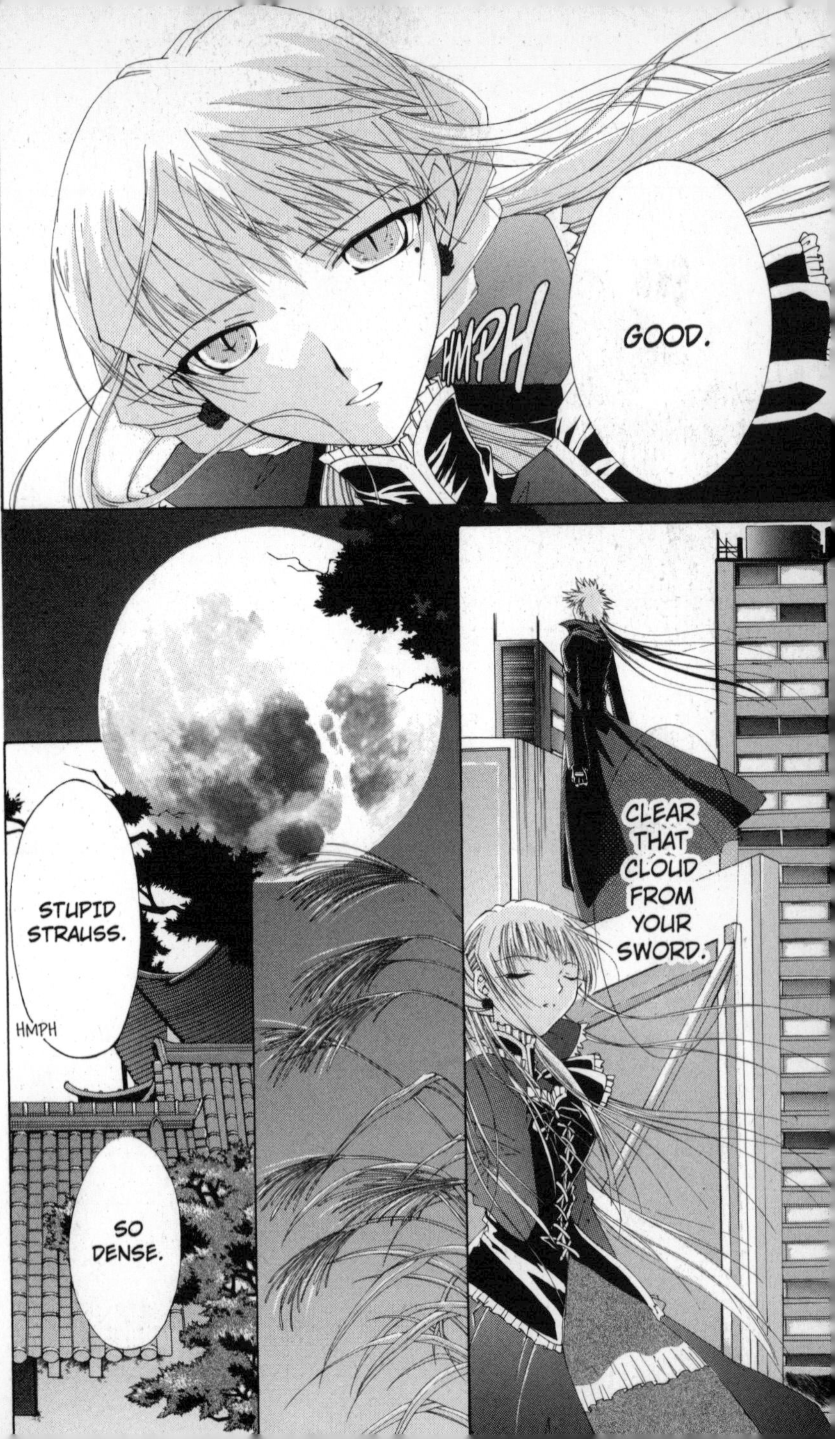
GOOD.
HMPH
CLEAR THAT CLOUD FROM YOUR SWORD.
STUPID STRAUSS.
HMPH
SO DENSE.

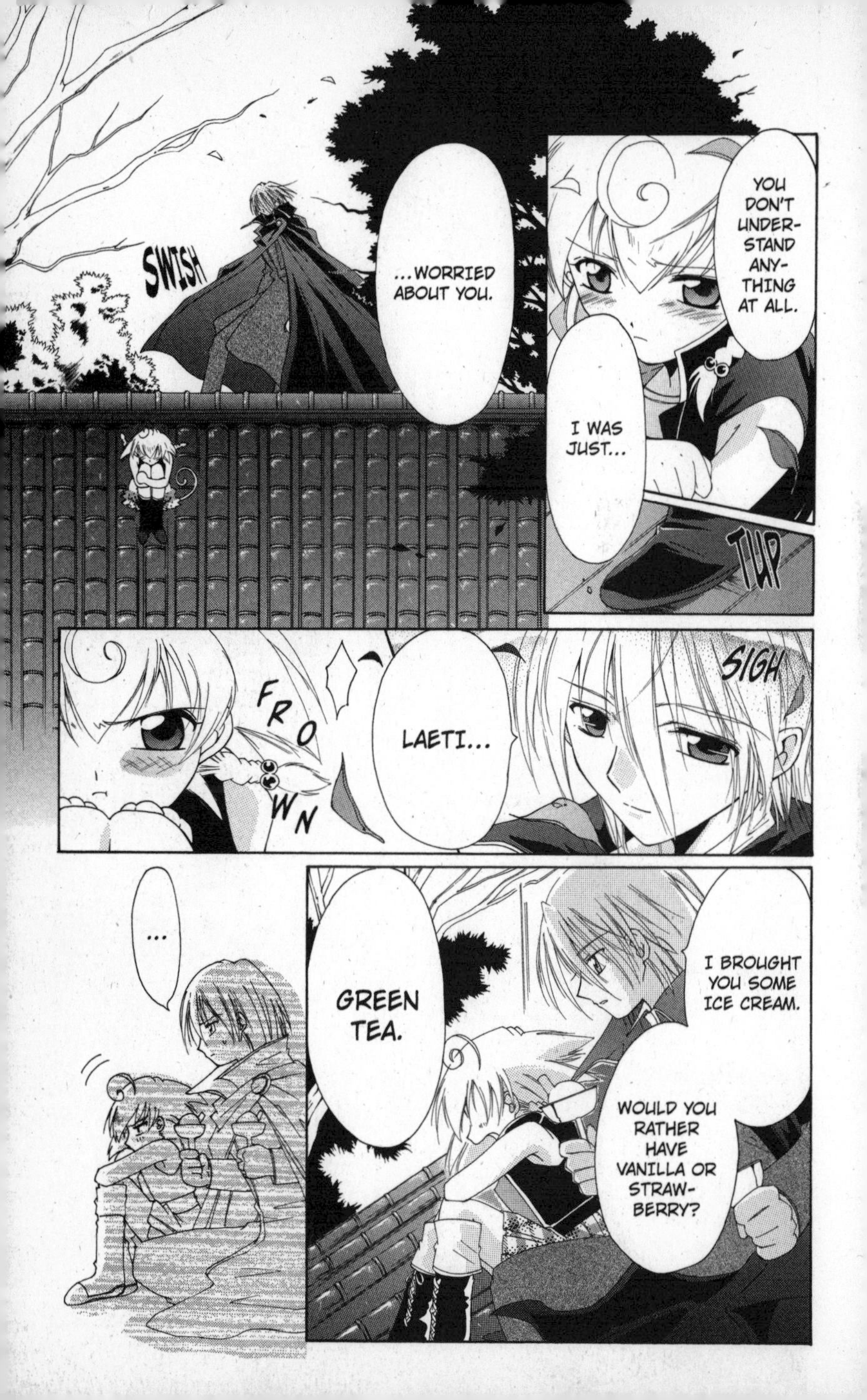
YOU DON'T UNDERSTAND ANYTHING AT ALL.
I WAS JUST...
TUP
...WORRIED ABOUT YOU.
SWISH
SIGH
LAETI...
FROWN
I BROUGHT YOU SOME ICE CREAM.
WOULD YOU RATHER HAVE VANILLA OR STRAWBERRY?
GREEN TEA.
...

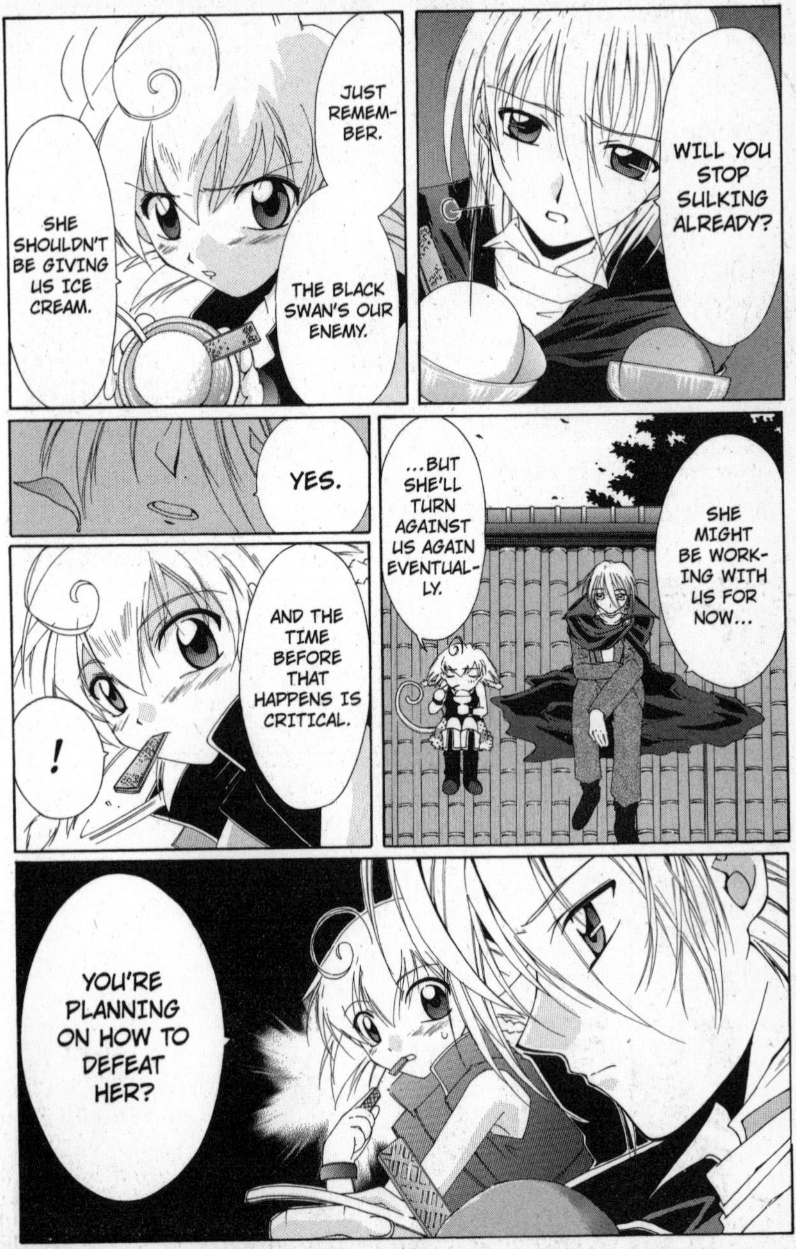
WILL YOU STOP SULKING ALREADY?
JUST REMEMBER.
THE BLACK SWAN'S OUR ENEMY.
SHE SHOULDN'T BE GIVING US ICE CREAM.
SHE MIGHT BE WORKING WITH US FOR NOW...
...BUT SHE'LL TURN AGAINST US AGAIN EVENTUALLY.
YES.
AND THE TIME BEFORE THAT HAPPENS IS CRITICAL.
!
YOU'RE PLANNING ON HOW TO DEFEAT HER?

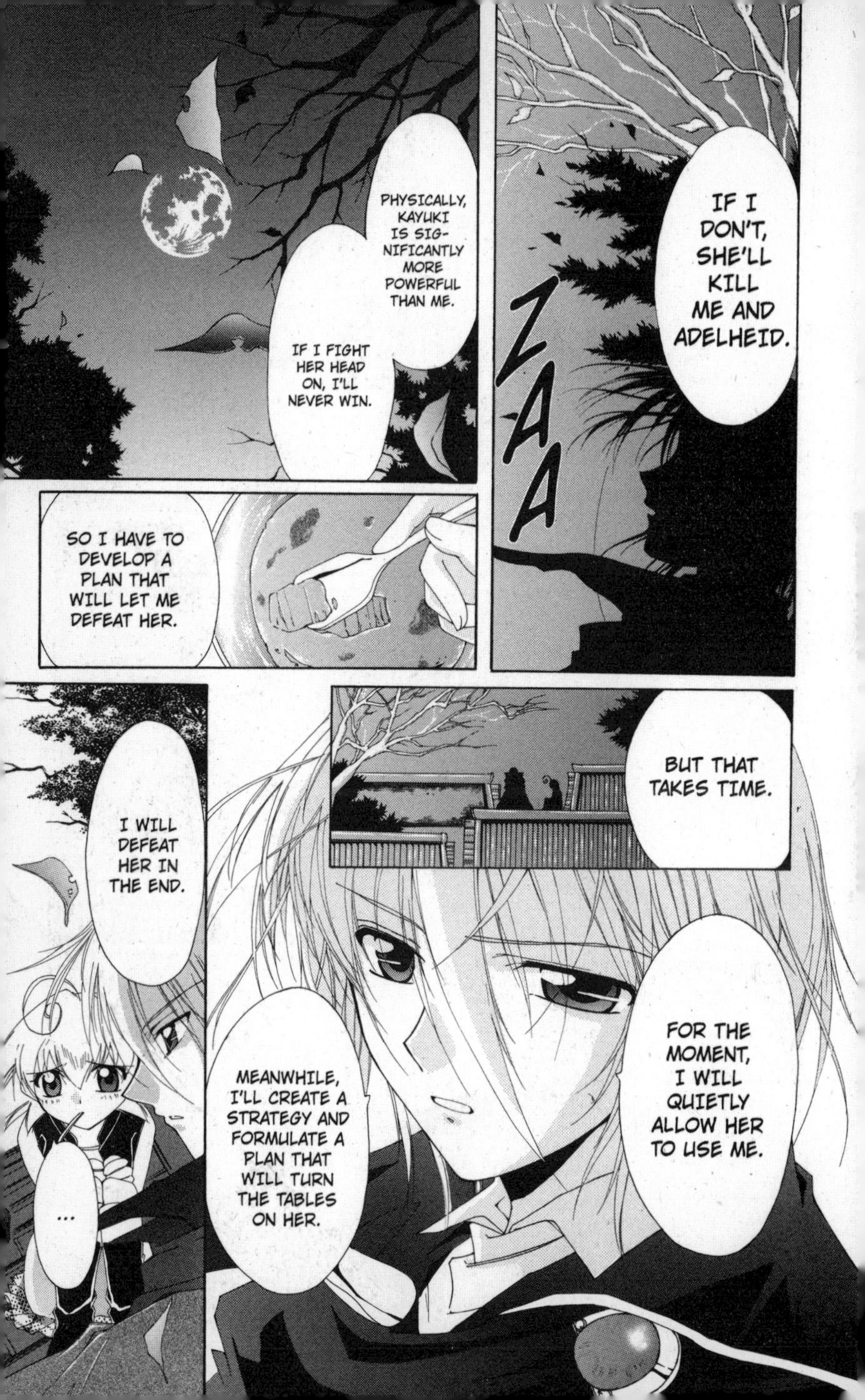
IF I DON'T, SHE'LL KILL ME AND ADELHEID.
ZAAA
PHYSICALLY, KAYUKI IS SIG-NIFICANTLY MORE POWERFUL THAN ME.
IF I FIGHT HER HEAD ON, I'LL NEVER WIN.
SO I HAVE TO DEVELOP A PLAN THAT WILL LET ME DEFEAT HER.
BUT THAT TAKES TIME.
FOR THE MOMENT, I WILL QUIETLY ALLOW HER TO USE ME.
MEANWHILE, I'LL CREATE A STRATEGY AND FORMULATE A PLAN THAT WILL TURN THE TABLES ON HER.
I WILL DEFEAT HER IN THE END.
...

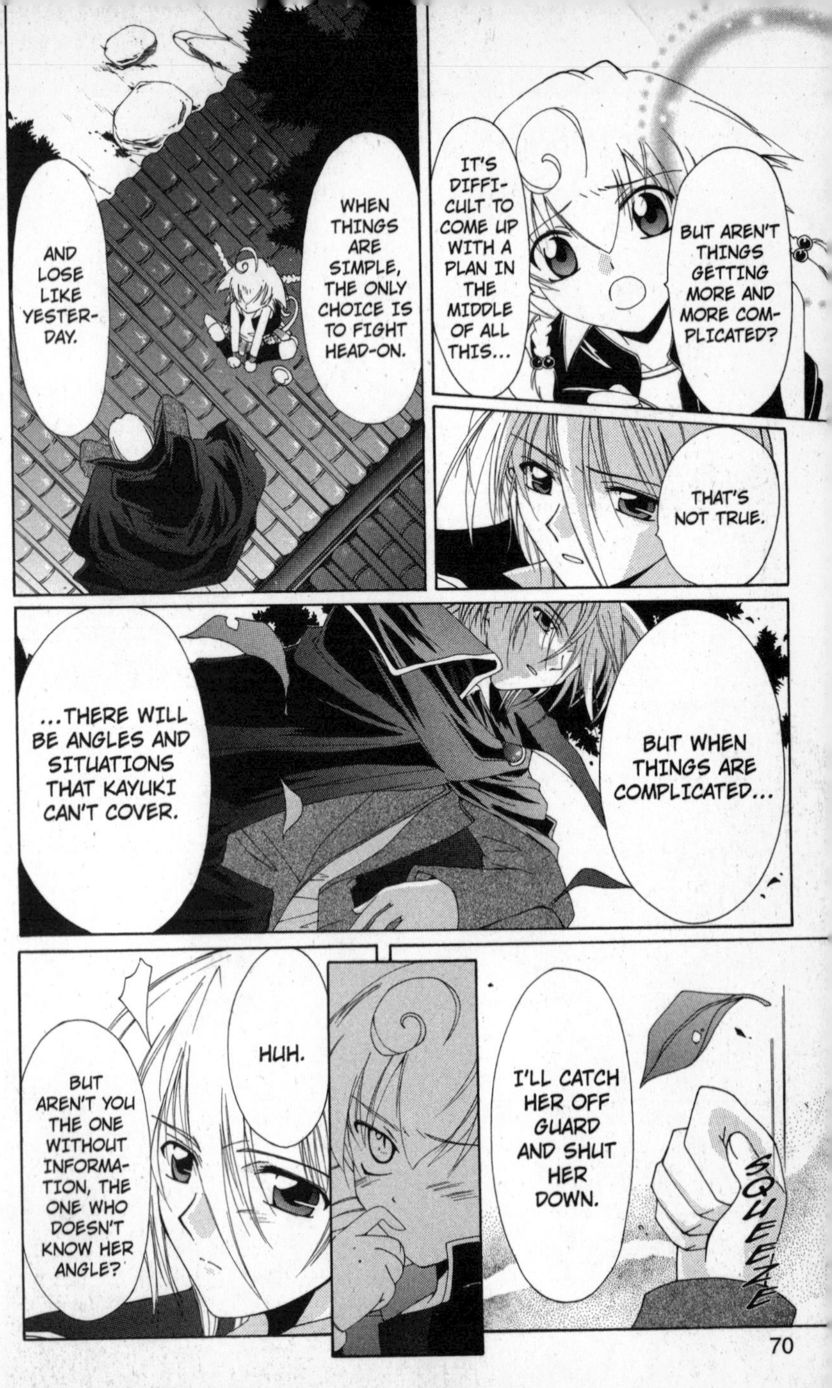
BUT AREN'T THINGS GETTING MORE AND MORE COMPLICATED?
IT'S DIFFICULT TO COME UP WITH A PLAN IN THE MIDDLE OF ALL THIS...
THAT'S NOT TRUE.
WHEN THINGS ARE SIMPLE, THE ONLY CHOICE IS TO FIGHT HEAD-ON.
AND LOSE LIKE YESTERDAY.
BUT WHEN THINGS ARE COMPLICATED...
...THERE WILL BE ANGLES AND SITUATIONS THAT KAYUKI CAN'T COVER.
SQUEEZE
I'LL CATCH HER OFF GUARD AND SHUT HER DOWN.
HUH.
BUT AREN'T YOU THE ONE WITHOUT INFORMATION, THE ONE WHO DOESN'T KNOW HER ANGLE?

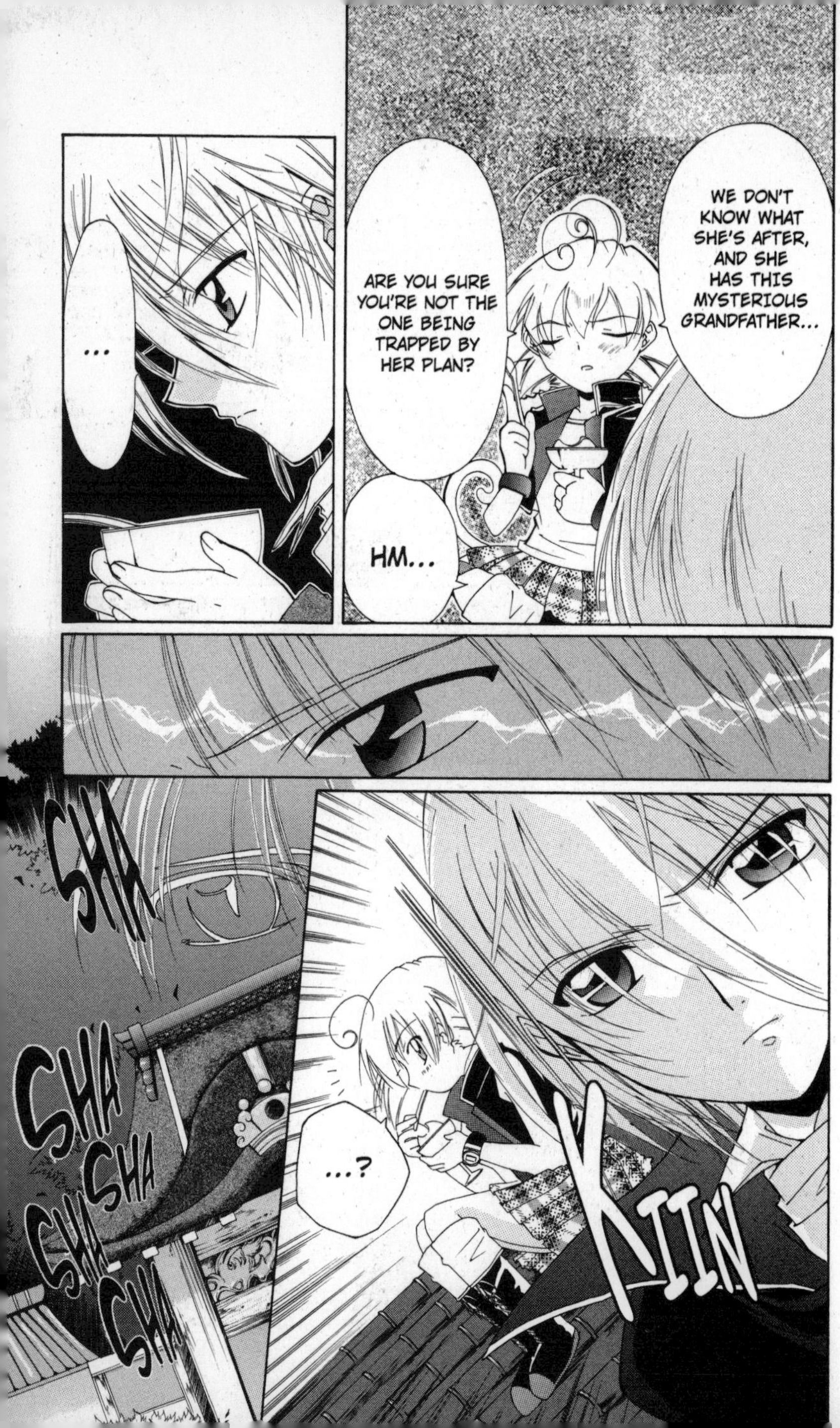
WE DON'T KNOW WHAT SHE'S AFTER, AND SHE HAS THIS MYSTERIOUS GRANDFATHER...
ARE YOU SURE YOU'RE NOT THE ONE BEING TRAPPED BY HER PLAN?
HM...
...
...?
KIIN
SHA
SHA SHA SHA SHA SHA

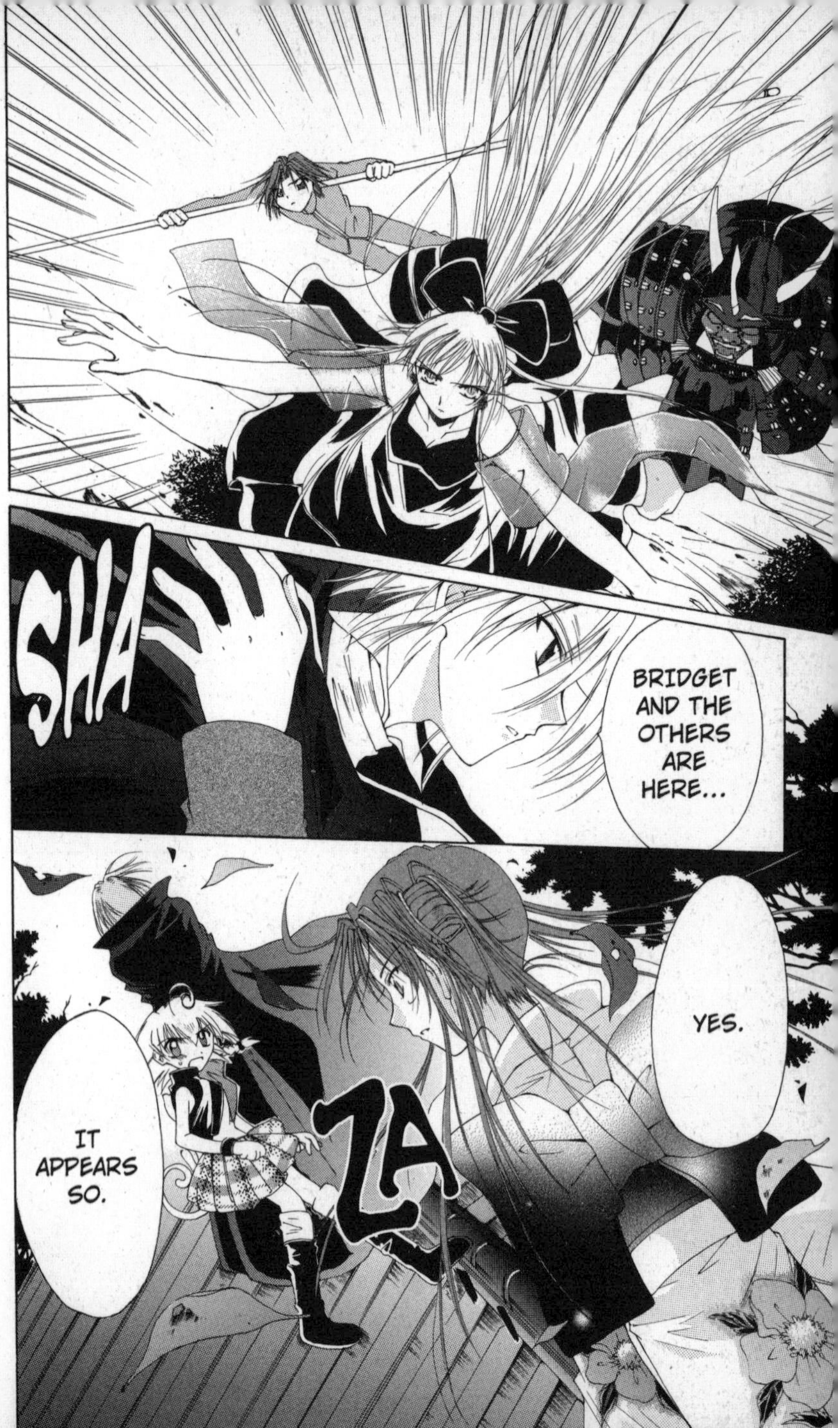
BRIDGET AND THE OTHERS ARE HERE...
SHA
YES.
ZA
IT APPEARS SO.

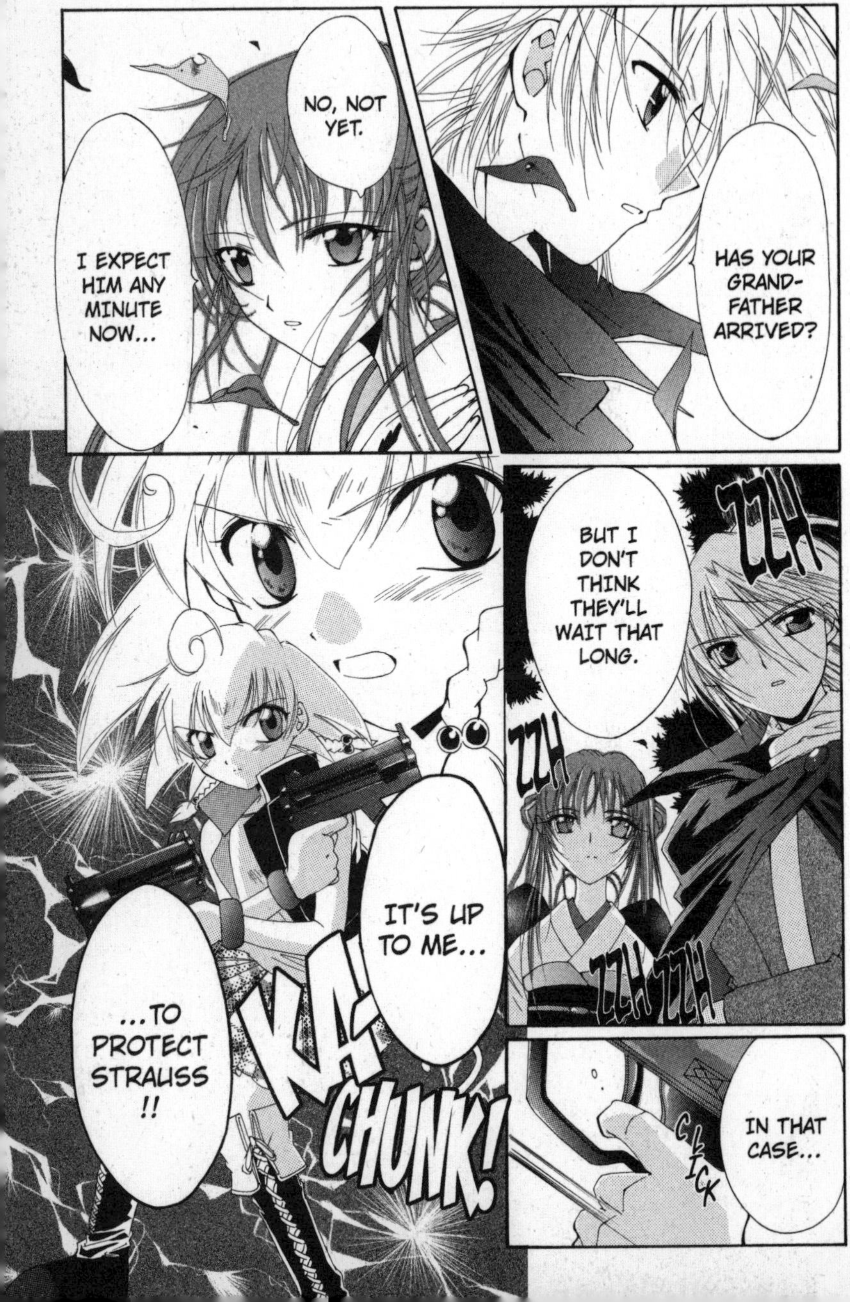
HAS YOUR GRAND-FATHER ARRIVED?
NO, NOT YET.
I EXPECT HIM ANY MINUTE NOW...
BUT I DON'T THINK THEY'LL WAIT THAT LONG.
ZZH
ZZH
ZZH ZZH
IN THAT CASE...
CLICK
IT'S UP TO ME...
...TO PROTECT STRAUSS!!
KA-CHUNK!

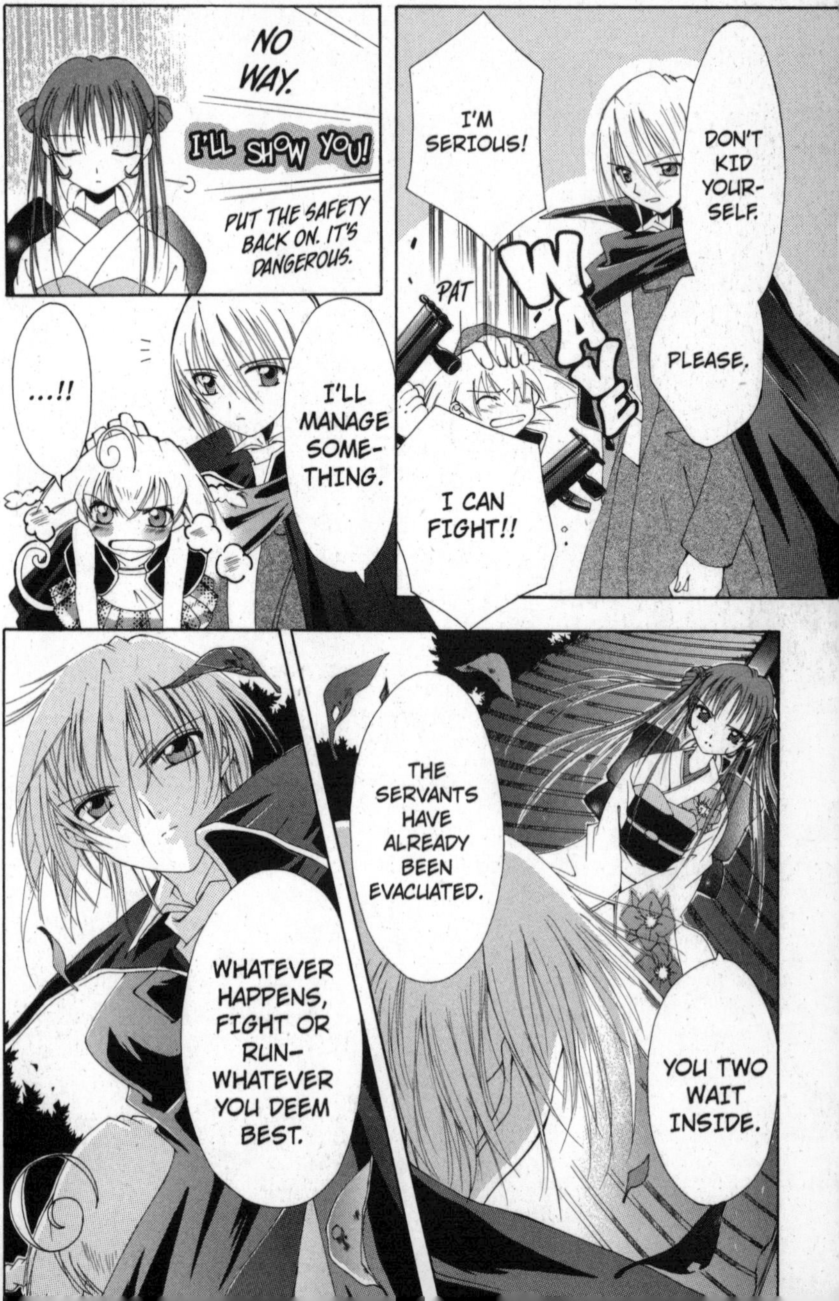
DON'T KID YOUR-SELF.
I'M SERIOUS!
PLEASE.
WAVE
PAT
I CAN FIGHT!!
NO WAY.
I'LL SHOW YOU!
PUT THE SAFETY BACK ON. IT'S DANGEROUS.
I'LL MANAGE SOME-THING.
...!!
THE SERVANTS HAVE ALREADY BEEN EVACUATED.
YOU TWO WAIT INSIDE.
WHATEVER HAPPENS, FIGHT OR RUN—WHATEVER YOU DEEM BEST.

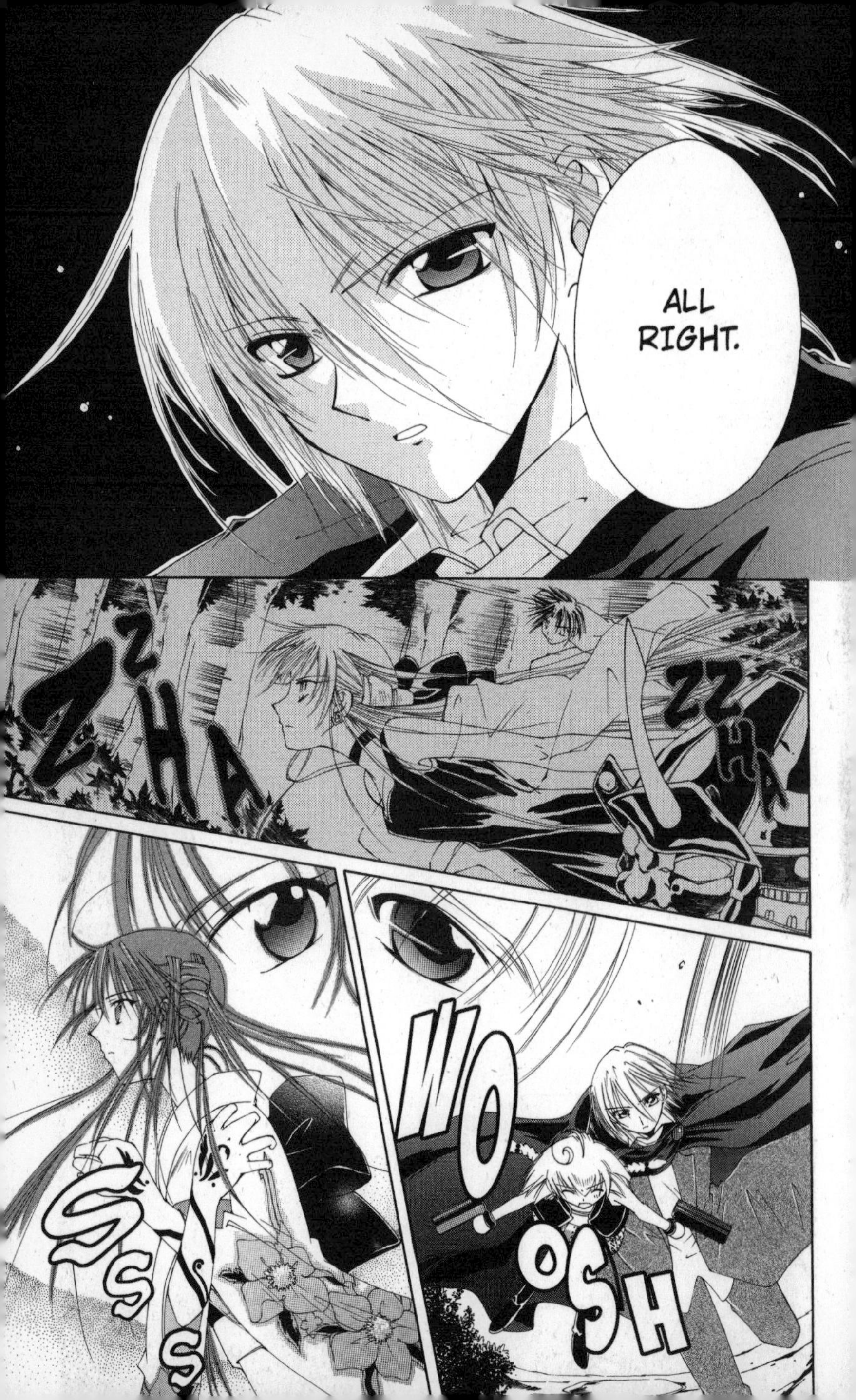
ALL RIGHT.
ZZHA
ZZHA
WOOSH
SSSS

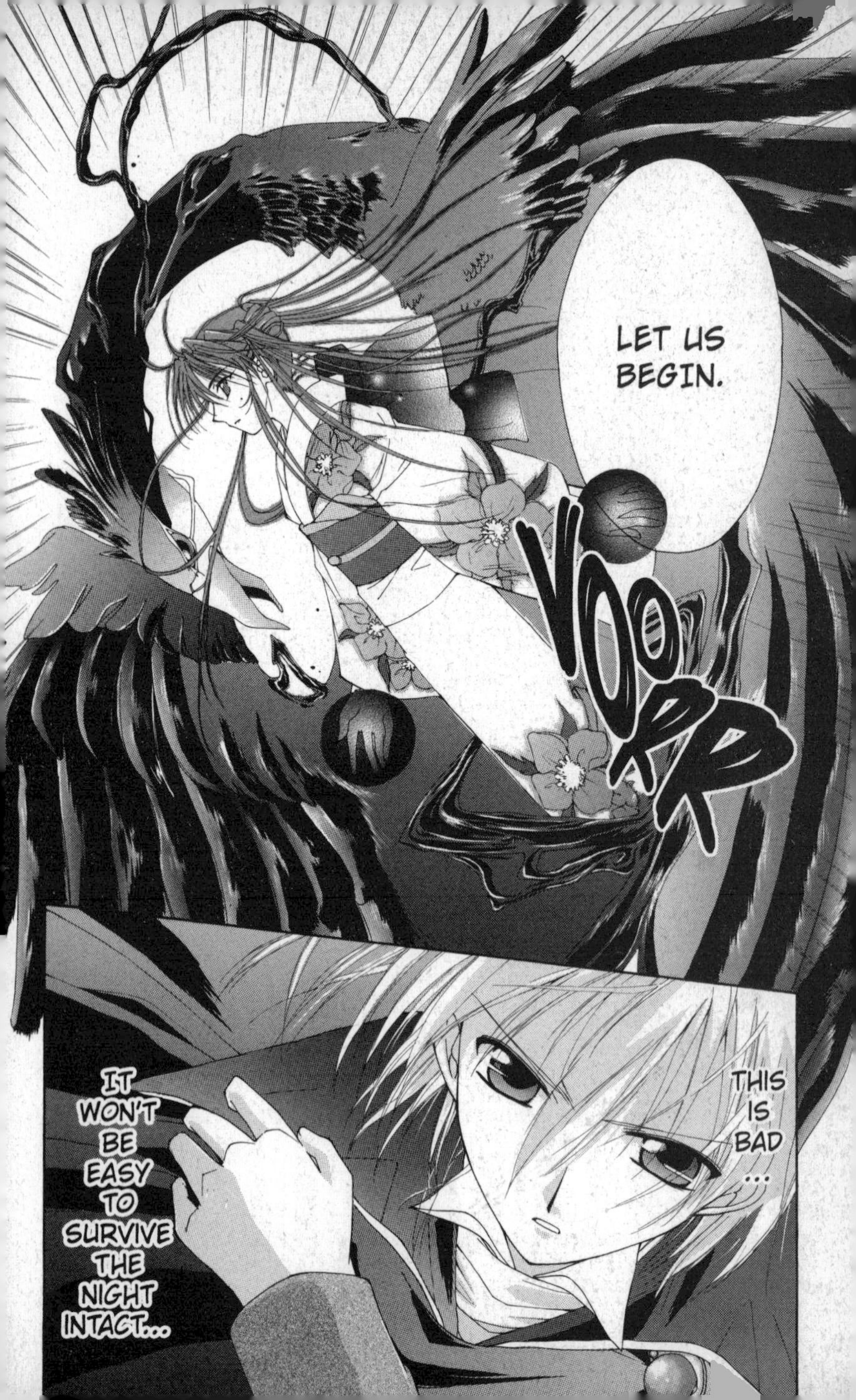
LET US BEGIN.
VOORR
THIS IS BAD...
IT WON'T BE EASY TO SURVIVE THE NIGHT INTACT...

THE RECORD OF A

FALLEN VAMPIRE

THE RECORD OF A
FALLEN VAMPIRE

CHAPTER 6: RENDEZVOUS

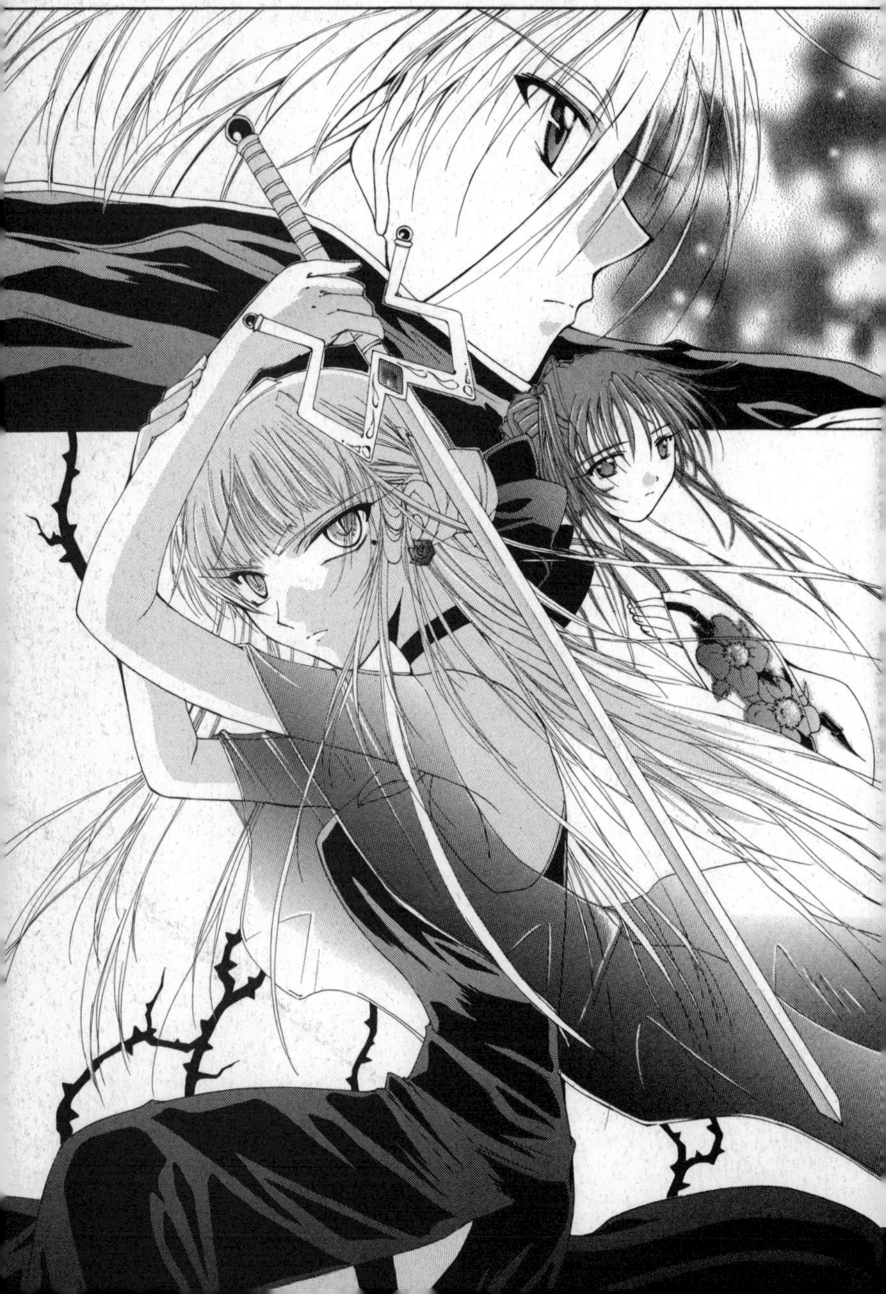

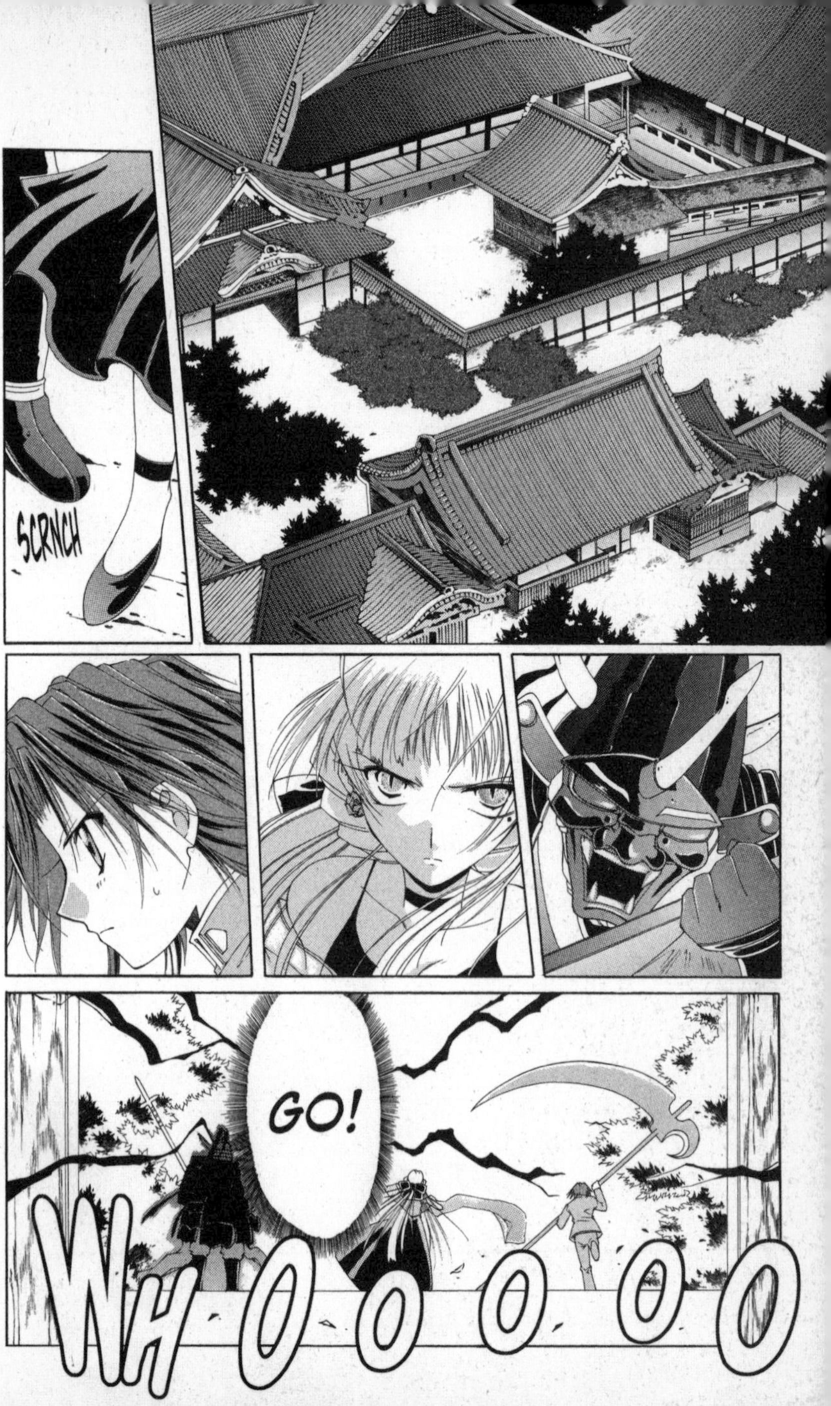
SCRNCH
GO!
WHOOOOOO

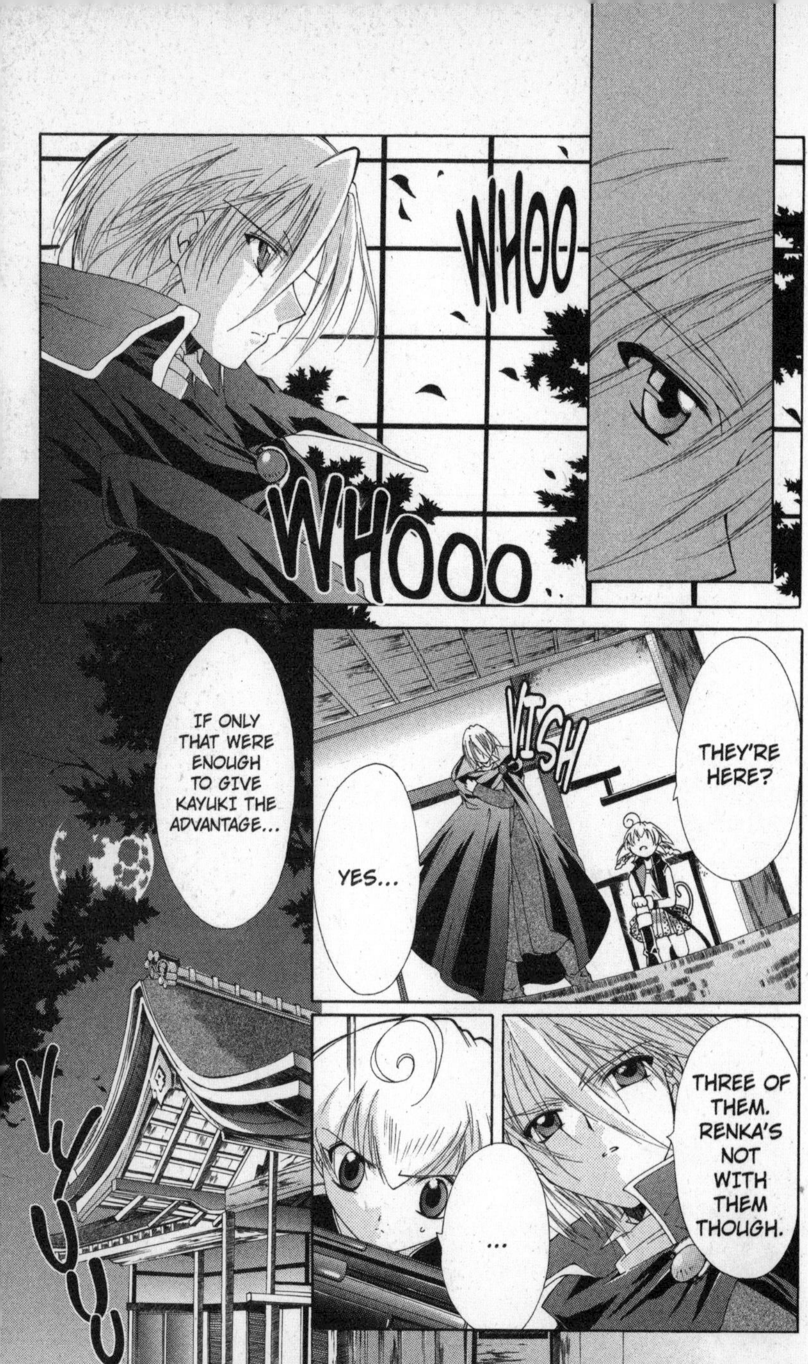
WHOO
WHOOO
VISH
THEY'RE HERE?
YES...
THREE OF THEM. RENKA'S NOT WITH THEM THOUGH.
...
IF ONLY THAT WERE ENOUGH TO GIVE KAYUKI THE ADVANTAGE...
VYUUUU

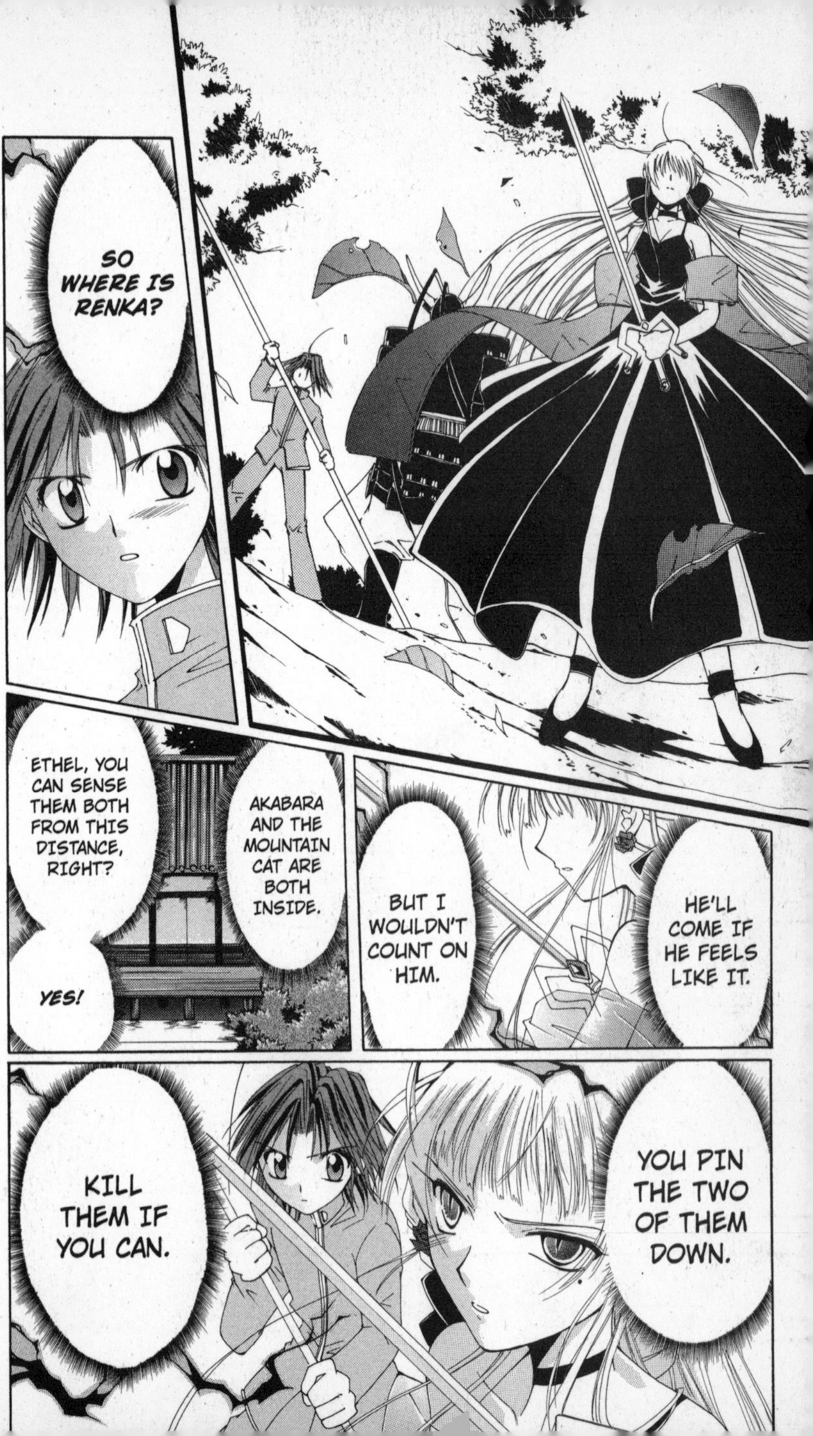
SO WHERE IS RENKA?
HE'LL COME IF HE FEELS LIKE IT.
BUT I WOULDN'T COUNT ON HIM.
AKABARA AND THE MOUNTAIN CAT ARE BOTH INSIDE.
ETHEL, YOU CAN SENSE THEM BOTH FROM THIS DISTANCE, RIGHT?
YES!
YOU PIN THE TWO OF THEM DOWN.
KILL THEM IF YOU CAN.

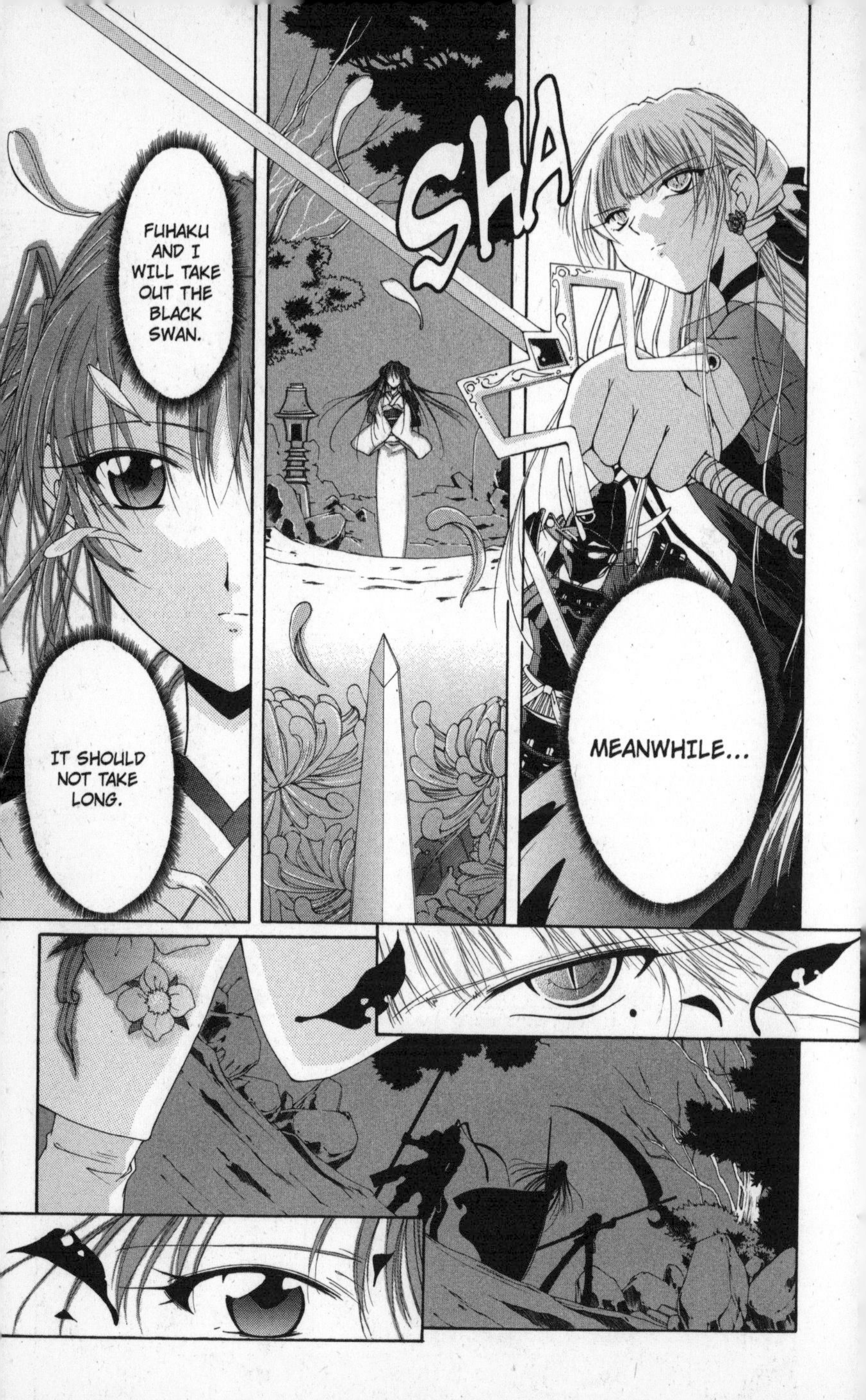
SHA
MEANWHILE...
FUHAKU AND I WILL TAKE OUT THE BLACK SWAN.
IT SHOULD NOT TAKE LONG.

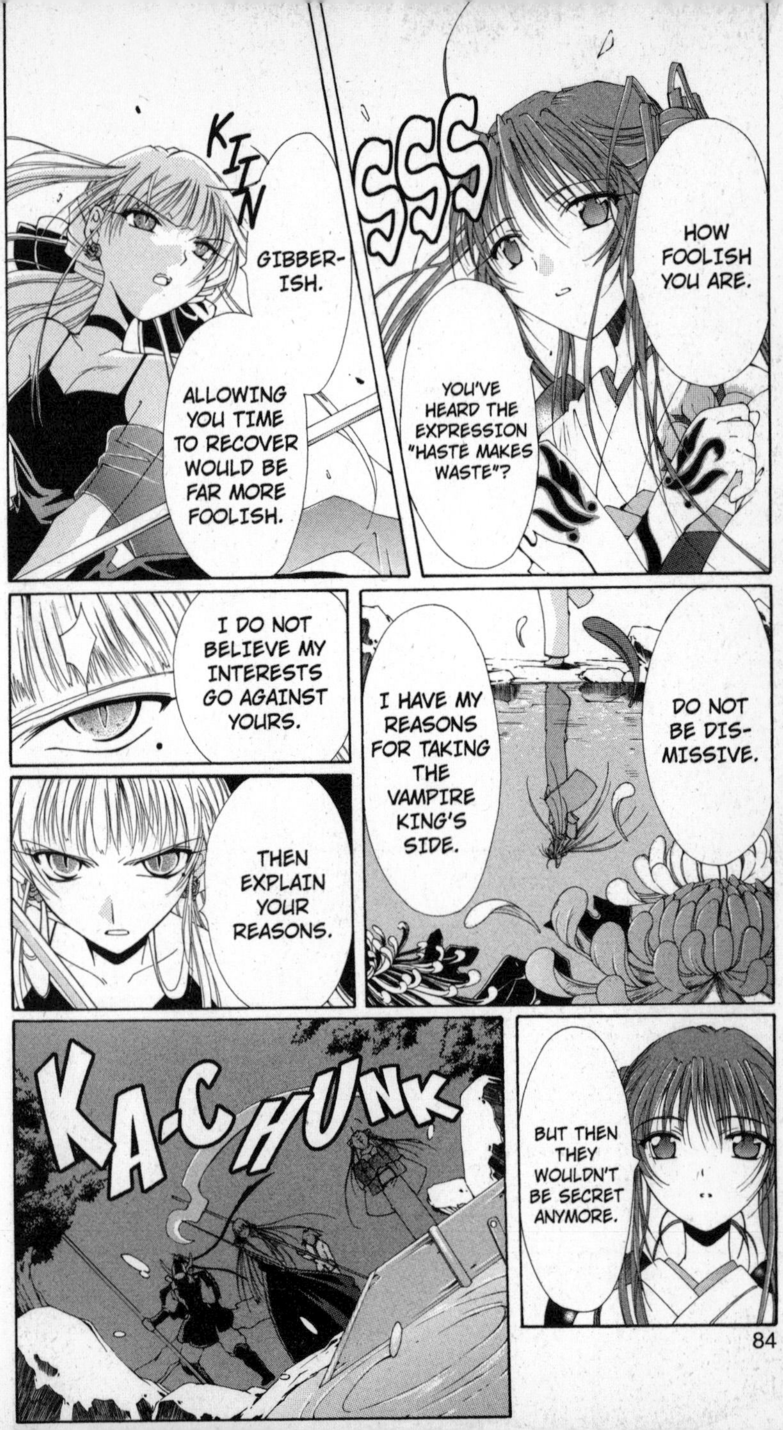

SSS
HOW FOOLISH YOU ARE.
YOU'VE HEARD THE EXPRESSION "HASTE MAKES WASTE"?
KIIIN
GIBBER-ISH.
ALLOWING YOU TIME TO RECOVER WOULD BE FAR MORE FOOLISH.
DO NOT BE DIS-MISSIVE.
I HAVE MY REASONS FOR TAKING THE VAMPIRE KING'S SIDE.
I DO NOT BELIEVE MY INTERESTS GO AGAINST YOURS.
THEN EXPLAIN YOUR REASONS.
BUT THEN THEY WOULDN'T BE SECRET ANYMORE.
KA-CHUNK

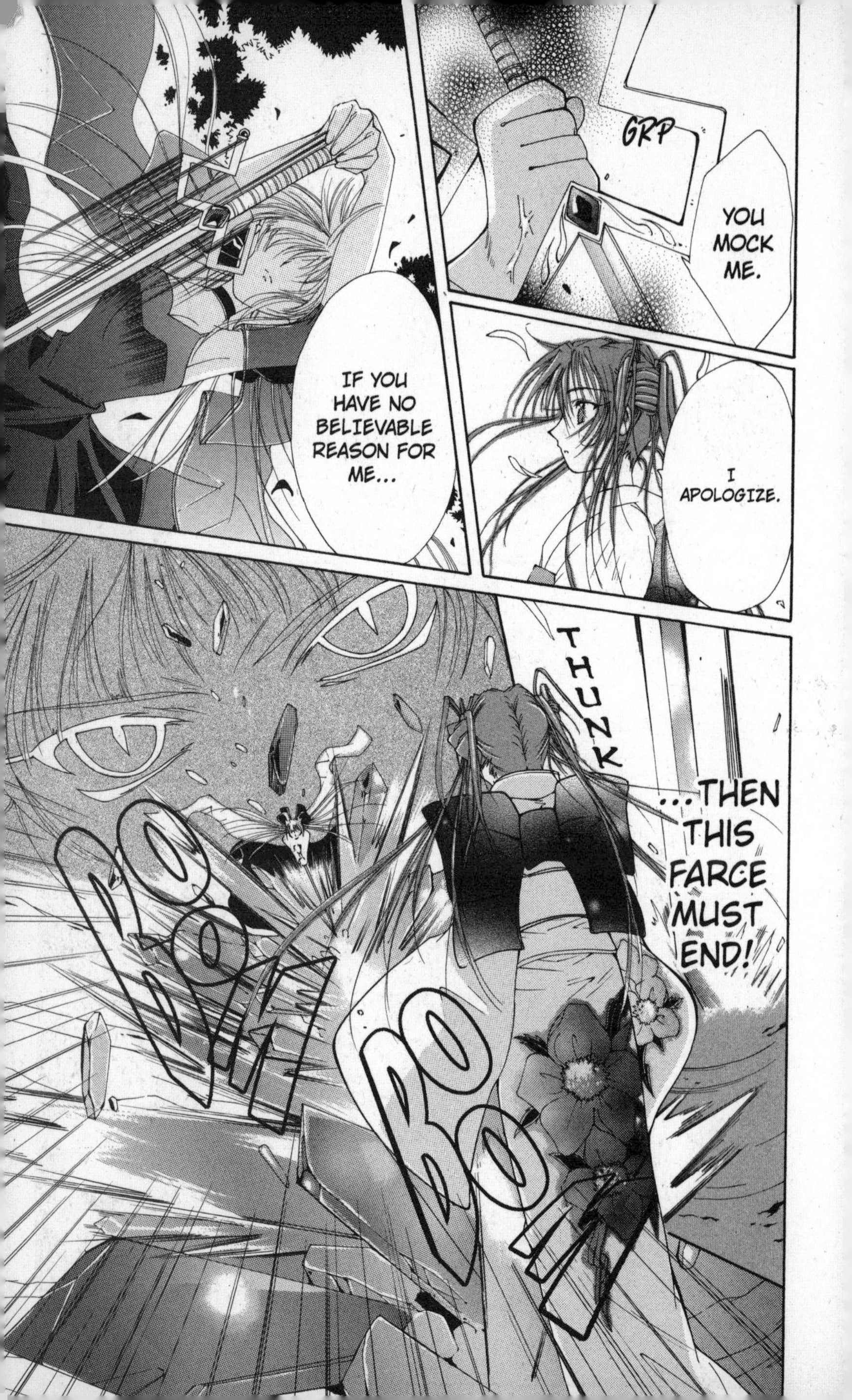
GRP
YOU MOCK ME.
I APOLOGIZE.
IF YOU HAVE NO BELIEVABLE REASON FOR ME...
THUNK
...THEN THIS FARCE MUST END!

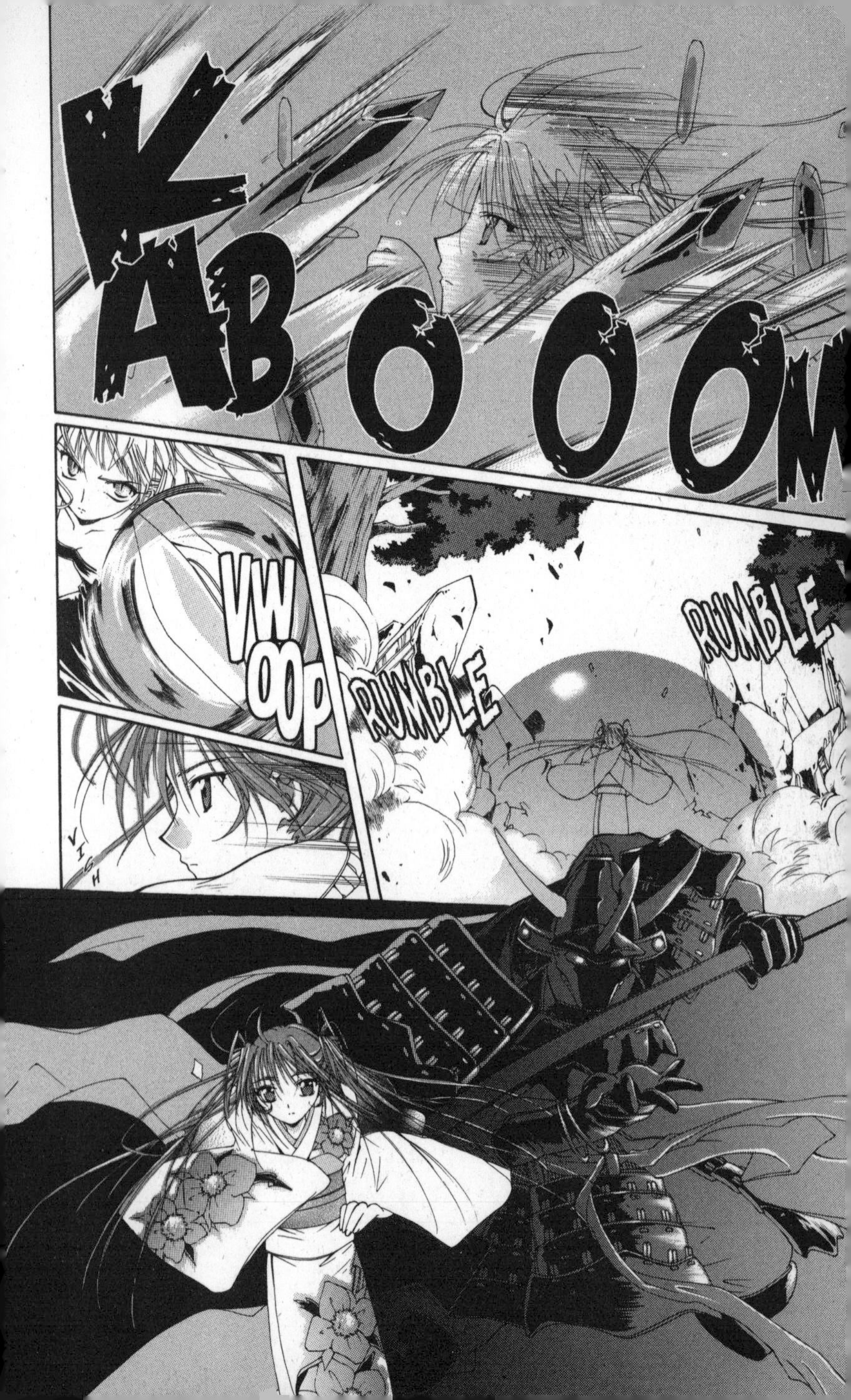
KABOOOM
RUMBLE
VWOOP
RUMBLE
VIGH

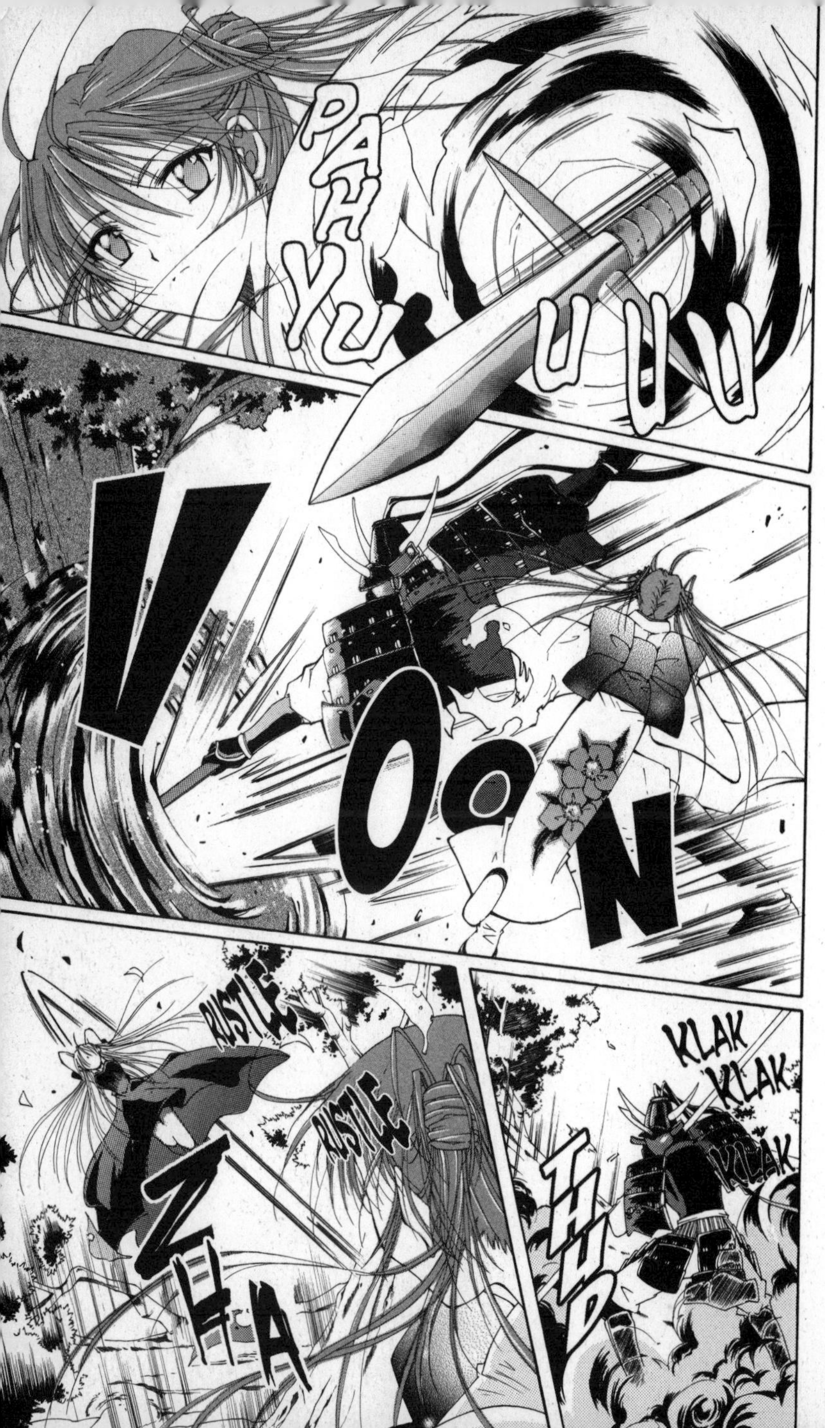
PAHYUUUU
VOOON
KLAK
KLAK
KLAK
THUD
RUSTLE
RUSTLE
ZHA

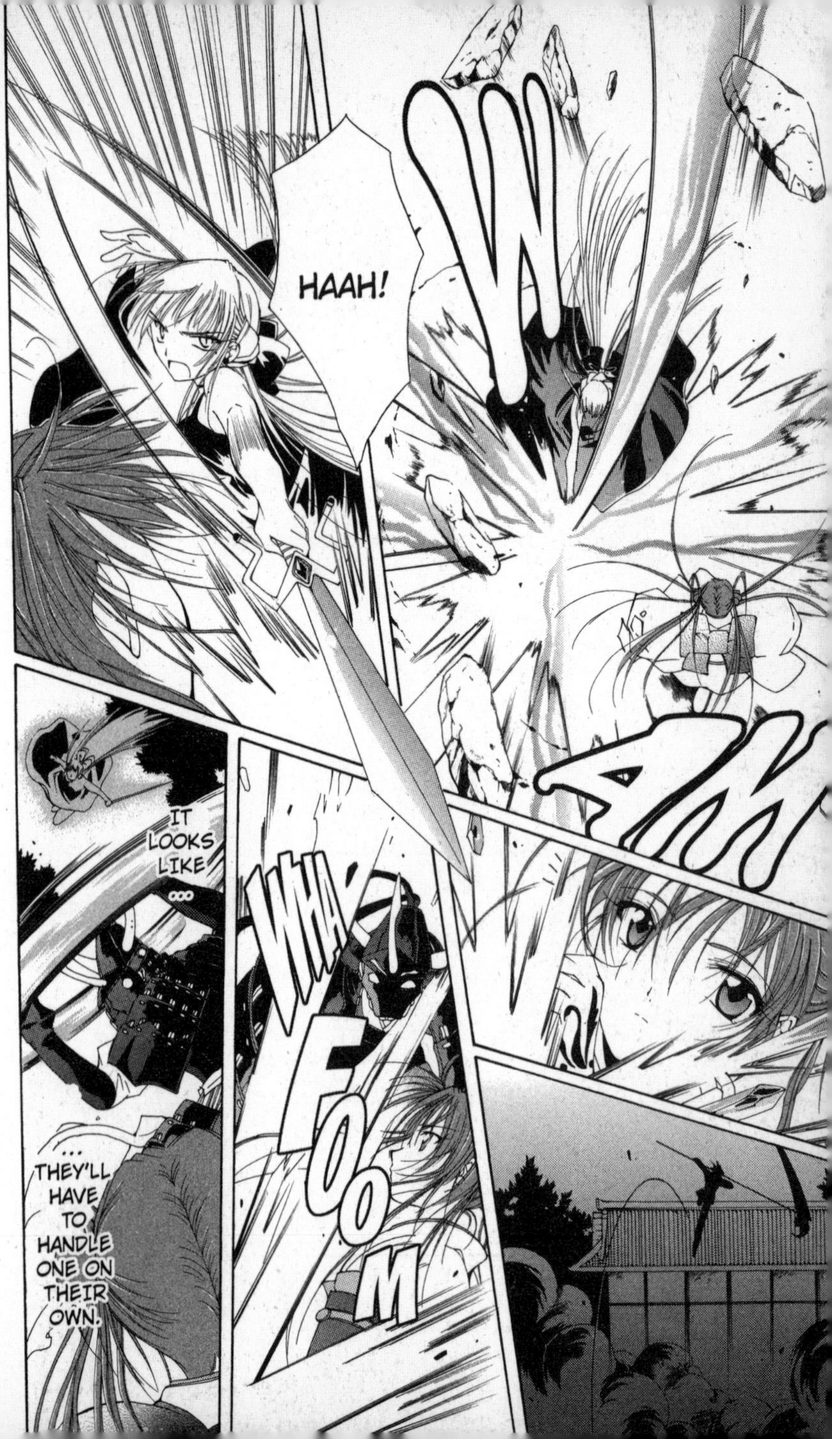
HAAH!
WHAFOOM
IT LOOKS LIKE...
...THEY'LL HAVE TO HANDLE ONE ON THEIR OWN.

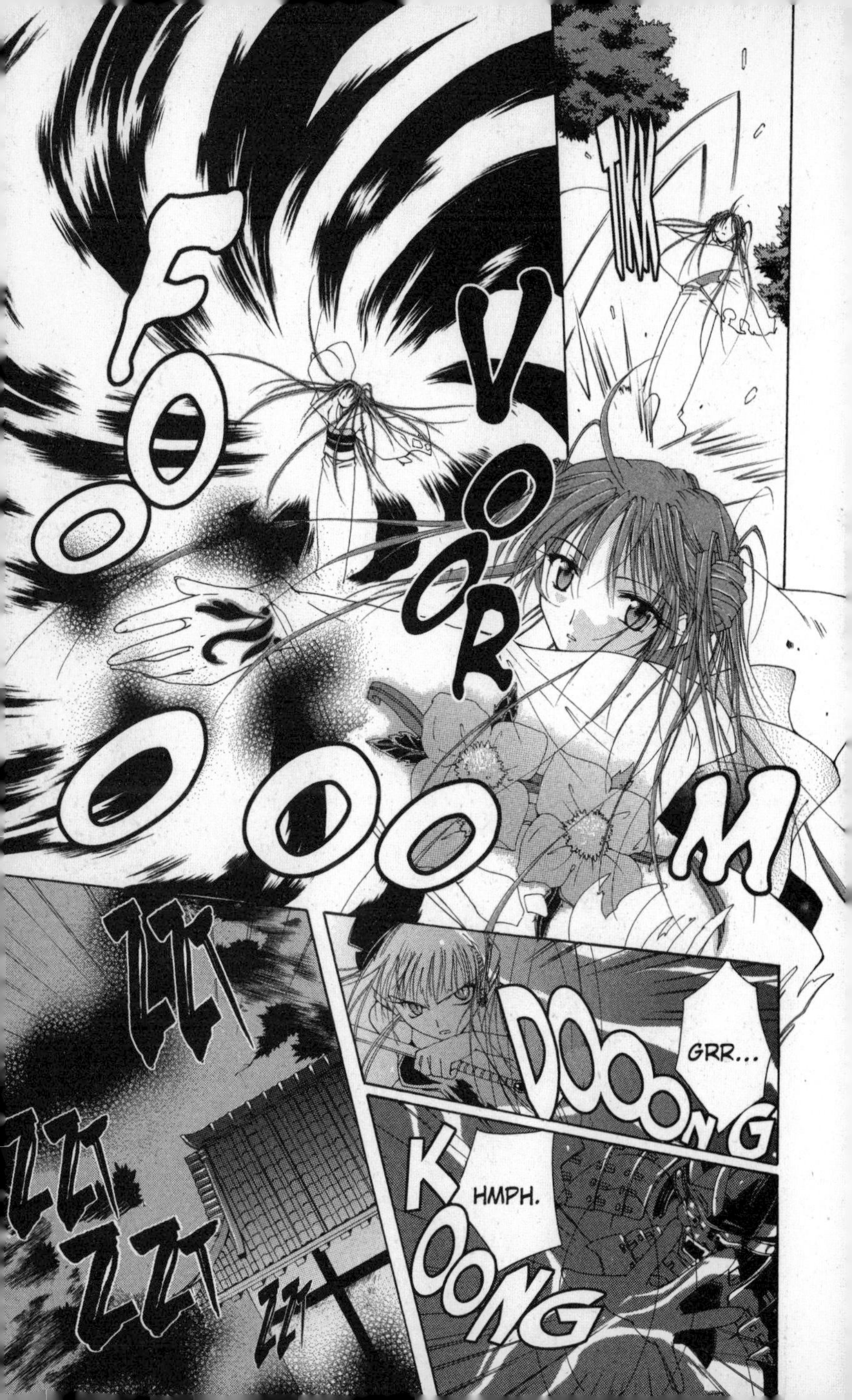
TINK
FOOO
VOOOR
OOOOM
DOOOONG
GRR...
KOOONG
HMPH.
ZZT
ZZT
ZZT
ZZT

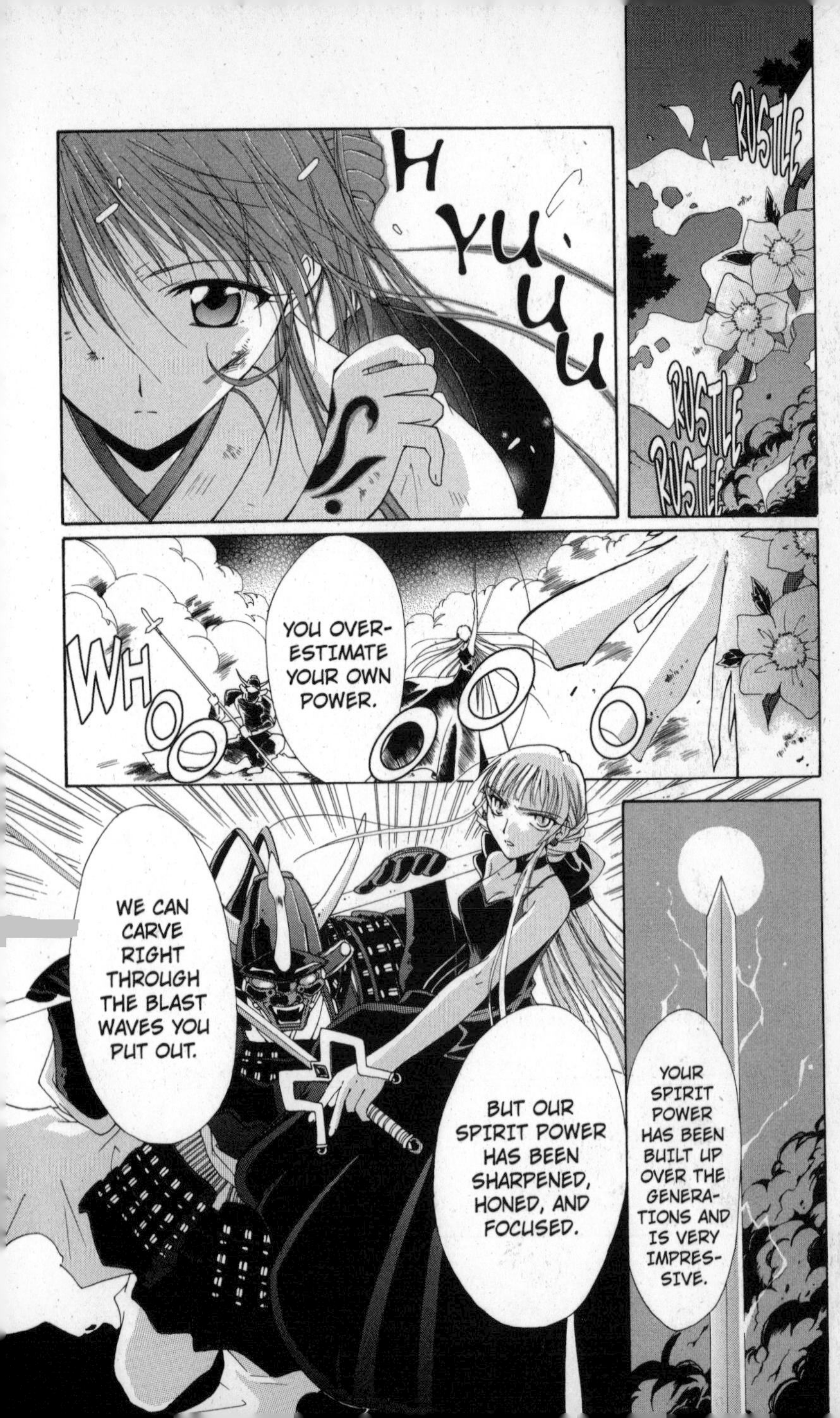
RUSTLE
RUSTLE
RUSTLE
HYUUUU
YOU OVER-ESTIMATE YOUR OWN POWER.
WHOOOOOO
YOUR SPIRIT POWER HAS BEEN BUILT UP OVER THE GENERA-TIONS AND IS VERY IMPRES-SIVE.
BUT OUR SPIRIT POWER HAS BEEN SHARPENED, HONED, AND FOCUSED.
WE CAN CARVE RIGHT THROUGH THE BLAST WAVES YOU PUT OUT.

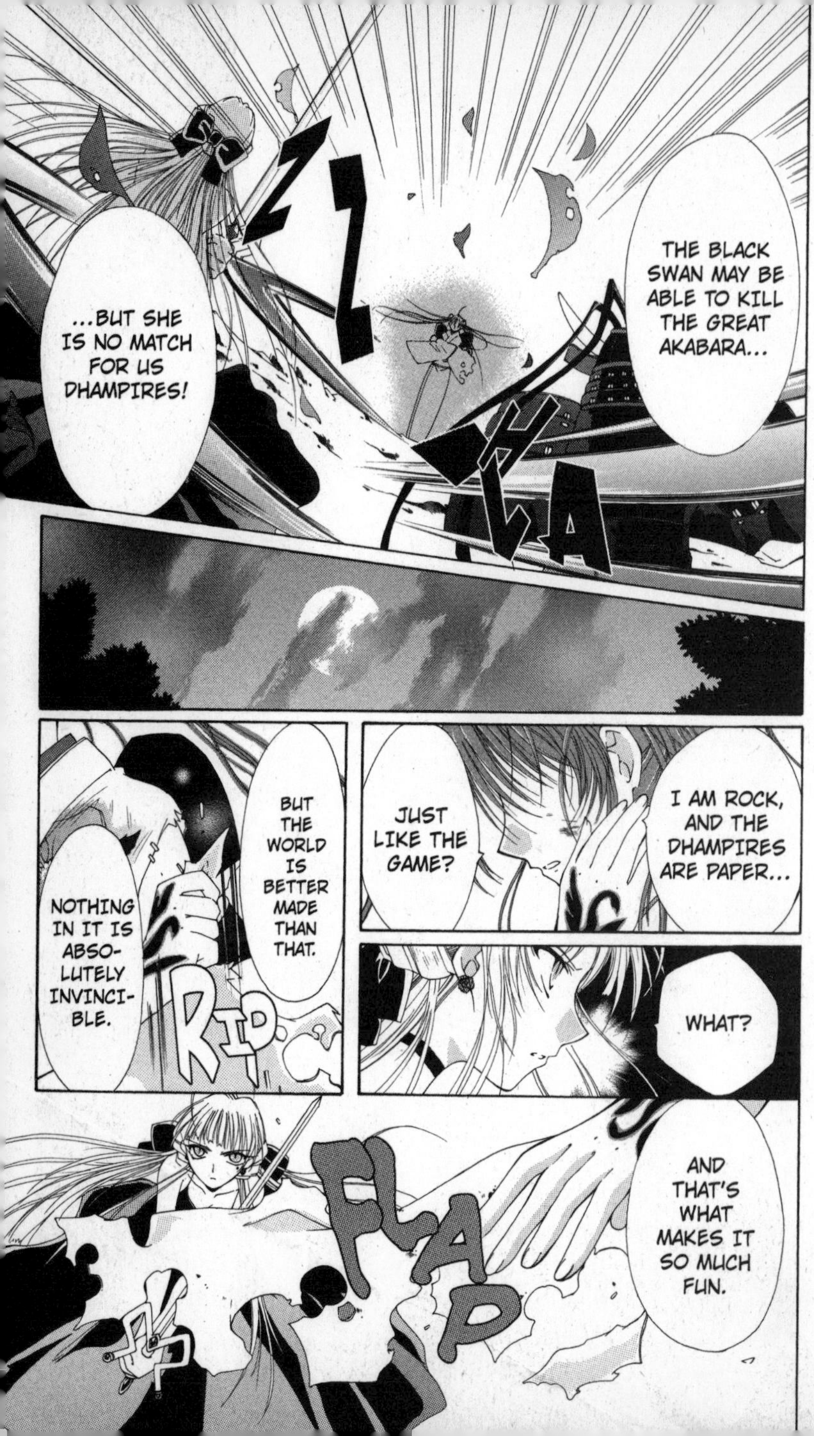
THE BLACK SWAN MAY BE ABLE TO KILL THE GREAT AKABARA...
...BUT SHE IS NO MATCH FOR US DHAMPIRES!
I AM ROCK, AND THE DHAMPIRES ARE PAPER...
JUST LIKE THE GAME?
WHAT?
BUT THE WORLD IS BETTER MADE THAN THAT.
NOTHING IN IT IS ABSO-LUTELY INVINCI-BLE.
RIP
AND THAT'S WHAT MAKES IT SO MUCH FUN.
FLAP

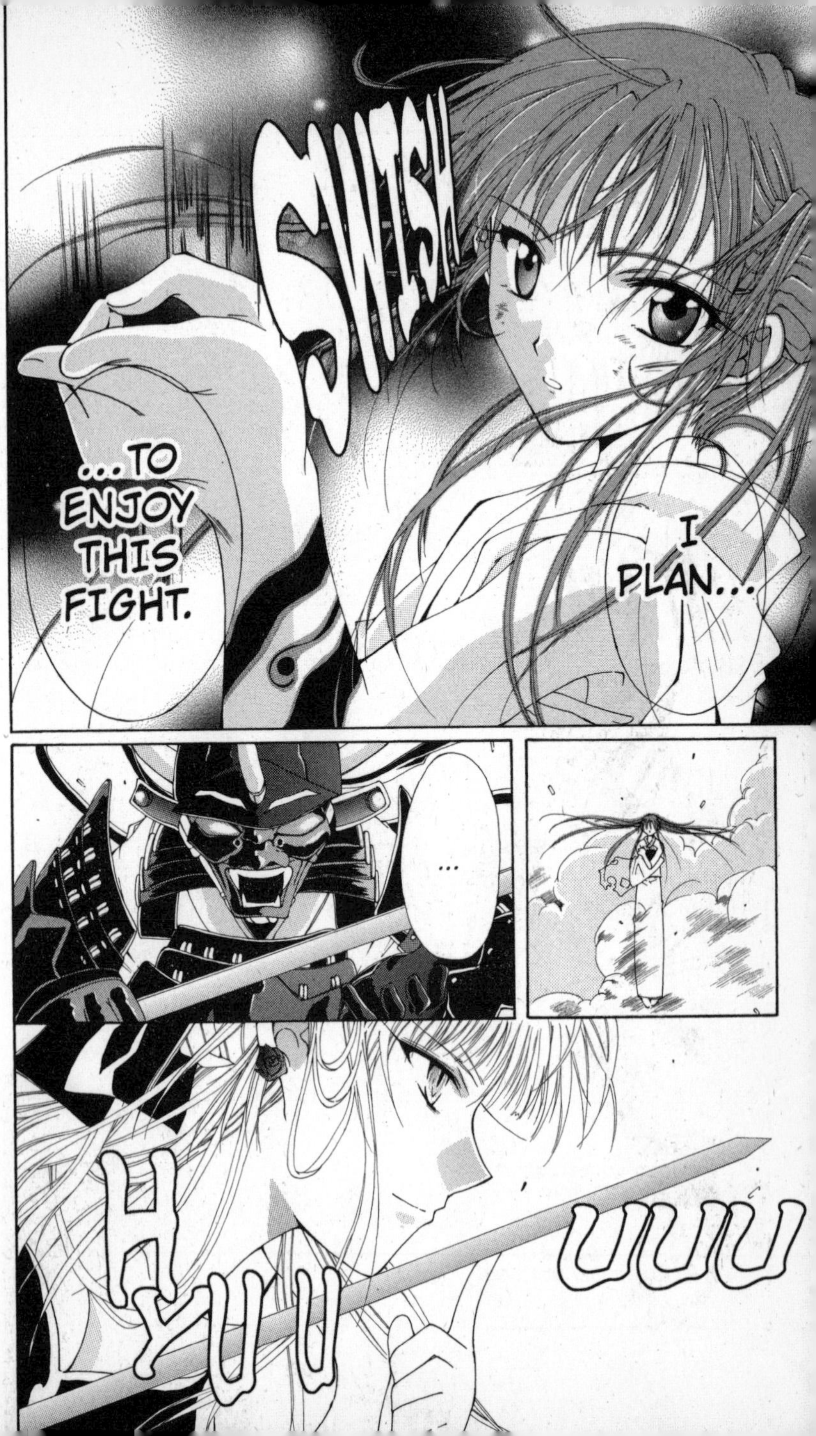
SWISH
I PLAN...
...TO ENJOY THIS FIGHT.
...
HYUU
UUUU

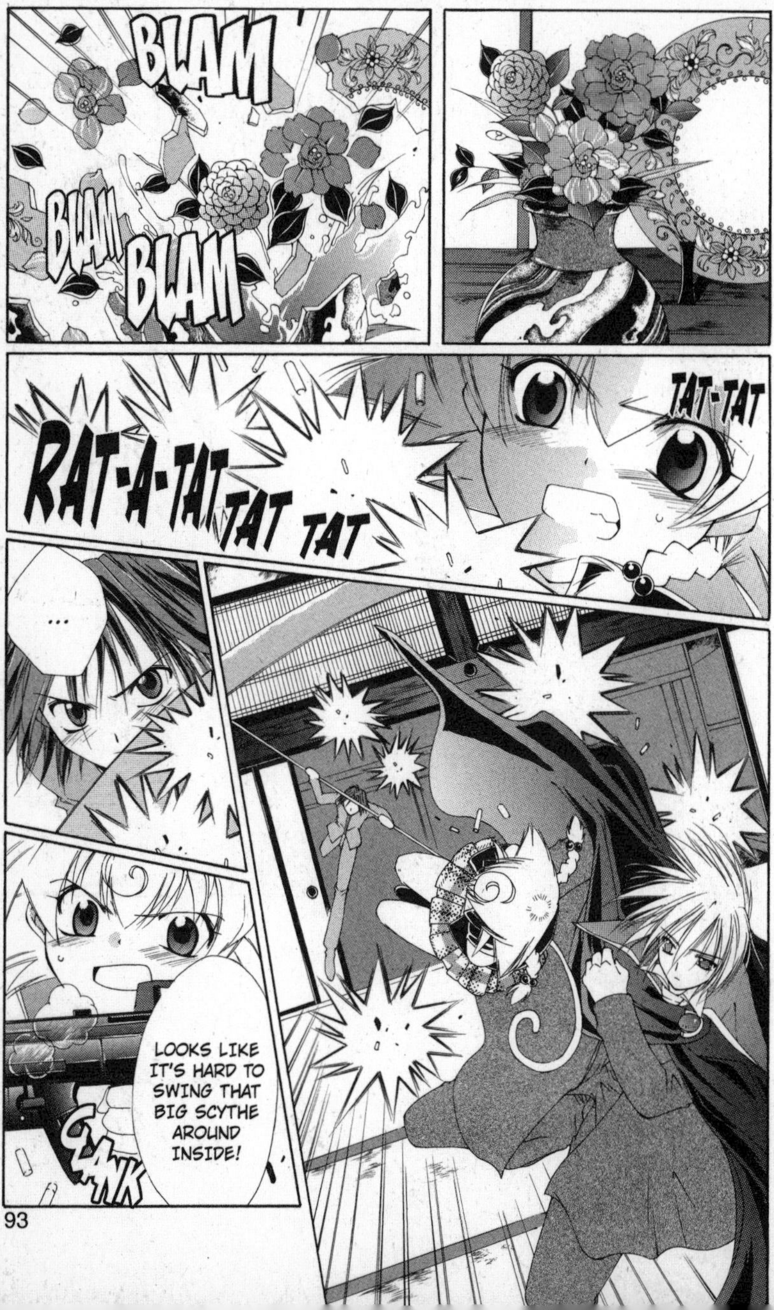
BLAM
BLAM
BLAM
TAT-TAT
RAT-A-TAT TAT TAT
...
LOOKS LIKE IT'S HARD TO SWING THAT BIG SCYTHE AROUND INSIDE!
CLANK

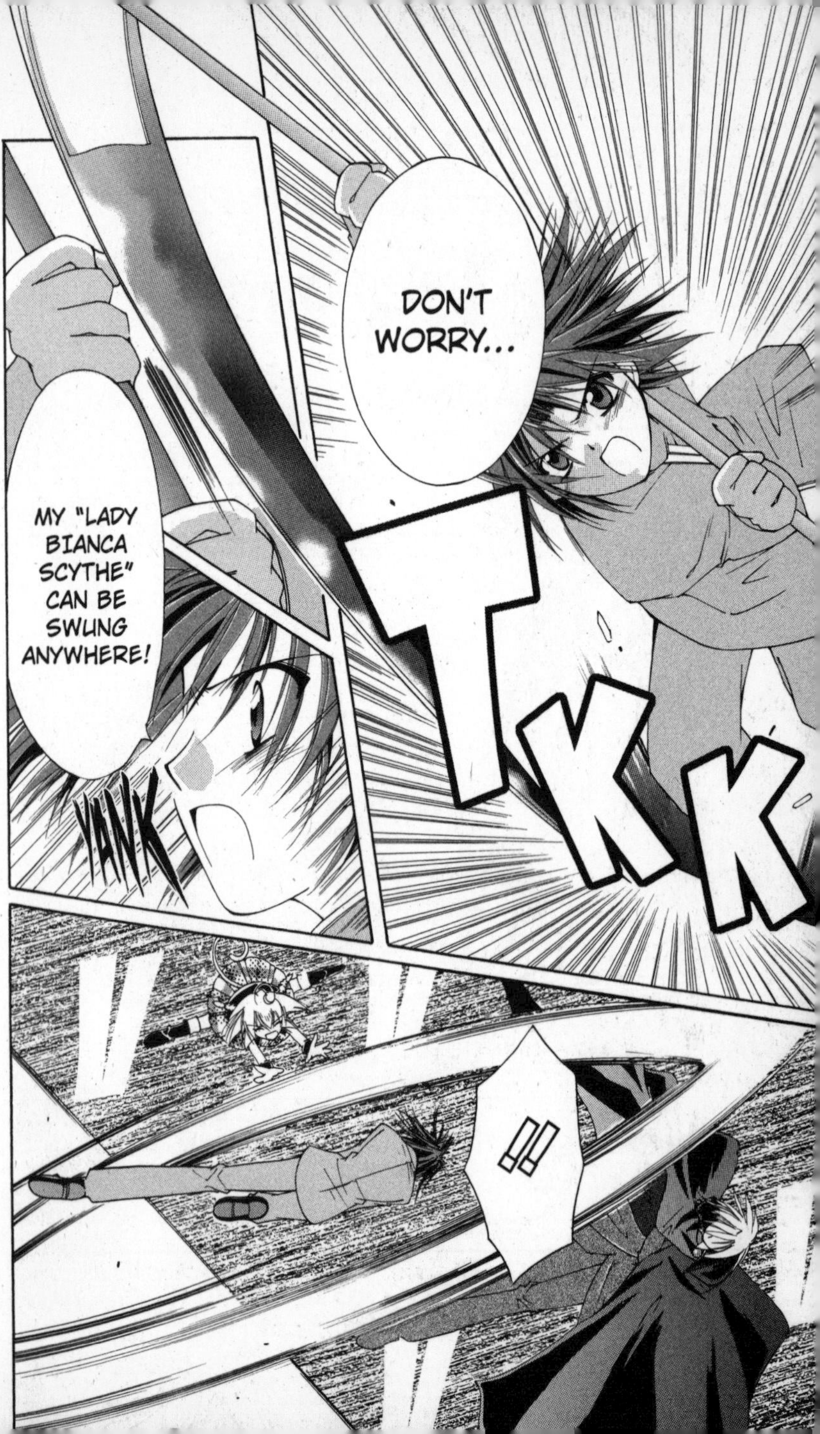
DON'T WORRY...
TKK
MY "LADY BIANCA SCYTHE" CAN BE SWUNG ANYWHERE!
YANK
!!

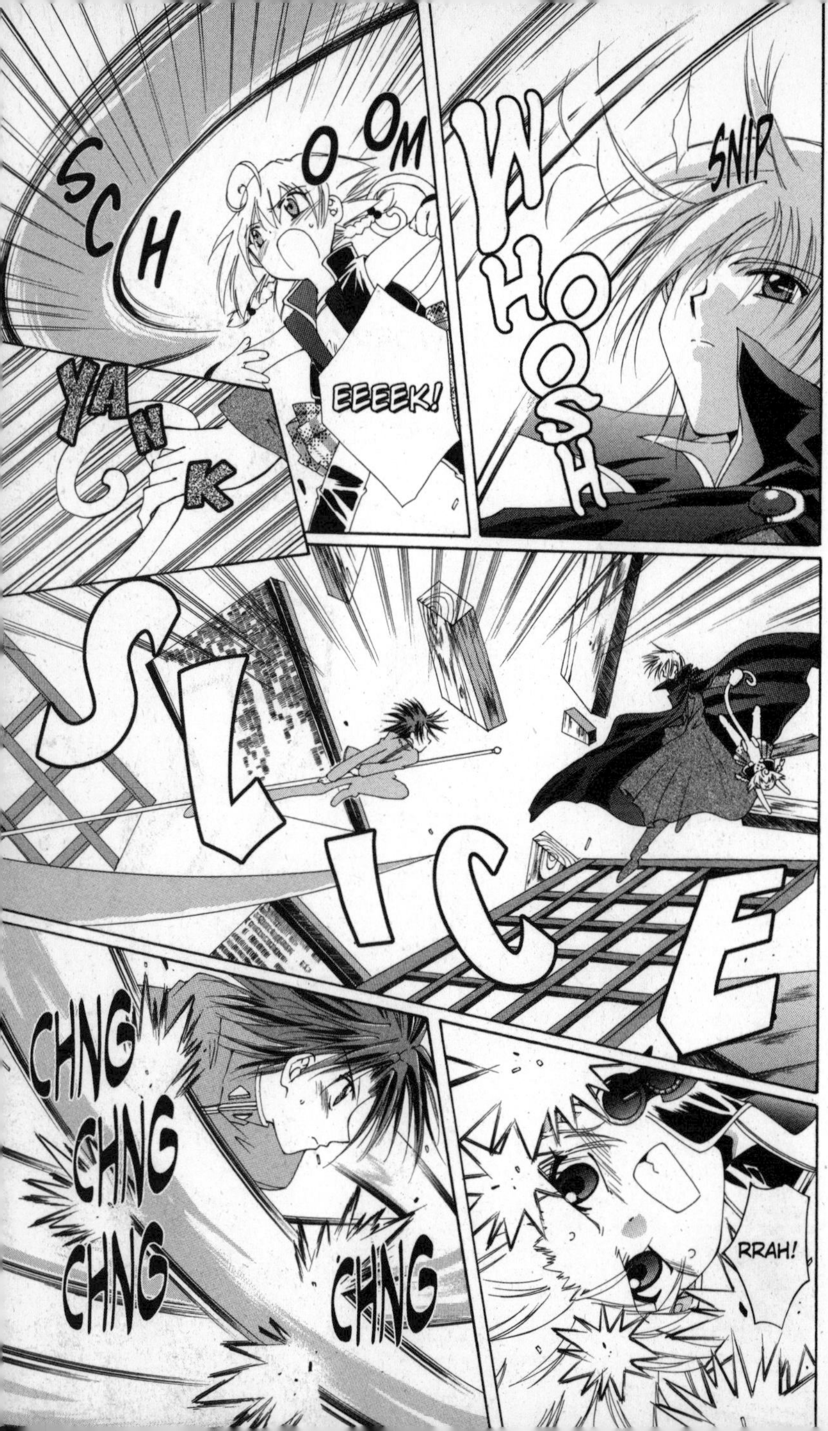
SNIP
WHOOSH
SCHOOOM
EEEEK!
YANK
SLICE
RRAH!
CHNG
CHNG CHNG CHNG CHNG

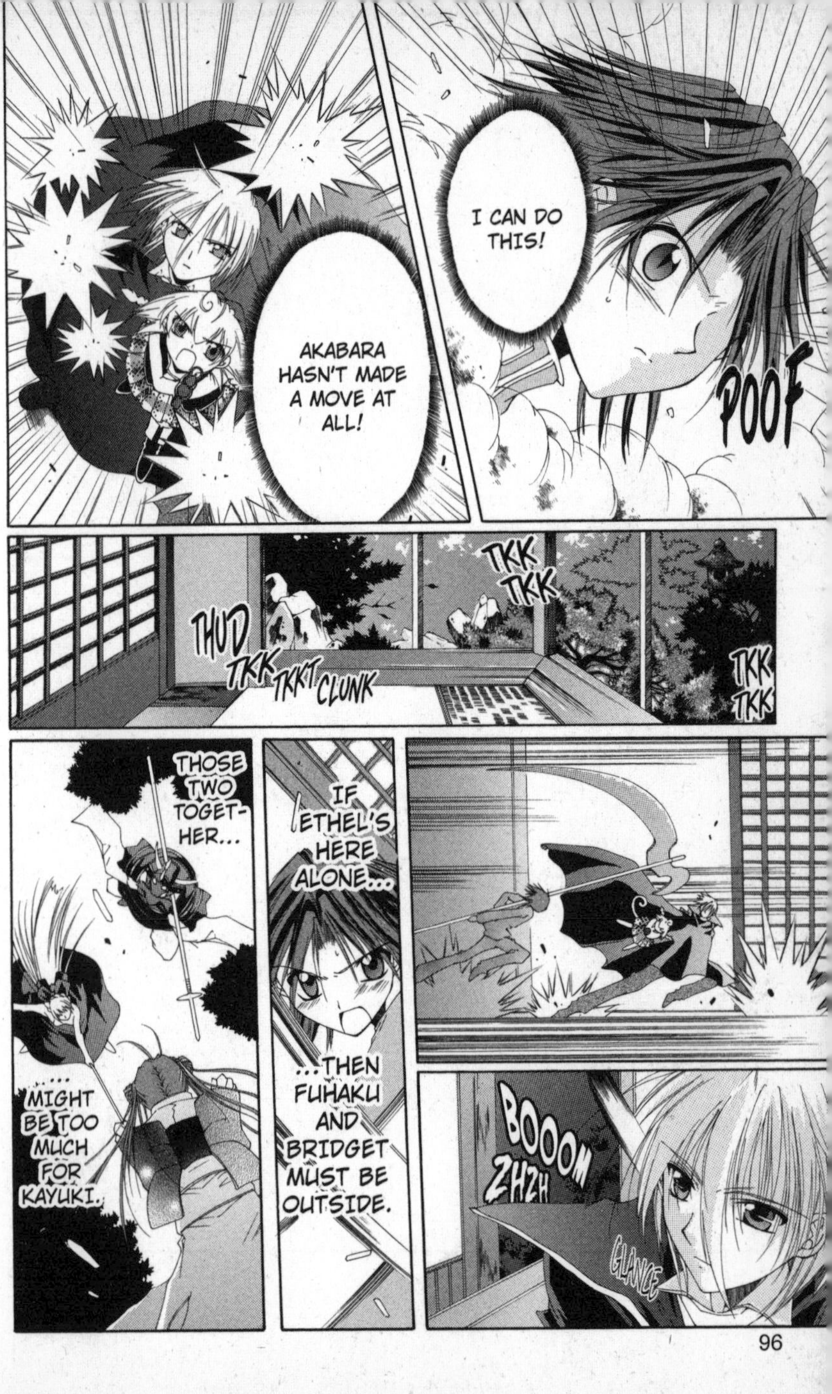
I CAN DO THIS!
POOF
AKABARA HASN'T MADE A MOVE AT ALL!
TKK TKK
TKK TKK
CLUNK
TKKT
TKK
THUD
BOOOM
ZHZH
GLANCE
IF ETHEL'S HERE ALONE...
...THEN FUHAKU AND BRIDGET MUST BE OUTSIDE.
THOSE TWO TOGET-HER...
...MIGHT BE TOO MUCH FOR KAYUKI.

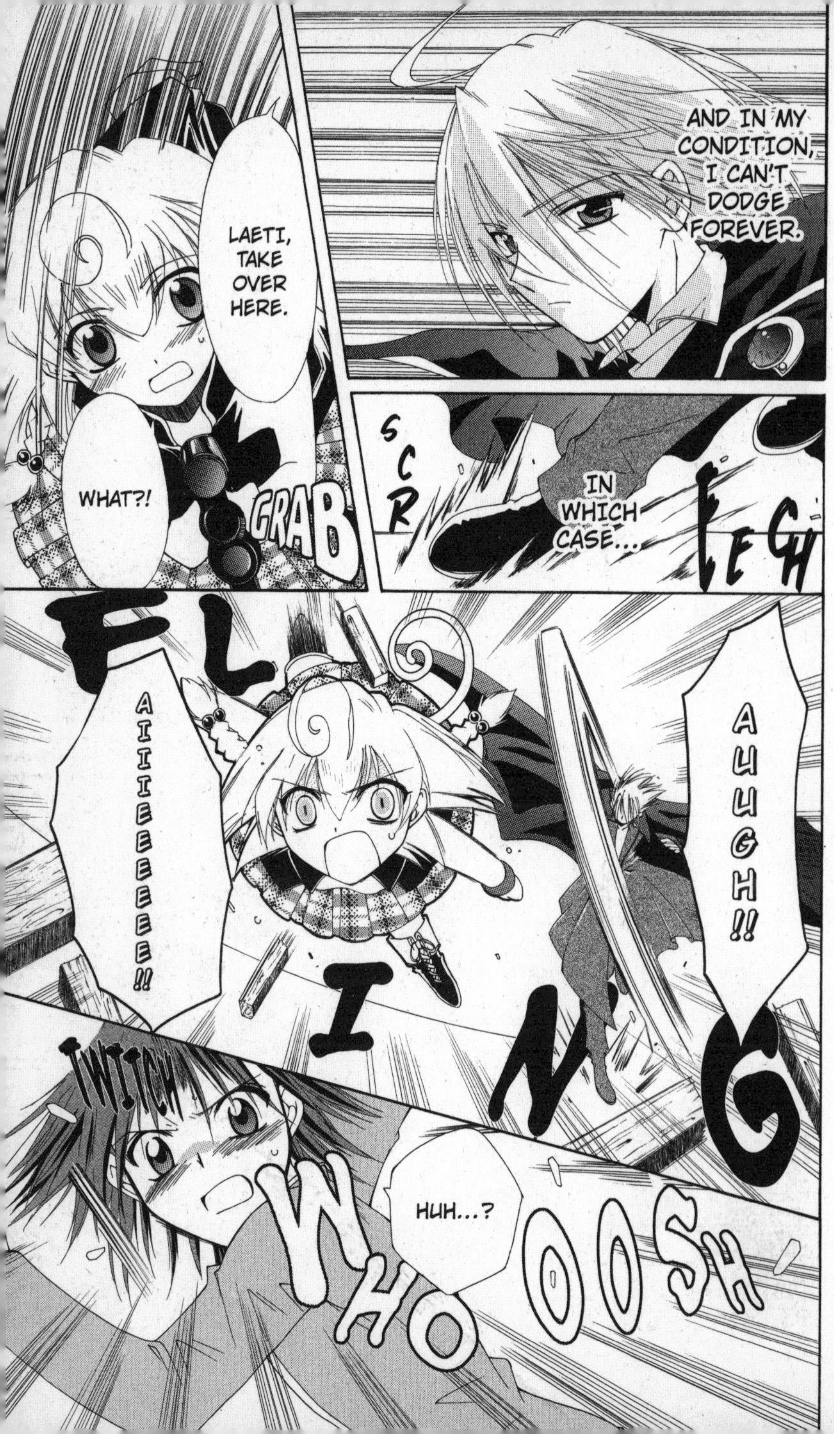
AND IN MY CONDITION, I CAN'T DODGE FOREVER.
SCR
IN WHICH CASE...
EECH
LAETI, TAKE OVER HERE.
WHAT?!
GRAB
FLING
AUUGH!!
AIIIEEEEEEEE!!
TWITCH
HUH...?
WHOOSH

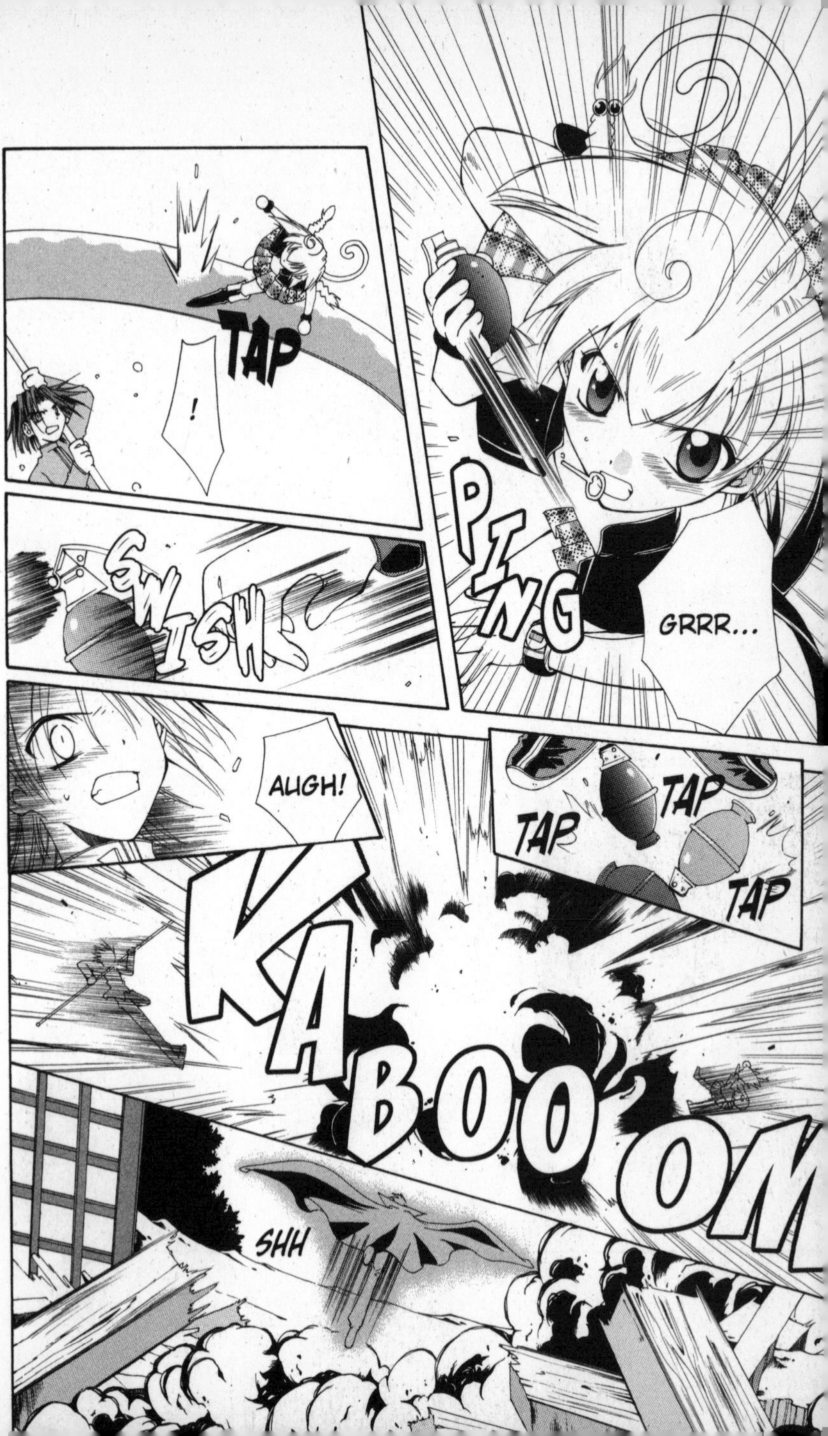
PING
GRRR...
TAP
!
SWISH
TAP
TAP
TAP
AUGH!
KABOOM
SHH

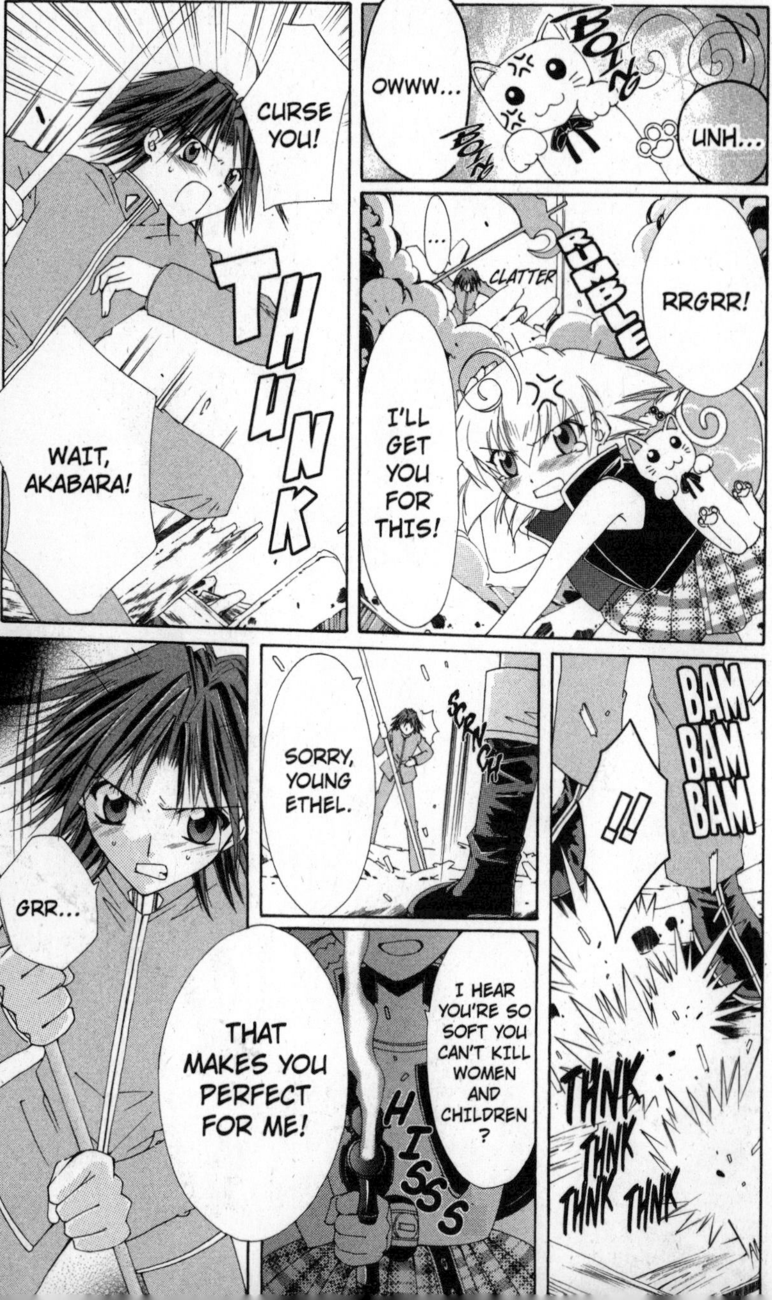
UNH...
BONK
OWWW...
BONK
RRGRR!
RUMBLE
...
CLATTER
I'LL GET YOU FOR THIS!
CURSE YOU!
THUNK
WAIT, AKABARA!
BAM BAM BAM
!!
THNK THNK THNK THNK
SCRNCH
SORRY, YOUNG ETHEL.
I HEAR YOU'RE SO SOFT YOU CAN'T KILL WOMEN AND CHILDREN?
HISSS
THAT MAKES YOU PERFECT FOR ME!
GRR...

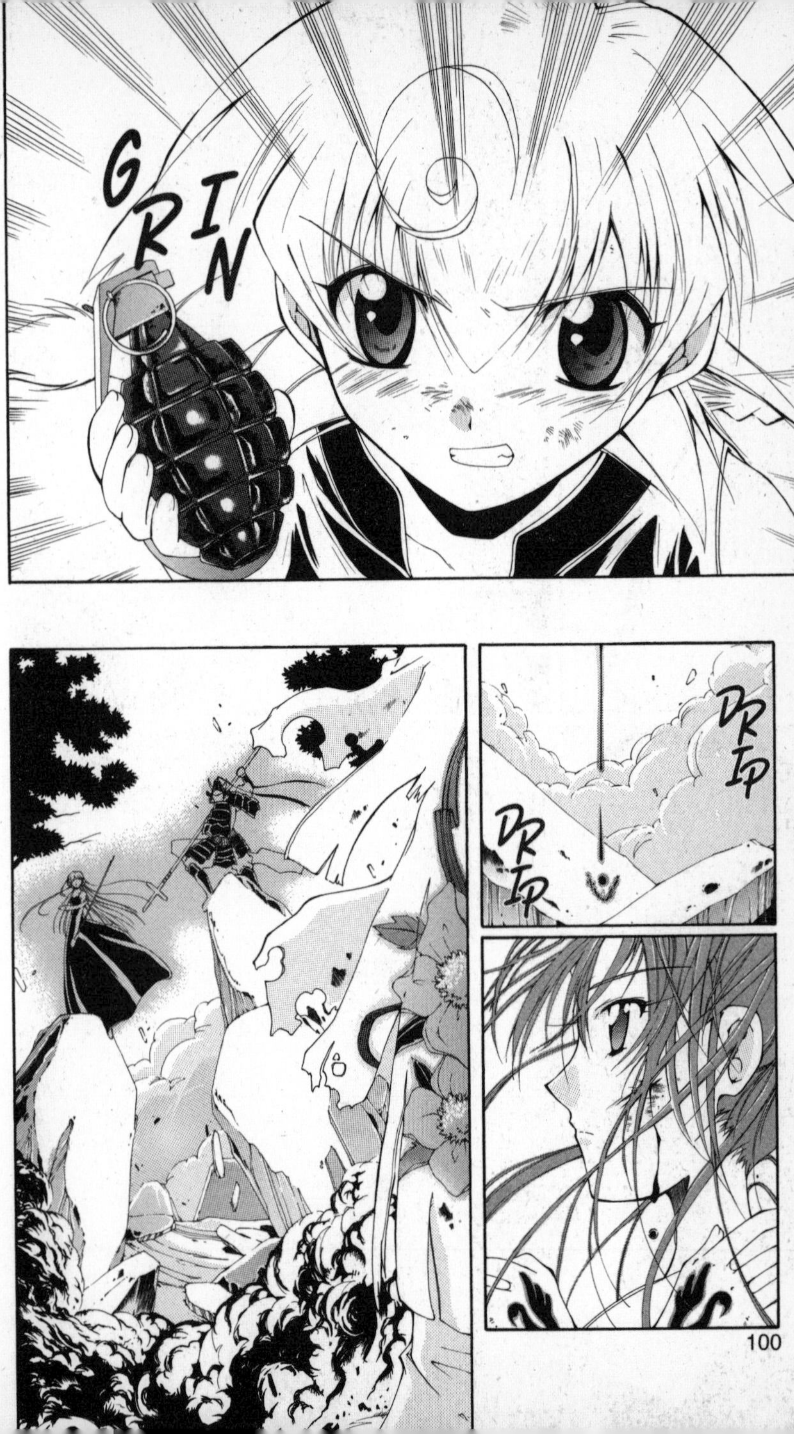
GRIN
DRIP
DRIP

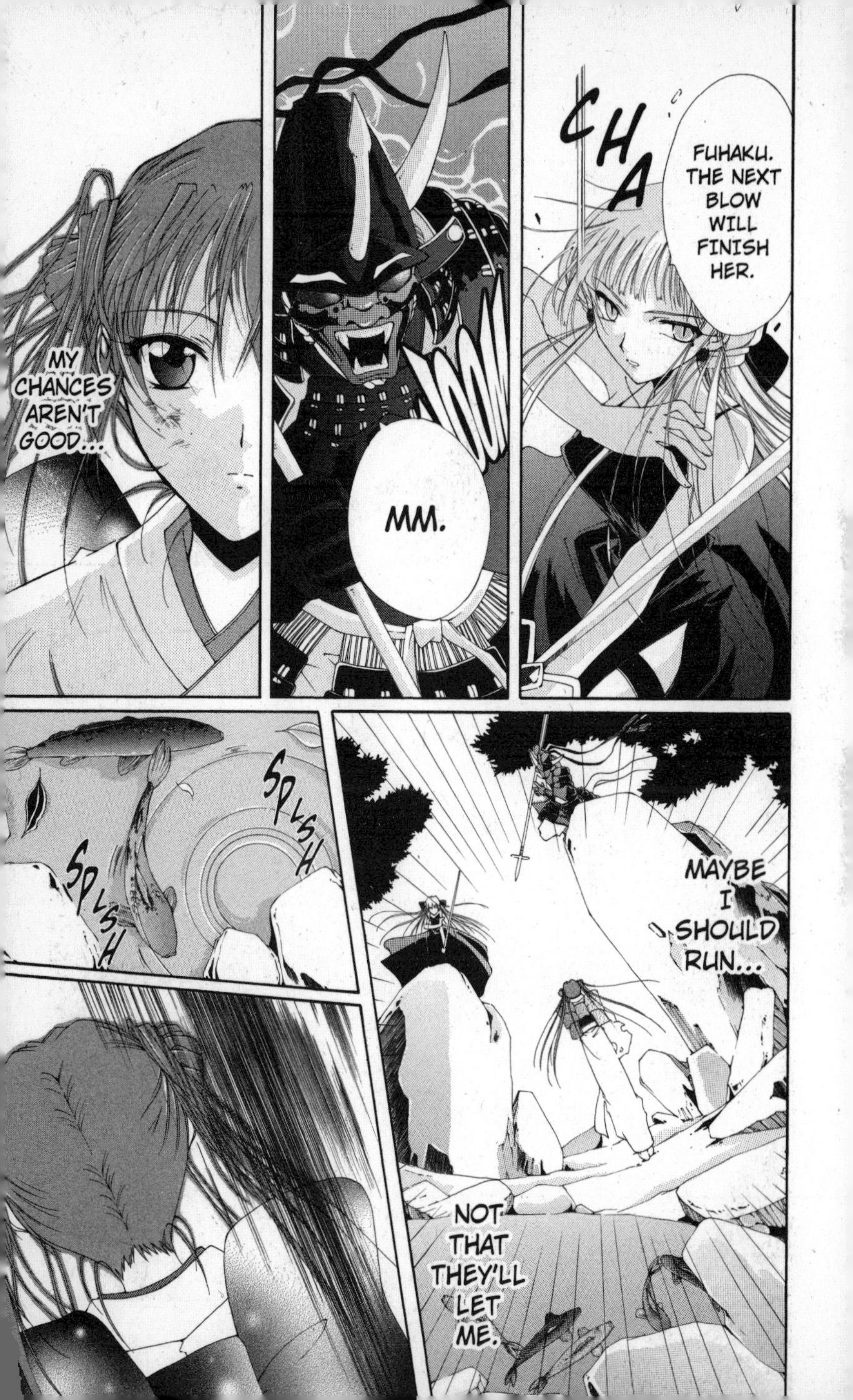
CHA
FUHAKU. THE NEXT BLOW WILL FINISH HER.
MM.
MY CHANCES AREN'T GOOD...
MAYBE I SHOULD RUN...
NOT THAT THEY'LL LET ME.
SPLSH
SPLSH

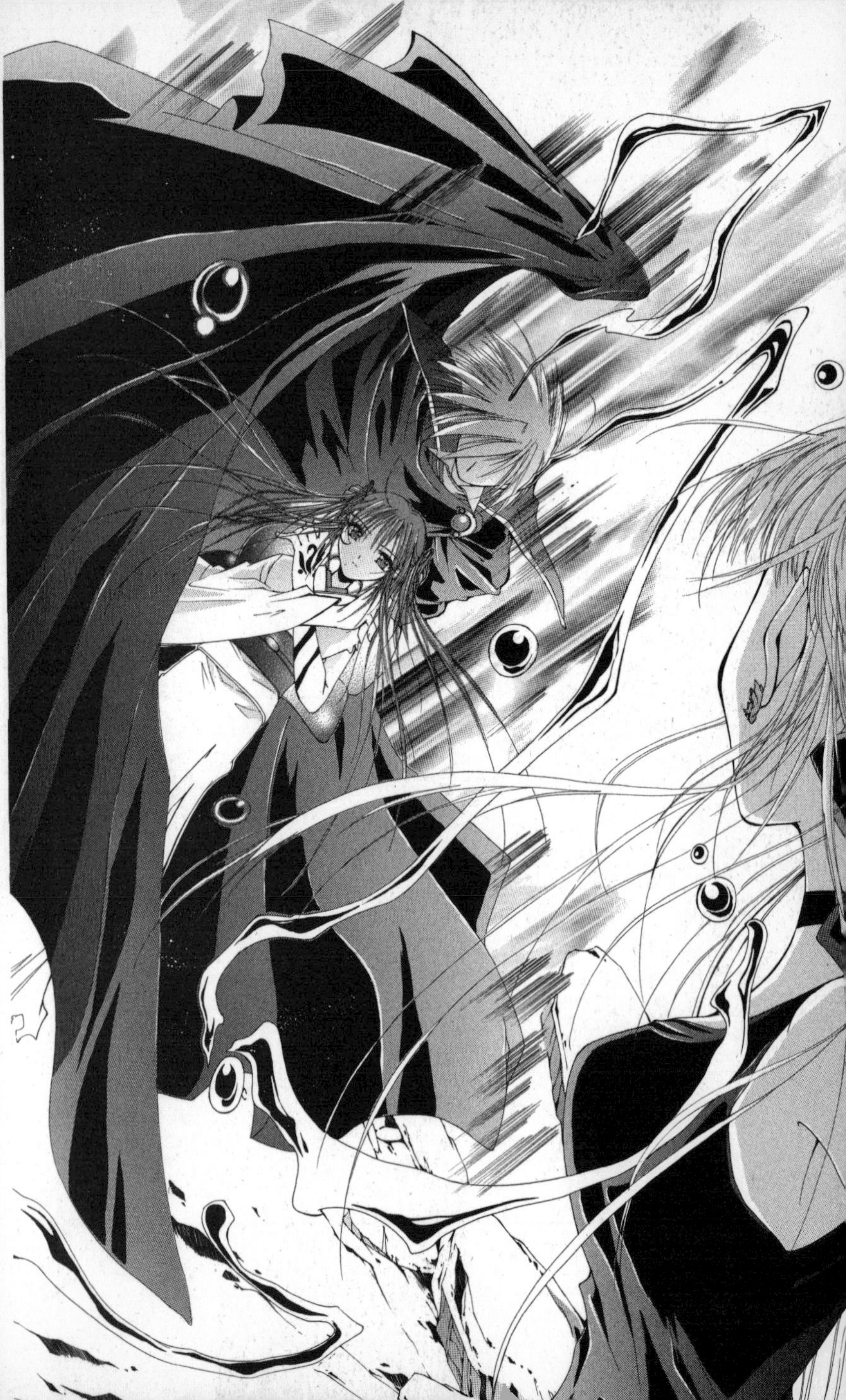

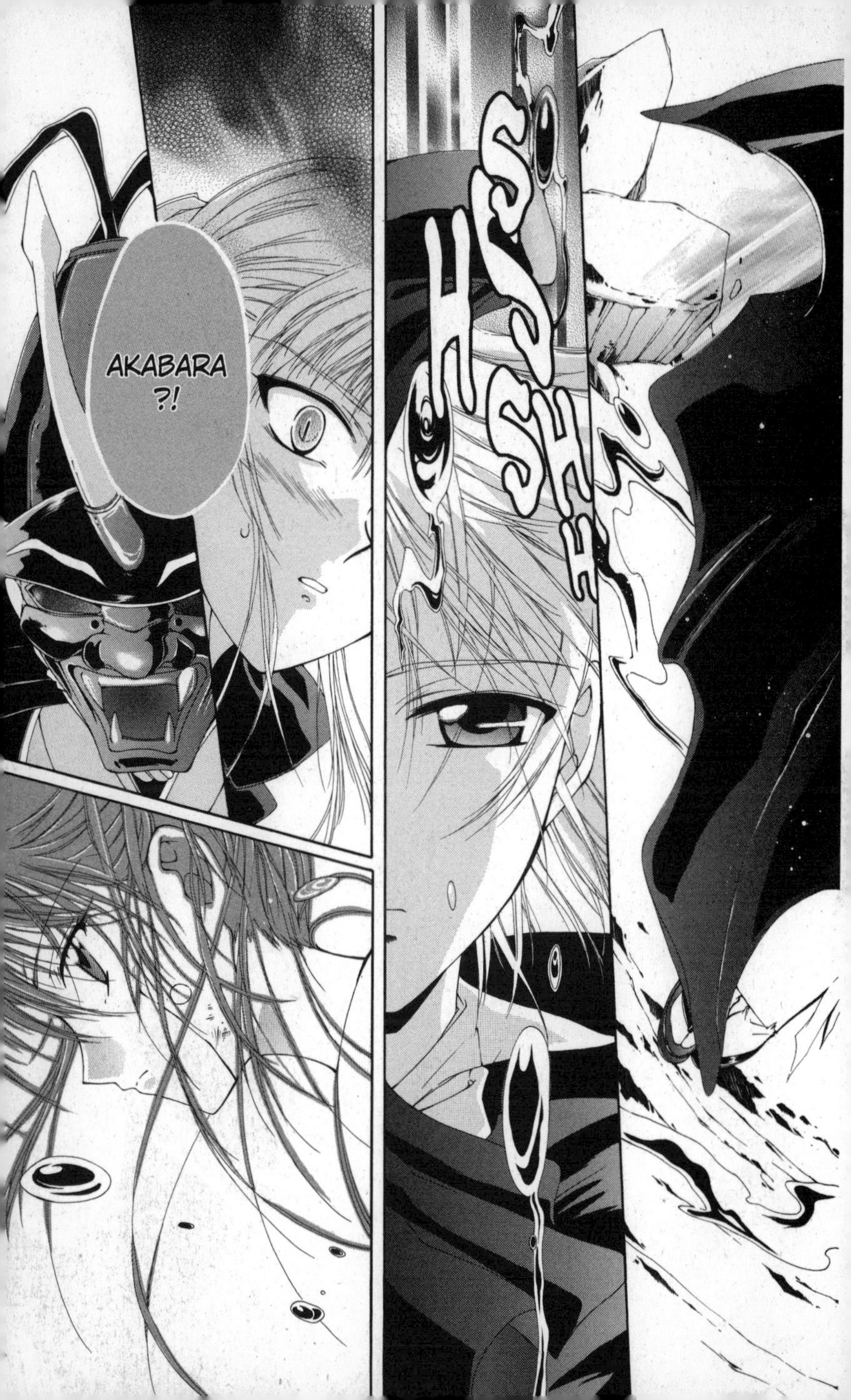
AKABARA ?!

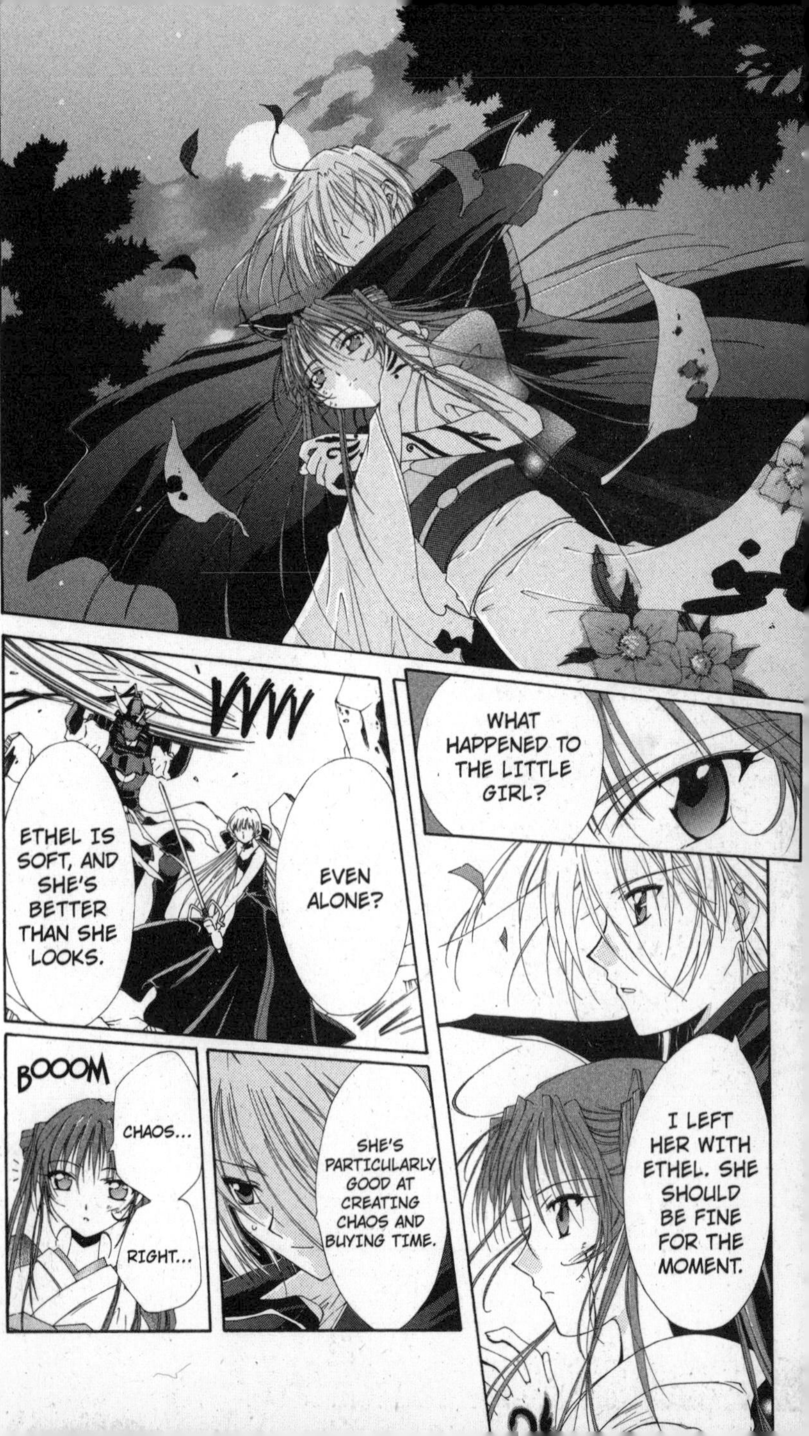
WHAT HAPPENED TO THE LITTLE GIRL?
I LEFT HER WITH ETHEL. SHE SHOULD BE FINE FOR THE MOMENT.
VVVV
EVEN ALONE?
ETHEL IS SOFT, AND SHE'S BETTER THAN SHE LOOKS.
SHE'S PARTICULARLY GOOD AT CREATING CHAOS AND BUYING TIME.
BOOOM
CHAOS...
RIGHT...

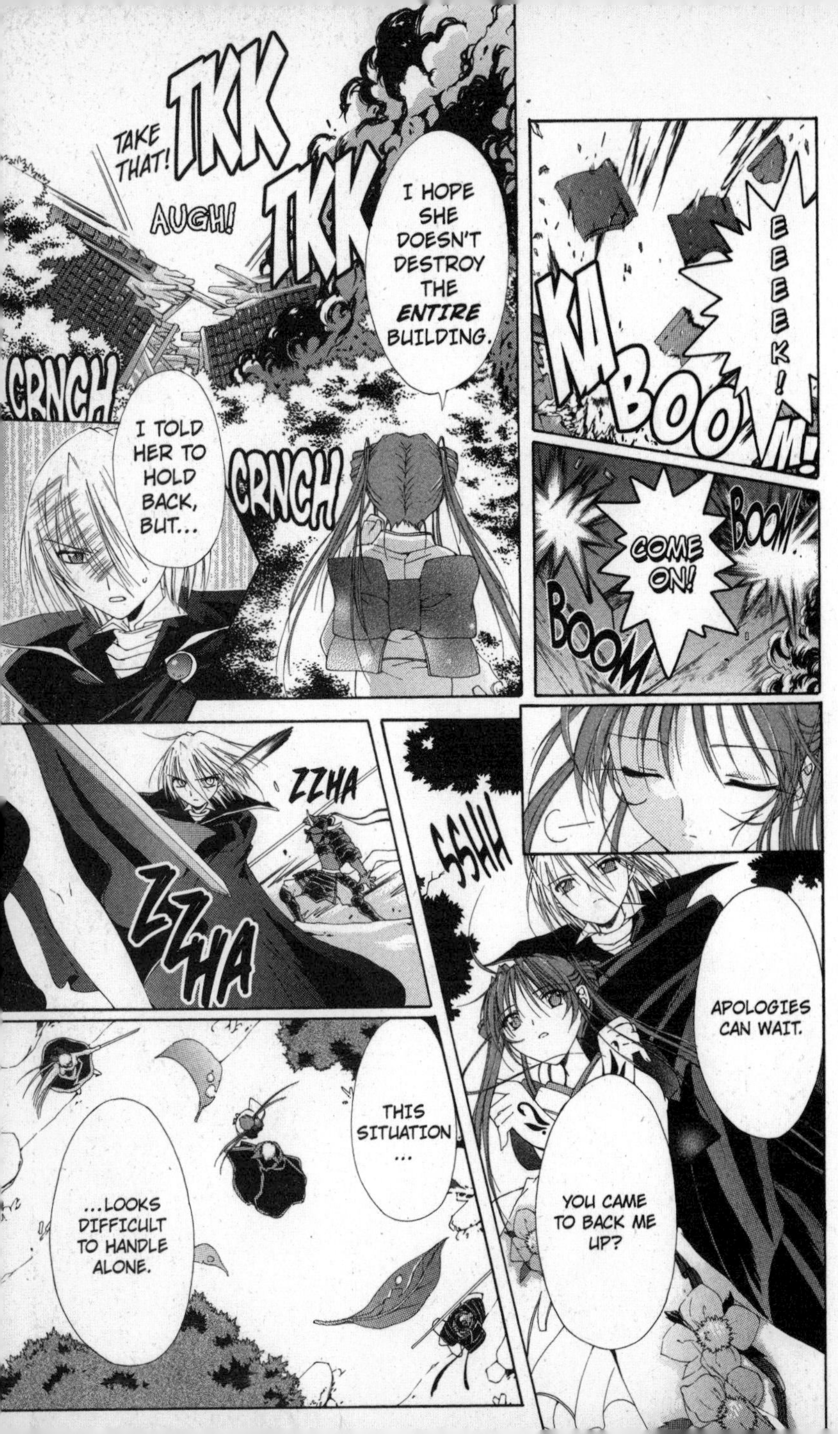
EEEEEK!
KA BOOM!
COME ON!
BOOM
BOOM
I HOPE SHE DOESN'T DESTROY THE *ENTIRE* BUILDING.
TKK
TKK
TAKE THAT!
AUGH!
CRNCH
I TOLD HER TO HOLD BACK, BUT...
CRNCH
SSHH
APOLOGIES CAN WAIT.
YOU CAME TO BACK ME UP?
ZZHA
ZZHA
THIS SITUATION ...
...LOOKS DIFFICULT TO HANDLE ALONE.

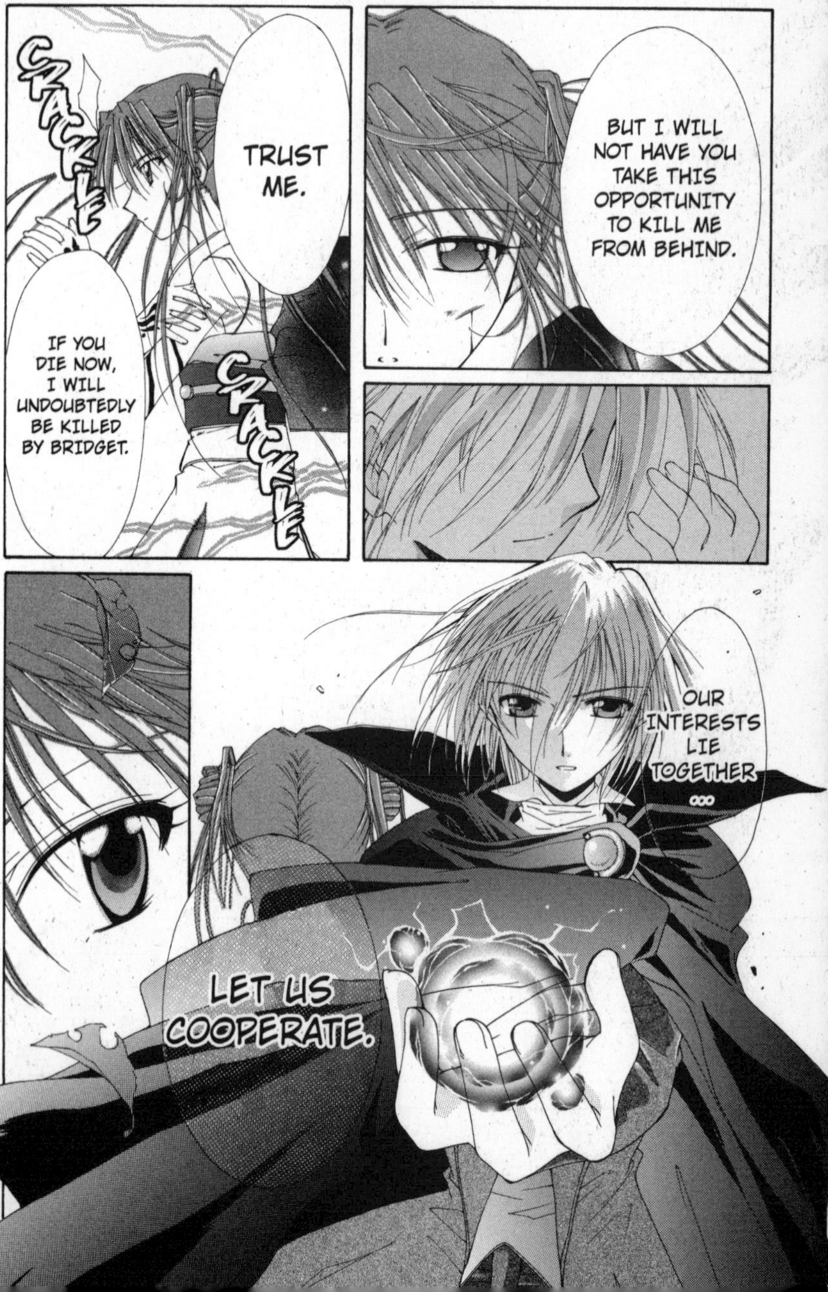
BUT I WILL NOT HAVE YOU TAKE THIS OPPORTUNITY TO KILL ME FROM BEHIND.
CRACKLE
TRUST ME.
IF YOU DIE NOW, I WILL UNDOUBTEDLY BE KILLED BY BRIDGET.
CRACKLE
OUR INTERESTS LIE TOGETHER...
LET US COOPERATE.

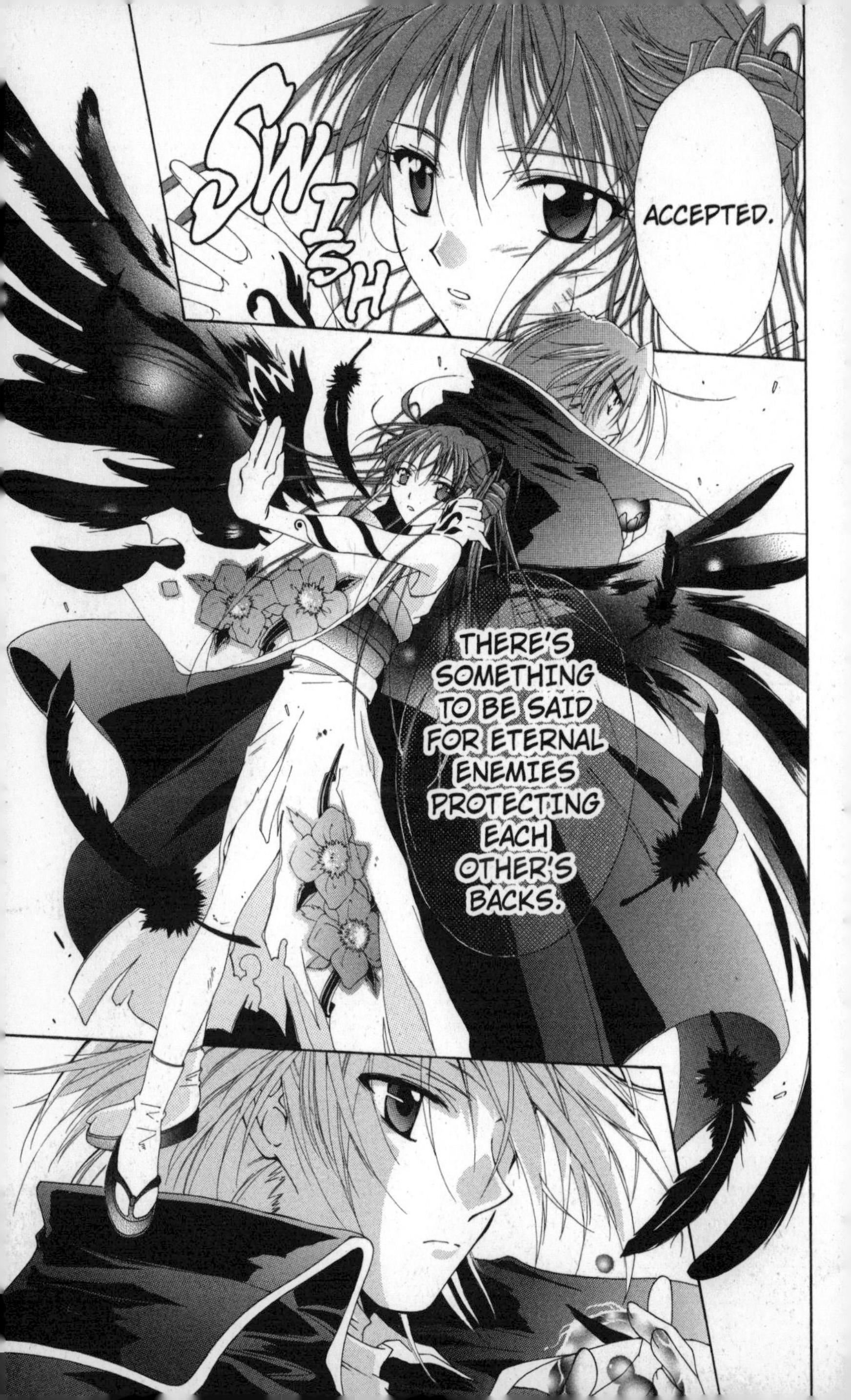
ACCEPTED.
SWISH
THERE'S SOMETHING TO BE SAID FOR ETERNAL ENEMIES PROTECTING EACH OTHER'S BACKS.

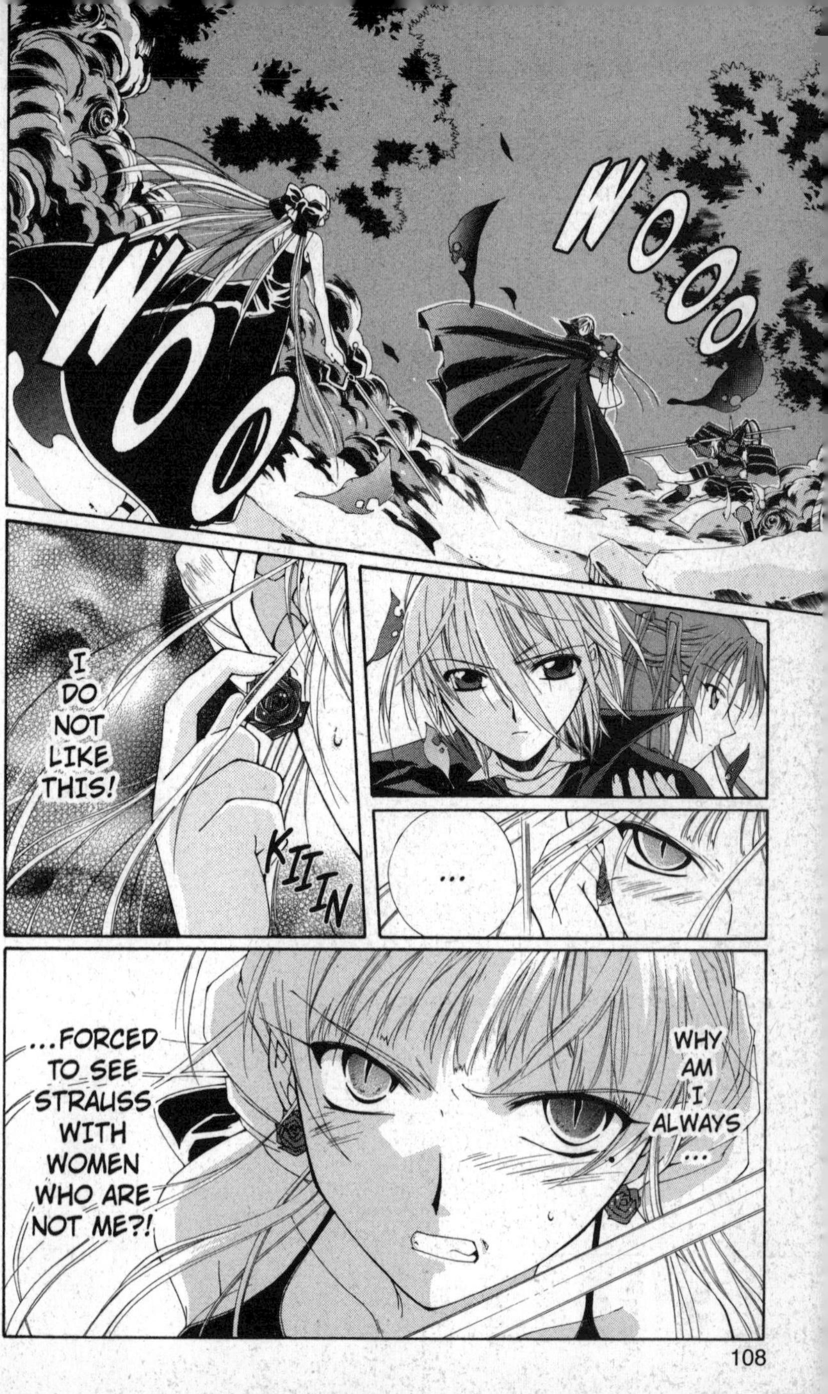
WOOOO
WOOO
...
I DO NOT LIKE THIS!
KIIIN
WHY AM I ALWAYS...
...FORCED TO SEE STRAUSS WITH WOMEN WHO ARE NOT ME?!

THE RECORD OF A

FALLEN VAMPIRE

THE RECORD OF A

FALLEN VAMPIRE

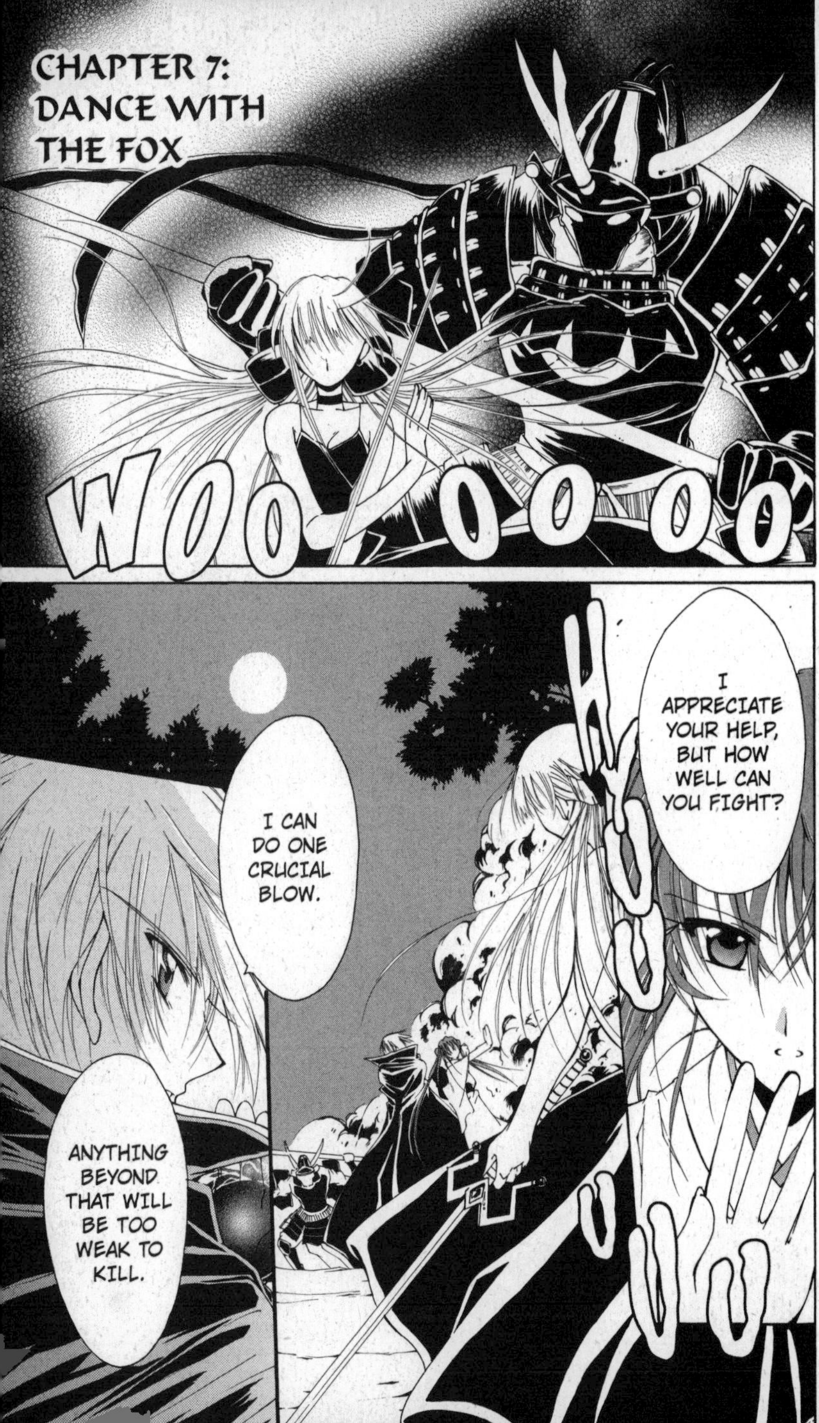
CHAPTER 7: DANCE WITH THE FOX
WOOOOOOO
I APPRECIATE YOUR HELP, BUT HOW WELL CAN YOU FIGHT?
I CAN DO ONE CRUCIAL BLOW.
ANYTHING BEYOND THAT WILL BE TOO WEAK TO KILL.

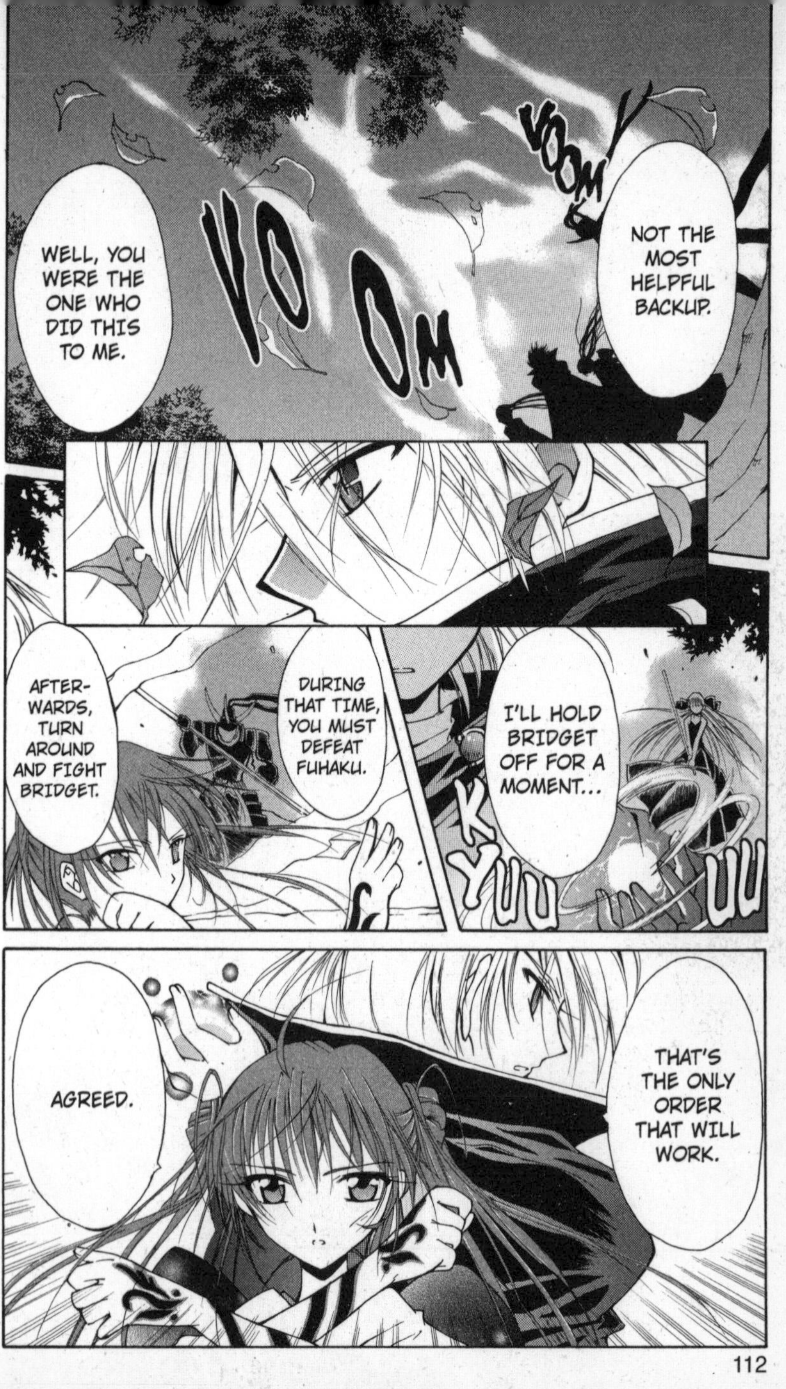
VOOM
NOT THE MOST HELPFUL BACKUP.
VOOM
WELL, YOU WERE THE ONE WHO DID THIS TO ME.
I'LL HOLD BRIDGET OFF FOR A MOMENT...
KYUUUU
DURING THAT TIME, YOU MUST DEFEAT FUHAKU.
AFTER-WARDS, TURN AROUND AND FIGHT BRIDGET.
THAT'S THE ONLY ORDER THAT WILL WORK.
AGREED.

CHAPTER 7: DANCE WITH THE FOX

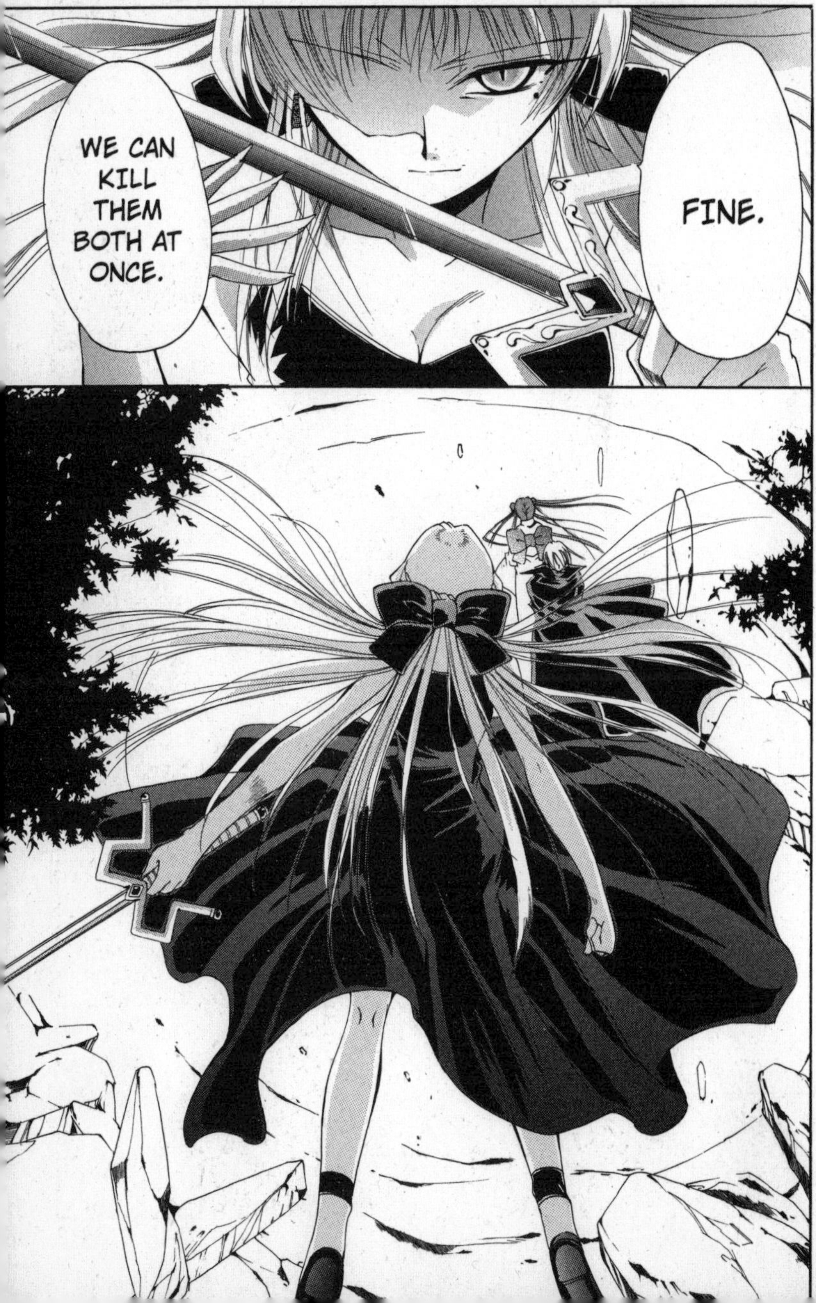
FINE.
WE CAN KILL THEM BOTH AT ONCE.

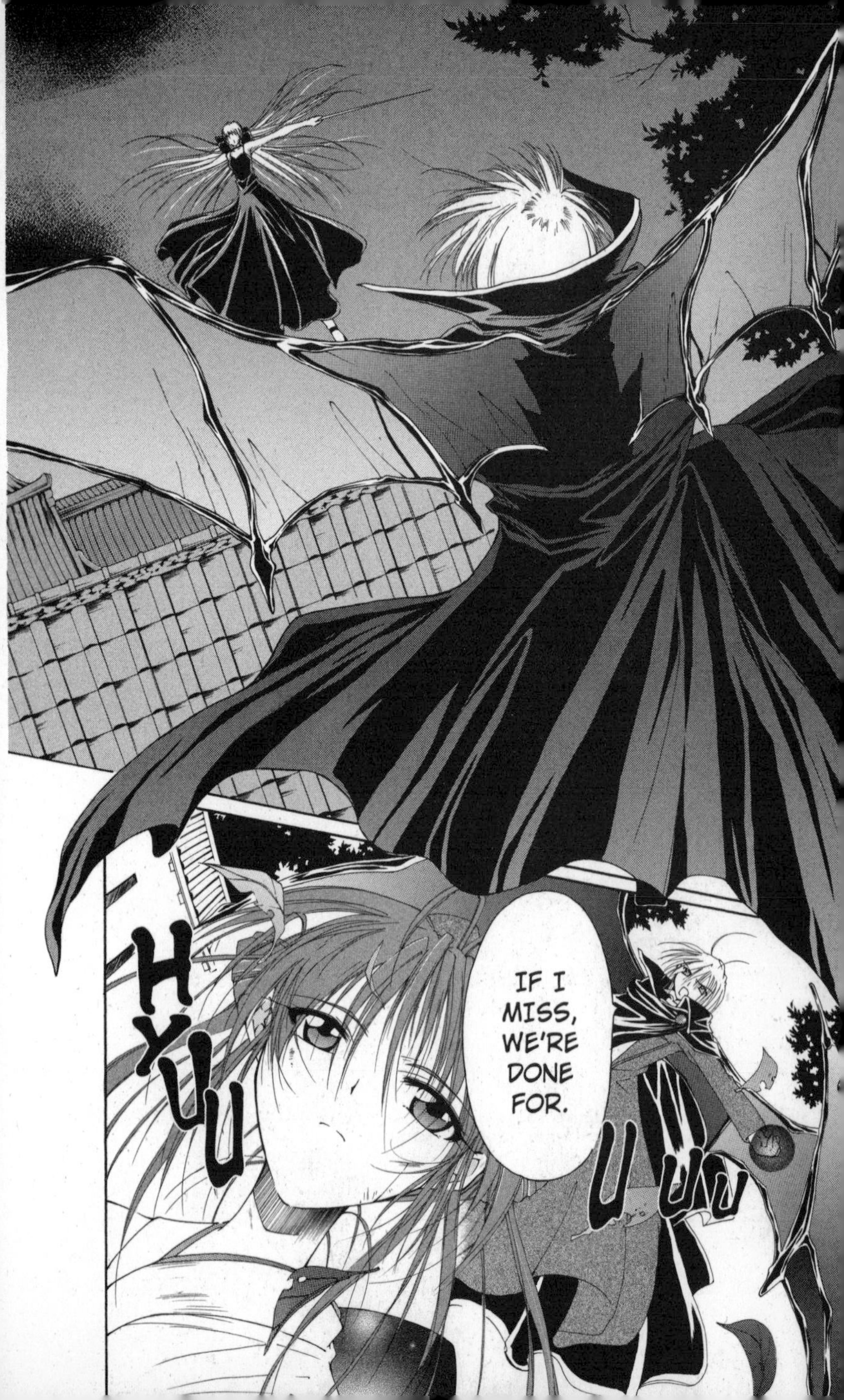
IF I MISS, WE'RE DONE FOR.
HYUUU
UUUU

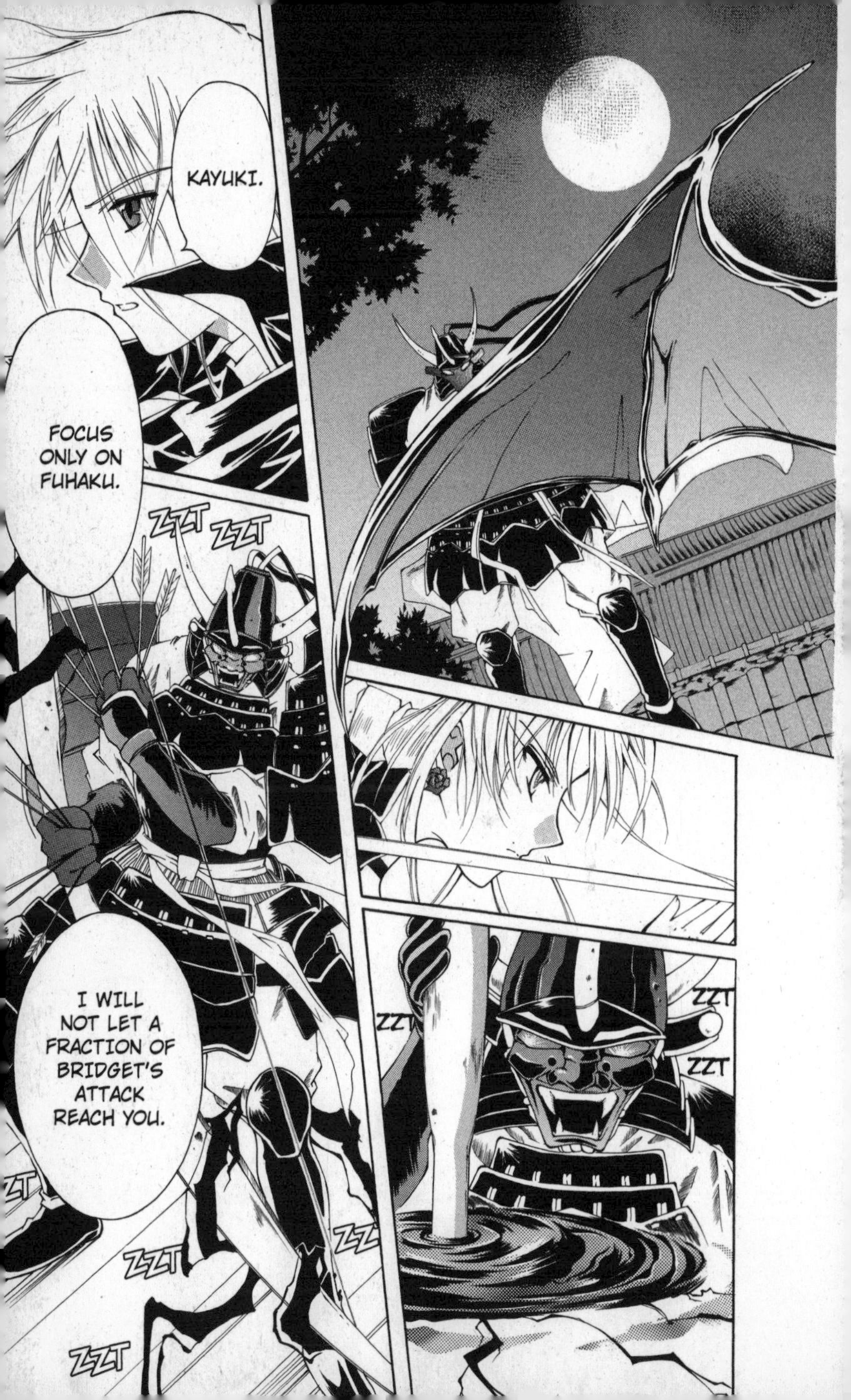
KAYUKI.
FOCUS ONLY ON FUHAKU.
ZZT
ZZT
ZZT
ZZT
ZZT
I WILL NOT LET A FRACTION OF BRIDGET'S ATTACK REACH YOU.
ZZT
ZZT
ZZT
ZZT

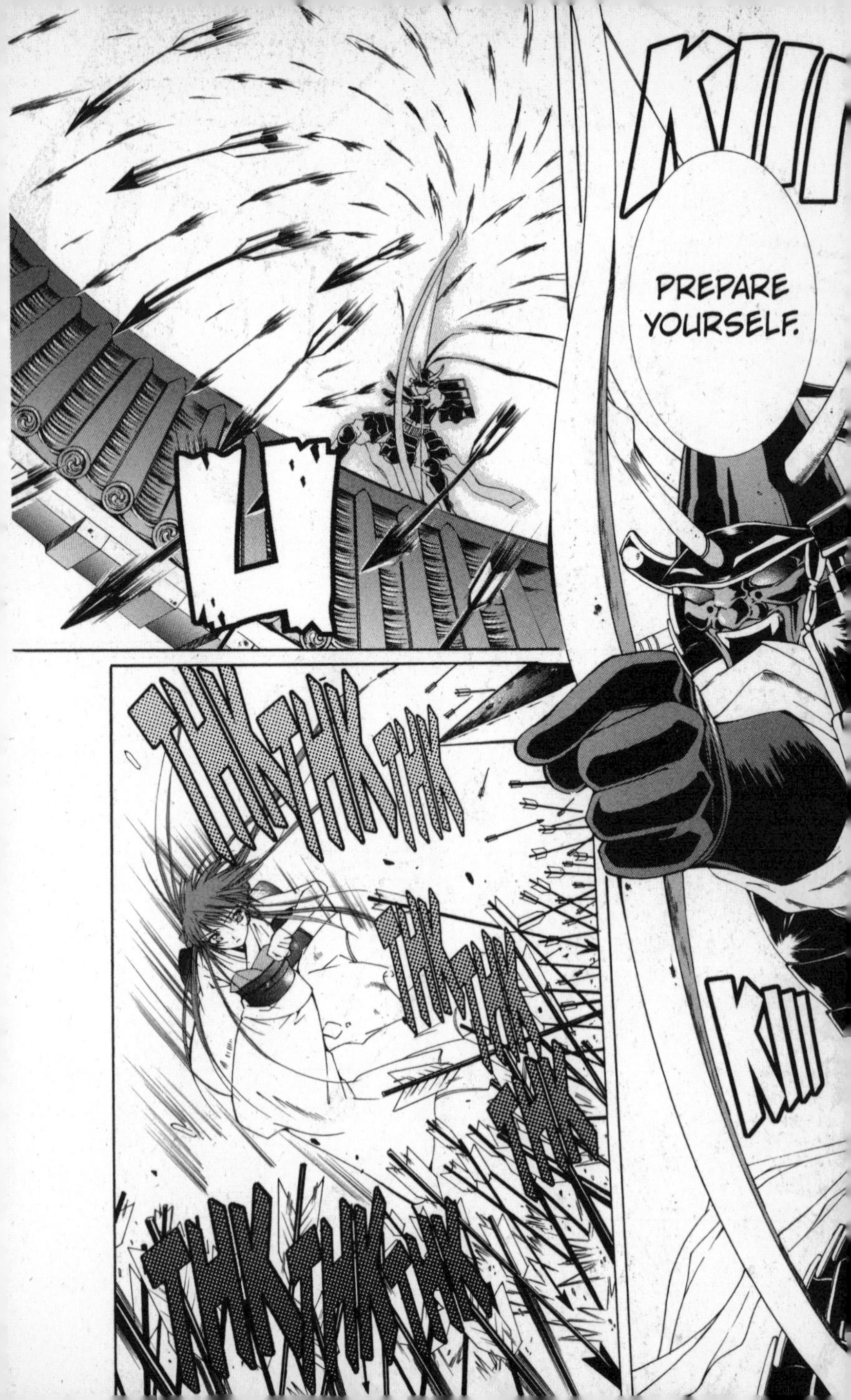
KIII
PREPARE YOURSELF.
KIII
U
THKTHKTHK
THKTHK
THK
THKTHKTHK

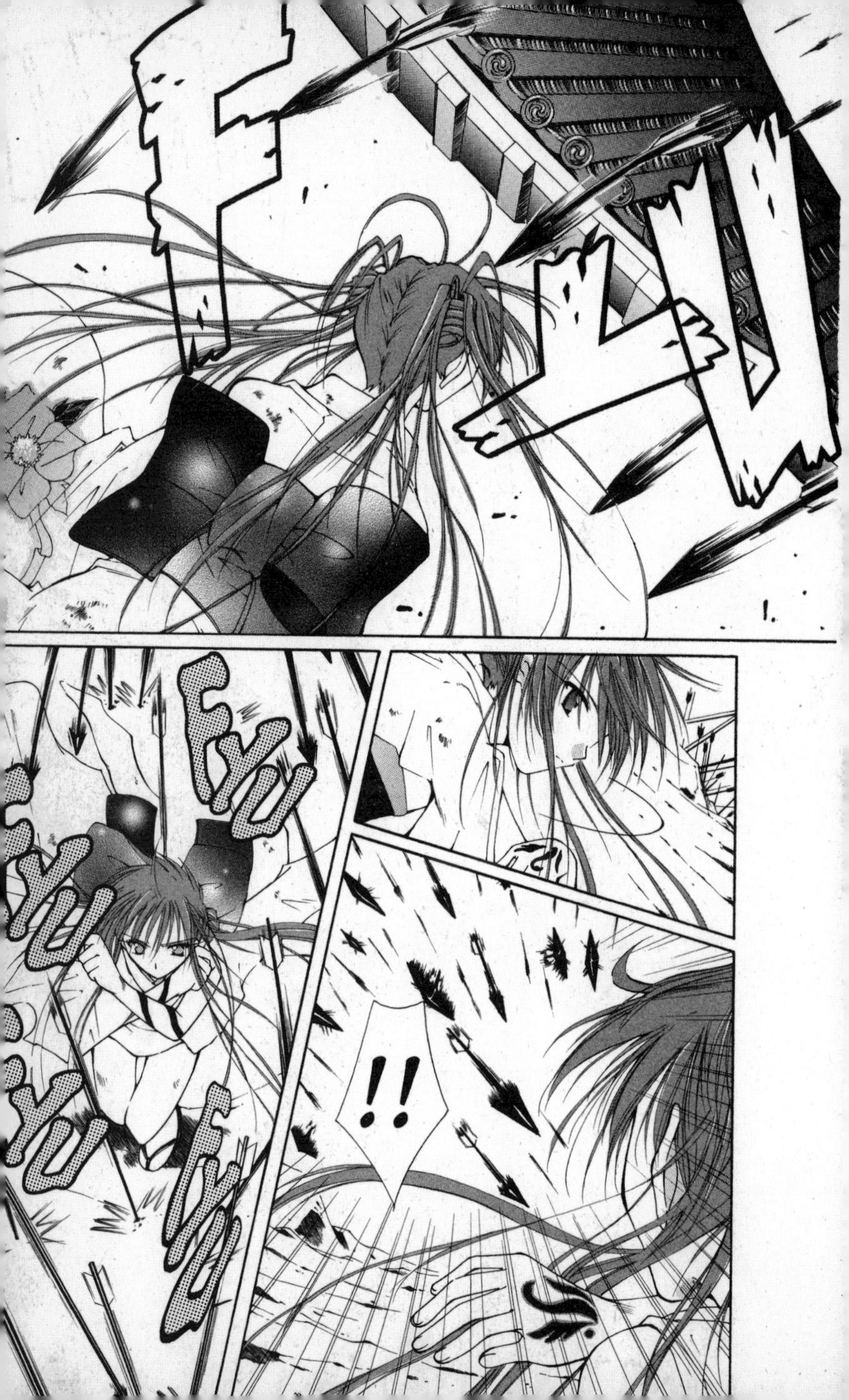
!!
FYU
FYU
FYU

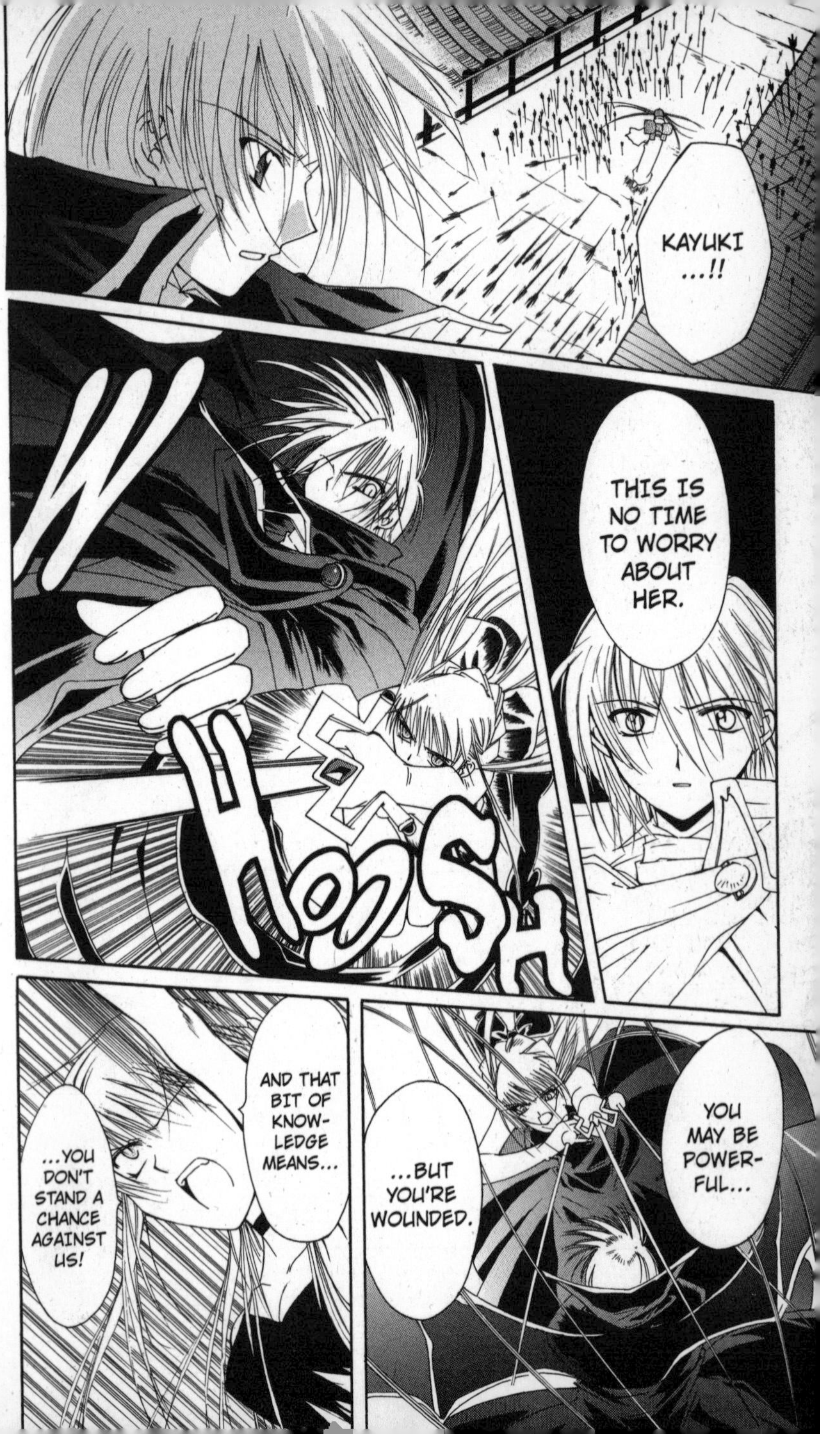
KAYUKI ...!!
THIS IS NO TIME TO WORRY ABOUT HER.
WHOOSH
YOU MAY BE POWER-FUL...
...BUT YOU'RE WOUNDED.
AND THAT BIT OF KNOW-LEDGE MEANS...
...YOU DON'T STAND A CHANCE AGAINST US!

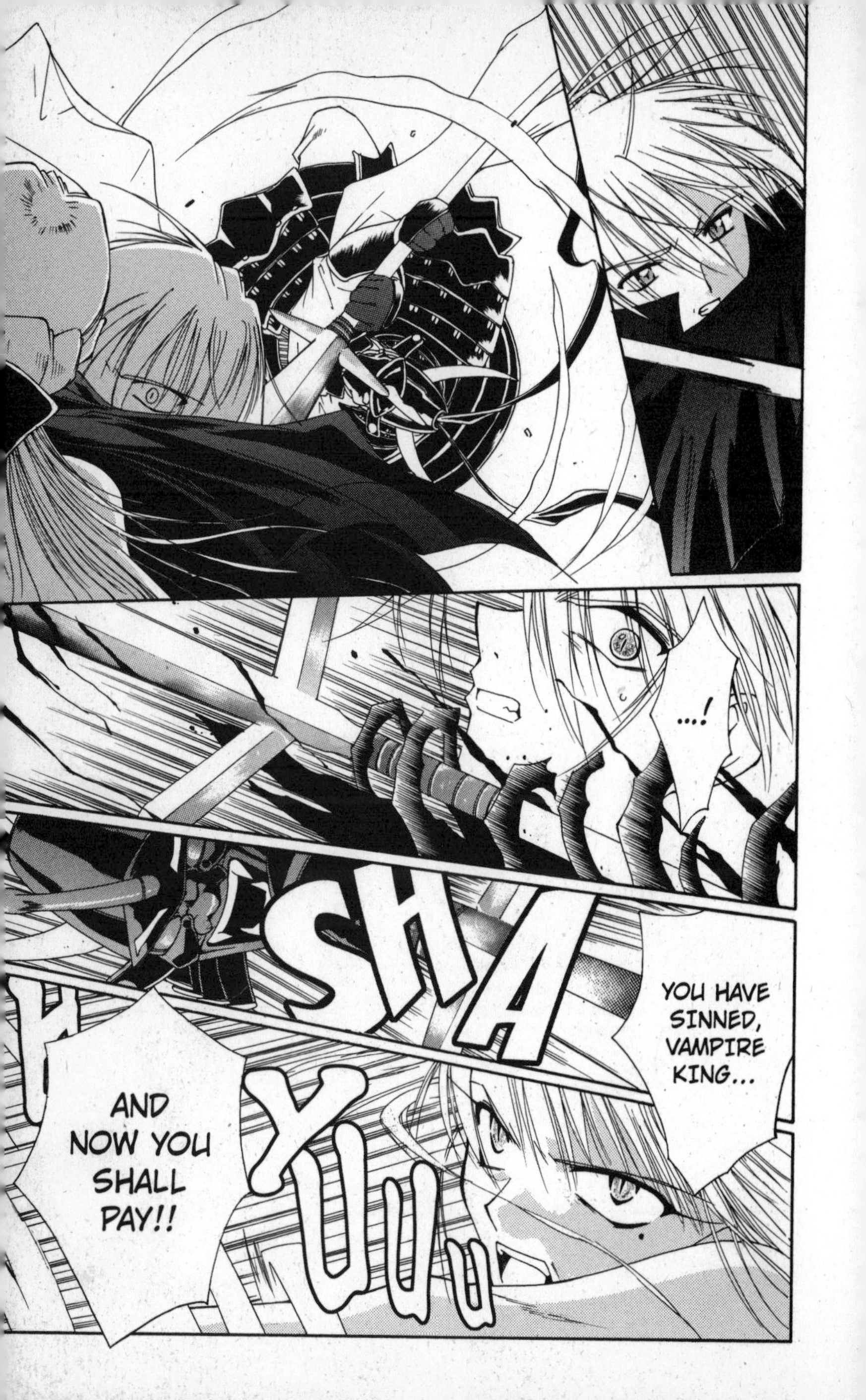
...!
SHA
YOU HAVE SINNED, VAMPIRE KING...
AND NOW YOU SHALL PAY!!
XYUUU

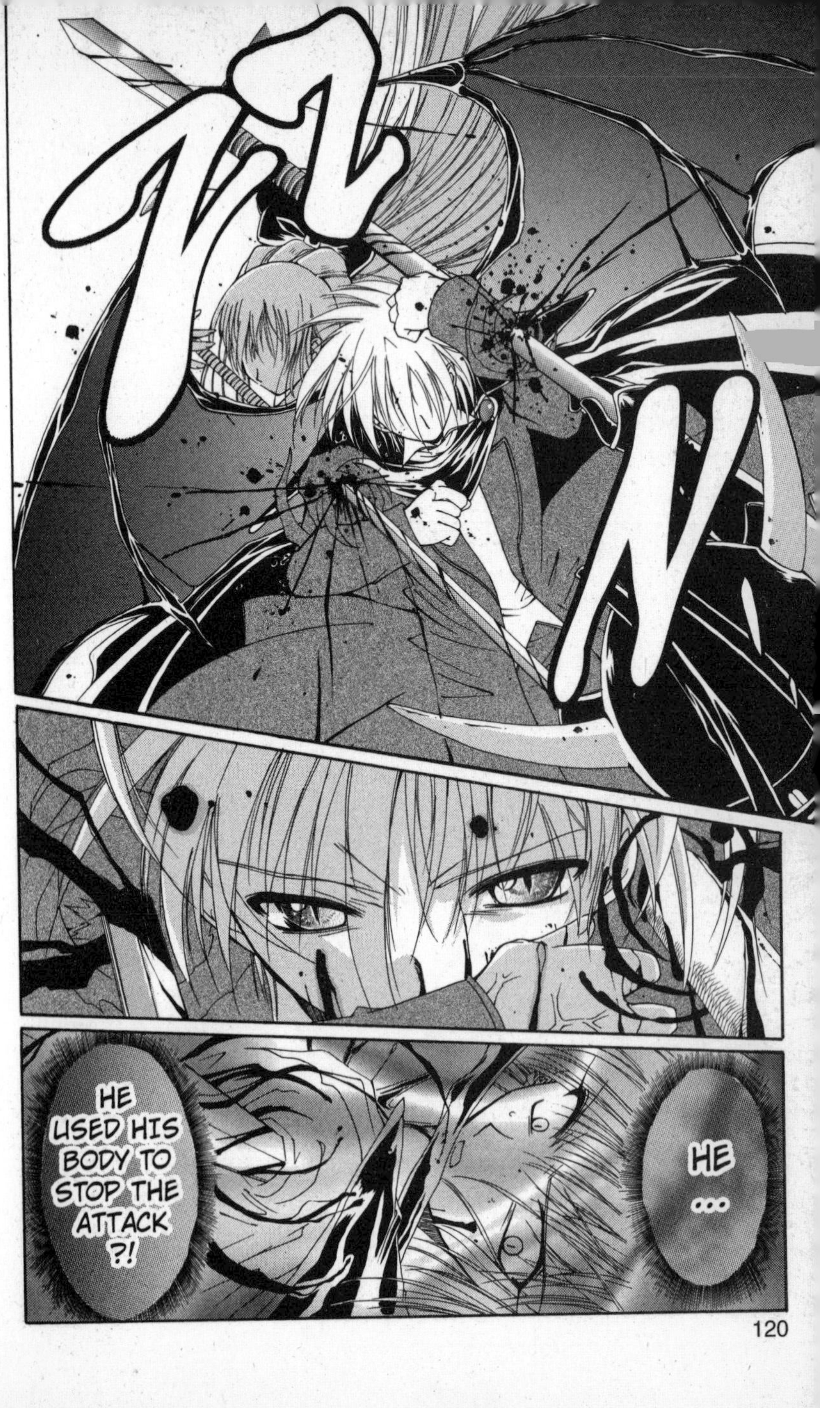
HE ...
HE USED HIS BODY TO STOP THE ATTACK ?!

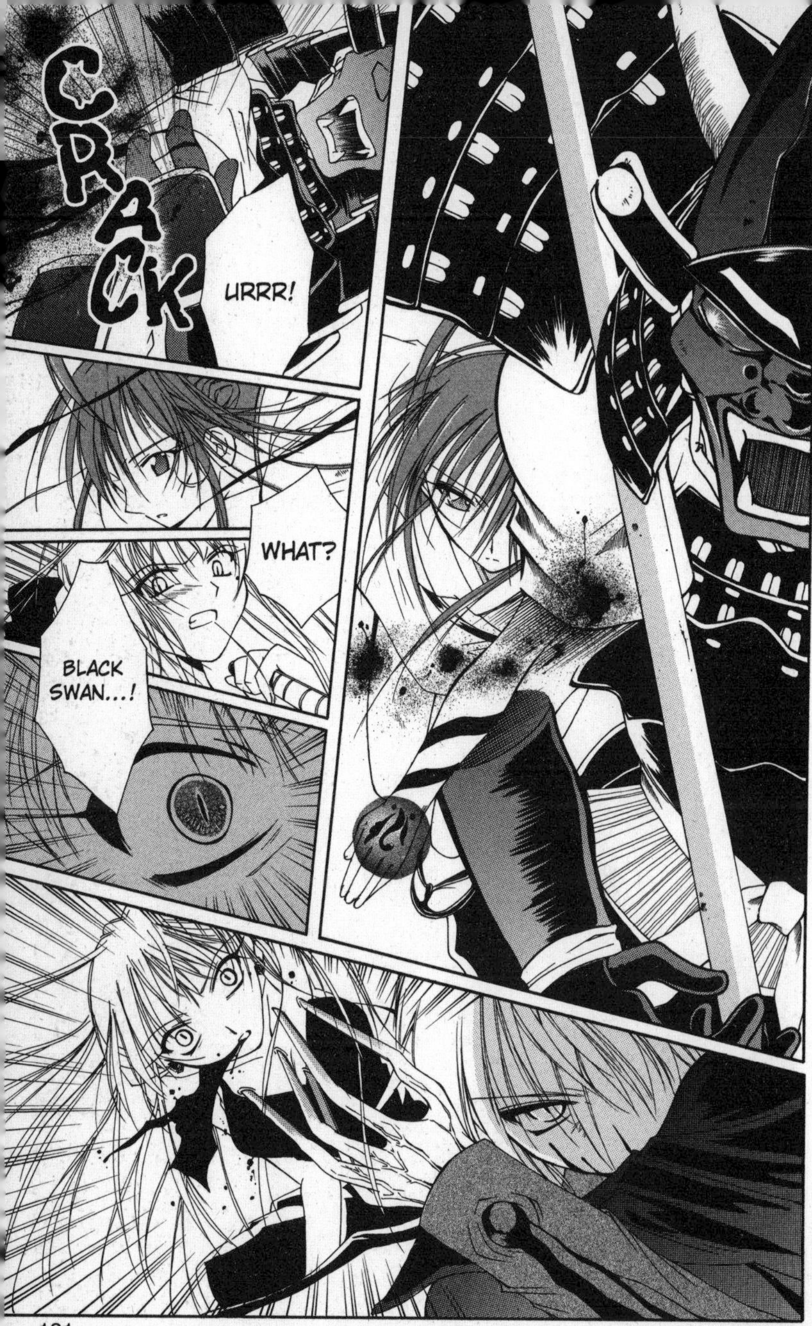
CRACK
URRR!
WHAT?
BLACK SWAN...!

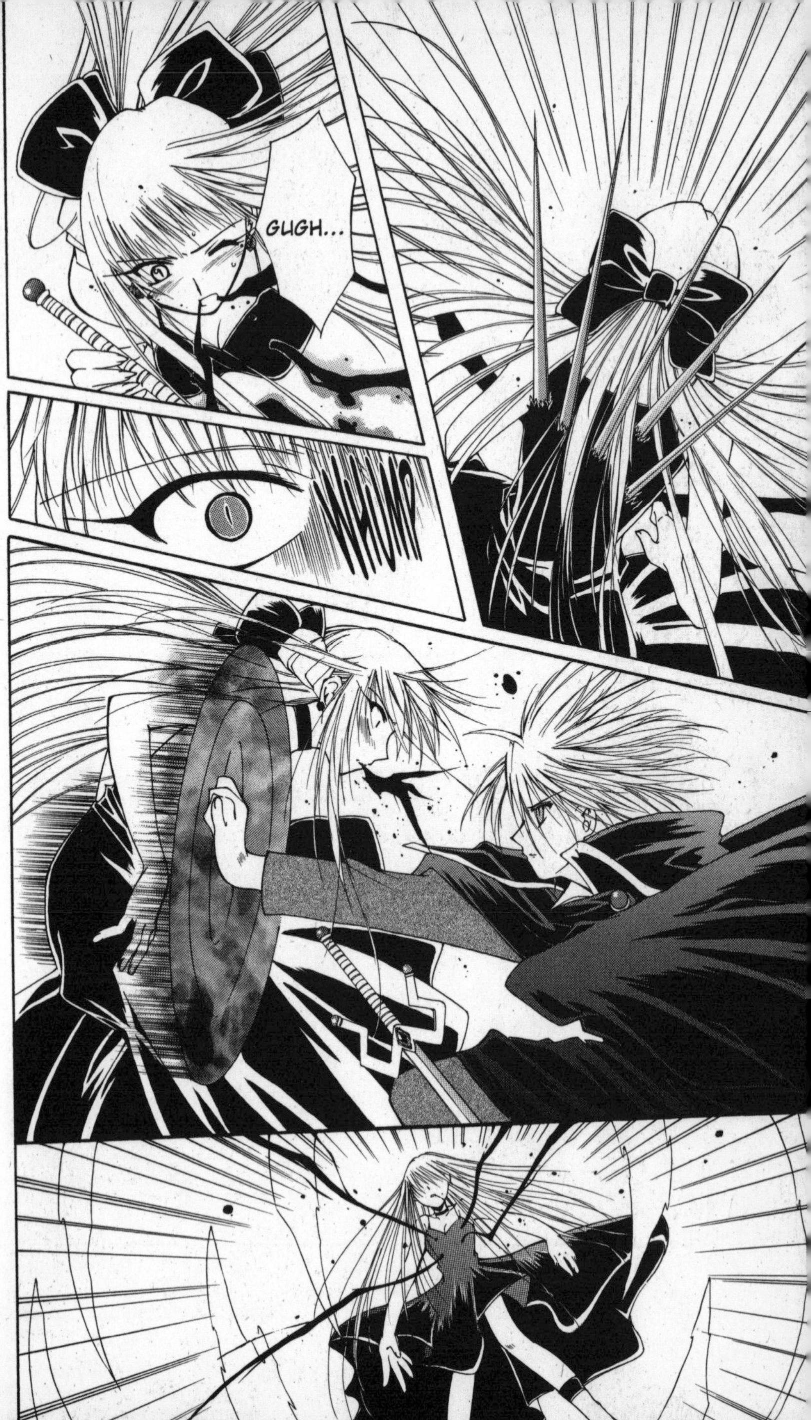
GUGH...
WHUMP

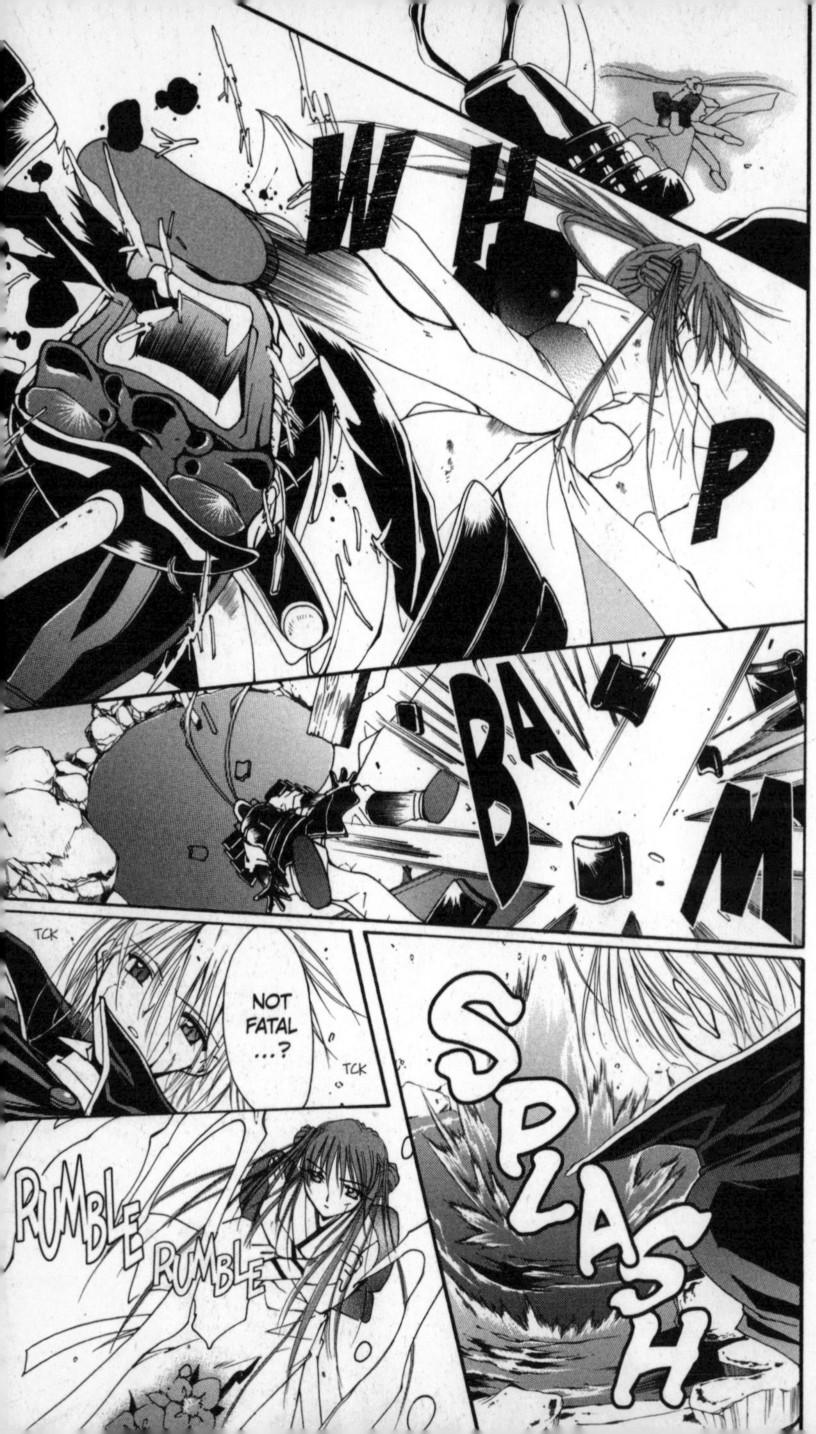
WH
P
BAM
SPLASH
TCK
NOT FATAL ...?
TCK
RUMBLE RUMBLE

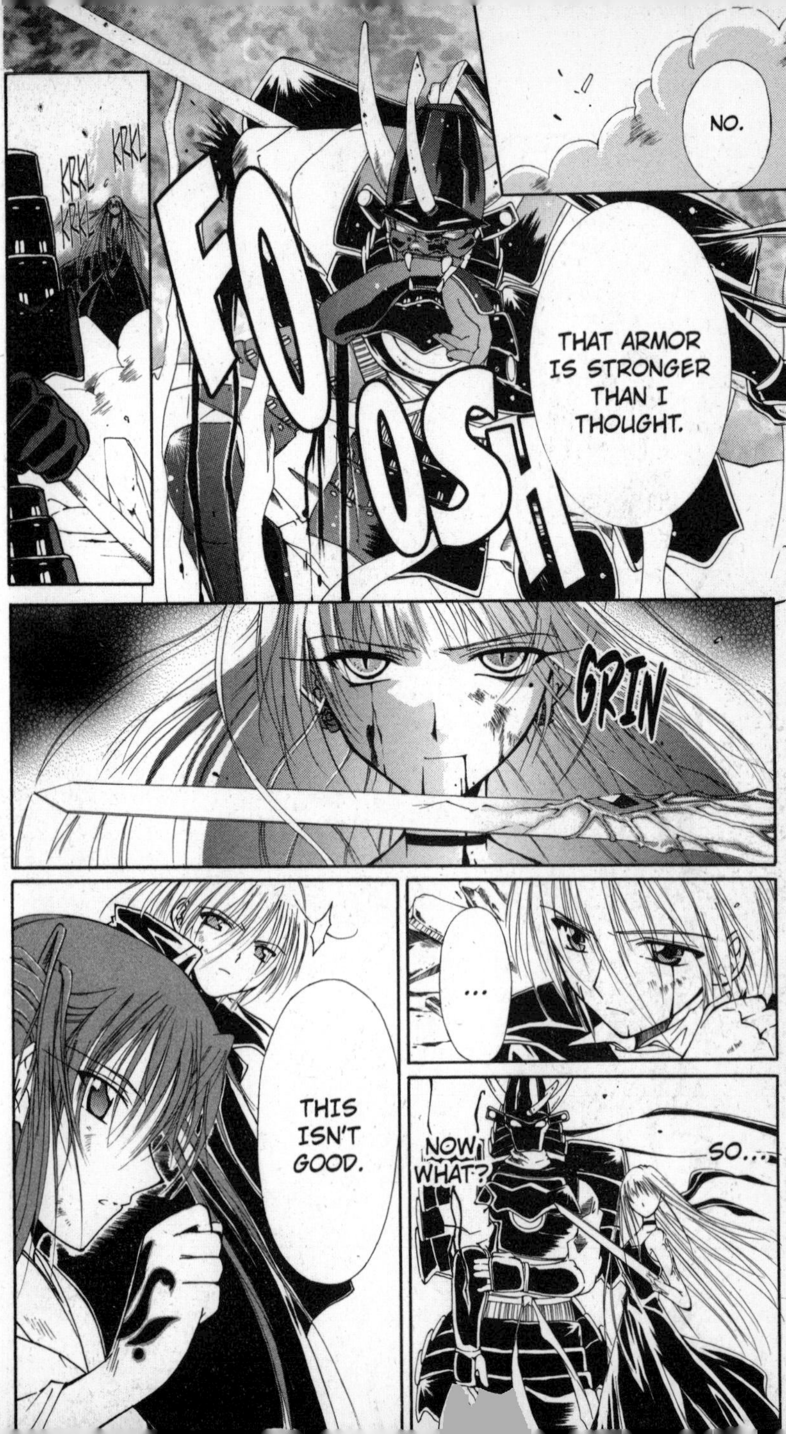
NO.
THAT ARMOR IS STRONGER THAN I THOUGHT.
FOOSH
KRKL KRKL KRKL
GRIN
...
SO...
NOW WHAT?
THIS ISN'T GOOD.

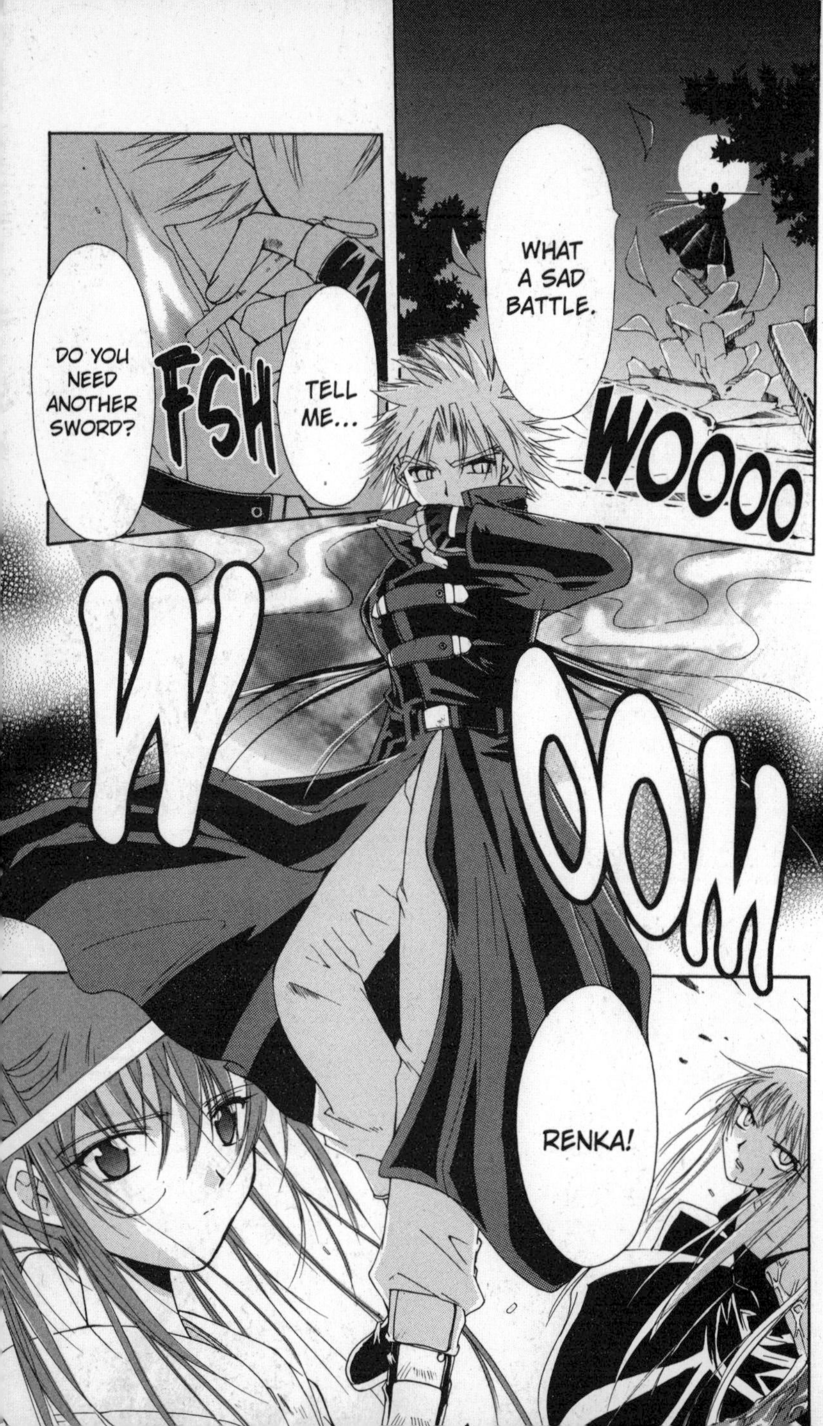
WHAT A SAD BATTLE.
WOOOO
TELL ME...
DO YOU NEED ANOTHER SWORD?
FSH
WOOOM
RENKA!

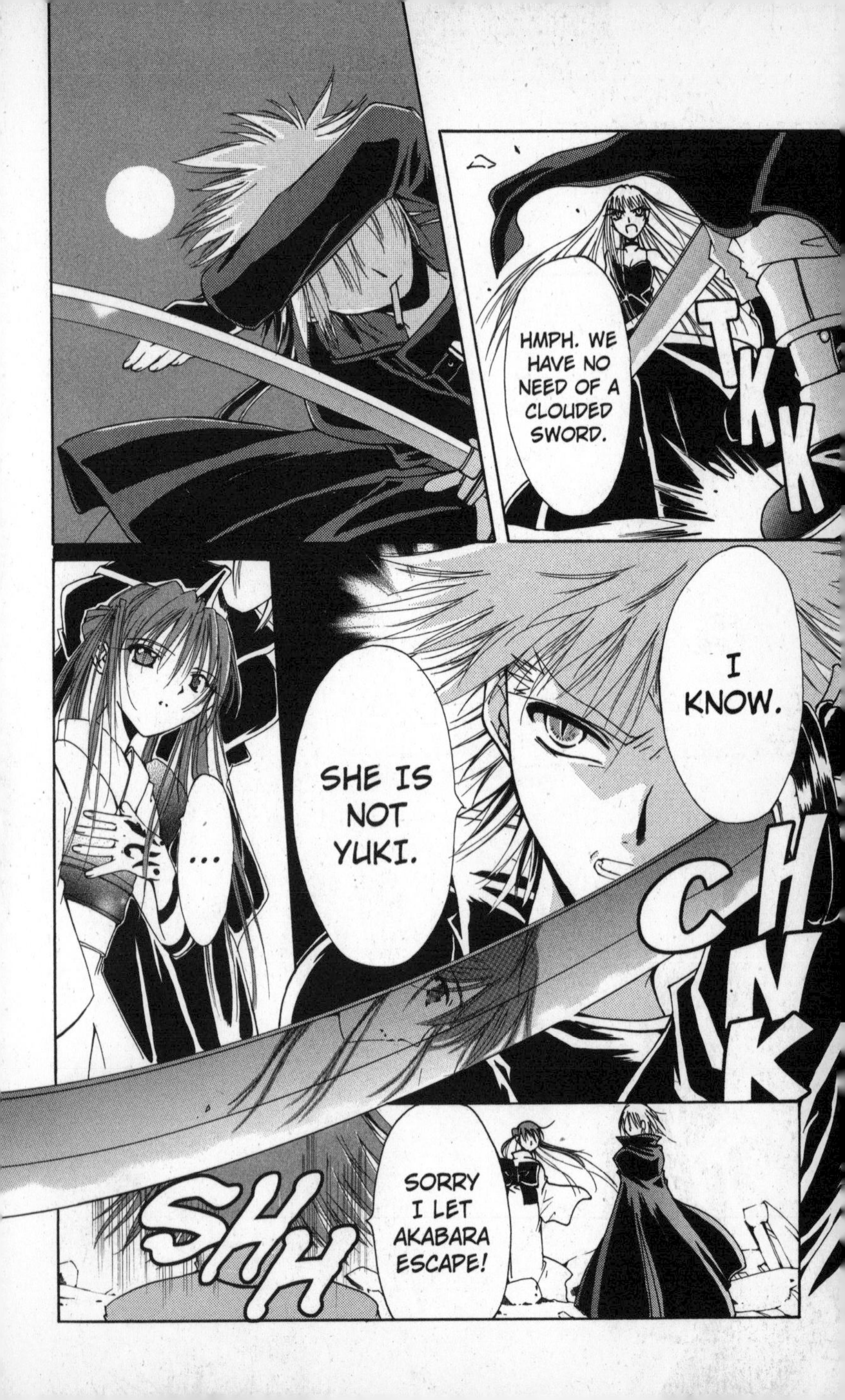
HMPH. WE HAVE NO NEED OF A CLOUDED SWORD.
TKK
I KNOW.
SHE IS NOT YUKI.
CHINK
...
SORRY I LET AKABARA ESCAPE!
SHH

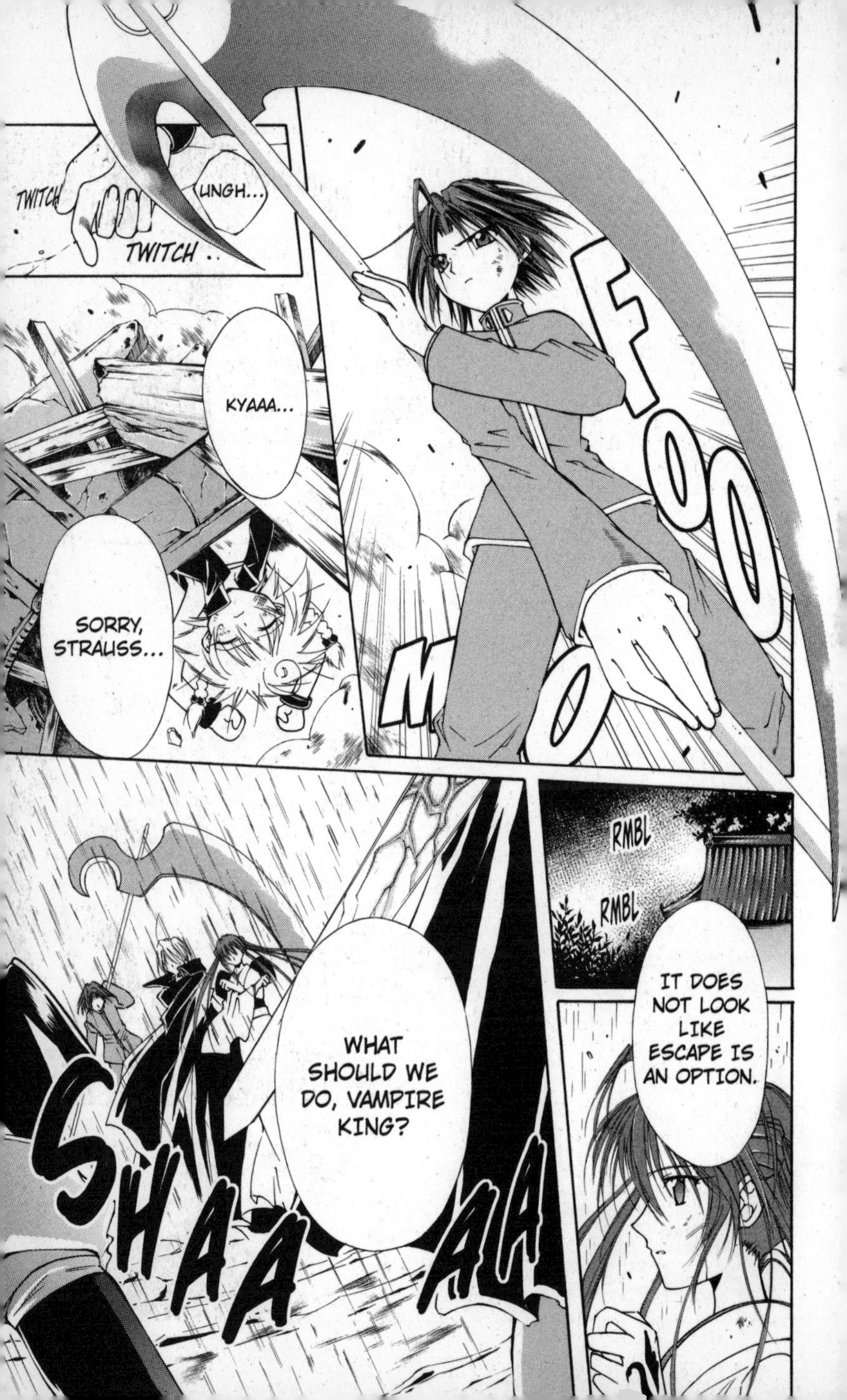
FOOOM
UNGH...
TWITCH
TWITCH...
KYAAA...
SORRY, STRAUSS...
RMBL
RMBL
IT DOES NOT LOOK LIKE ESCAPE IS AN OPTION.
WHAT SHOULD WE DO, VAMPIRE KING?
SHAAAAAA

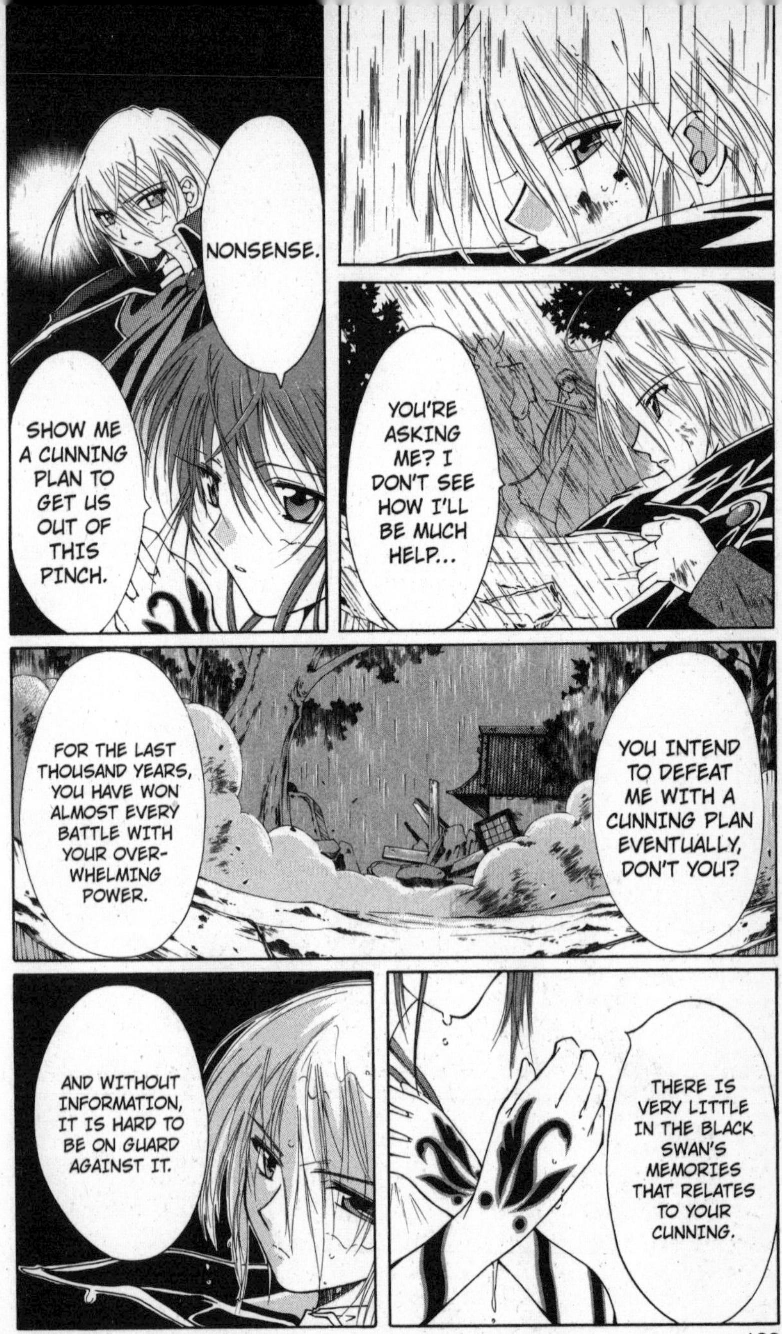
YOU'RE ASKING ME? I DON'T SEE HOW I'LL BE MUCH HELP...
NONSENSE.
SHOW ME A CUNNING PLAN TO GET US OUT OF THIS PINCH.
YOU INTEND TO DEFEAT ME WITH A CUNNING PLAN EVENTUALLY, DON'T YOU?
FOR THE LAST THOUSAND YEARS, YOU HAVE WON ALMOST EVERY BATTLE WITH YOUR OVER-WHELMING POWER.
THERE IS VERY LITTLE IN THE BLACK SWAN'S MEMORIES THAT RELATES TO YOUR CUNNING.
AND WITHOUT INFORMATION, IT IS HARD TO BE ON GUARD AGAINST IT.

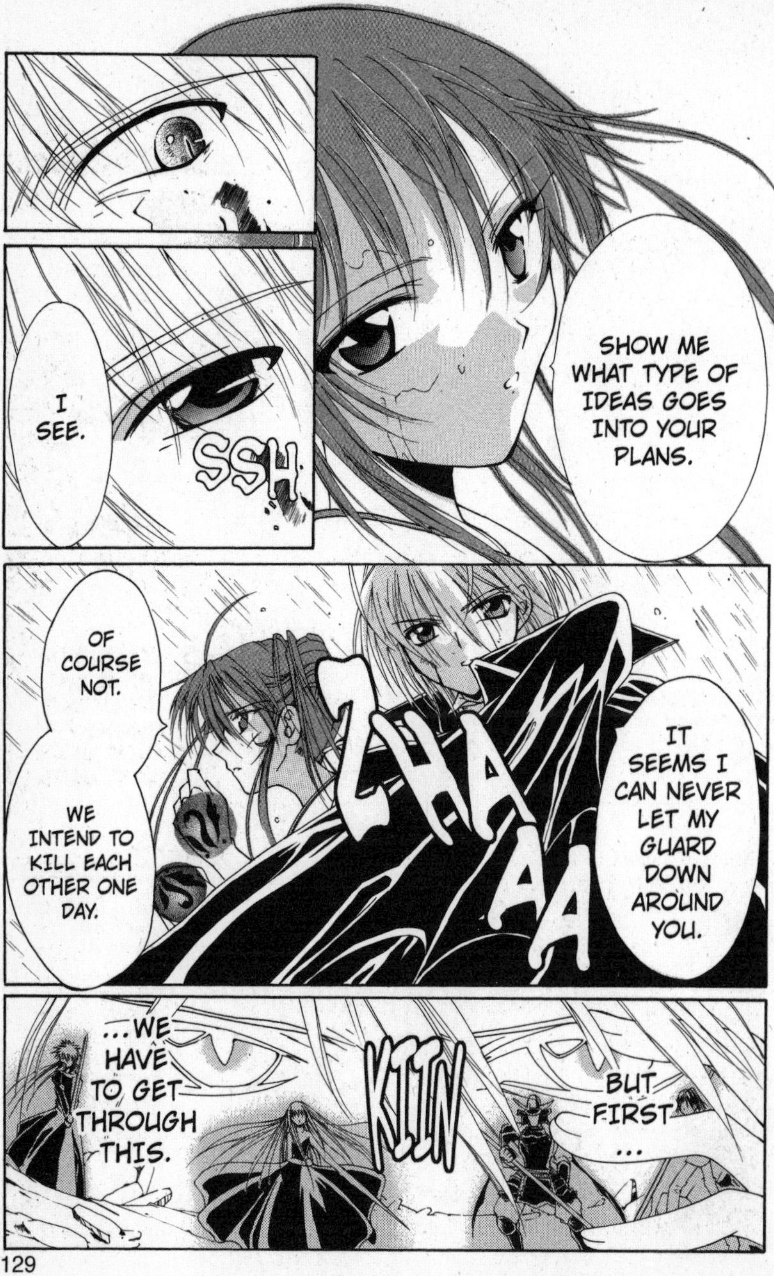
SHOW ME WHAT TYPE OF IDEAS GOES INTO YOUR PLANS.
I SEE.
SSH
IT SEEMS I CAN NEVER LET MY GUARD DOWN AROUND YOU.
ZHAAA
OF COURSE NOT.
WE INTEND TO KILL EACH OTHER ONE DAY.
BUT FIRST ...
KIIN
...WE HAVE TO GET THROUGH THIS.

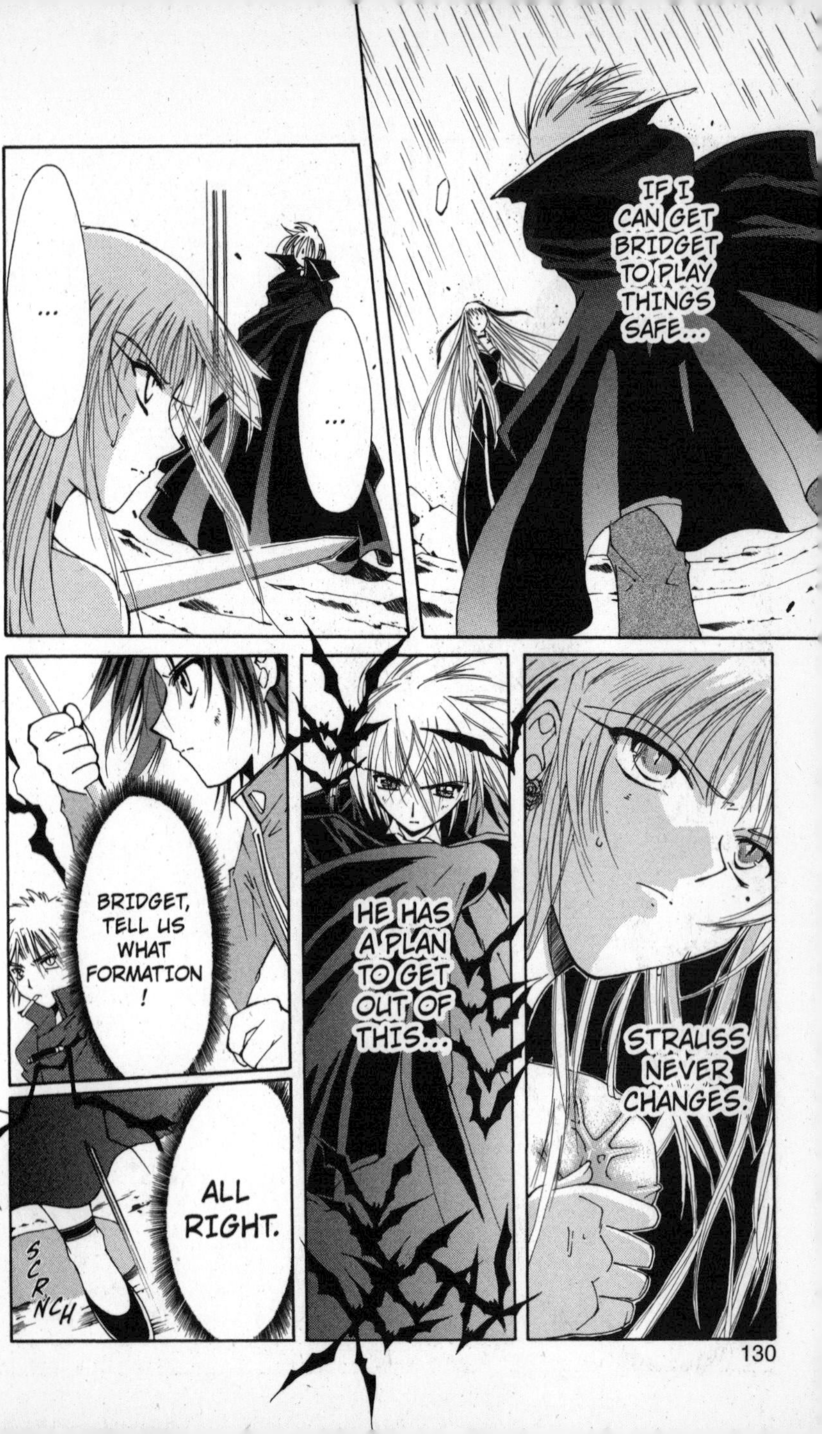
IF I CAN GET BRIDGET TO PLAY THINGS SAFE...
...
...
STRAUSS NEVER CHANGES.
HE HAS A PLAN TO GET OUT OF THIS...
BRIDGET, TELL US WHAT FORMATION!
ALL RIGHT.
SCRNCH

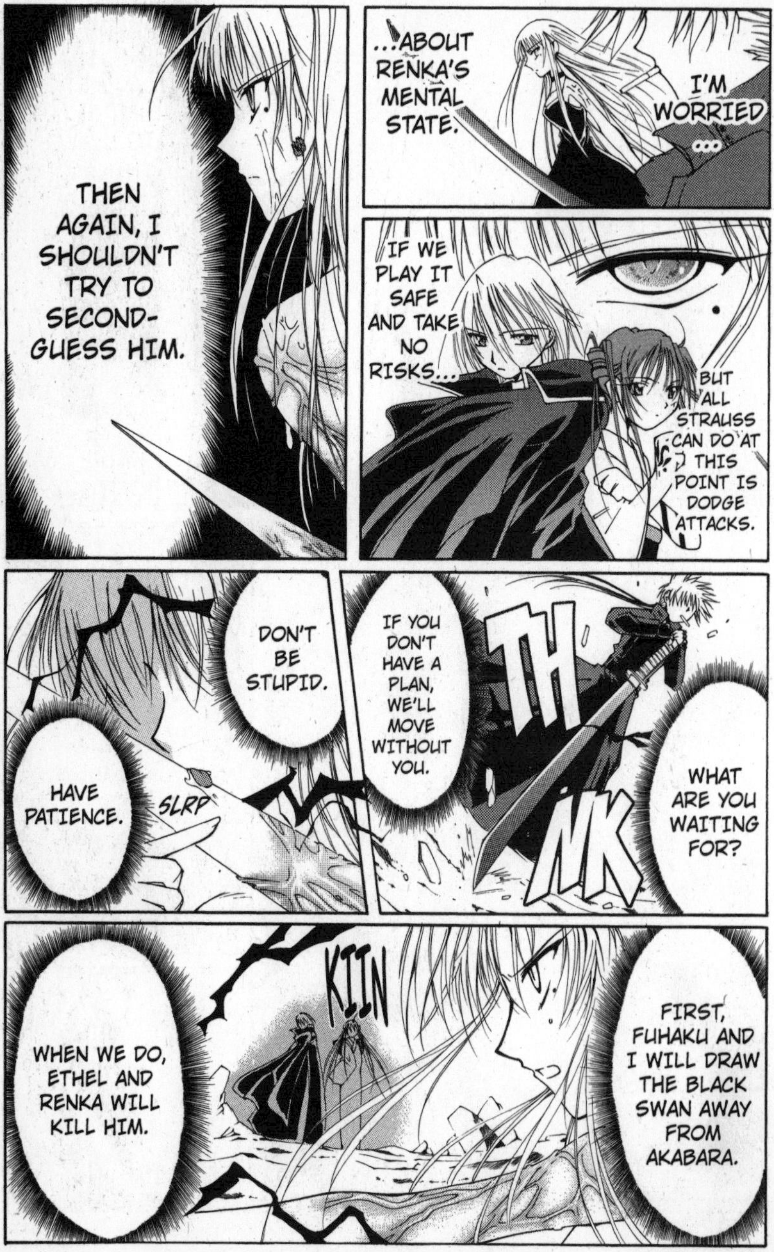
I'M WORRIED ...
...ABOUT RENKA'S MENTAL STATE.
IF WE PLAY IT SAFE AND TAKE NO RISKS...
BUT ALL STRAUSS CAN DO AT THIS POINT IS DODGE ATTACKS.
THEN AGAIN, I SHOULDN'T TRY TO SECOND-GUESS HIM.
WHAT ARE YOU WAITING FOR?
THNK
IF YOU DON'T HAVE A PLAN, WE'LL MOVE WITHOUT YOU.
DON'T BE STUPID.
SLRP
HAVE PATIENCE.
FIRST, FUHAKU AND I WILL DRAW THE BLACK SWAN AWAY FROM AKABARA.
KIIN
WHEN WE DO, ETHEL AND RENKA WILL KILL HIM.

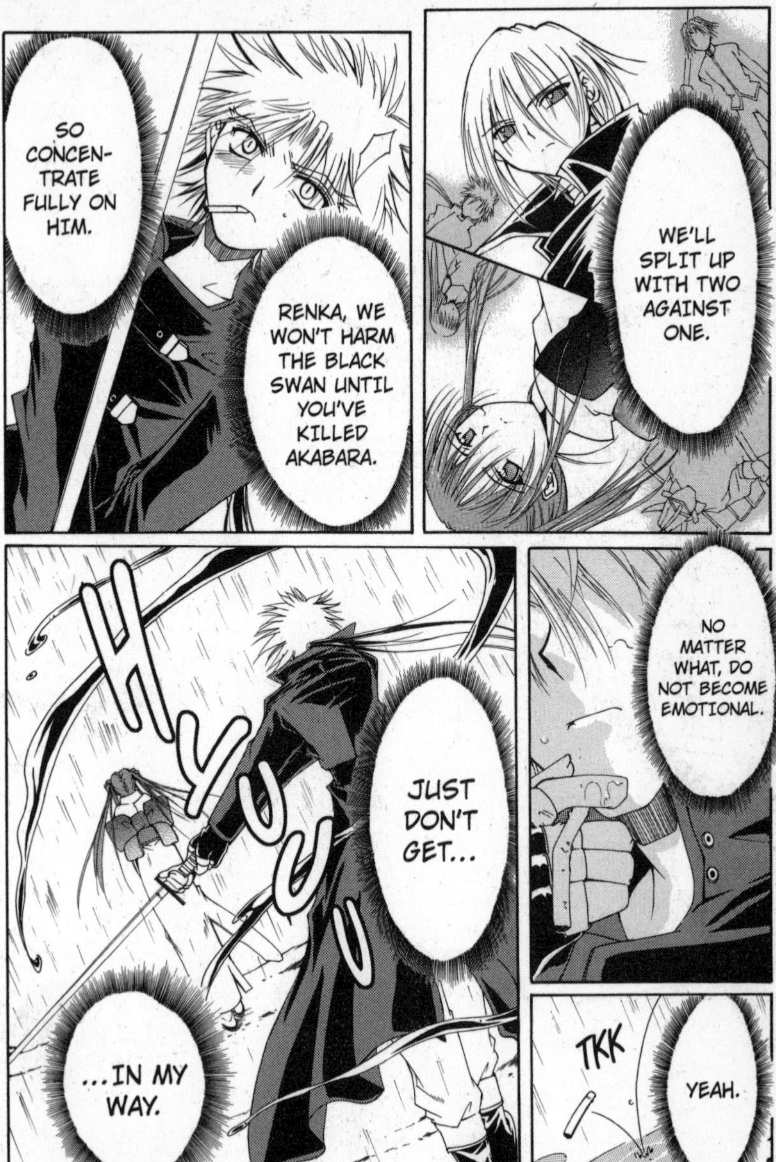
WE'LL SPLIT UP WITH TWO AGAINST ONE.
RENKA, WE WON'T HARM THE BLACK SWAN UNTIL YOU'VE KILLED AKABARA.
SO CONCEN-TRATE FULLY ON HIM.
NO MATTER WHAT, DO NOT BECOME EMOTIONAL.
YEAH.
TKK
HYUUU
JUST DON'T GET...
...IN MY WAY.

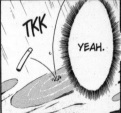

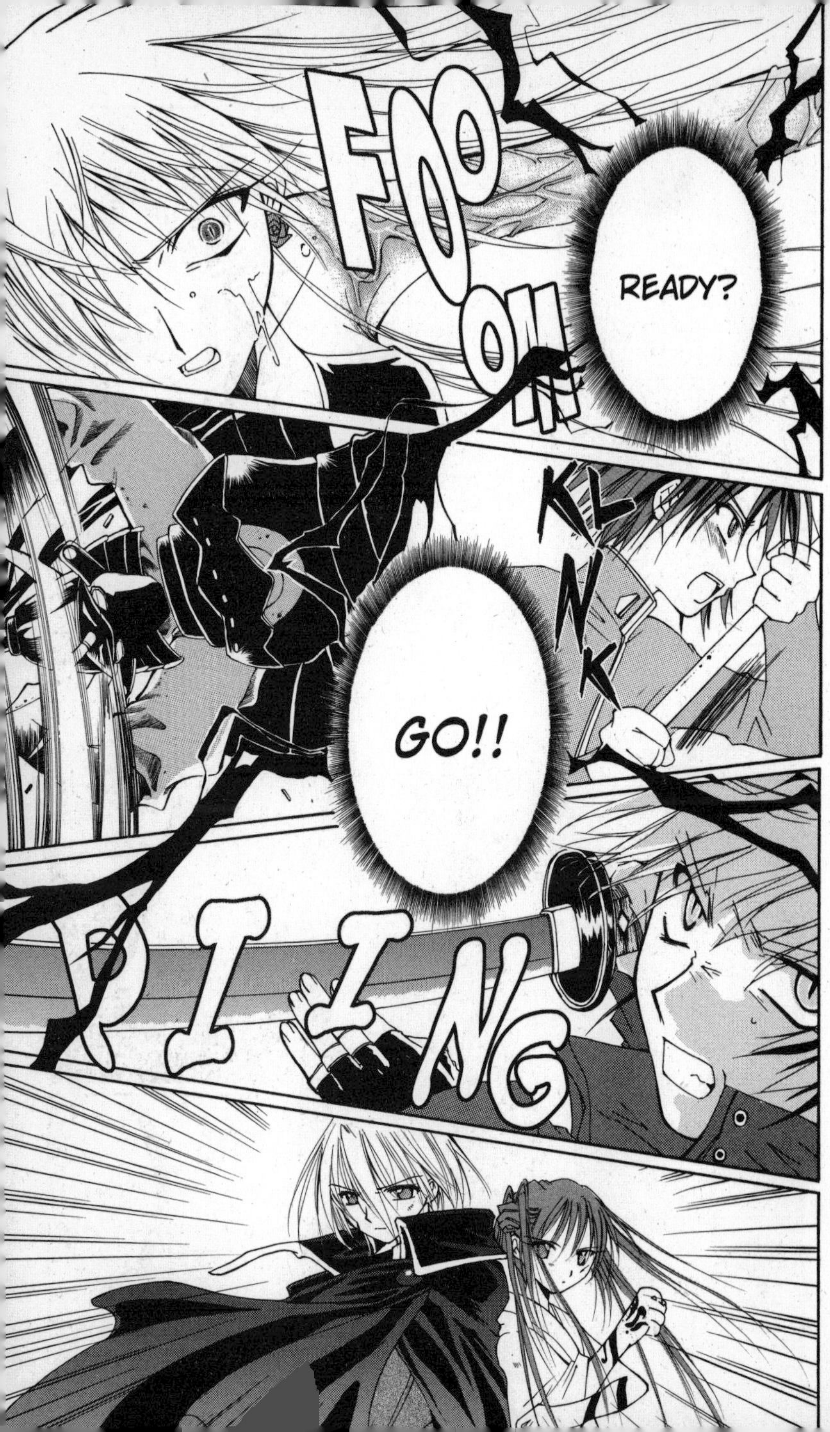
READY?
FOOOM!!
KLNK
GO!!
RIING

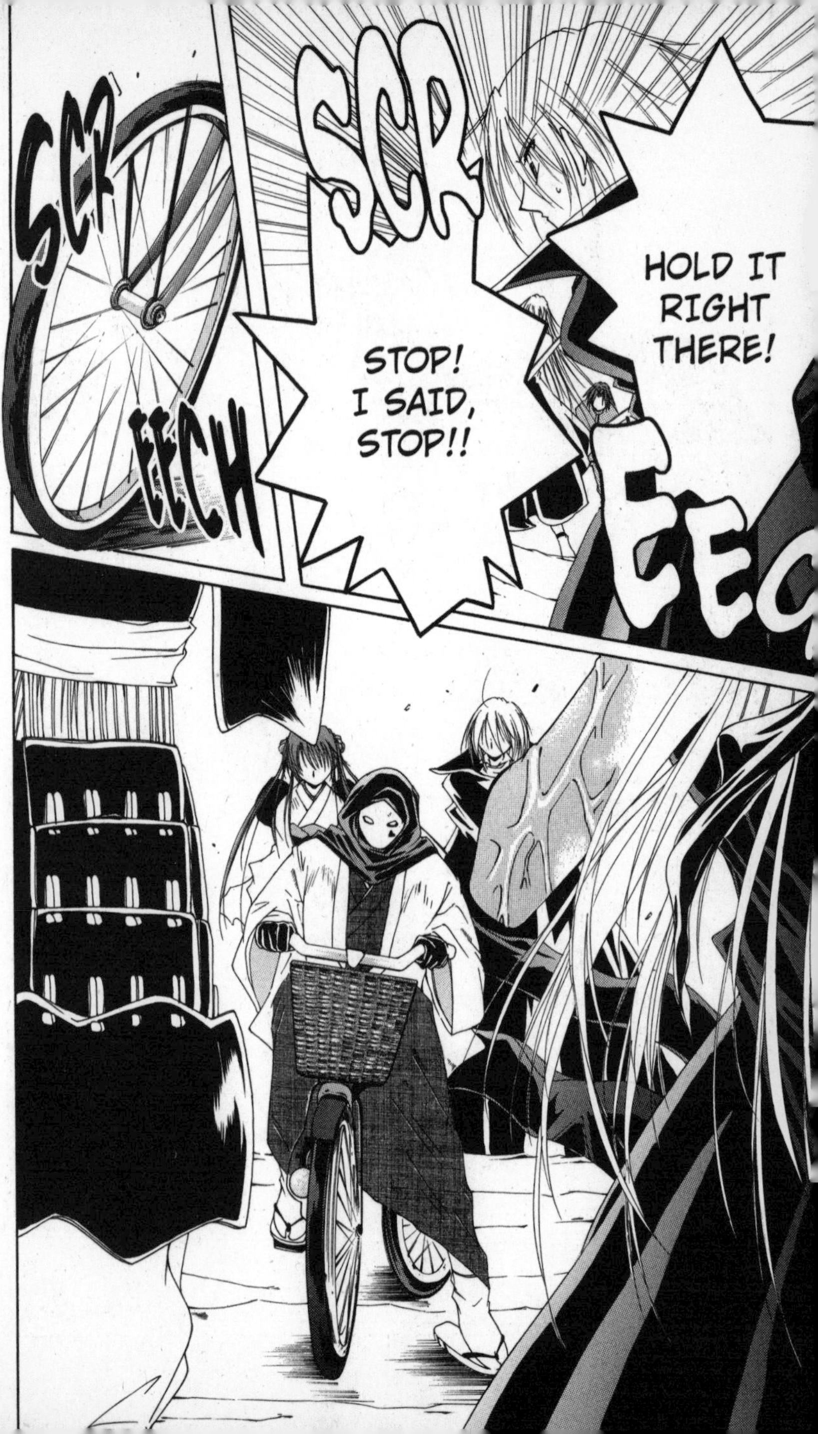
SCR
HOLD IT RIGHT THERE!
STOP! I SAID, STOP!!
EEC
SCR
EECH

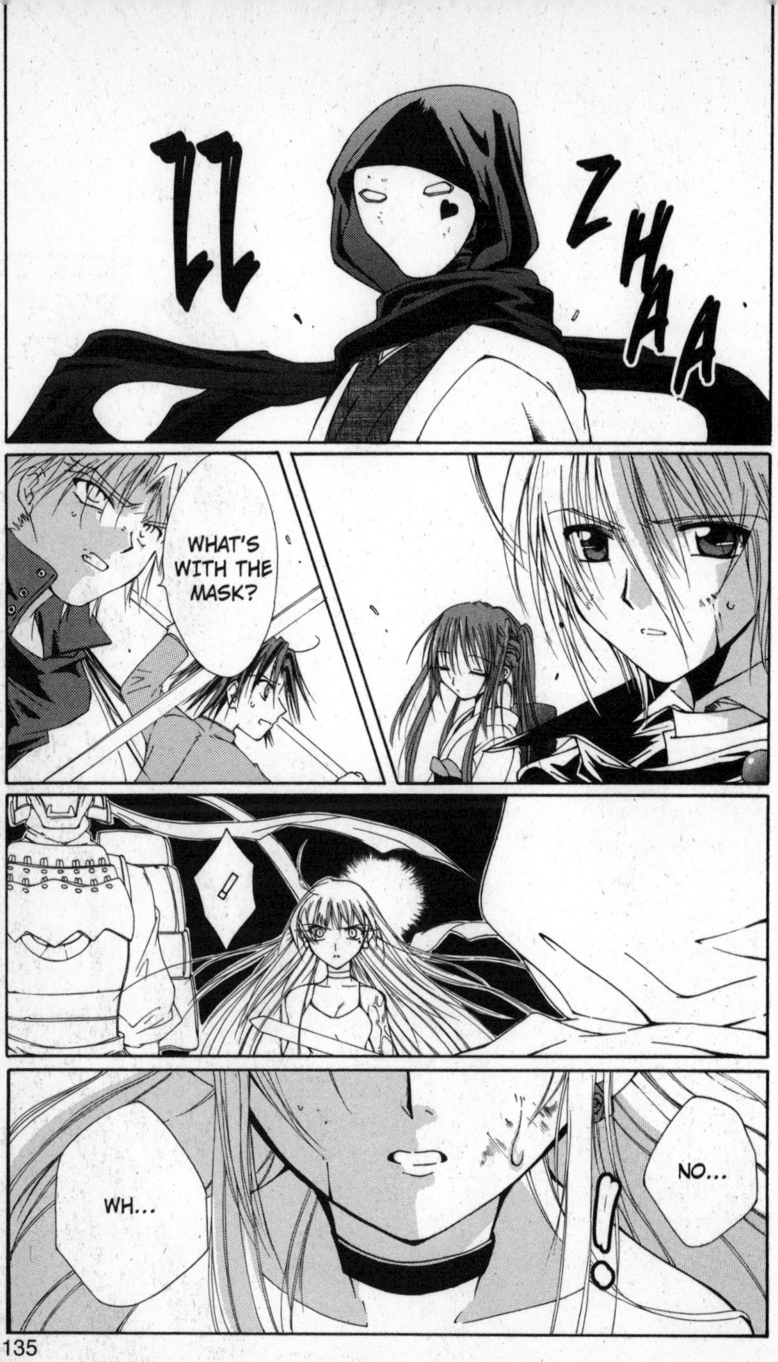
ZHAA
ZZ
WHAT'S WITH THE MASK?
!
NO...
!
WH...

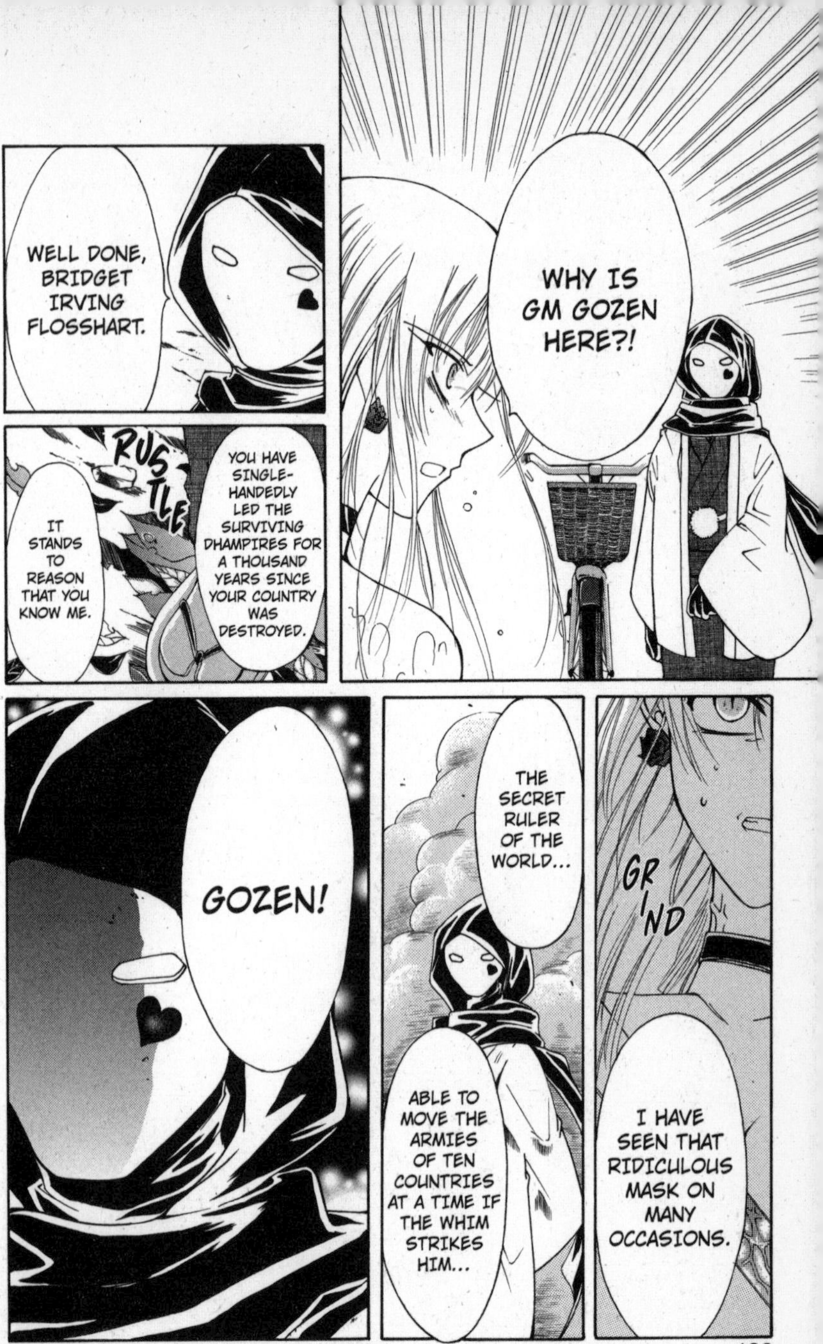
WHY IS GM GOZEN HERE?!
WELL DONE, BRIDGET IRVING FLOSSHART.
YOU HAVE SINGLE-HANDEDLY LED THE SURVIVING DHAMPIRES FOR A THOUSAND YEARS SINCE YOUR COUNTRY WAS DESTROYED.
RUSTLE
IT STANDS TO REASON THAT YOU KNOW ME.
GRIND
I HAVE SEEN THAT RIDICULOUS MASK ON MANY OCCASIONS.
THE SECRET RULER OF THE WORLD...
ABLE TO MOVE THE ARMIES OF TEN COUNTRIES AT A TIME IF THE WHIM STRIKES HIM...
GOZEN!

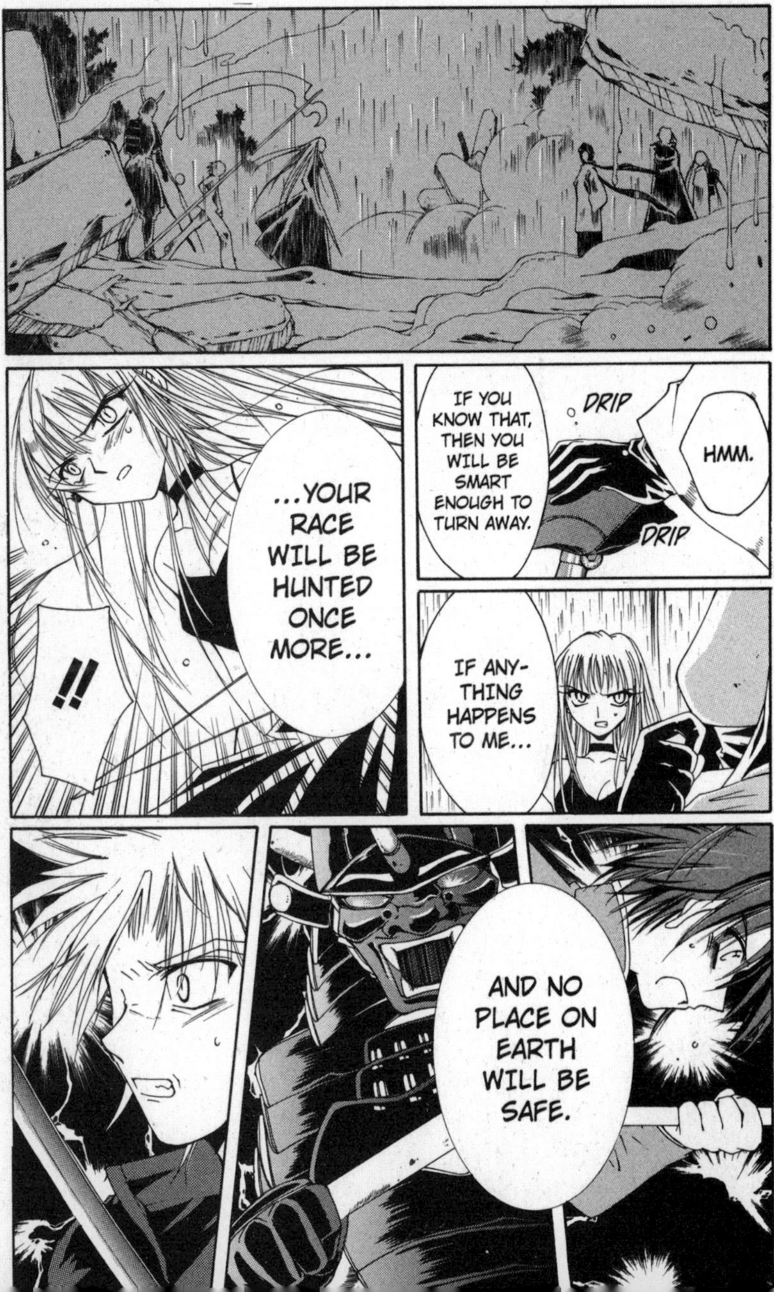
HMM.
DRIP
IF YOU KNOW THAT, THEN YOU WILL BE SMART ENOUGH TO TURN AWAY.
DRIP
IF ANYTHING HAPPENS TO ME...
...YOUR RACE WILL BE HUNTED ONCE MORE...
!!
AND NO PLACE ON EARTH WILL BE SAFE.

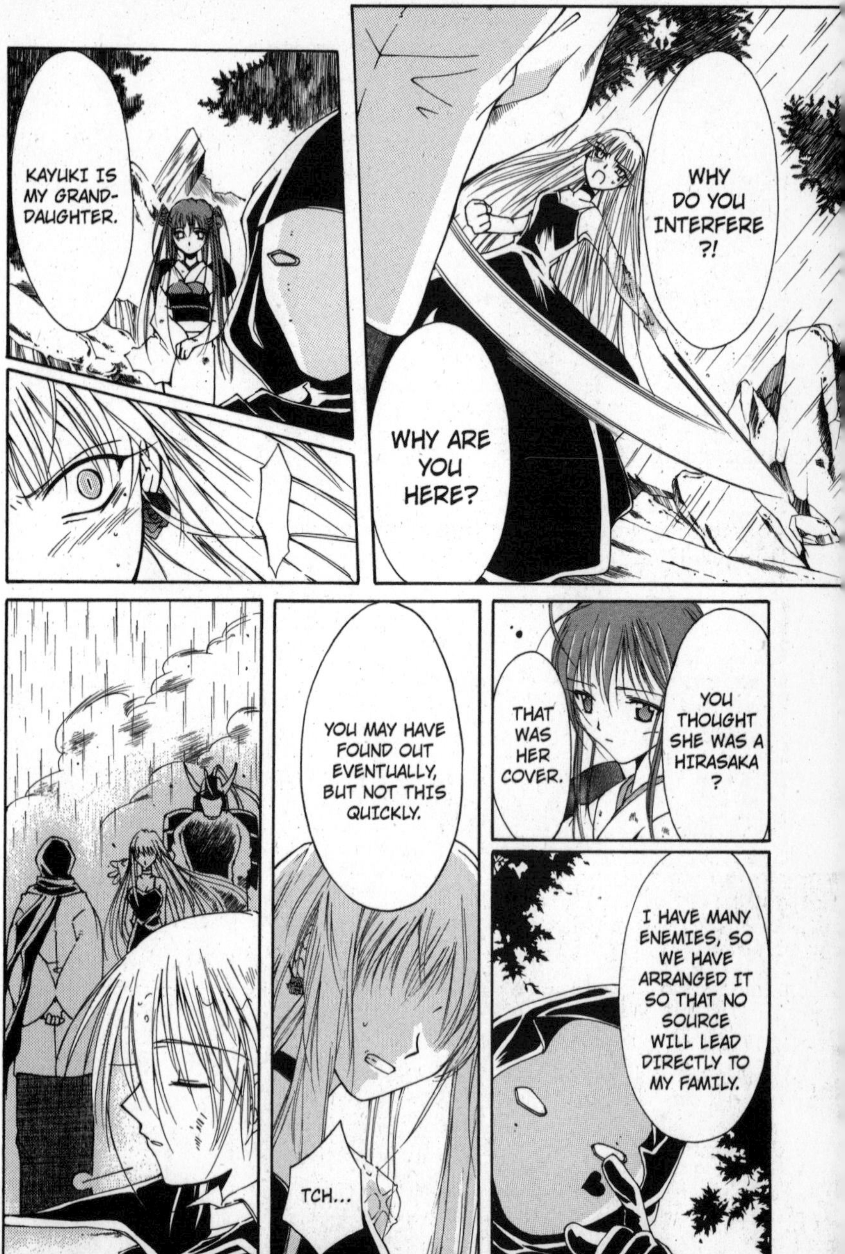
WHY DO YOU INTERFERE?!
WHY ARE YOU HERE?
KAYUKI IS MY GRAND-DAUGHTER.
YOU THOUGHT SHE WAS A HIRASAKA?
THAT WAS HER COVER.
I HAVE MANY ENEMIES, SO WE HAVE ARRANGED IT SO THAT NO SOURCE WILL LEAD DIRECTLY TO MY FAMILY.
YOU MAY HAVE FOUND OUT EVENTUALLY, BUT NOT THIS QUICKLY.
TCH...

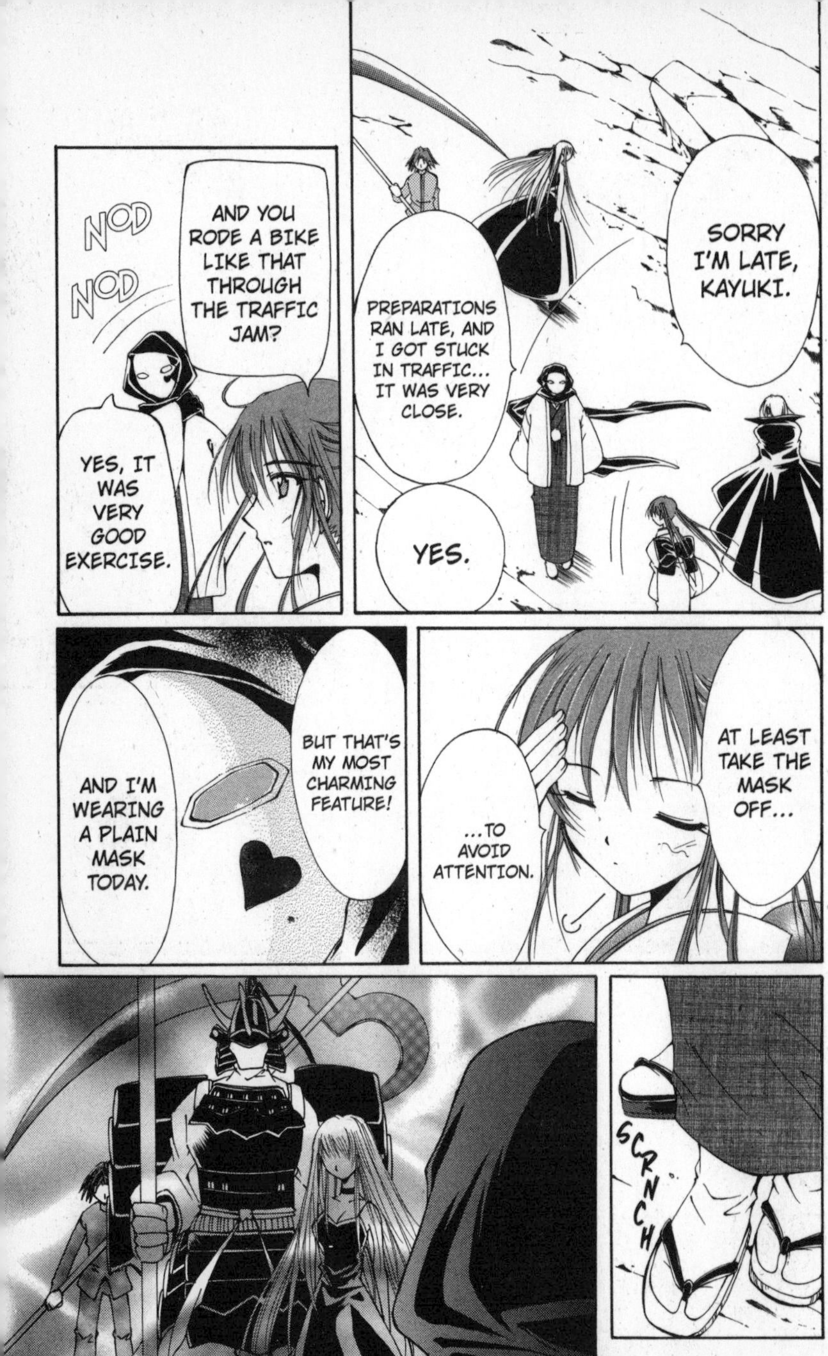
SORRY I'M LATE, KAYUKI.
PREPARATIONS RAN LATE, AND I GOT STUCK IN TRAFFIC... IT WAS VERY CLOSE.
YES.
AND YOU RODE A BIKE LIKE THAT THROUGH THE TRAFFIC JAM?
NOD NOD
YES, IT WAS VERY GOOD EXERCISE.
AT LEAST TAKE THE MASK OFF...
...TO AVOID ATTENTION.
BUT THAT'S MY MOST CHARMING FEATURE!
AND I'M WEARING A PLAIN MASK TODAY.
SCRNCH

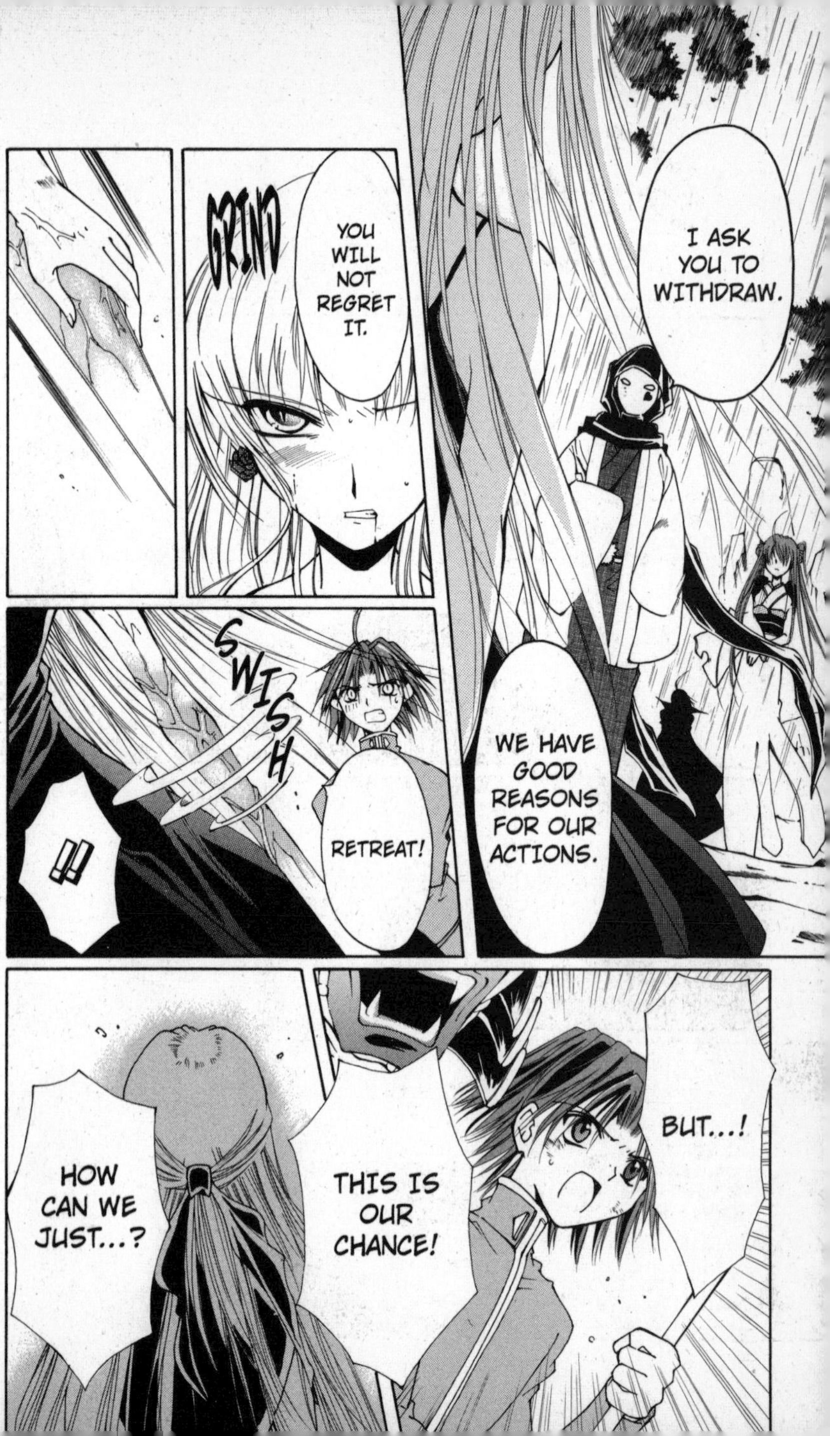
I ASK YOU TO WITHDRAW.
WE HAVE GOOD REASONS FOR OUR ACTIONS.
GRIND
YOU WILL NOT REGRET IT.
SWISH
RETREAT!
!!
BUT...!
THIS IS OUR CHANCE!
HOW CAN WE JUST...?

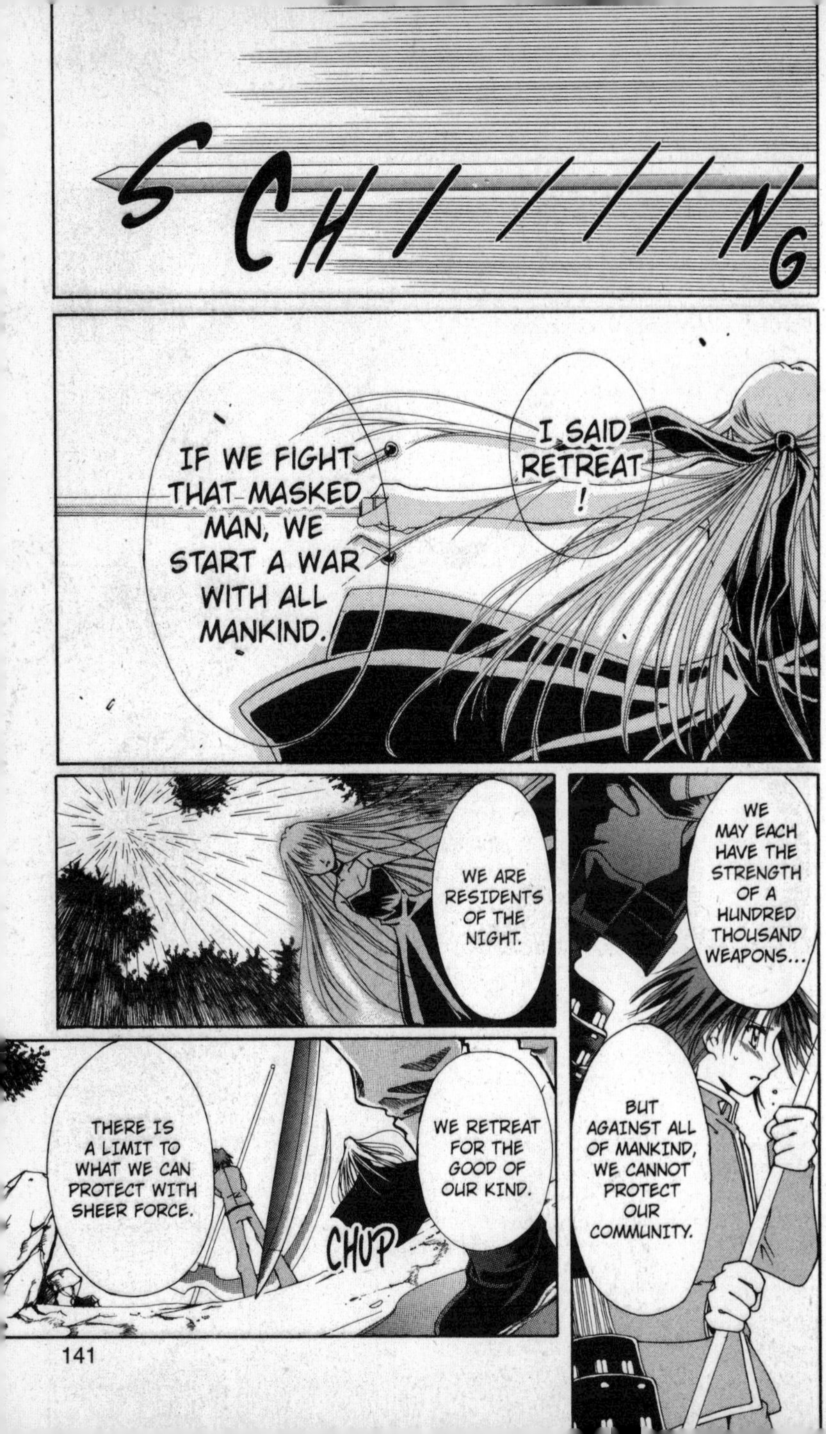
SCHIIIING
I SAID RETREAT!
IF WE FIGHT THAT MASKED MAN, WE START A WAR WITH ALL MANKIND.
WE MAY EACH HAVE THE STRENGTH OF A HUNDRED THOUSAND WEAPONS...
BUT AGAINST ALL OF MANKIND, WE CANNOT PROTECT OUR COMMUNITY.
WE ARE RESIDENTS OF THE NIGHT.
WE RETREAT FOR THE GOOD OF OUR KIND.
CHUP
THERE IS A LIMIT TO WHAT WE CAN PROTECT WITH SHEER FORCE.

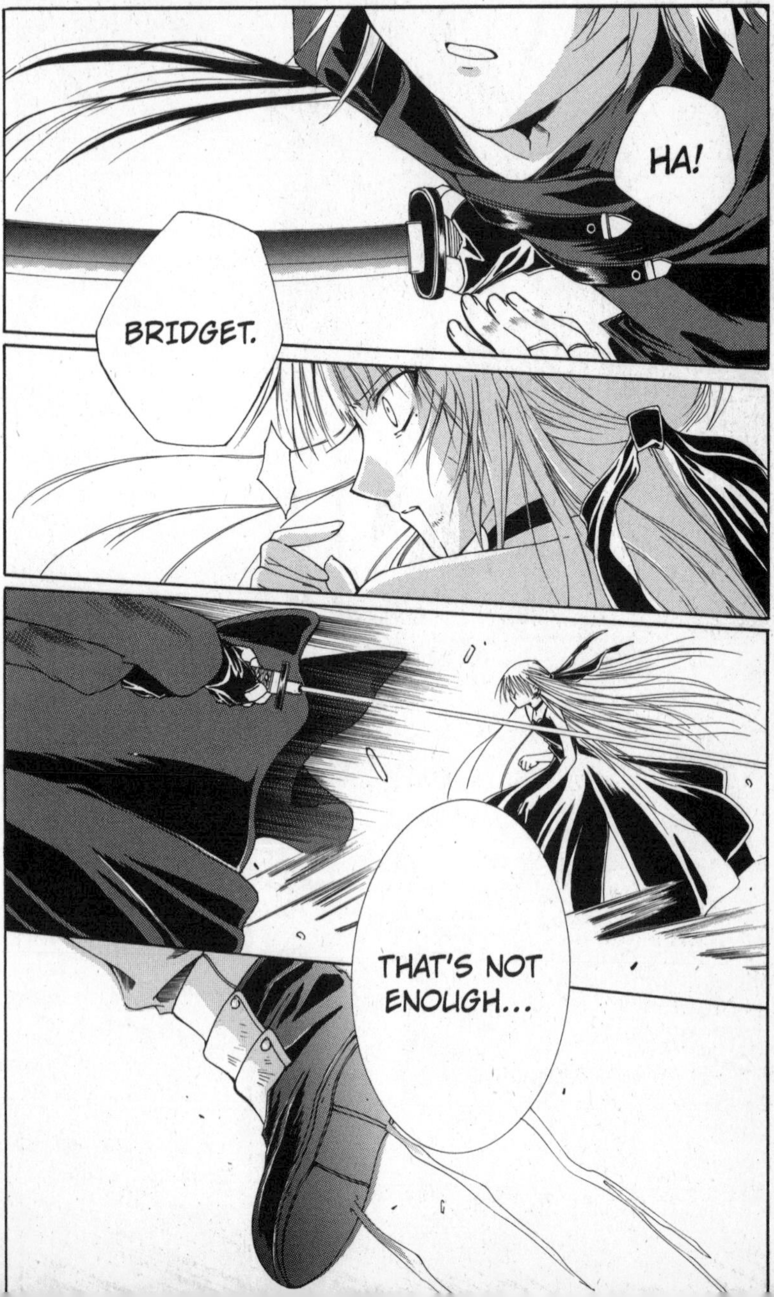
HA!
BRIDGET.
THAT'S NOT ENOUGH...

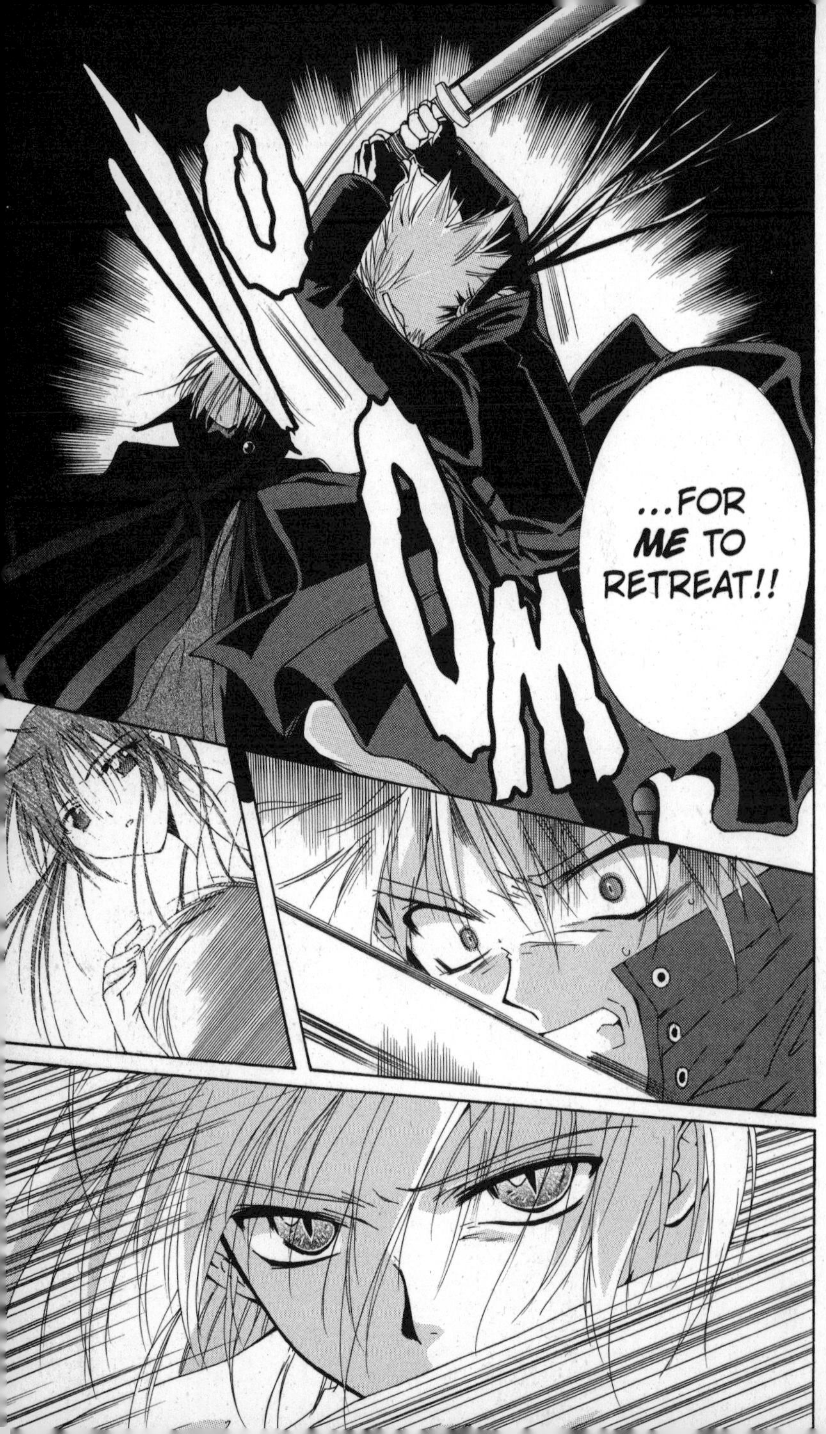
...FOR ME TO RETREAT!!

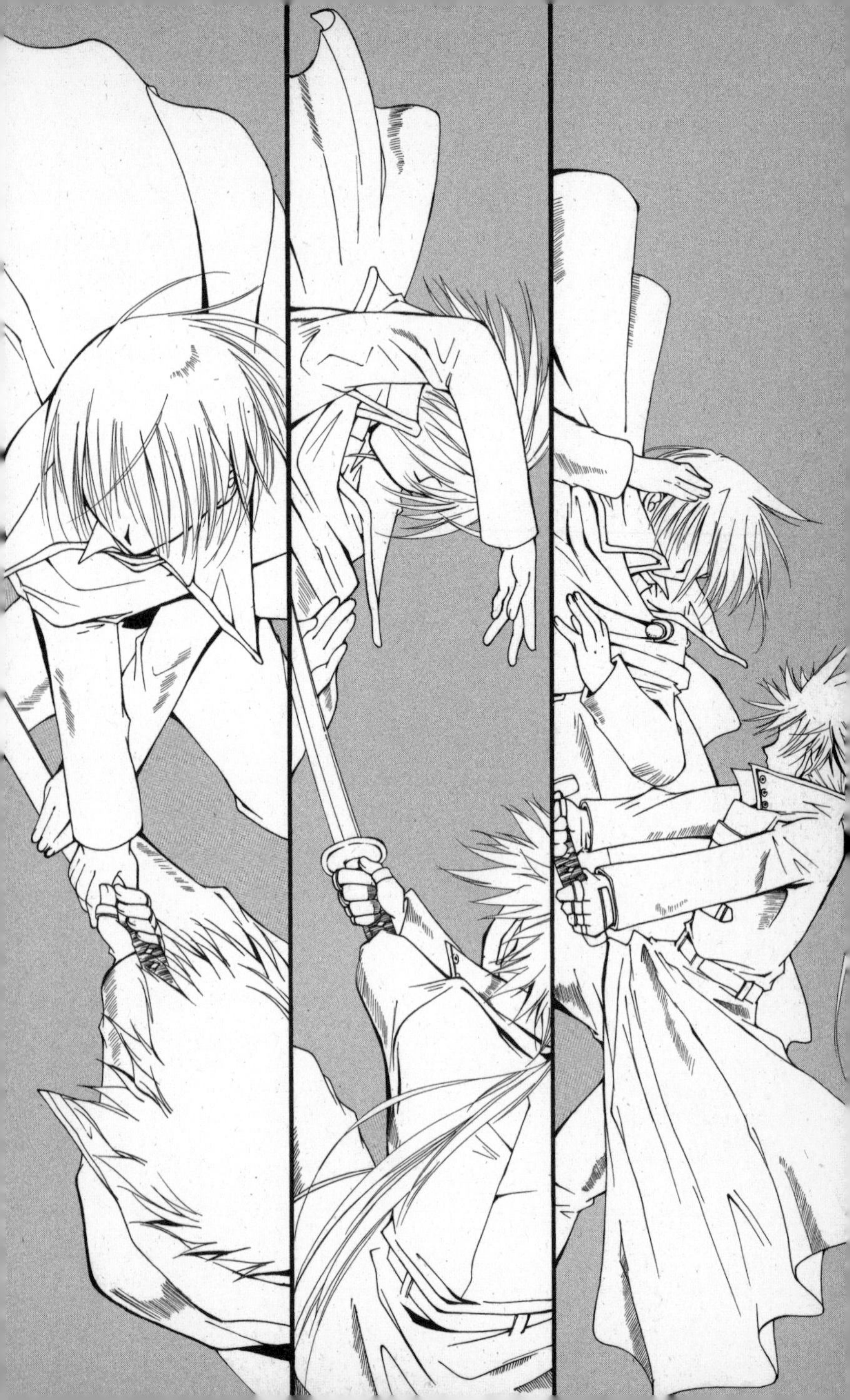

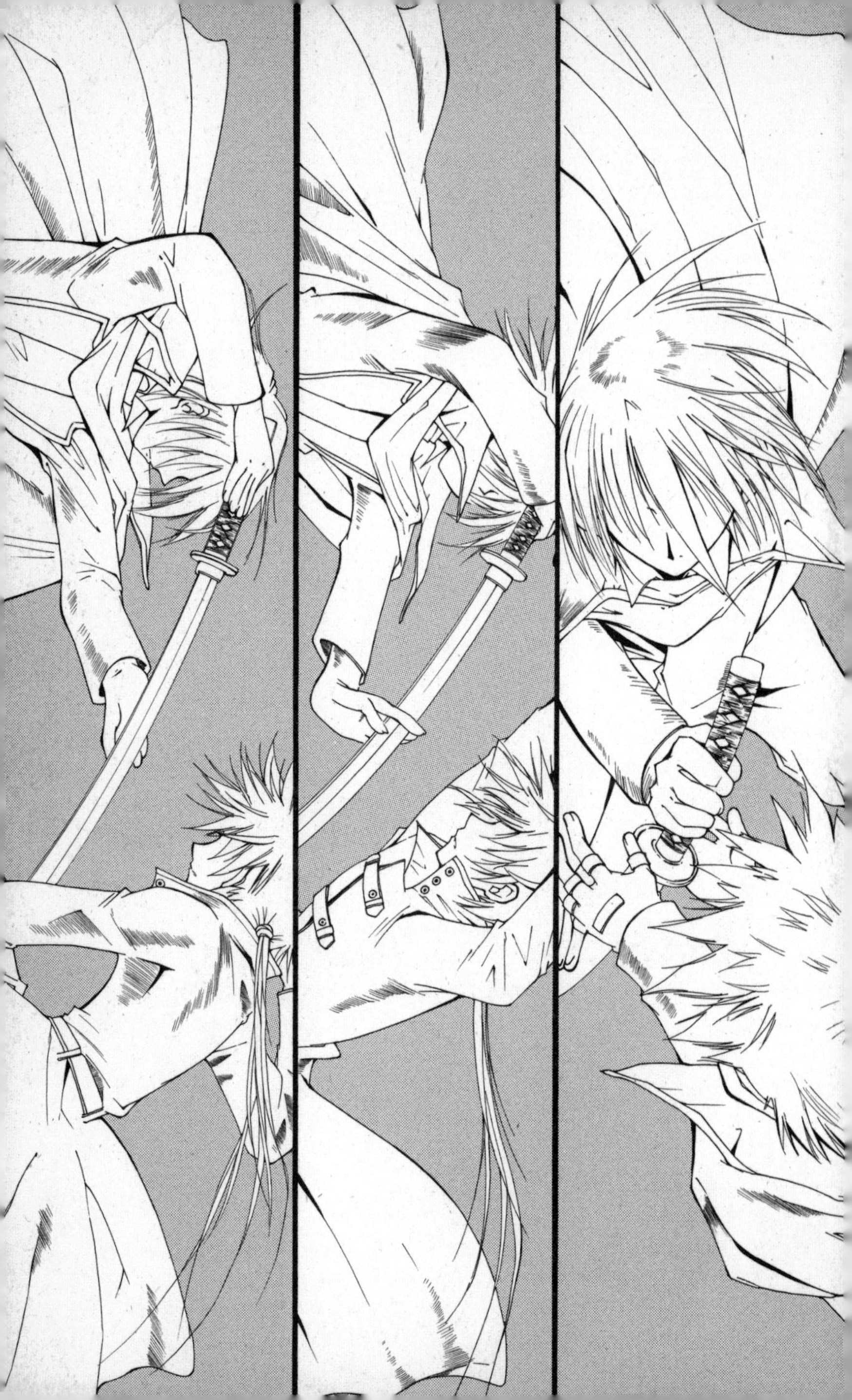

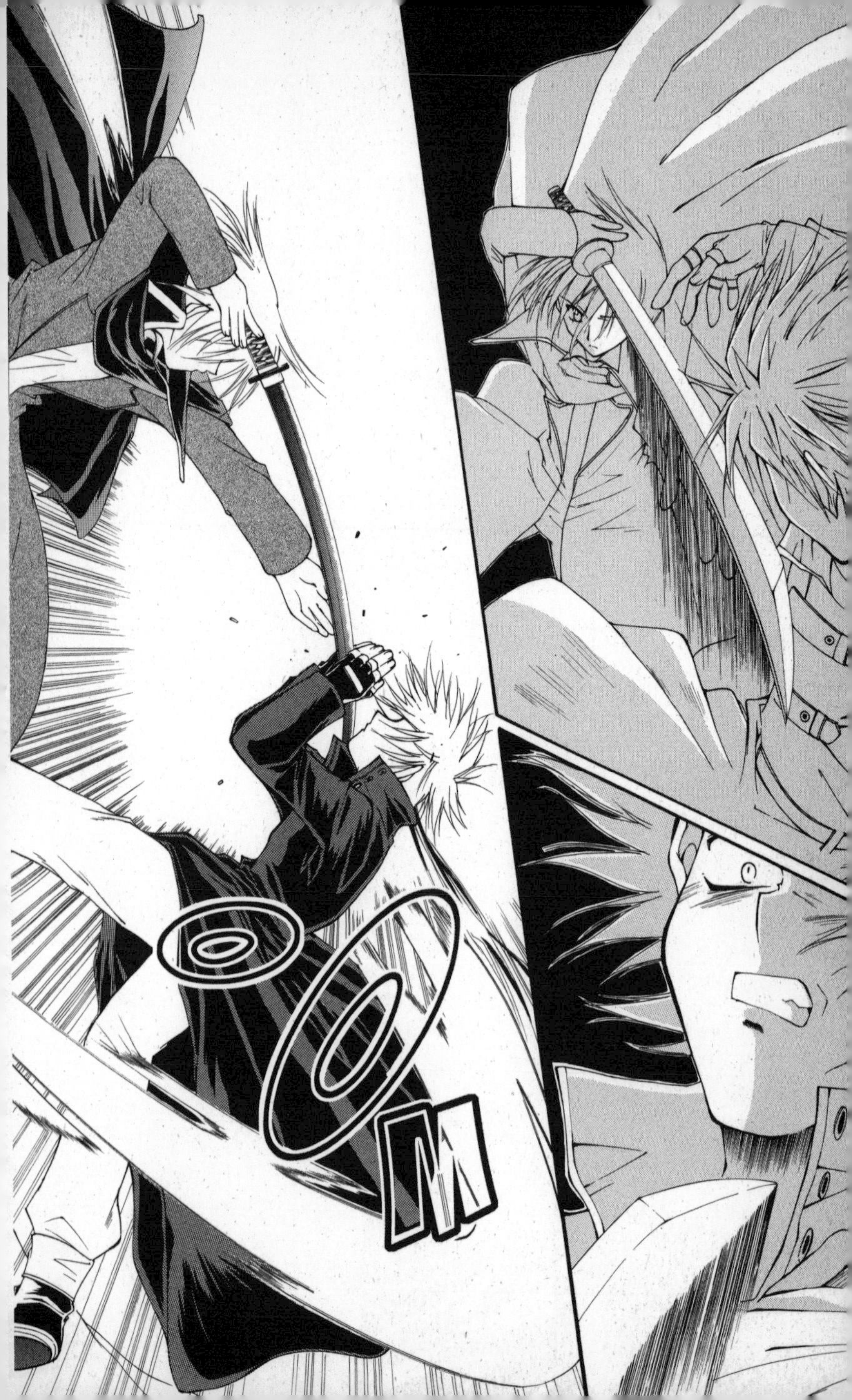
OOOM

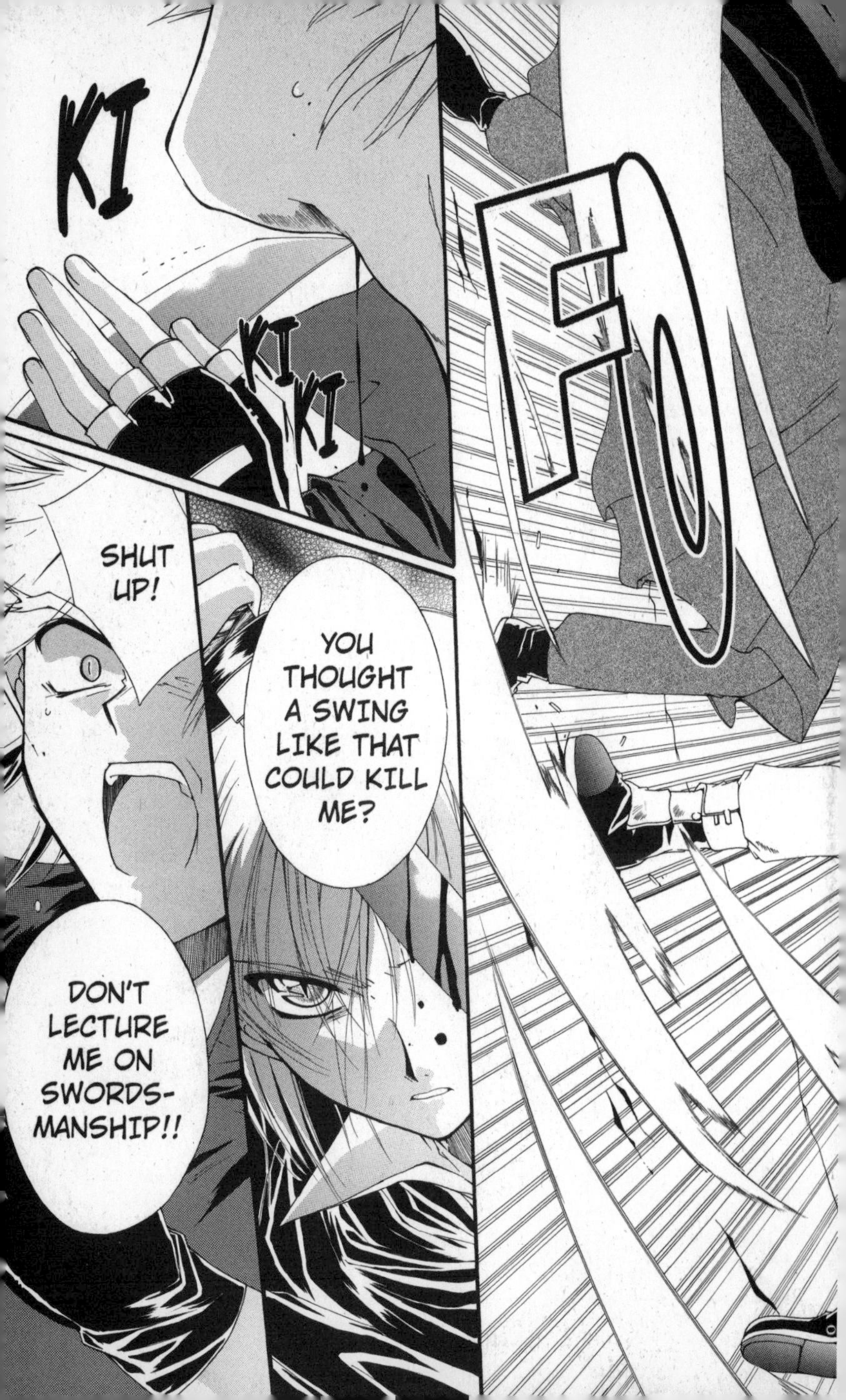
FO
KI
KI KI
YOU THOUGHT A SWING LIKE THAT COULD KILL ME?
SHUT UP!
DON'T LECTURE ME ON SWORDS-MANSHIP!!

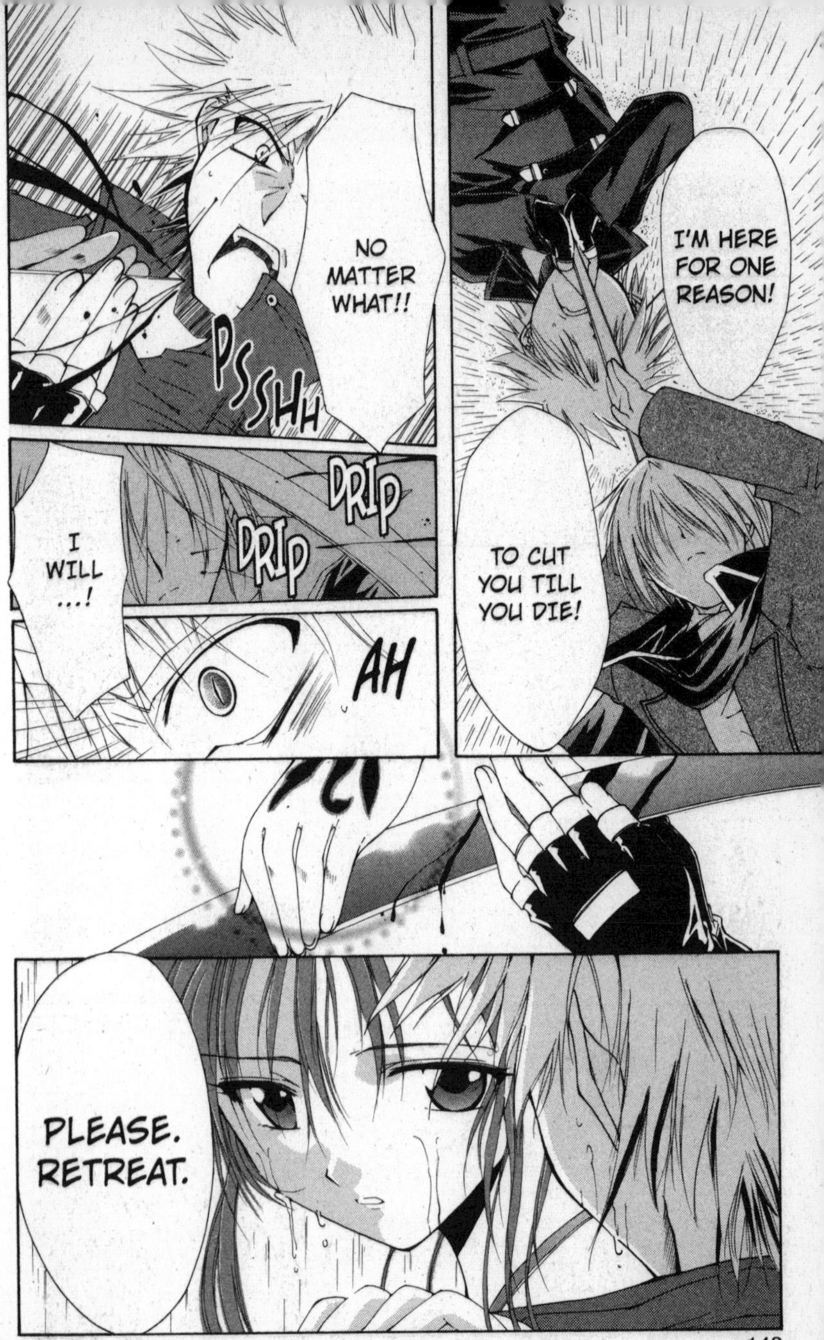
I'M HERE FOR ONE REASON!
TO CUT YOU TILL YOU DIE!
NO MATTER WHAT!!
PSSHH
I WILL ...!
DRIP
DRIP
AH
PLEASE. RETREAT.

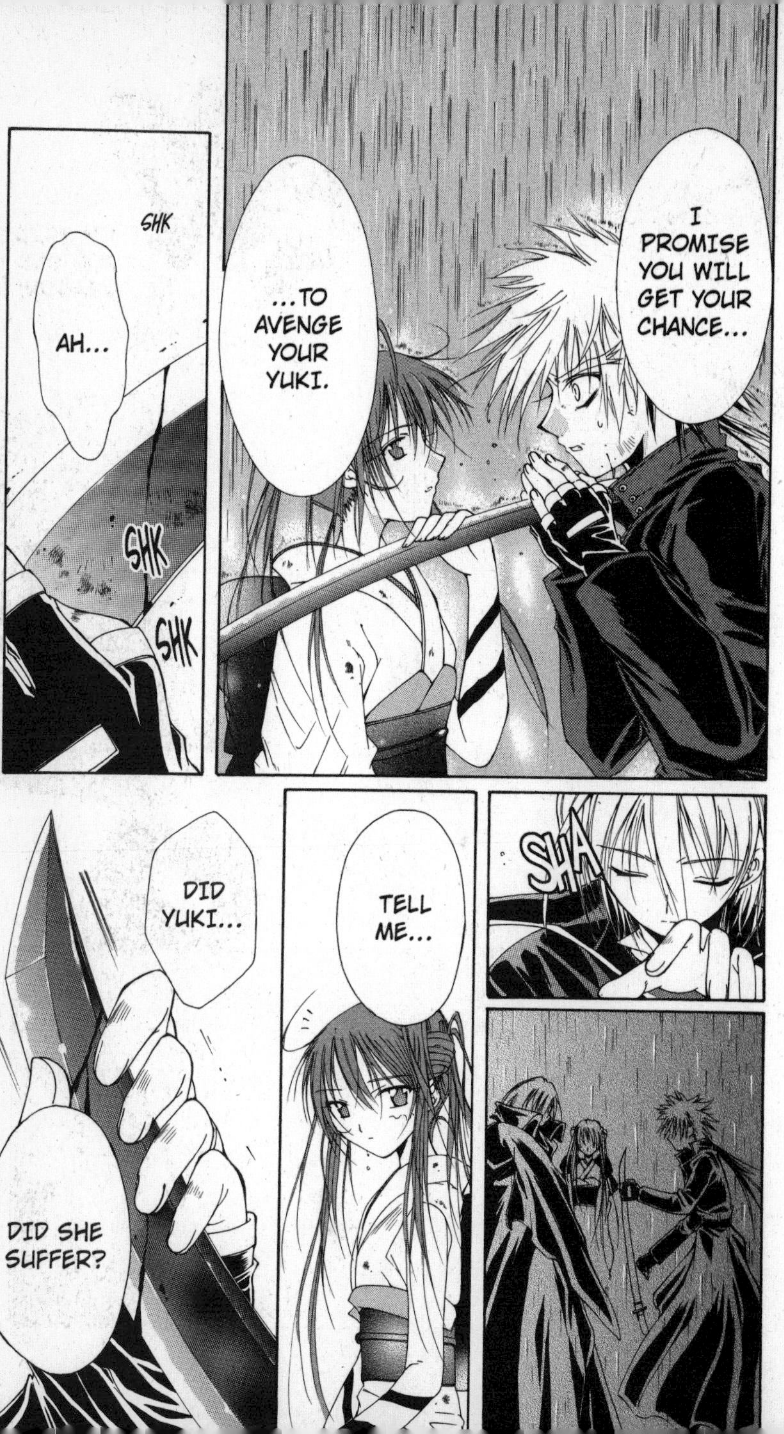
I PROMISE YOU WILL GET YOUR CHANCE...
...TO AVENGE YOUR YUKI.
SHK
AH...
SHK
SHK
SHA
TELL ME...
DID YUKI...
DID SHE SUFFER?

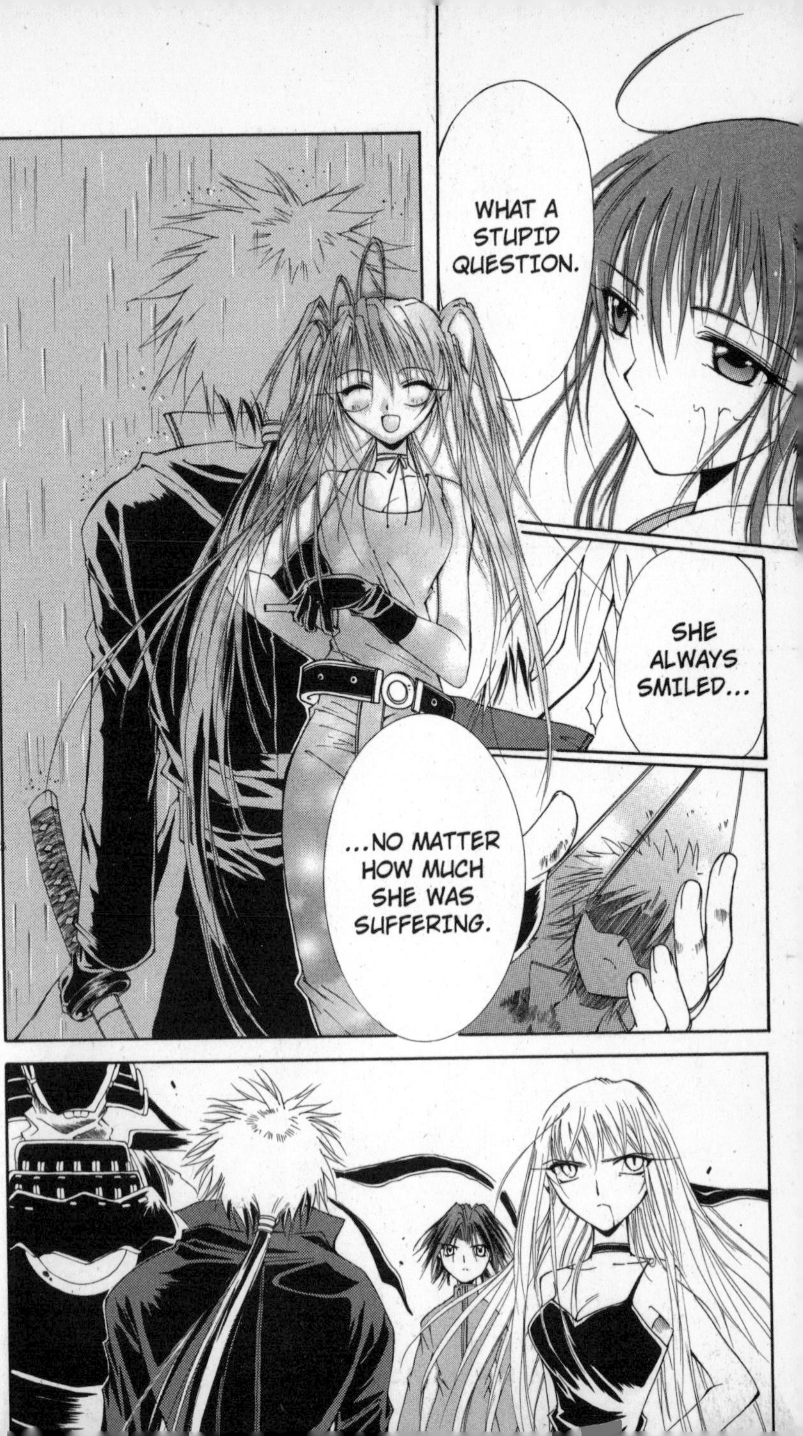
WHAT A STUPID QUESTION.
SHE ALWAYS SMILED...
...NO MATTER HOW MUCH SHE WAS SUFFERING.

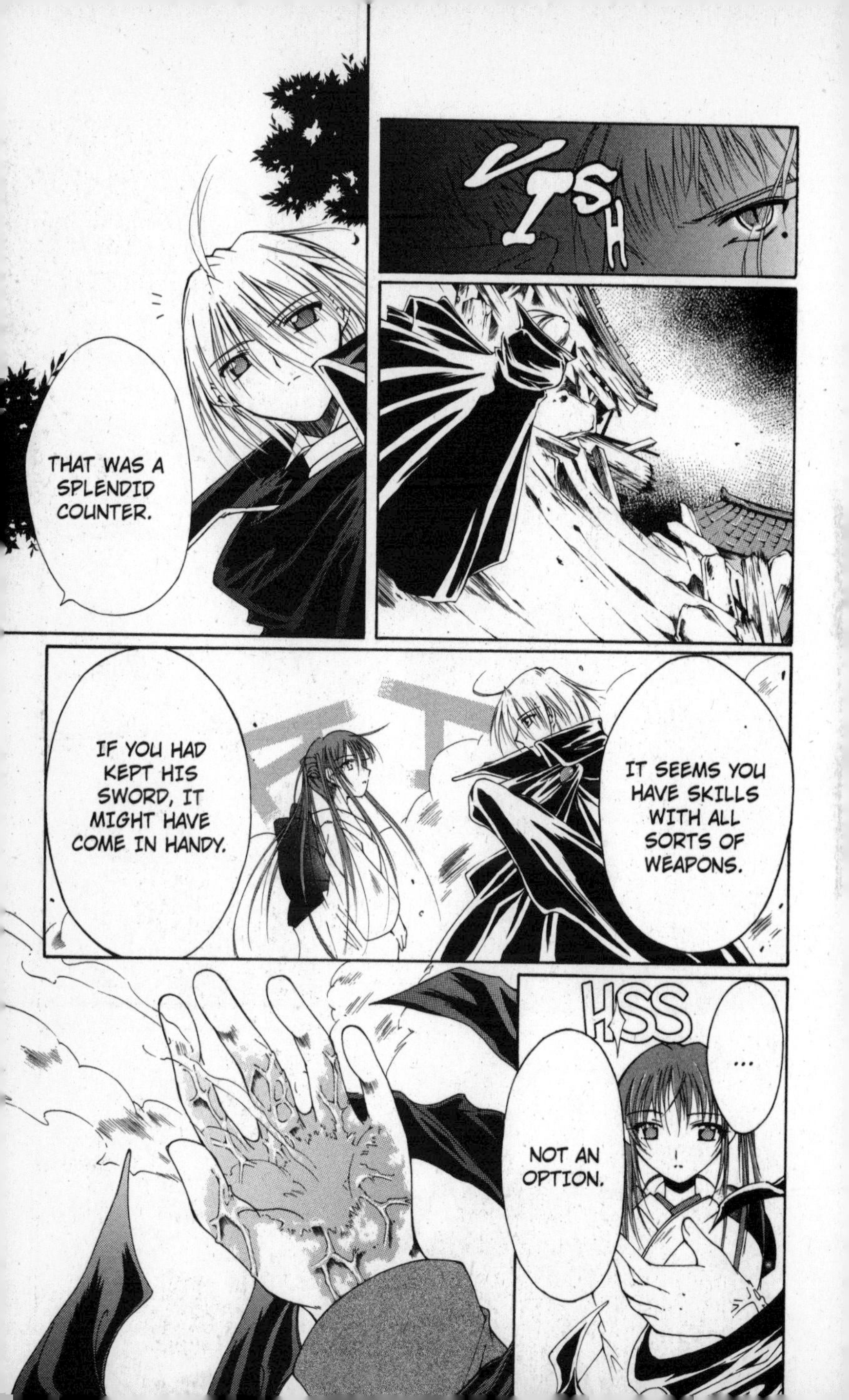
VISH
THAT WAS A SPLENDID COUNTER.
IT SEEMS YOU HAVE SKILLS WITH ALL SORTS OF WEAPONS.
IF YOU HAD KEPT HIS SWORD, IT MIGHT HAVE COME IN HANDY.
HSS
...
NOT AN OPTION.

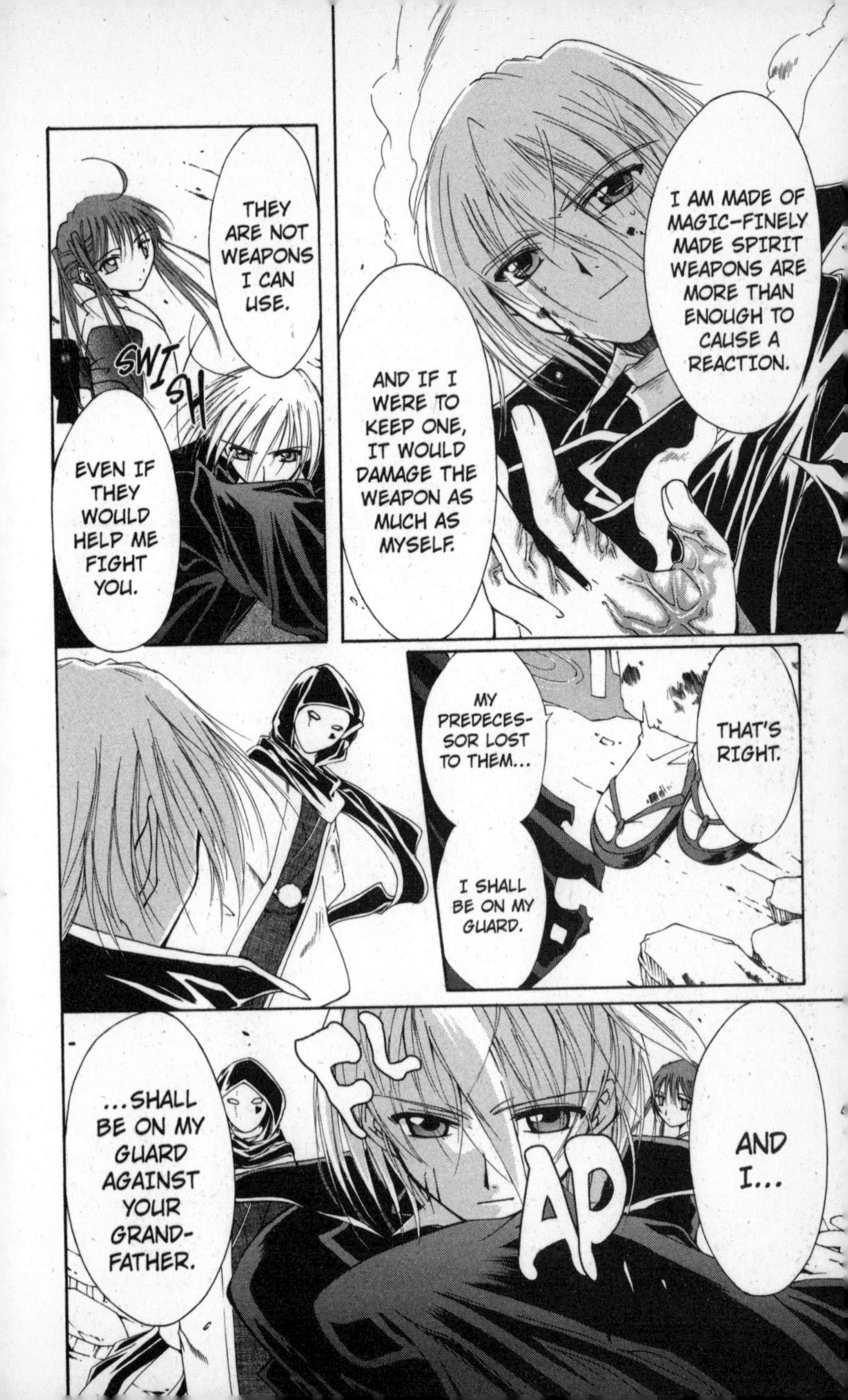
I AM MADE OF MAGIC—FINELY MADE SPIRIT WEAPONS ARE MORE THAN ENOUGH TO CAUSE A REACTION.
AND IF I WERE TO KEEP ONE, IT WOULD DAMAGE THE WEAPON AS MUCH AS MYSELF.
THEY ARE NOT WEAPONS I CAN USE.
SWISH
EVEN IF THEY WOULD HELP ME FIGHT YOU.
THAT'S RIGHT.
MY PREDECES-SOR LOST TO THEM...
I SHALL BE ON MY GUARD.
AND I...
FLAP
...SHALL BE ON MY GUARD AGAINST YOUR GRAND-FATHER.

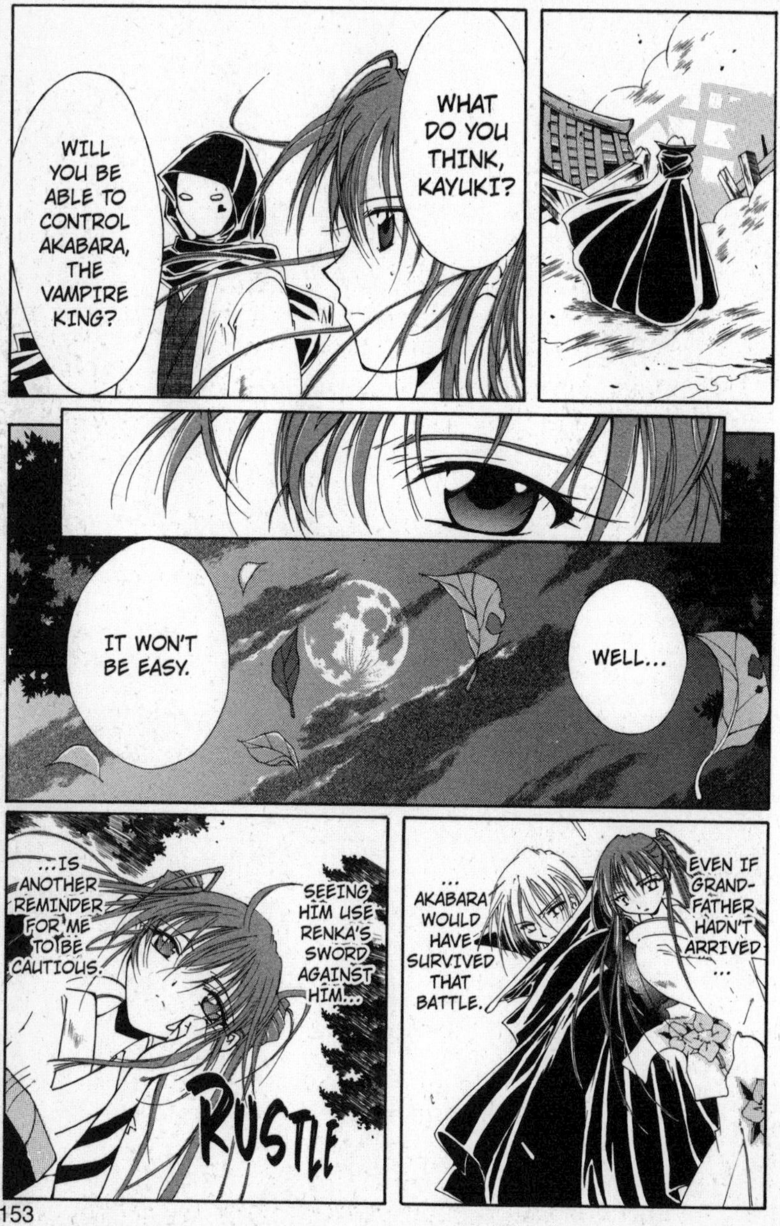
WHAT DO YOU THINK, KAYUKI?
WILL YOU BE ABLE TO CONTROL AKABARA, THE VAMPIRE KING?
WELL...
IT WON'T BE EASY.
EVEN IF GRAND-FATHER HADN'T ARRIVED...
...AKABARA WOULD HAVE SURVIVED THAT BATTLE.
SEEING HIM USE RENKA'S SWORD AGAINST HIM...
...IS ANOTHER REMINDER FOR ME TO BE CAUTIOUS.
RUSTLE

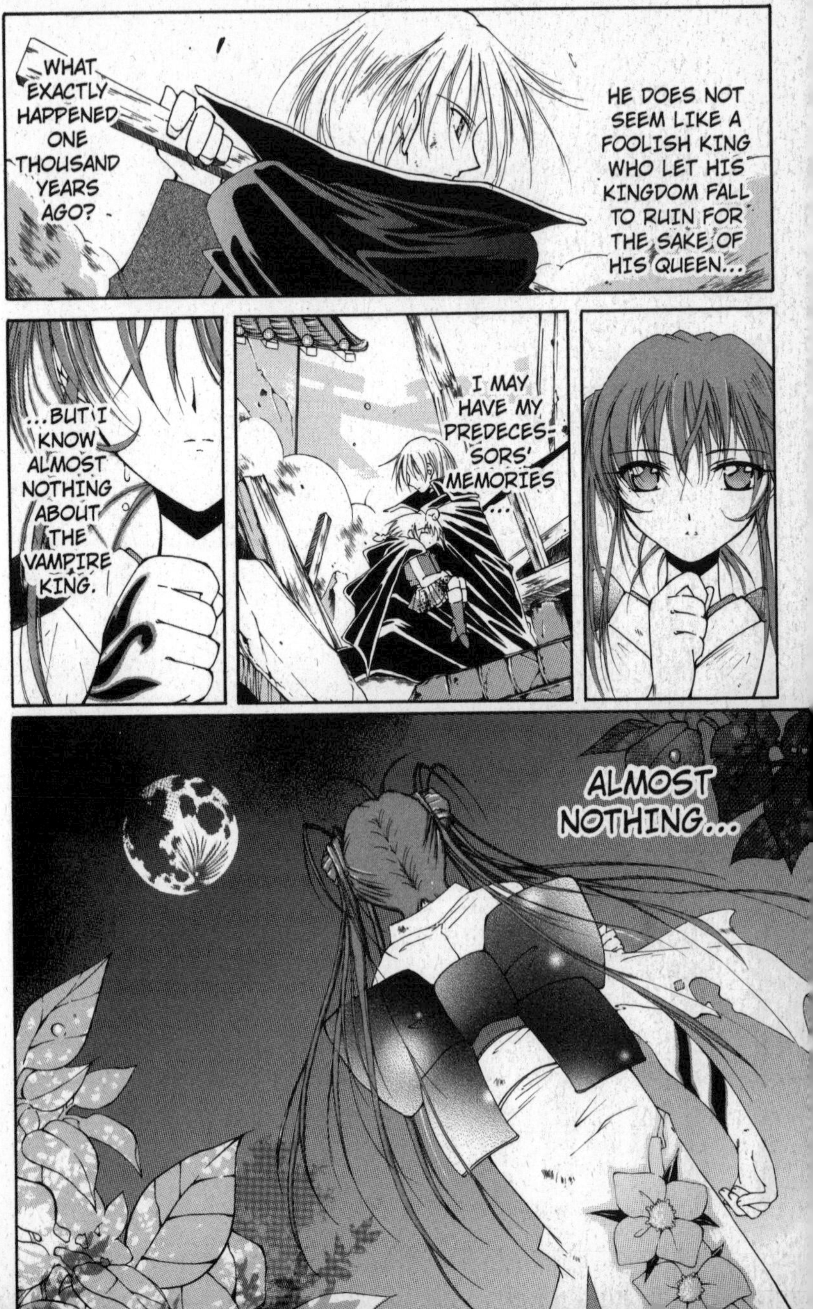
HE DOES NOT SEEM LIKE A FOOLISH KING WHO LET HIS KINGDOM FALL TO RUIN FOR THE SAKE OF HIS QUEEN...
WHAT EXACTLY HAPPENED ONE THOUSAND YEARS AGO?
I MAY HAVE MY PREDECES-SORS' MEMORIES...
...BUT I KNOW ALMOST NOTHING ABOUT THE VAMPIRE KING.
ALMOST NOTHING...

THE RECORD OF A

FALLEN VAMPIRE

THE RECORD OF A

FALLEN VAMPIRE

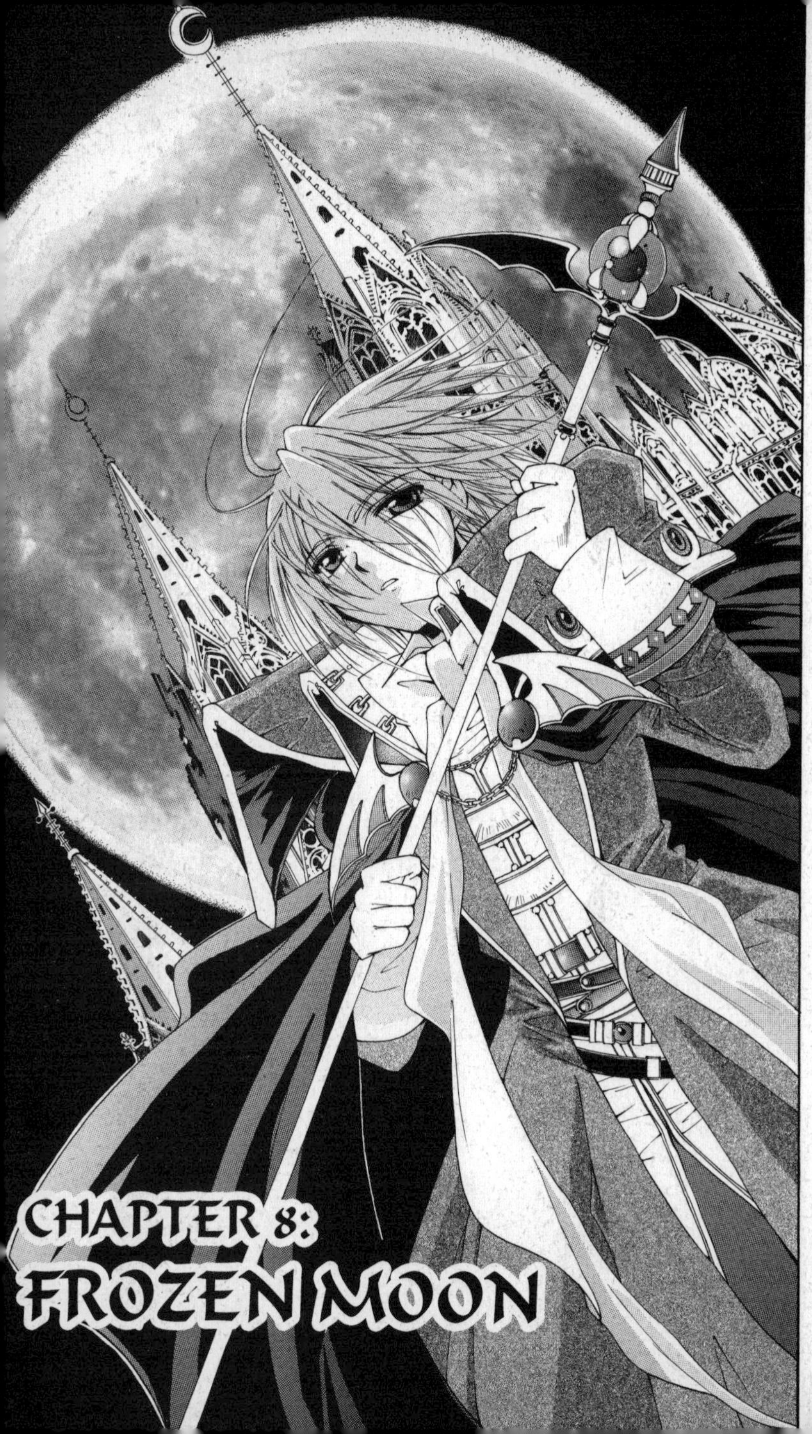
CHAPTER 8:
FROZEN MOON

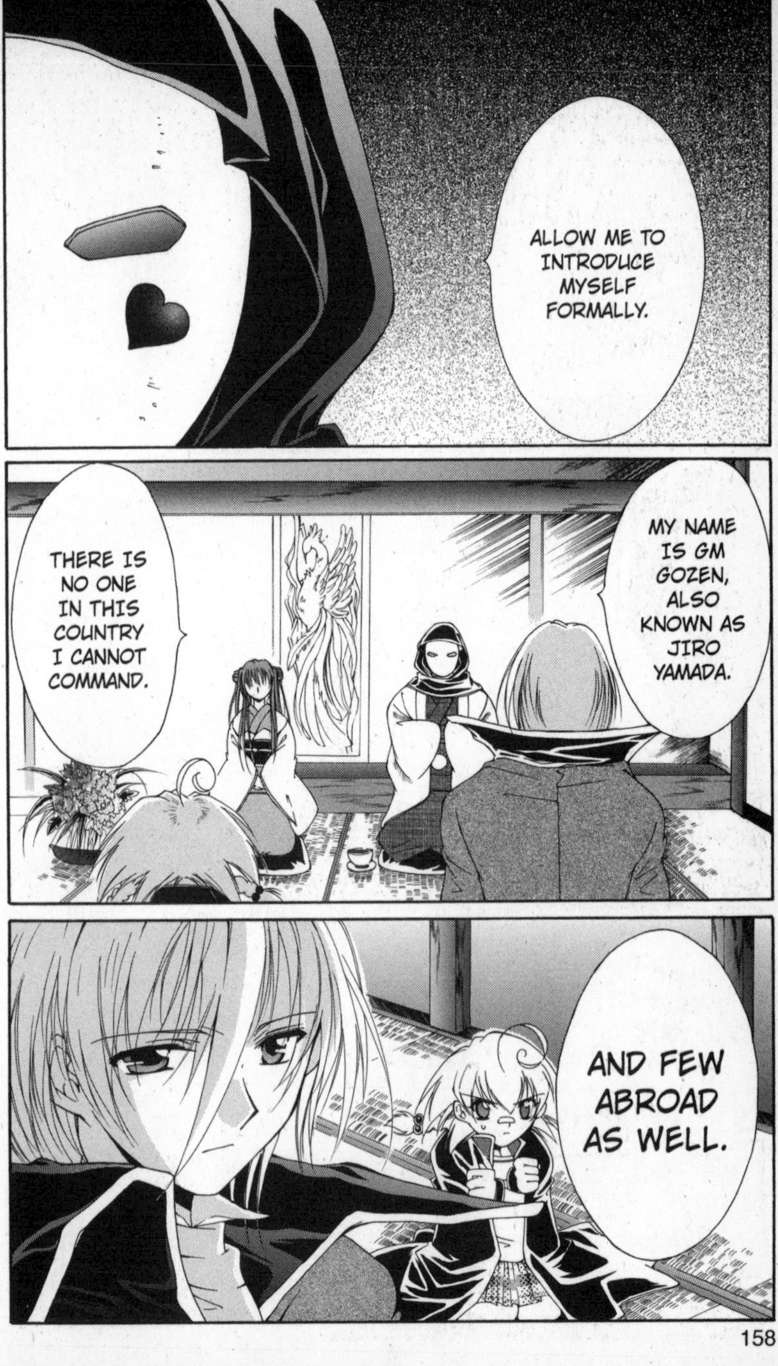
ALLOW ME TO INTRODUCE MYSELF FORMALLY.
MY NAME IS GM GOZEN, ALSO KNOWN AS JIRO YAMADA.
THERE IS NO ONE IN THIS COUNTRY I CANNOT COMMAND.
AND FEW ABROAD AS WELL.

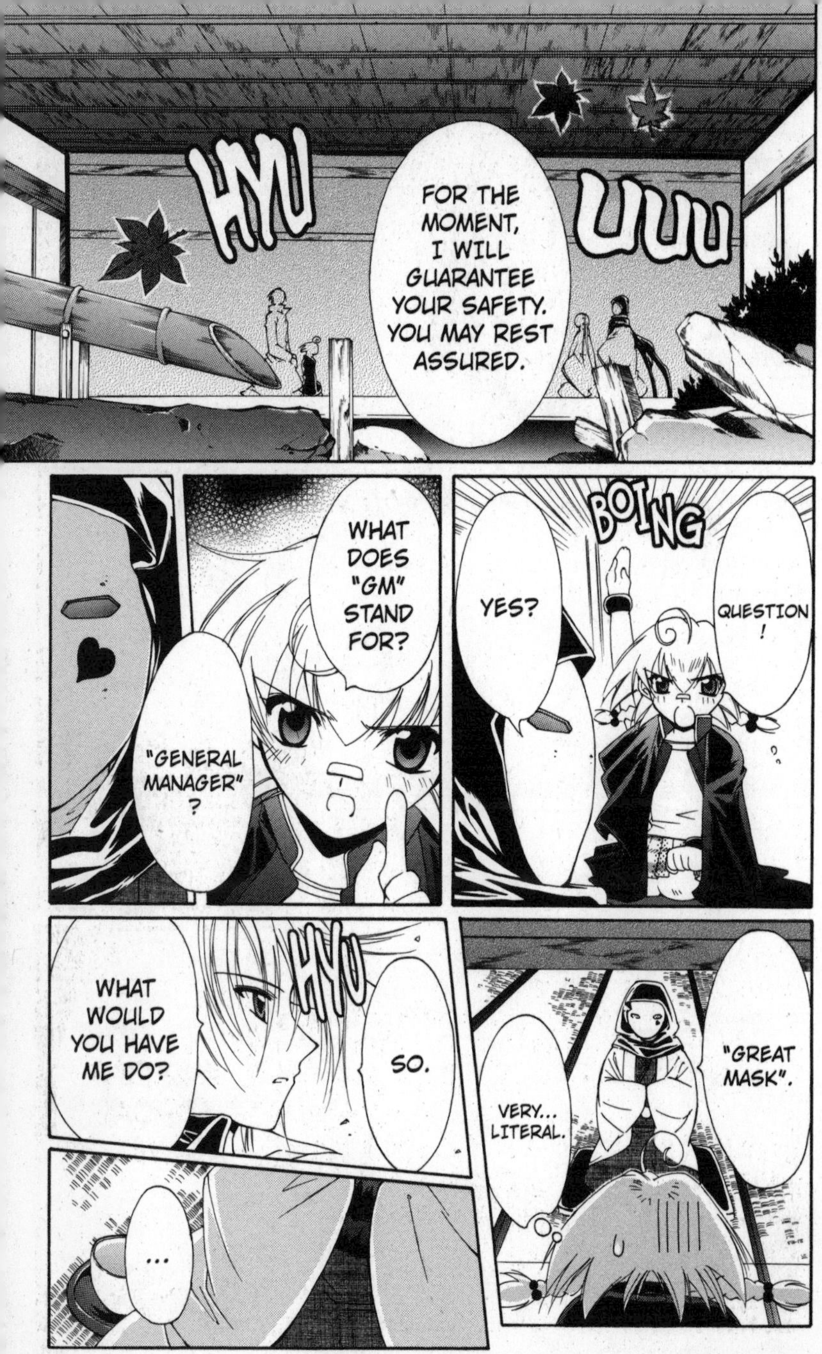
HYU
FOR THE MOMENT, I WILL GUARANTEE YOUR SAFETY. YOU MAY REST ASSURED.
UUU
BOING
QUESTION!
YES?
WHAT DOES "GM" STAND FOR?
"GENERAL MANAGER"?
"GREAT MASK".
VERY... LITERAL.
HYU
SO.
WHAT WOULD YOU HAVE ME DO?
...

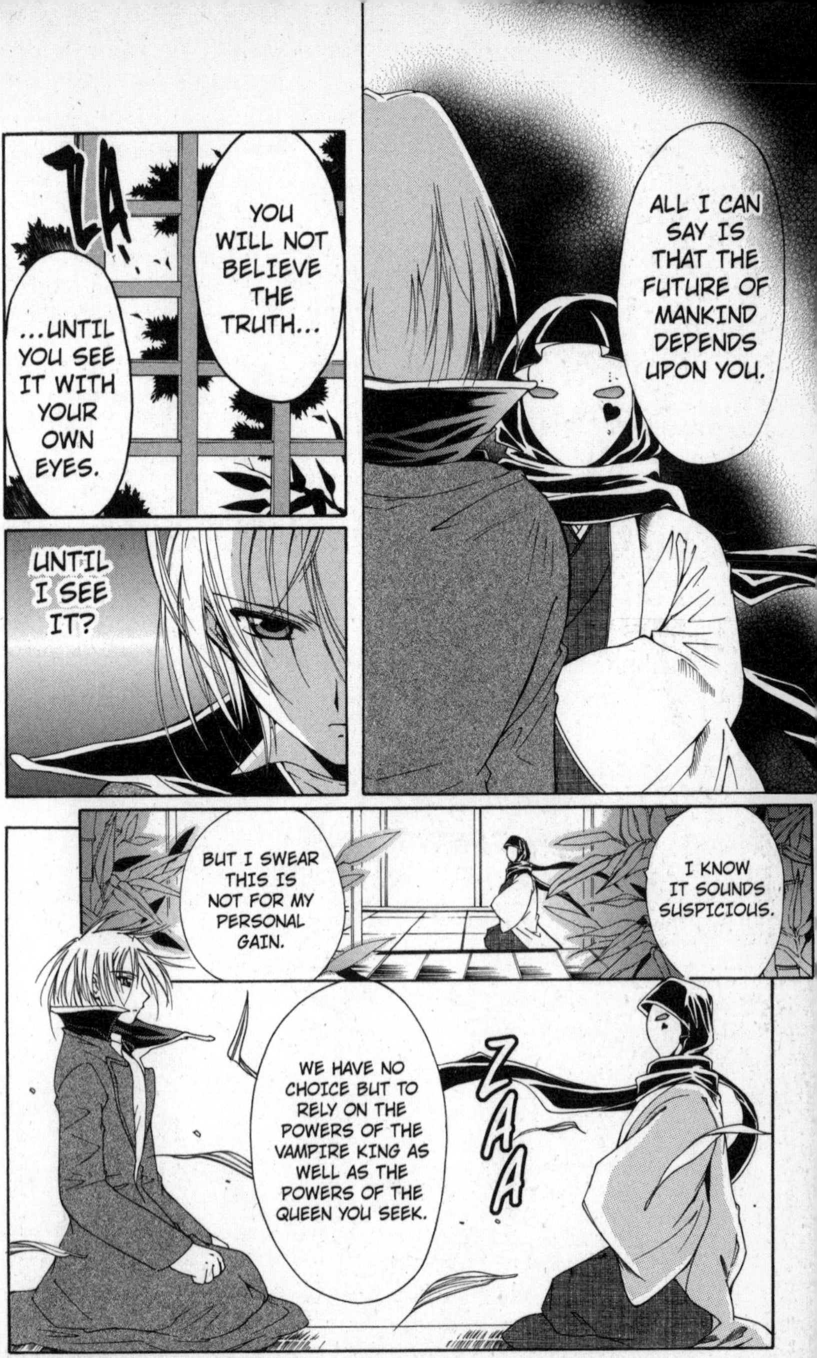
ALL I CAN SAY IS THAT THE FUTURE OF MANKIND DEPENDS UPON YOU.
ZA
YOU WILL NOT BELIEVE THE TRUTH...
...UNTIL YOU SEE IT WITH YOUR OWN EYES.
UNTIL I SEE IT?
I KNOW IT SOUNDS SUSPICIOUS.
BUT I SWEAR THIS IS NOT FOR MY PERSONAL GAIN.
ZAA
WE HAVE NO CHOICE BUT TO RELY ON THE POWERS OF THE VAMPIRE KING AS WELL AS THE POWERS OF THE QUEEN YOU SEEK.

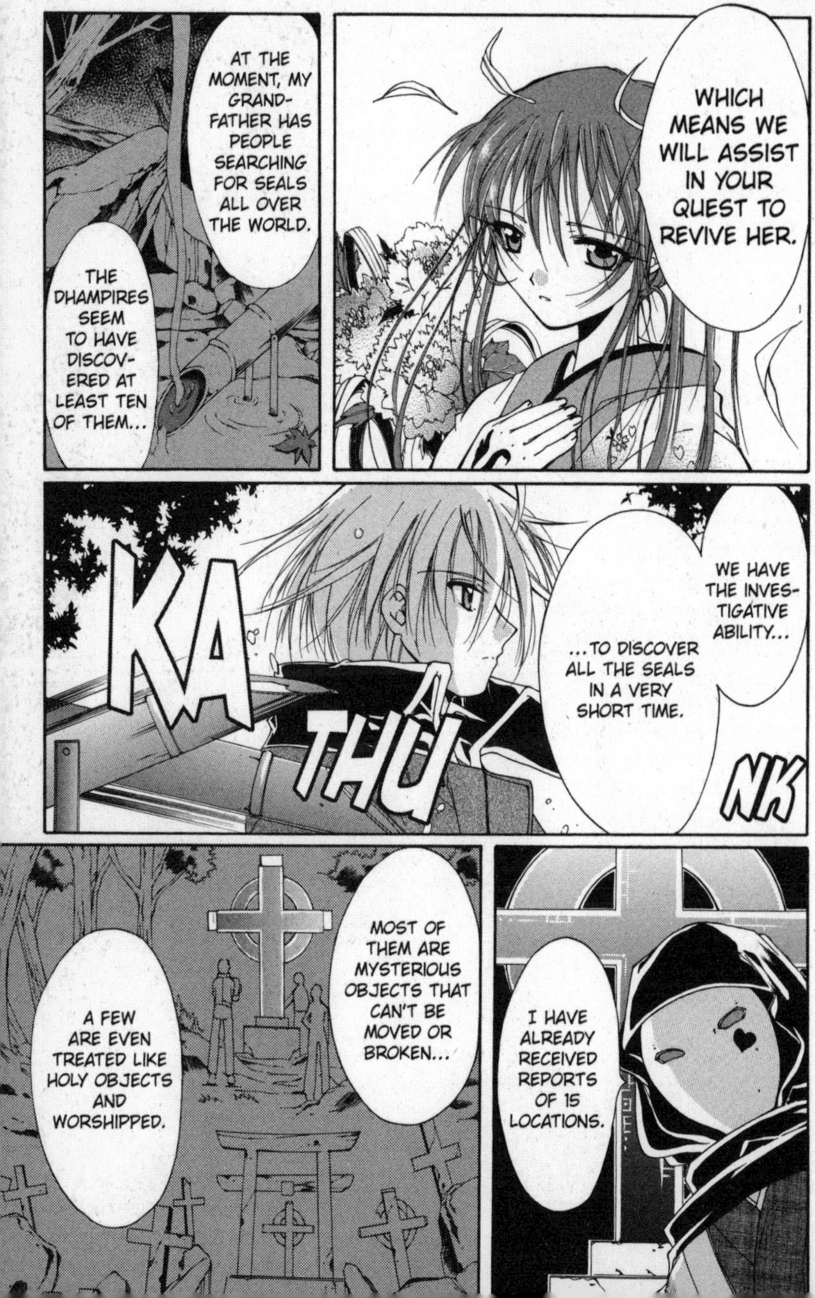
WHICH MEANS WE WILL ASSIST IN YOUR QUEST TO REVIVE HER.
AT THE MOMENT, MY GRAND-FATHER HAS PEOPLE SEARCHING FOR SEALS ALL OVER THE WORLD.
THE DHAMPIRES SEEM TO HAVE DISCOV-ERED AT LEAST TEN OF THEM...
WE HAVE THE INVES-TIGATIVE ABILITY...
...TO DISCOVER ALL THE SEALS IN A VERY SHORT TIME.
KA THUNK
I HAVE ALREADY RECEIVED REPORTS OF 15 LOCATIONS.
MOST OF THEM ARE MYSTERIOUS OBJECTS THAT CAN'T BE MOVED OR BROKEN...
A FEW ARE EVEN TREATED LIKE HOLY OBJECTS AND WORSHIPPED.

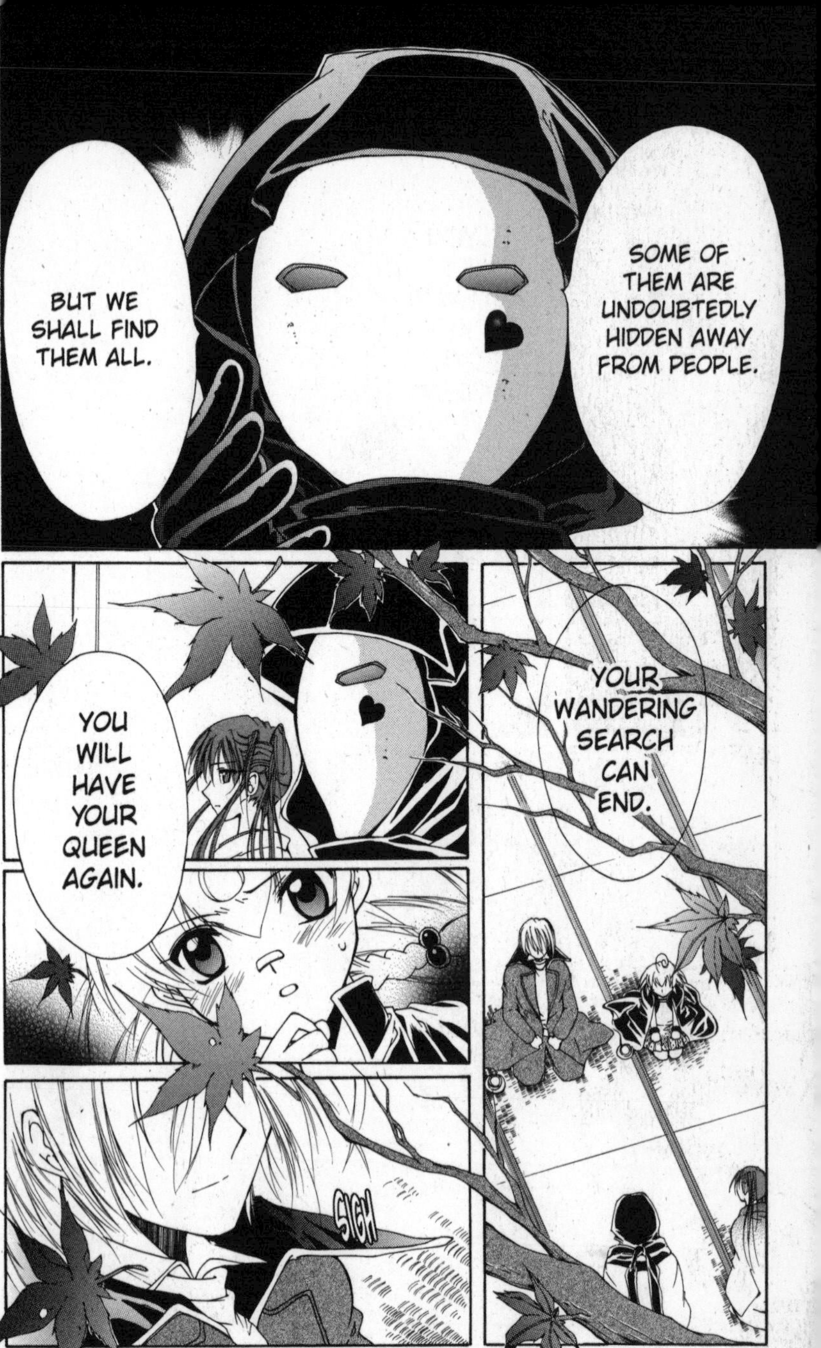
SOME OF THEM ARE UNDOUBTEDLY HIDDEN AWAY FROM PEOPLE.
BUT WE SHALL FIND THEM ALL.
YOUR WANDERING SEARCH CAN END.
YOU WILL HAVE YOUR QUEEN AGAIN.
SIGH

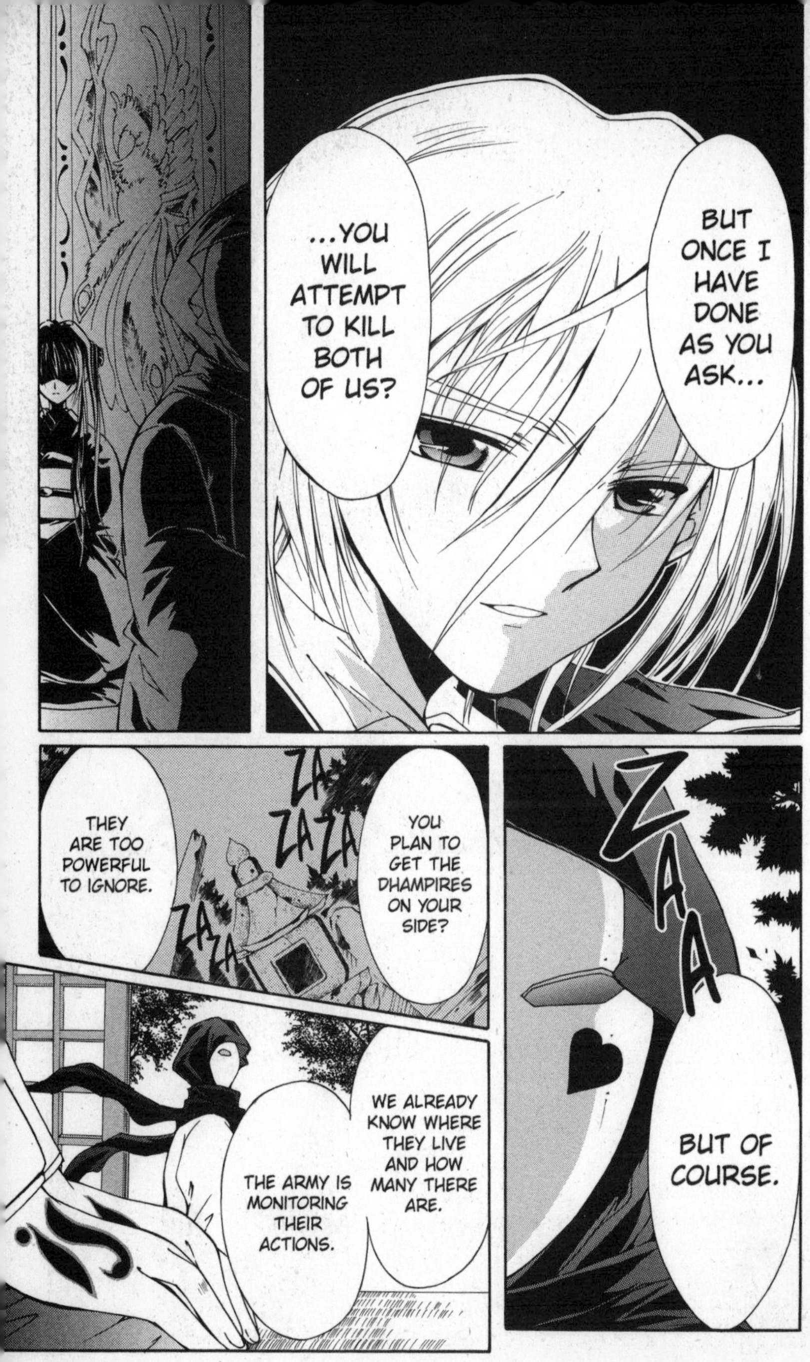
BUT ONCE I HAVE DONE AS YOU ASK...
...YOU WILL ATTEMPT TO KILL BOTH OF US?
ZAA
BUT OF COURSE.
ZA ZAZA
YOU PLAN TO GET THE DHAMPIRES ON YOUR SIDE?
ZAZA
THEY ARE TOO POWERFUL TO IGNORE.
WE ALREADY KNOW WHERE THEY LIVE AND HOW MANY THERE ARE.
THE ARMY IS MONITORING THEIR ACTIONS.

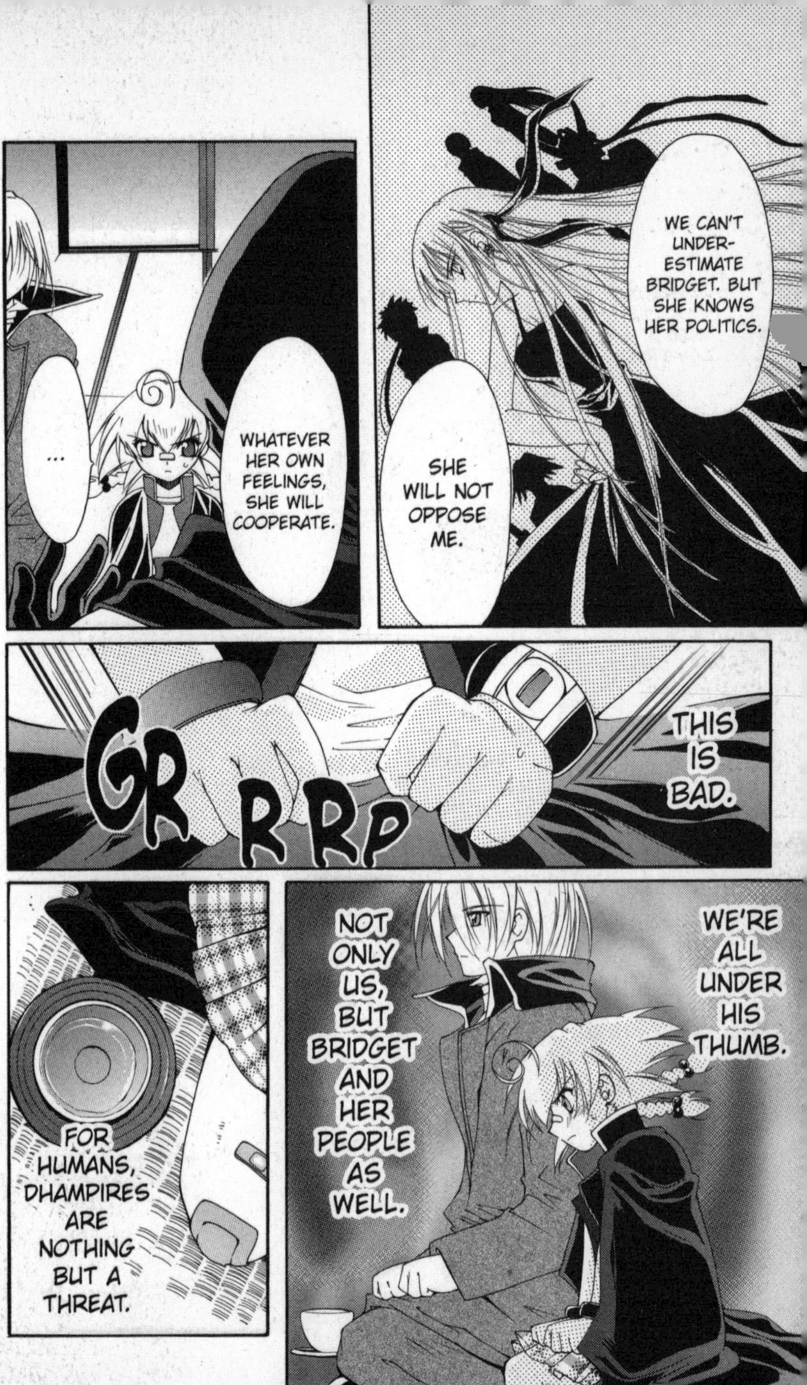
WE CAN'T UNDER-ESTIMATE BRIDGET. BUT SHE KNOWS HER POLITICS.
SHE WILL NOT OPPOSE ME.
WHATEVER HER OWN FEELINGS, SHE WILL COOPERATE.
...
THIS IS BAD.
GRRRP
WE'RE ALL UNDER HIS THUMB.
NOT ONLY US, BUT BRIDGET AND HER PEOPLE AS WELL.
FOR HUMANS, DHAMPIRES ARE NOTHING BUT A THREAT.

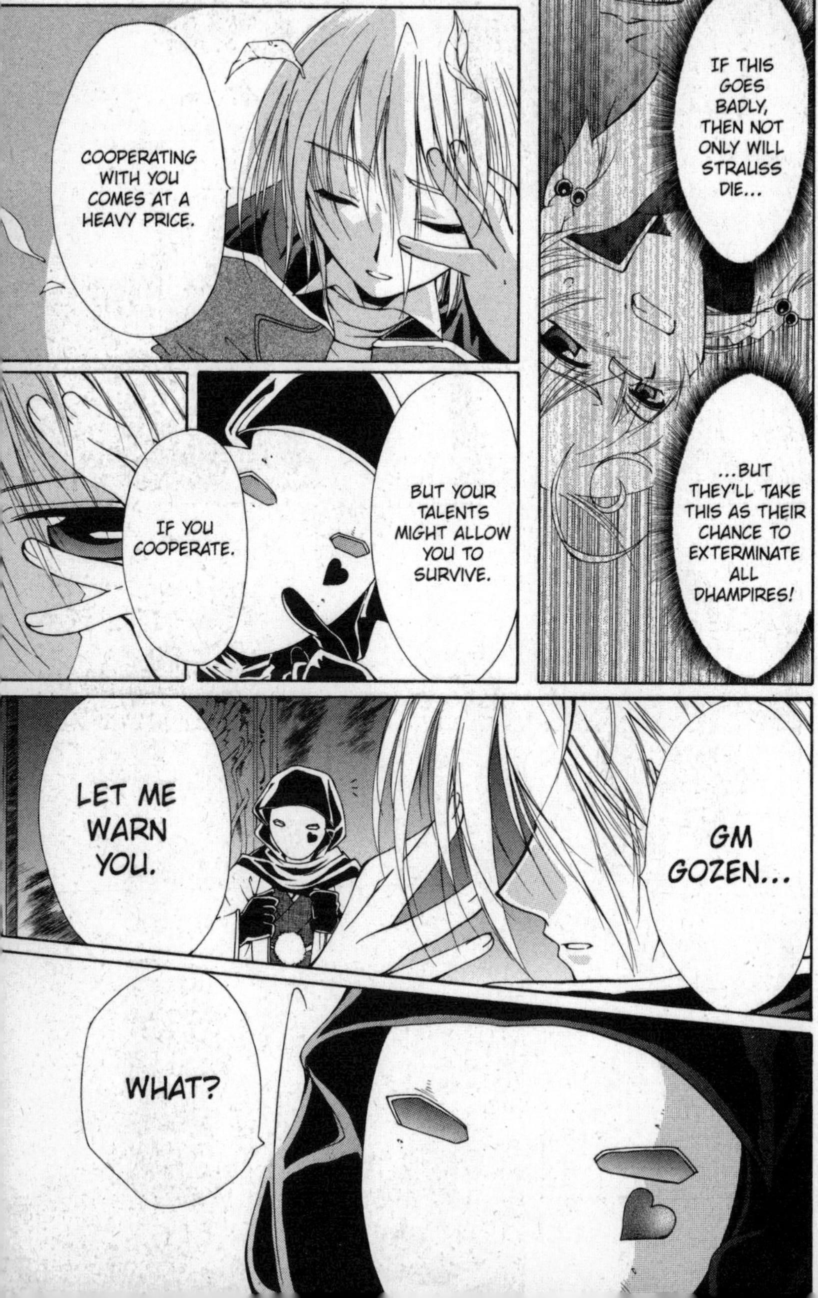
IF THIS GOES BADLY, THEN NOT ONLY WILL STRAUSS DIE...
...BUT THEY'LL TAKE THIS AS THEIR CHANCE TO EXTERMINATE ALL DHAMPIRES!
COOPERATING WITH YOU COMES AT A HEAVY PRICE.
BUT YOUR TALENTS MIGHT ALLOW YOU TO SURVIVE.
IF YOU COOPERATE.
GM GOZEN...
LET ME WARN YOU.
WHAT?

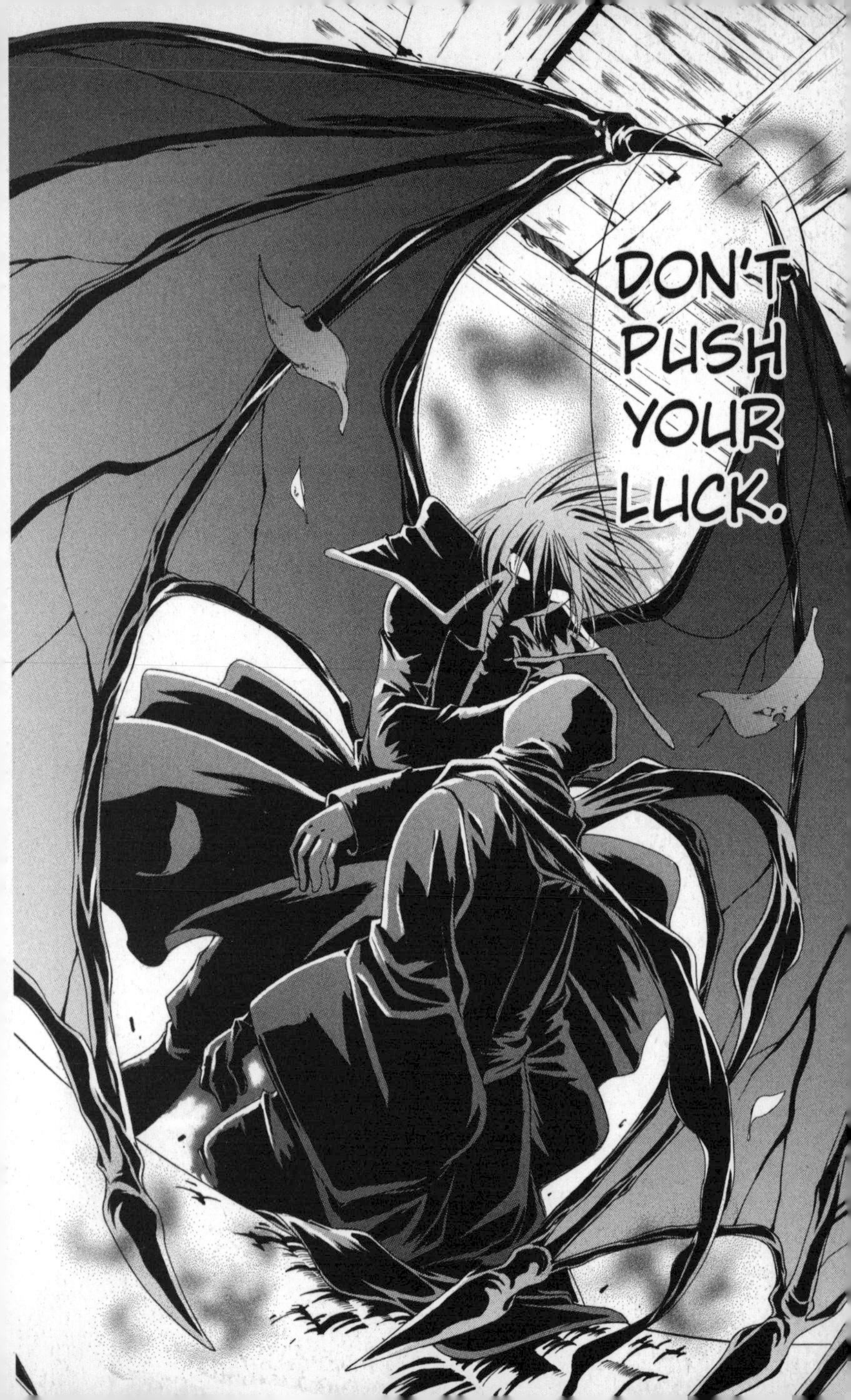
DON'T PUSH YOUR LUCK.

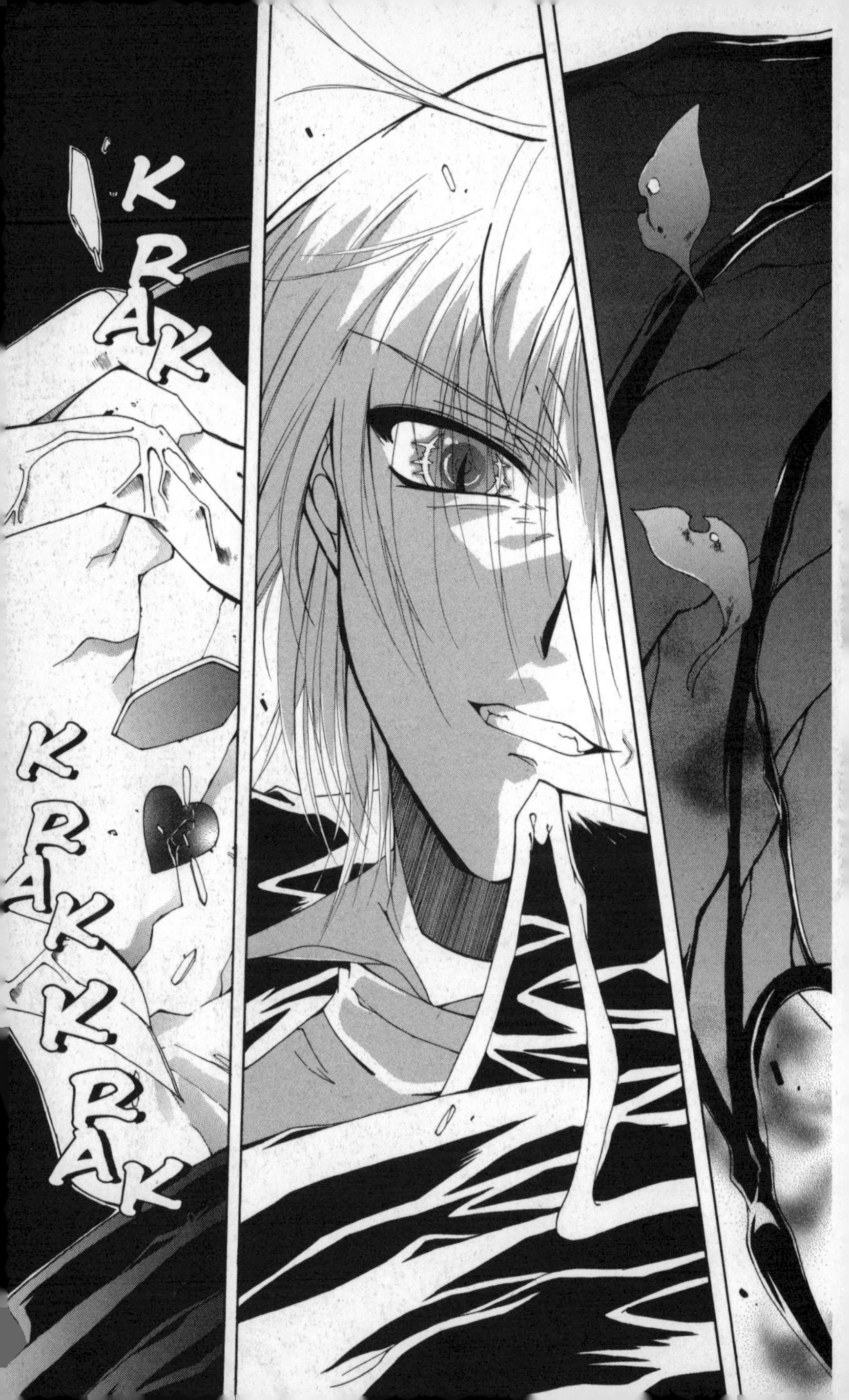
KRAK
KRAKKRAK

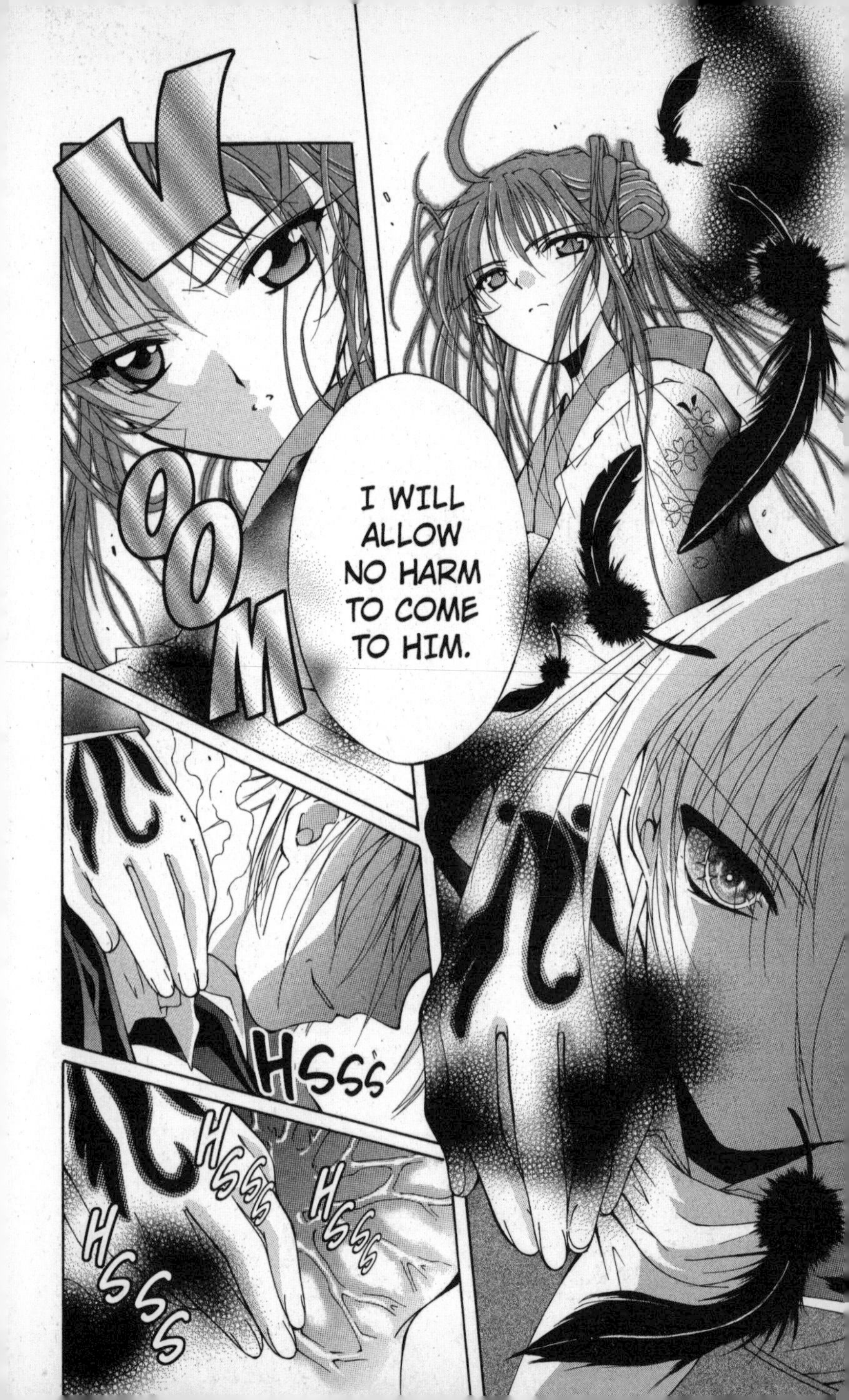
I WILL ALLOW NO HARM TO COME TO HIM.
VOOOM
HSSS
HSSS
HSSS
HSSS

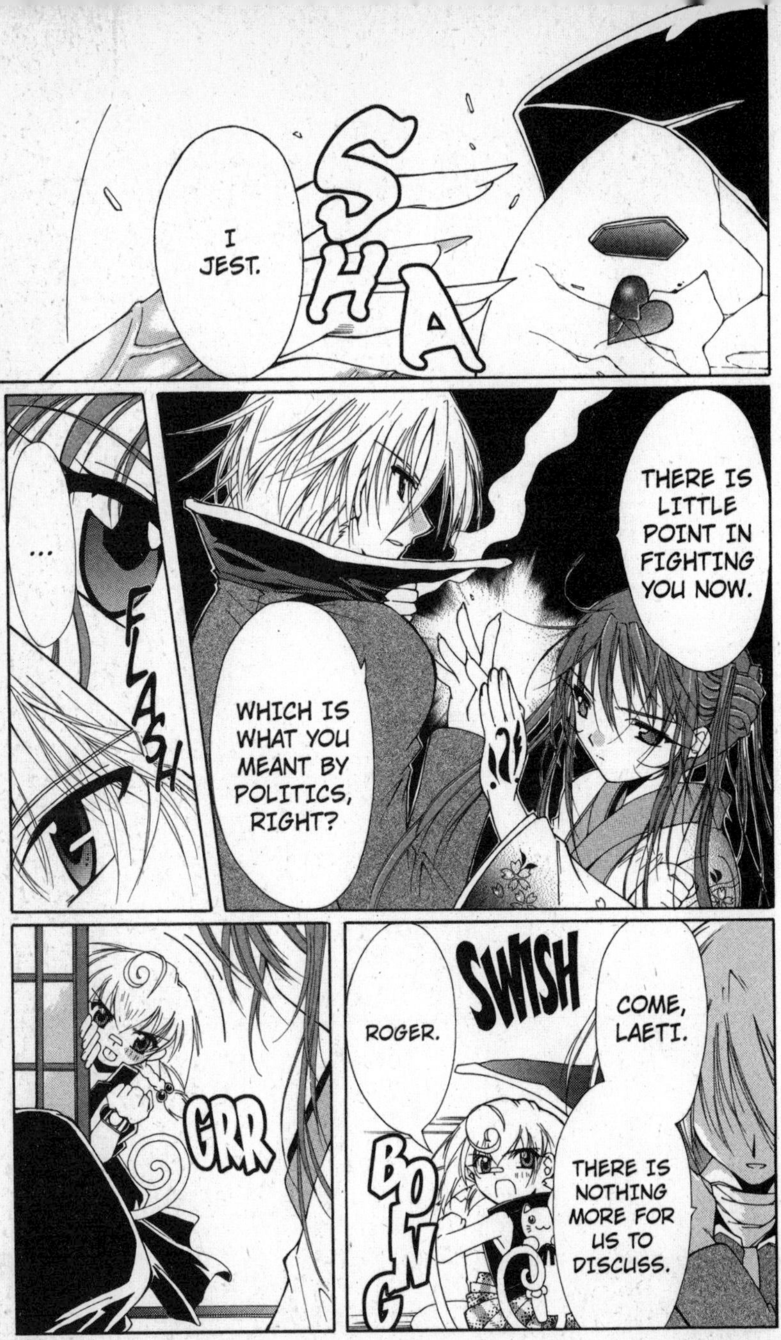
SHA
I JEST.
THERE IS LITTLE POINT IN FIGHTING YOU NOW.
WHICH IS WHAT YOU MEANT BY POLITICS, RIGHT?
...
FLASH
COME, LAETI.
SWISH
ROGER.
THERE IS NOTHING MORE FOR US TO DISCUSS.
BOING
GRR

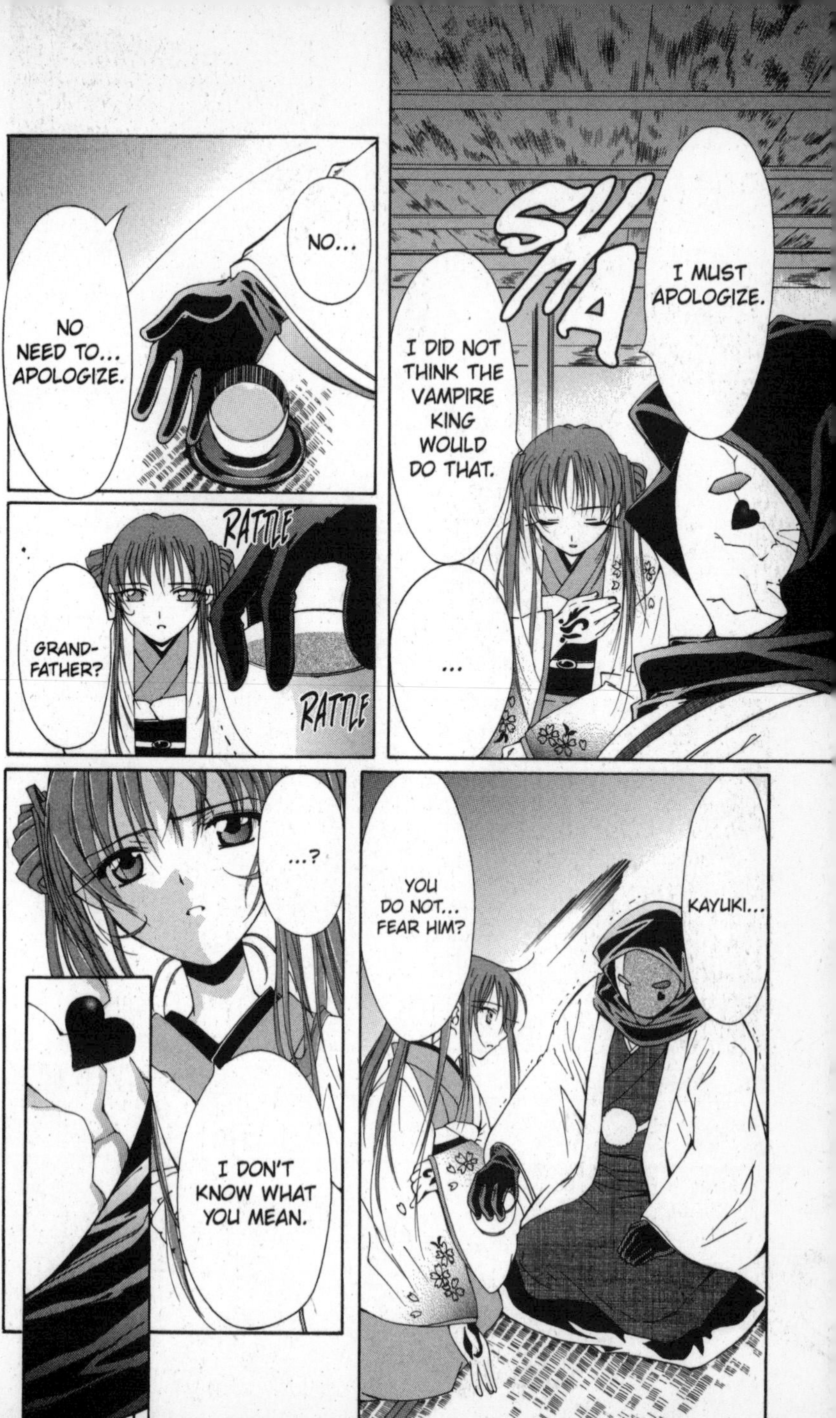
SHA
I MUST APOLOGIZE.
I DID NOT THINK THE VAMPIRE KING WOULD DO THAT.
...
NO...
NO NEED TO... APOLOGIZE.
RATTLE
RATTLE
GRAND-FATHER?
KAYUKI...
YOU DO NOT... FEAR HIM?
...?
I DON'T KNOW WHAT YOU MEAN.

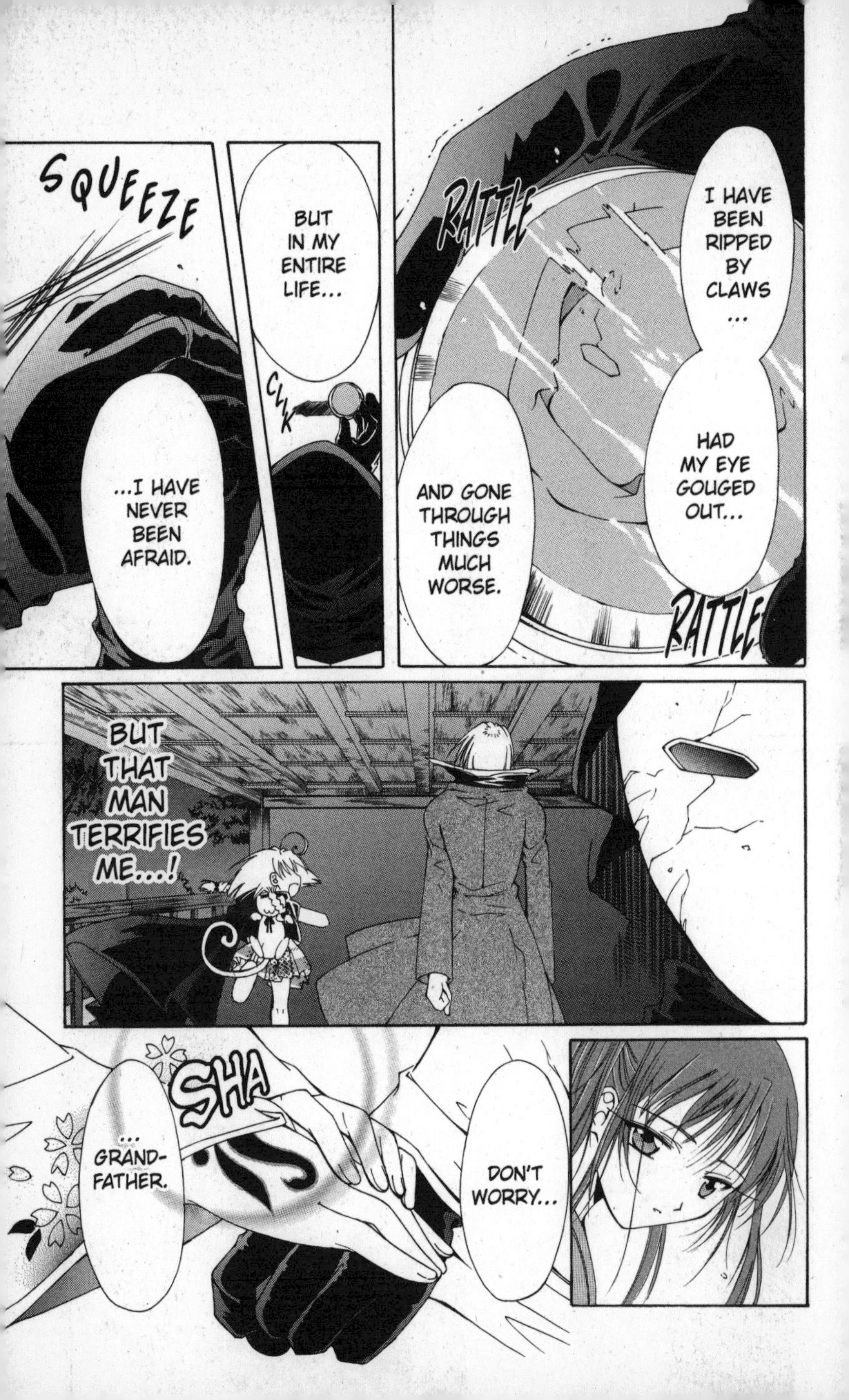
RATTLE
I HAVE BEEN RIPPED BY CLAWS...
HAD MY EYE GOUGED OUT...
AND GONE THROUGH THINGS MUCH WORSE.
RATTLE
BUT IN MY ENTIRE LIFE...
CLIK
SQUEEZE
...I HAVE NEVER BEEN AFRAID.
BUT THAT MAN TERRIFIES ME...!
DON'T WORRY...
SHA
...GRANDFATHER.

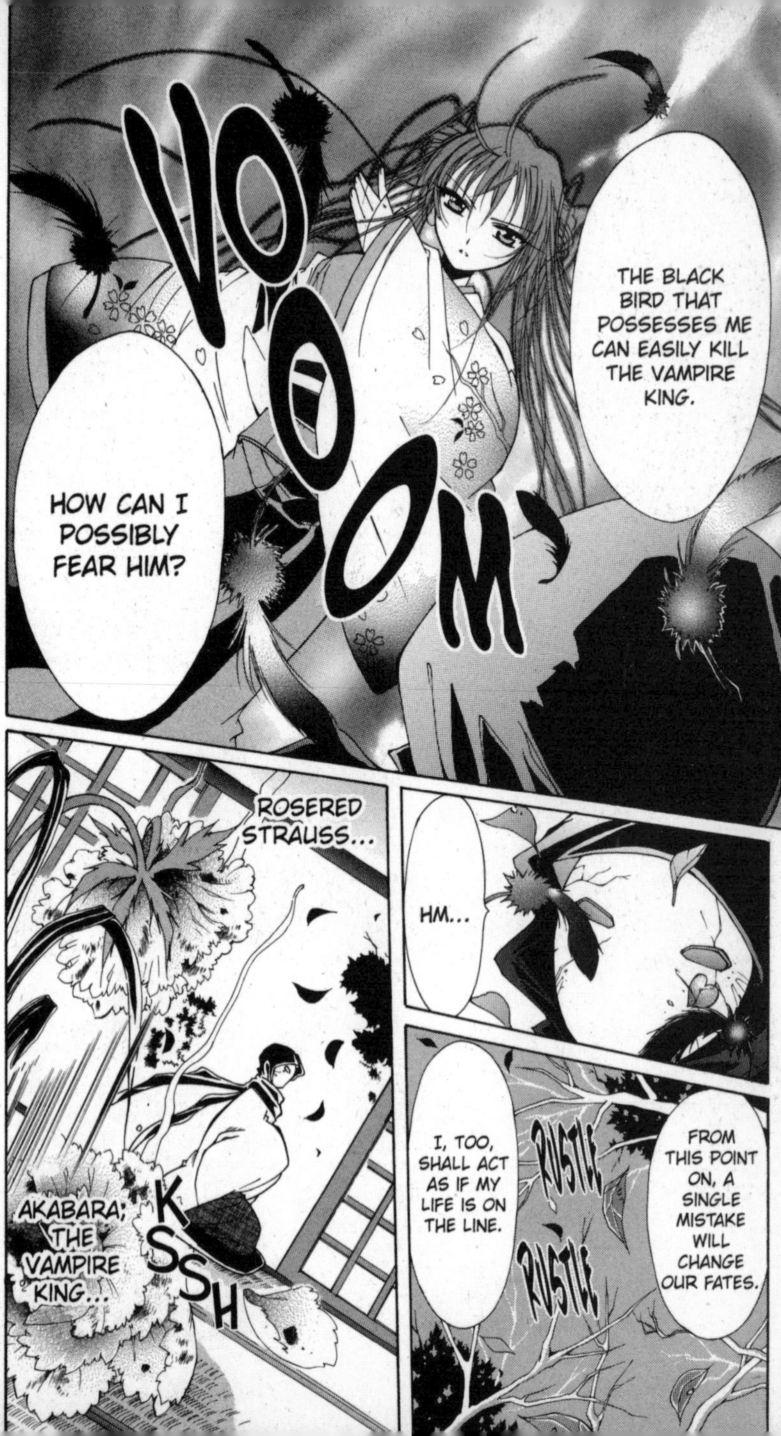
THE BLACK BIRD THAT POSSESSES ME CAN EASILY KILL THE VAMPIRE KING.
VOOOM
HOW CAN I POSSIBLY FEAR HIM?
HM...
FROM THIS POINT ON, A SINGLE MISTAKE WILL CHANGE OUR FATES.
RUSTLE
I, TOO, SHALL ACT AS IF MY LIFE IS ON THE LINE.
RUSTLE
ROSERED STRAUSS...
KSSH
AKABARA; THE VAMPIRE KING...

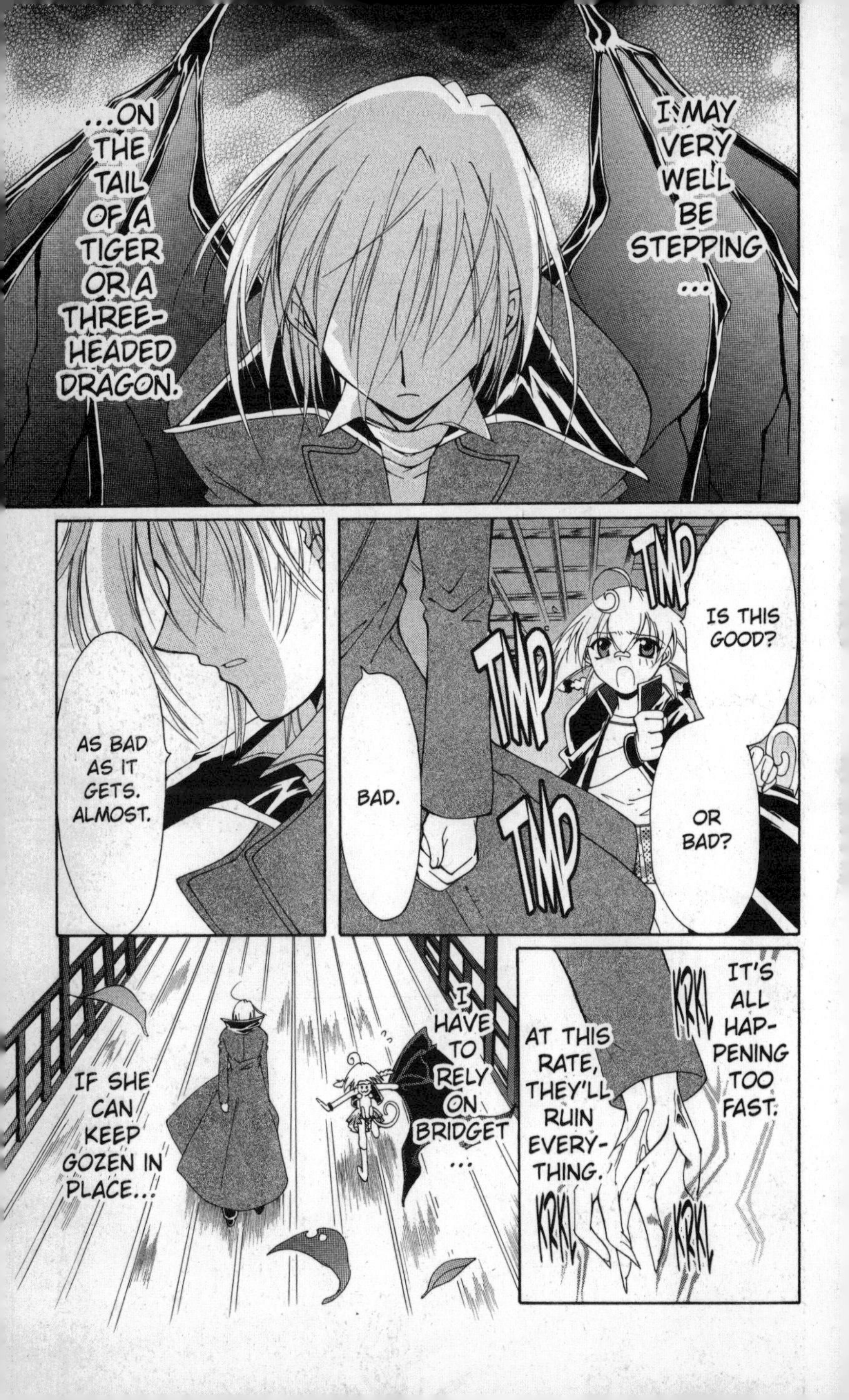
I MAY VERY WELL BE STEPPING...
...ON THE TAIL OF A TIGER OR A THREE-HEADED DRAGON.
TMP
IS THIS GOOD?
TMP
OR BAD?
TMP
BAD.
AS BAD AS IT GETS. ALMOST.
KRKL
IT'S ALL HAPPENING TOO FAST.
AT THIS RATE, THEY'LL RUIN EVERYTHING.
KRKL
KRKL
I HAVE TO RELY ON BRIDGET...
IF SHE CAN KEEP GOZEN IN PLACE...

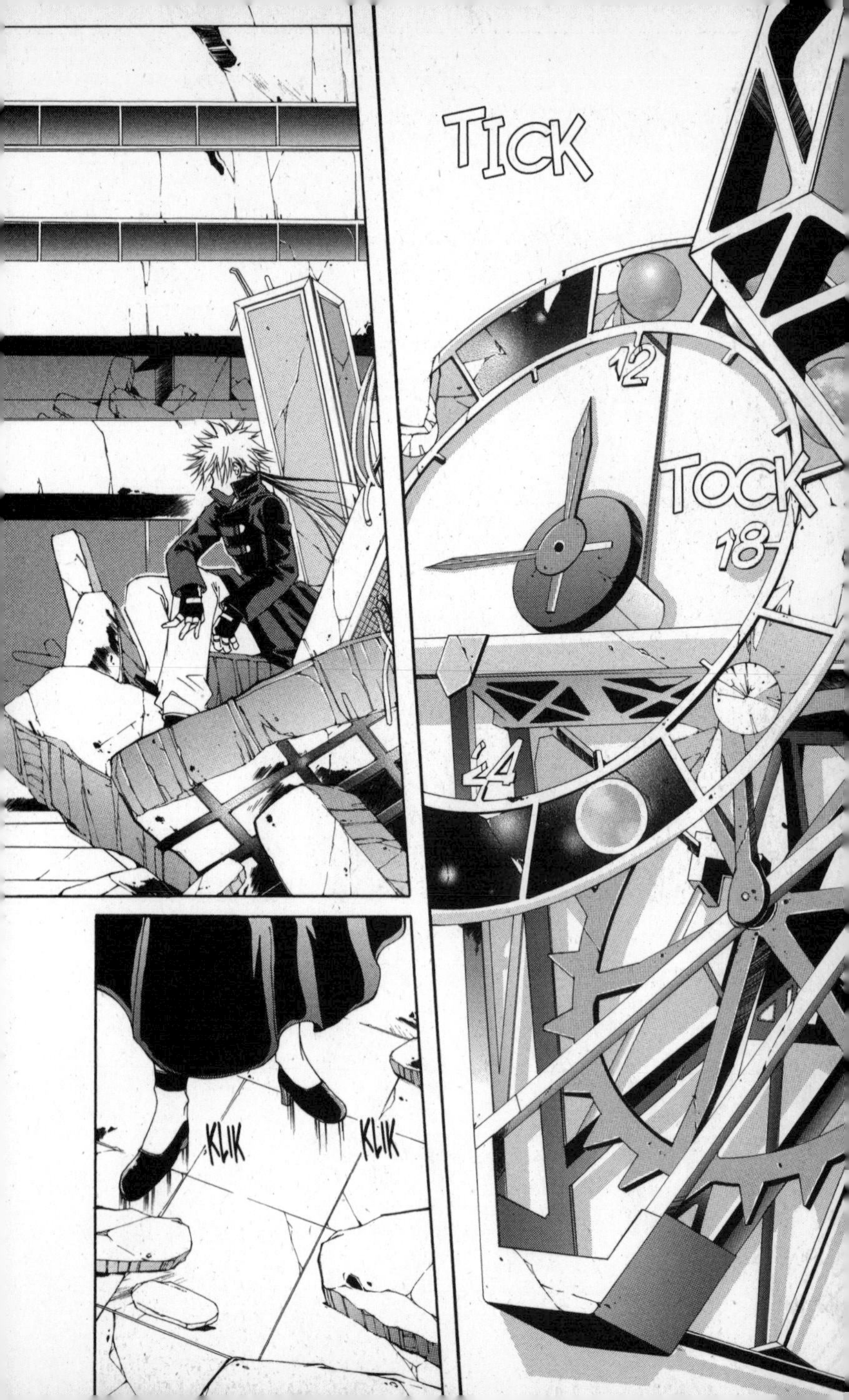
TICK
TOCK
KLIK
KLIK

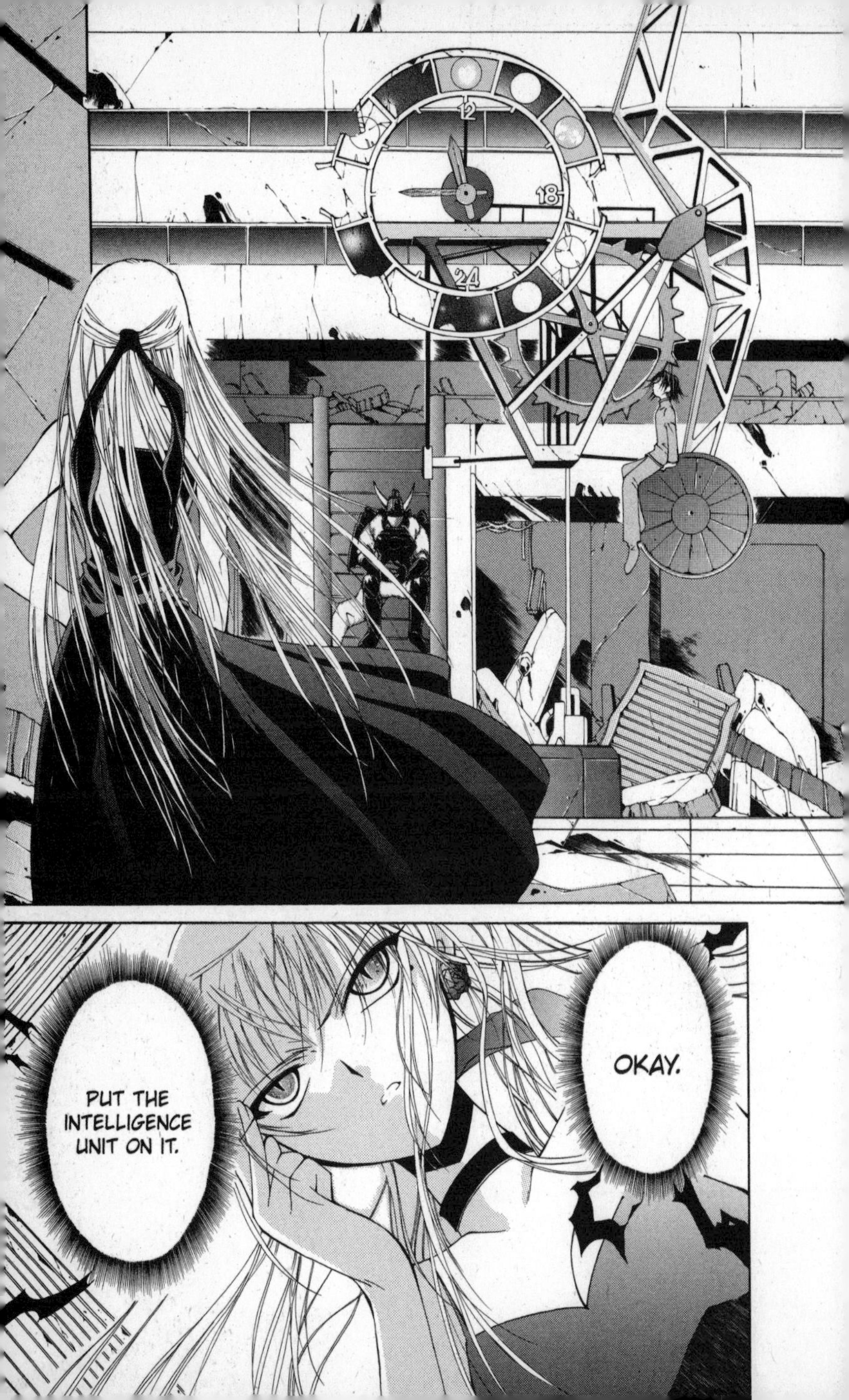
12
18
24
OKAY.
PUT THE INTELLIGENCE UNIT ON IT.

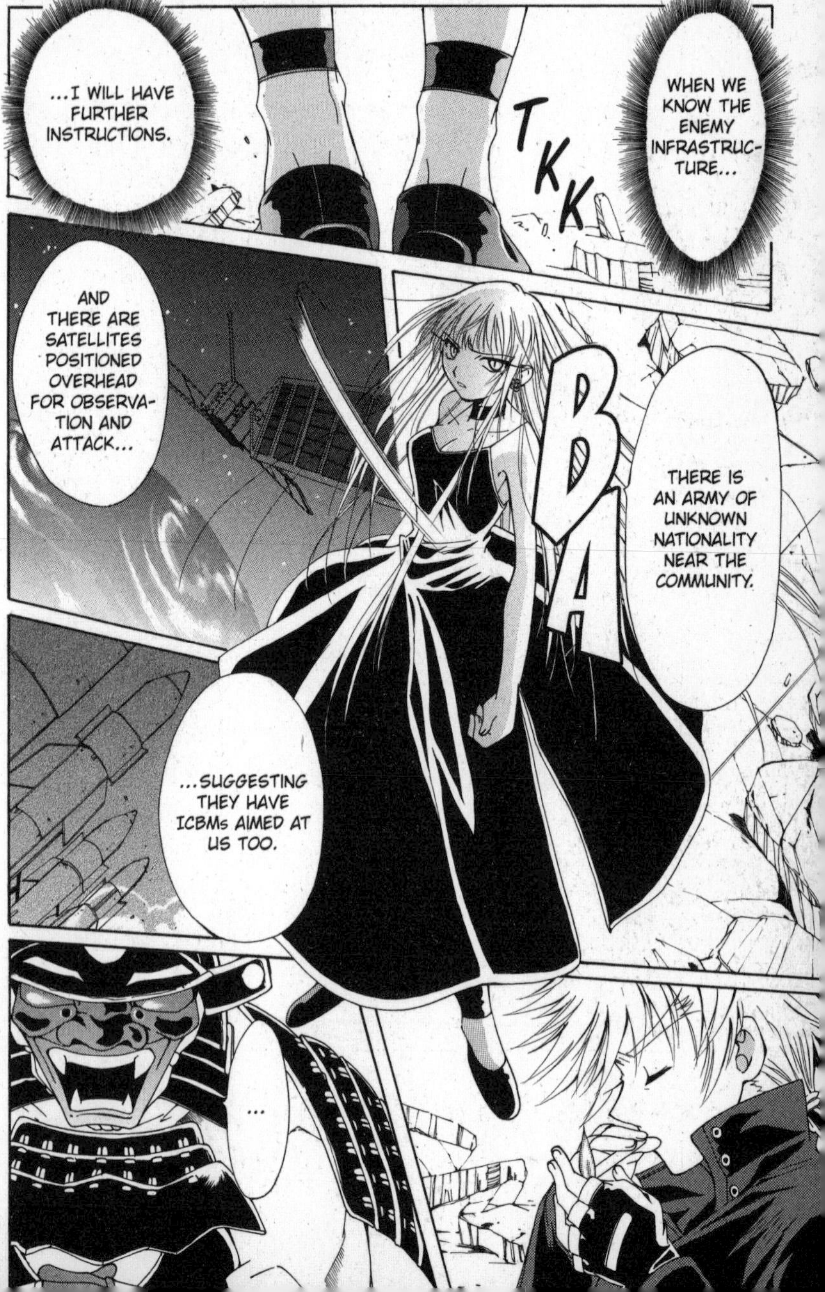
WHEN WE KNOW THE ENEMY INFRASTRUCTURE...
TKK
...I WILL HAVE FURTHER INSTRUCTIONS.
THERE IS AN ARMY OF UNKNOWN NATIONALITY NEAR THE COMMUNITY.
BA
AND THERE ARE SATELLITES POSITIONED OVERHEAD FOR OBSERVATION AND ATTACK...
...SUGGESTING THEY HAVE ICBMs AIMED AT US TOO.
...

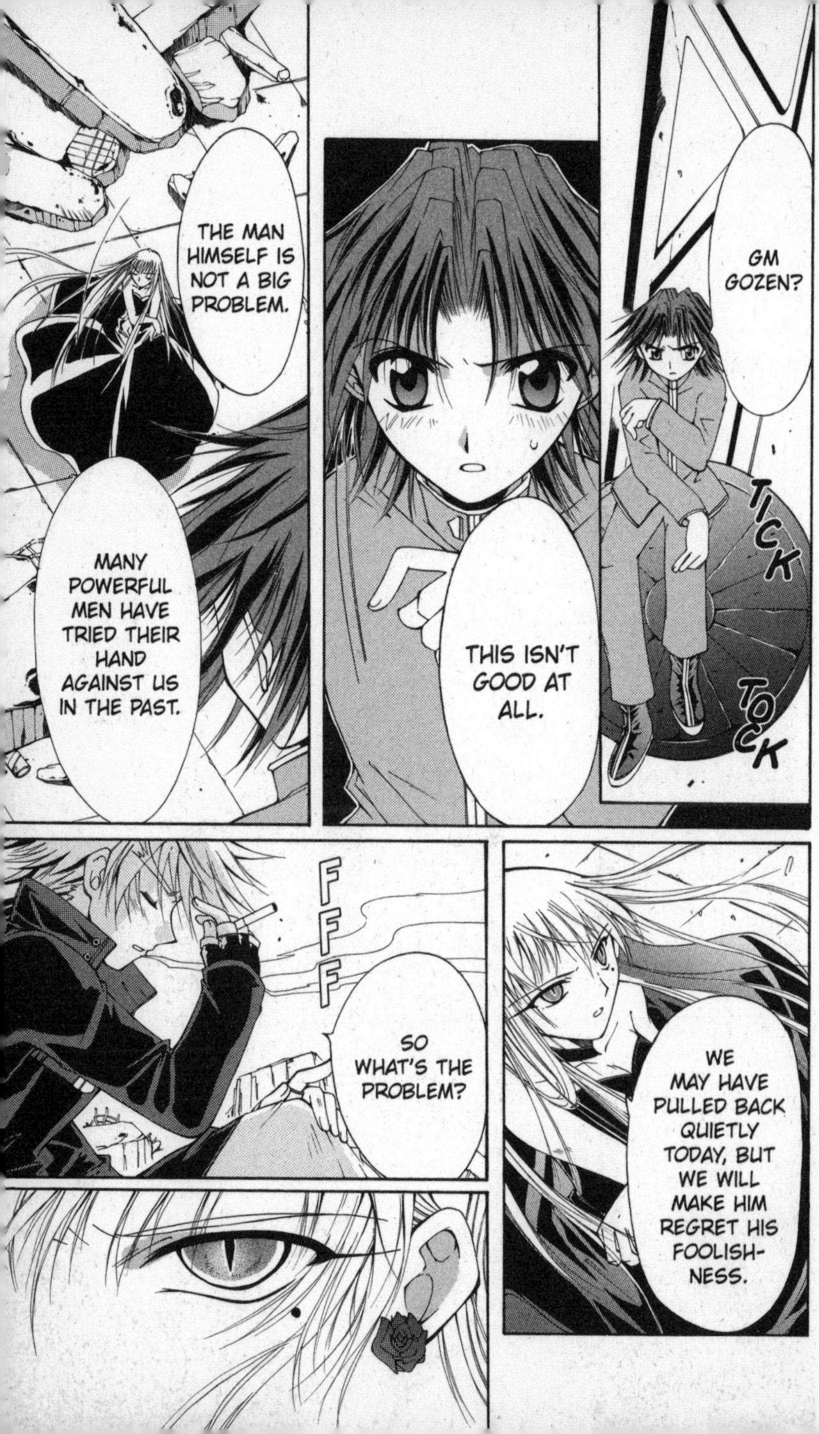
GM GOZEN?
TICK
TOCK
THIS ISN'T GOOD AT ALL.
THE MAN HIMSELF IS NOT A BIG PROBLEM.
MANY POWERFUL MEN HAVE TRIED THEIR HAND AGAINST US IN THE PAST.
WE MAY HAVE PULLED BACK QUIETLY TODAY, BUT WE WILL MAKE HIM REGRET HIS FOOLISH-NESS.
FFF
SO WHAT'S THE PROBLEM?

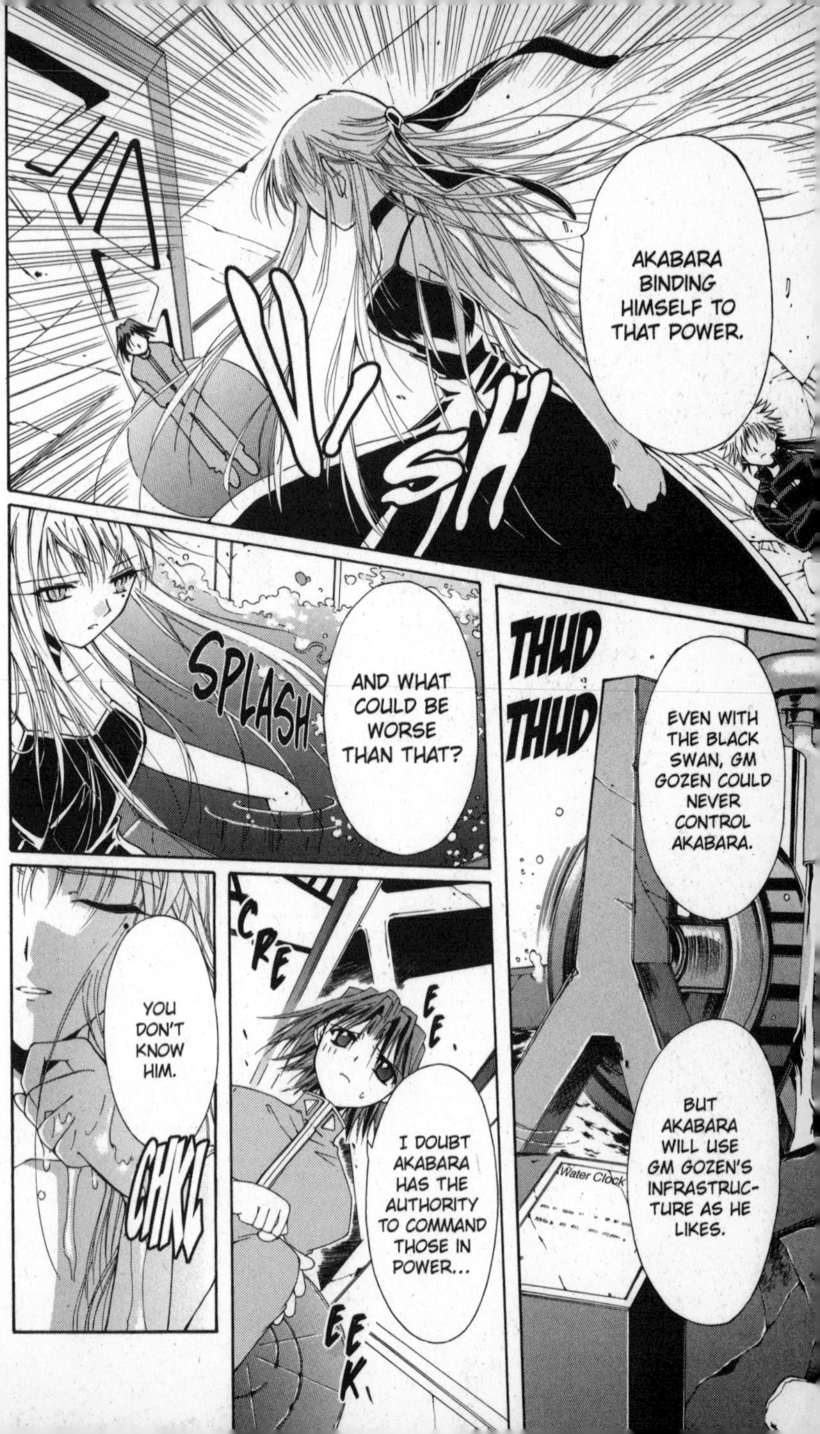
AKABARA BINDING HIMSELF TO THAT POWER.
VISH
THUD THUD
EVEN WITH THE BLACK SWAN, GM GOZEN COULD NEVER CONTROL AKABARA.
SPLASH
AND WHAT COULD BE WORSE THAN THAT?
BUT AKABARA WILL USE GM GOZEN'S INFRASTRUCTURE AS HE LIKES.
Water Clock
CREEEEK
I DOUBT AKABARA HAS THE AUTHORITY TO COMMAND THOSE IN POWER...
YOU DON'T KNOW HIM.
CHKL

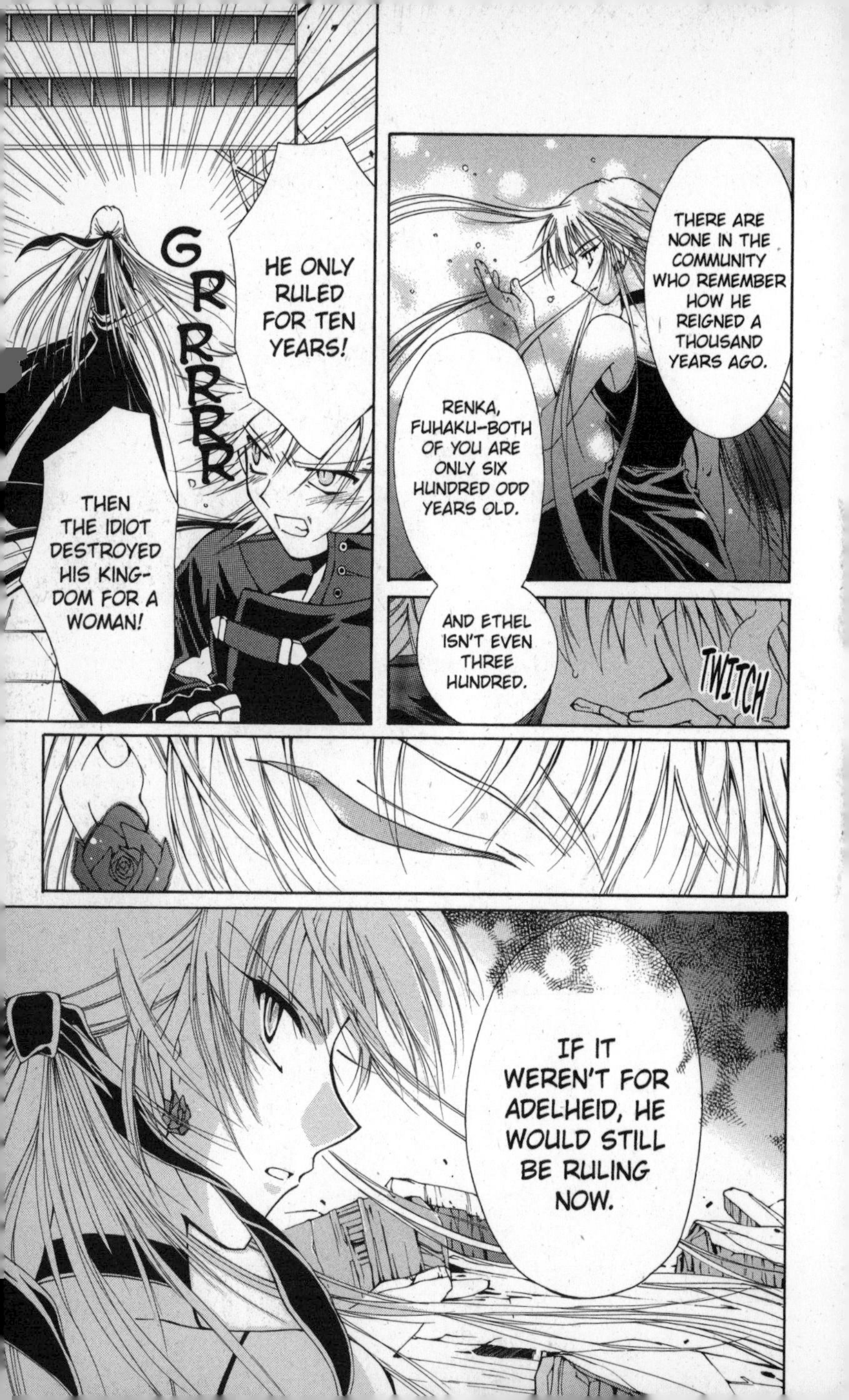
THERE ARE NONE IN THE COMMUNITY WHO REMEMBER HOW HE REIGNED A THOUSAND YEARS AGO.
RENKA, FUHAKU–BOTH OF YOU ARE ONLY SIX HUNDRED ODD YEARS OLD.
AND ETHEL ISN'T EVEN THREE HUNDRED.
TWITCH
HE ONLY RULED FOR TEN YEARS!
GRRRRR
THEN THE IDIOT DESTROYED HIS KING-DOM FOR A WOMAN!
IF IT WEREN'T FOR ADELHEID, HE WOULD STILL BE RULING NOW.

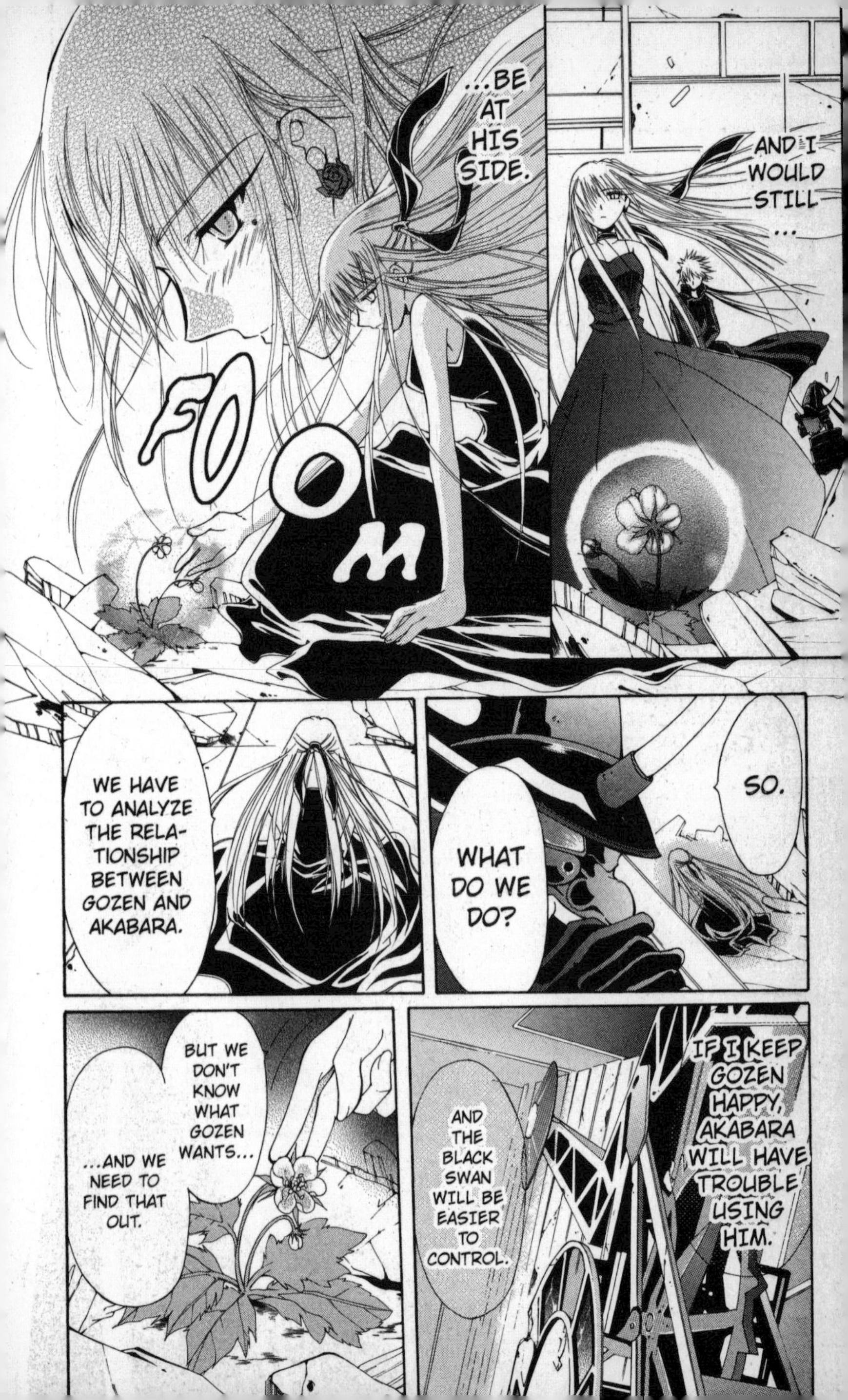
AND I WOULD STILL ...
...BE AT HIS SIDE.
FOOM
SO.
WHAT DO WE DO?
WE HAVE TO ANALYZE THE RELA-TIONSHIP BETWEEN GOZEN AND AKABARA.
IF I KEEP GOZEN HAPPY, AKABARA WILL HAVE TROUBLE USING HIM.
AND THE BLACK SWAN WILL BE EASIER TO CONTROL.
BUT WE DON'T KNOW WHAT GOZEN WANTS...
...AND WE NEED TO FIND THAT OUT.

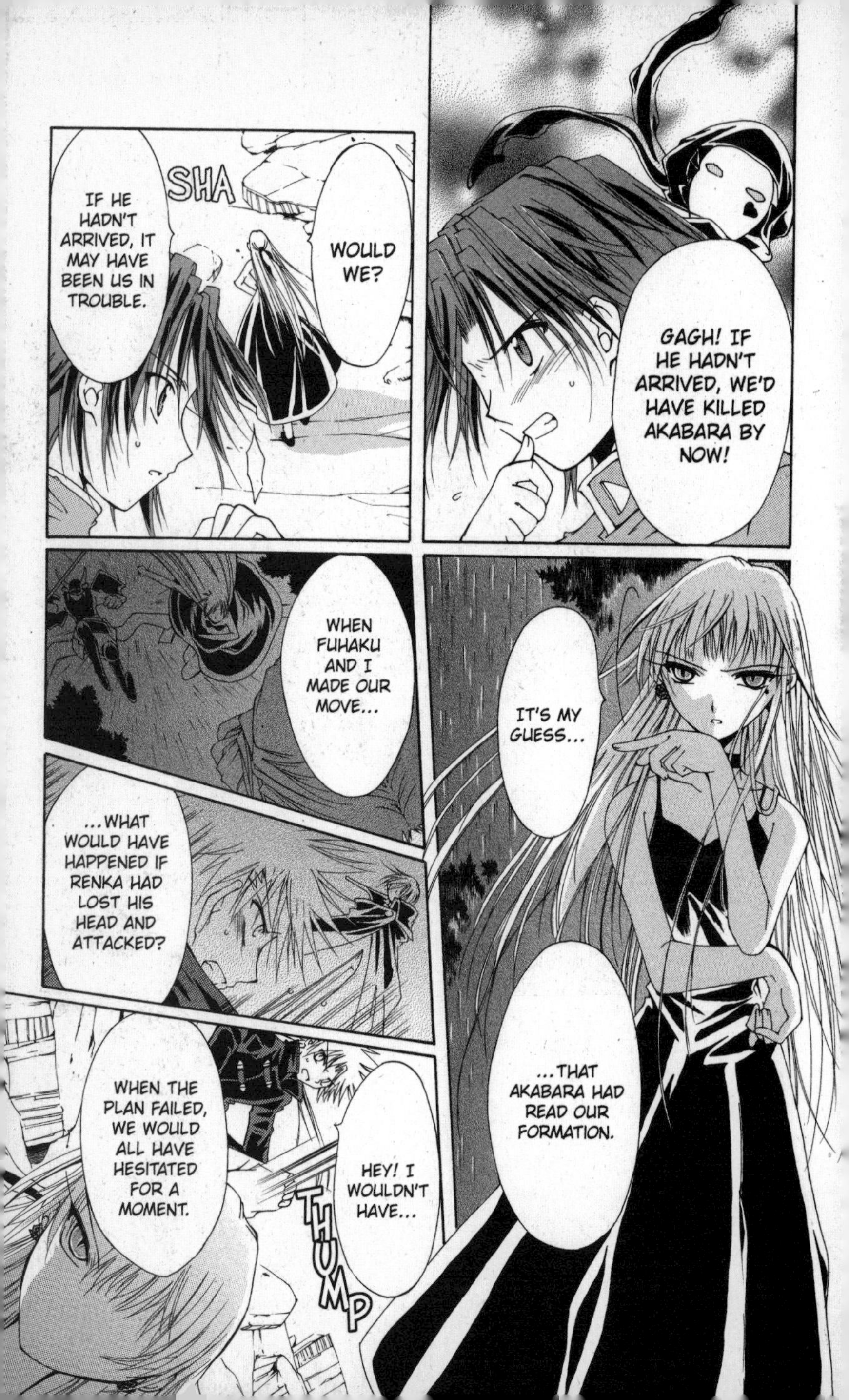
GAGH! IF HE HADN'T ARRIVED, WE'D HAVE KILLED AKABARA BY NOW!
WOULD WE?
SHA
IF HE HADN'T ARRIVED, IT MAY HAVE BEEN US IN TROUBLE.
IT'S MY GUESS...
...THAT AKABARA HAD READ OUR FORMATION.
WHEN FUHAKU AND I MADE OUR MOVE...
...WHAT WOULD HAVE HAPPENED IF RENKA HAD LOST HIS HEAD AND ATTACKED?
HEY! I WOULDN'T HAVE...
THUMP
WHEN THE PLAN FAILED, WE WOULD ALL HAVE HESITATED FOR A MOMENT.

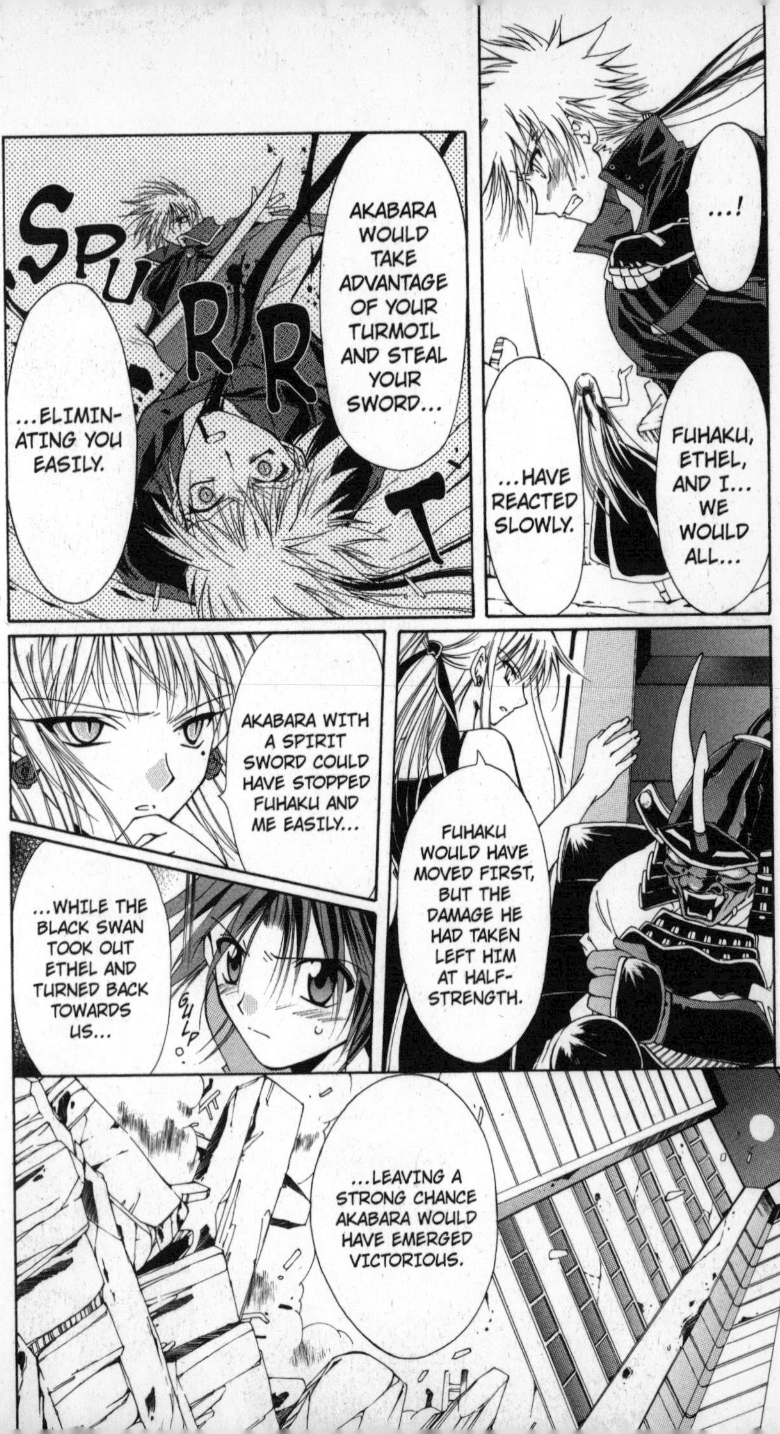
...!
FUHAKU, ETHEL, AND I... WE WOULD ALL...
...HAVE REACTED SLOWLY.
AKABARA WOULD TAKE ADVANTAGE OF YOUR TURMOIL AND STEAL YOUR SWORD...
SPURRRT
...ELIMIN-ATING YOU EASILY.
FUHAKU WOULD HAVE MOVED FIRST, BUT THE DAMAGE HE HAD TAKEN LEFT HIM AT HALF-STRENGTH.
AKABARA WITH A SPIRIT SWORD COULD HAVE STOPPED FUHAKU AND ME EASILY...
...WHILE THE BLACK SWAN TOOK OUT ETHEL AND TURNED BACK TOWARDS US...
GULP
...LEAVING A STRONG CHANCE AKABARA WOULD HAVE EMERGED VICTORIOUS.

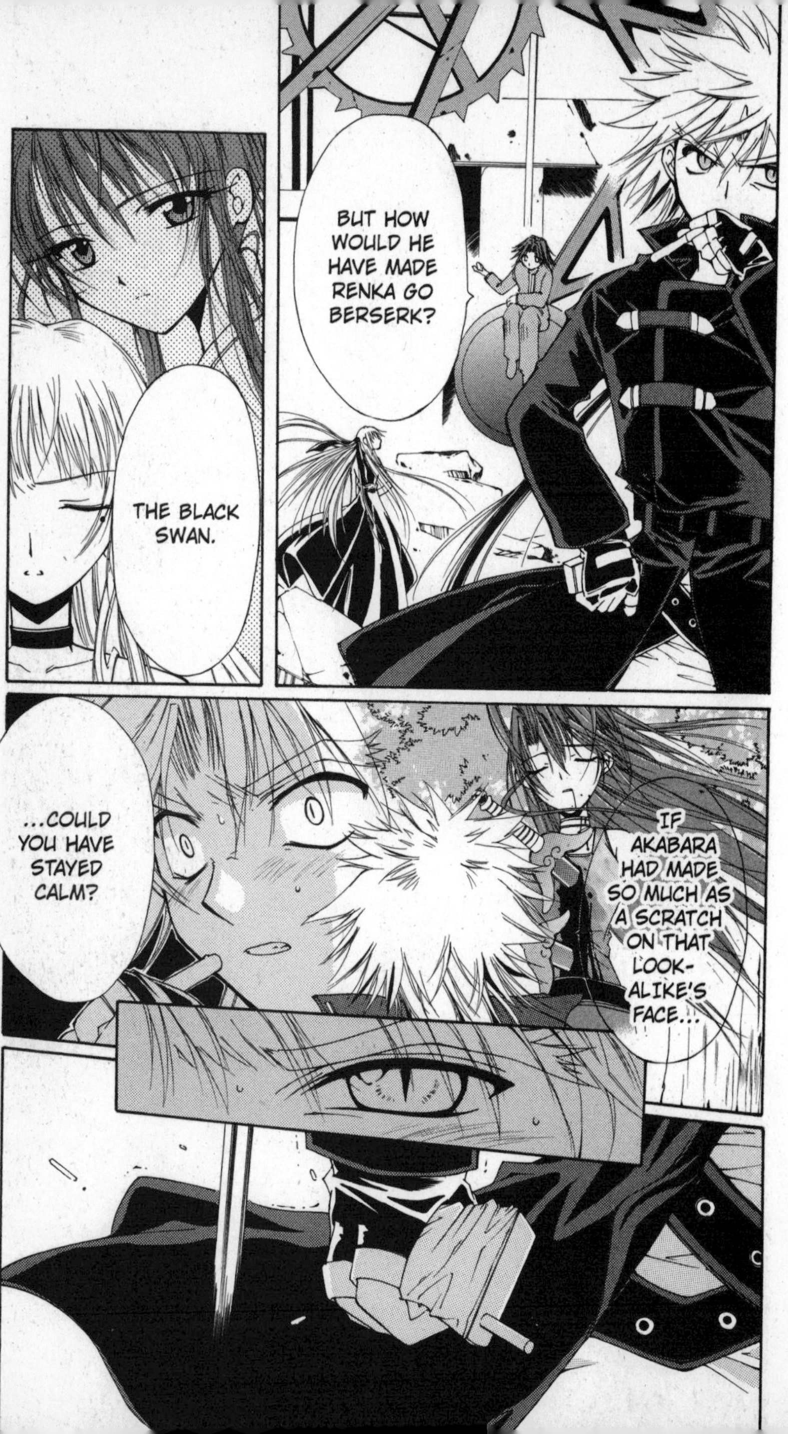
BUT HOW WOULD HE HAVE MADE RENKA GO BERSERK?
THE BLACK SWAN.
IF AKABARA HAD MADE SO MUCH AS A SCRATCH ON THAT LOOK-ALIKE'S FACE...
...COULD YOU HAVE STAYED CALM?

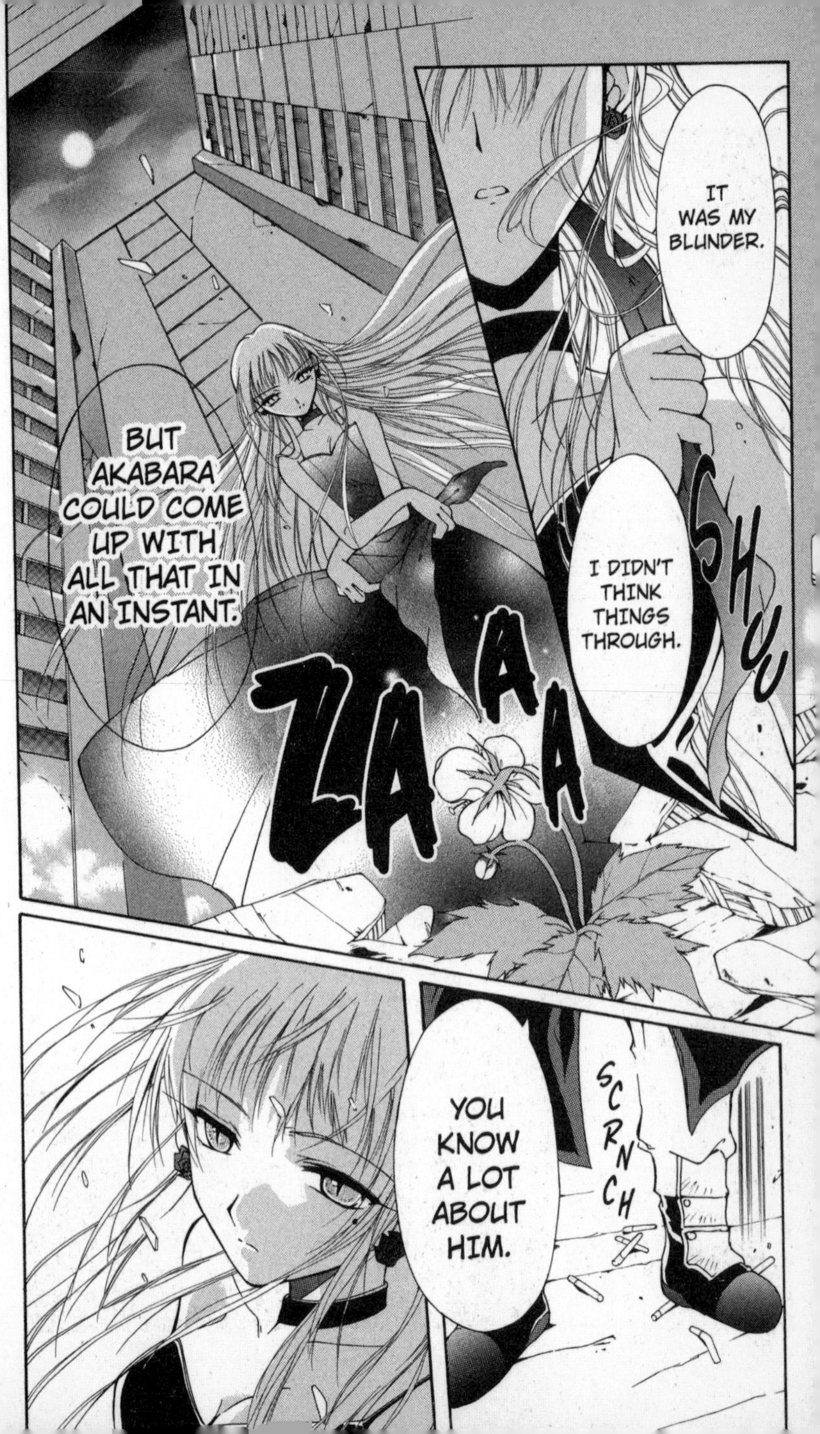
IT WAS MY BLUNDER.
SHUU
I DIDN'T THINK THINGS THROUGH.
BUT AKABARA COULD COME UP WITH ALL THAT IN AN INSTANT.
ZAAA
SCRNCH
YOU KNOW A LOT ABOUT HIM.

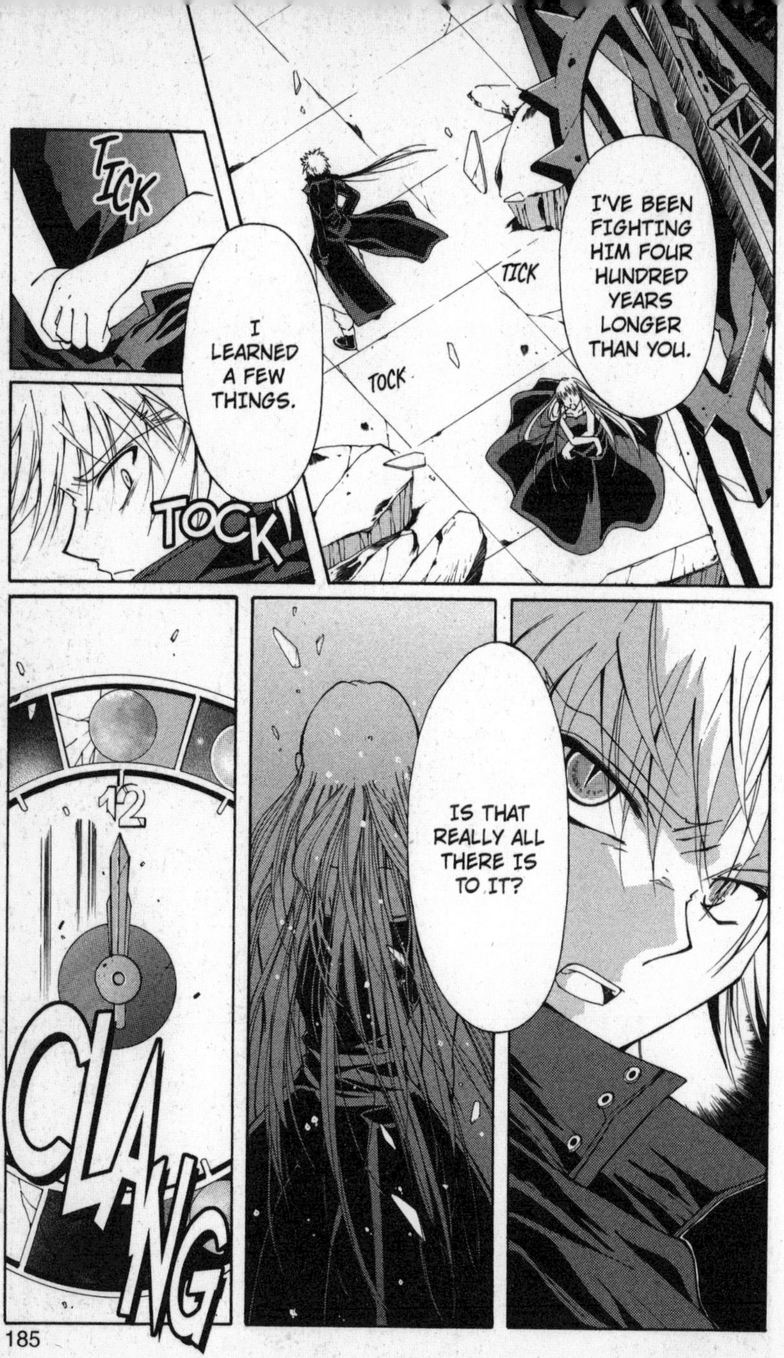
I'VE BEEN FIGHTING HIM FOUR HUNDRED YEARS LONGER THAN YOU.
TICK
TOCK
I LEARNED A FEW THINGS.
TICK
TOCK
IS THAT REALLY ALL THERE IS TO IT?
12
CLANG

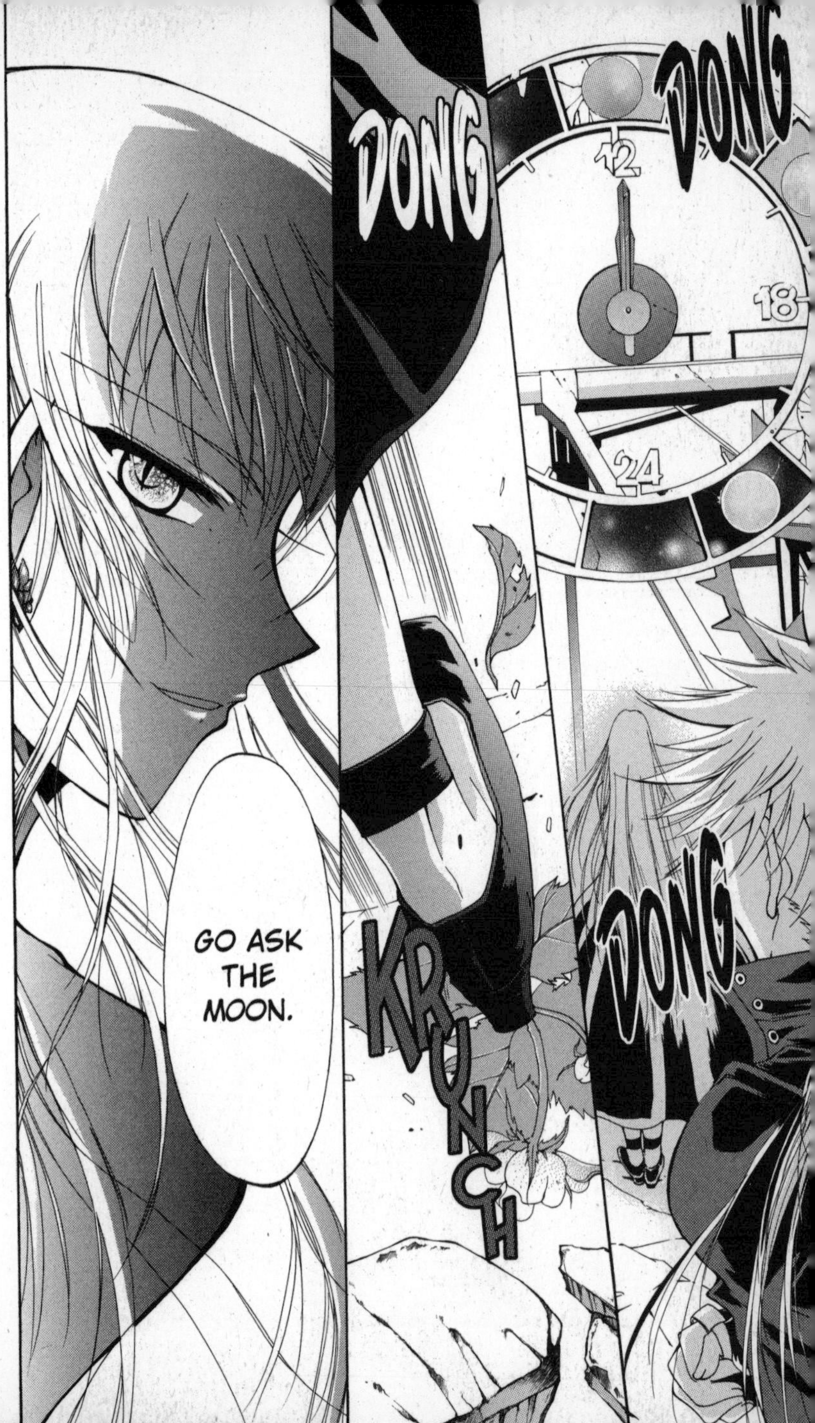
DONG
DONG
DONG
KRUNCH
GO ASK THE MOON.

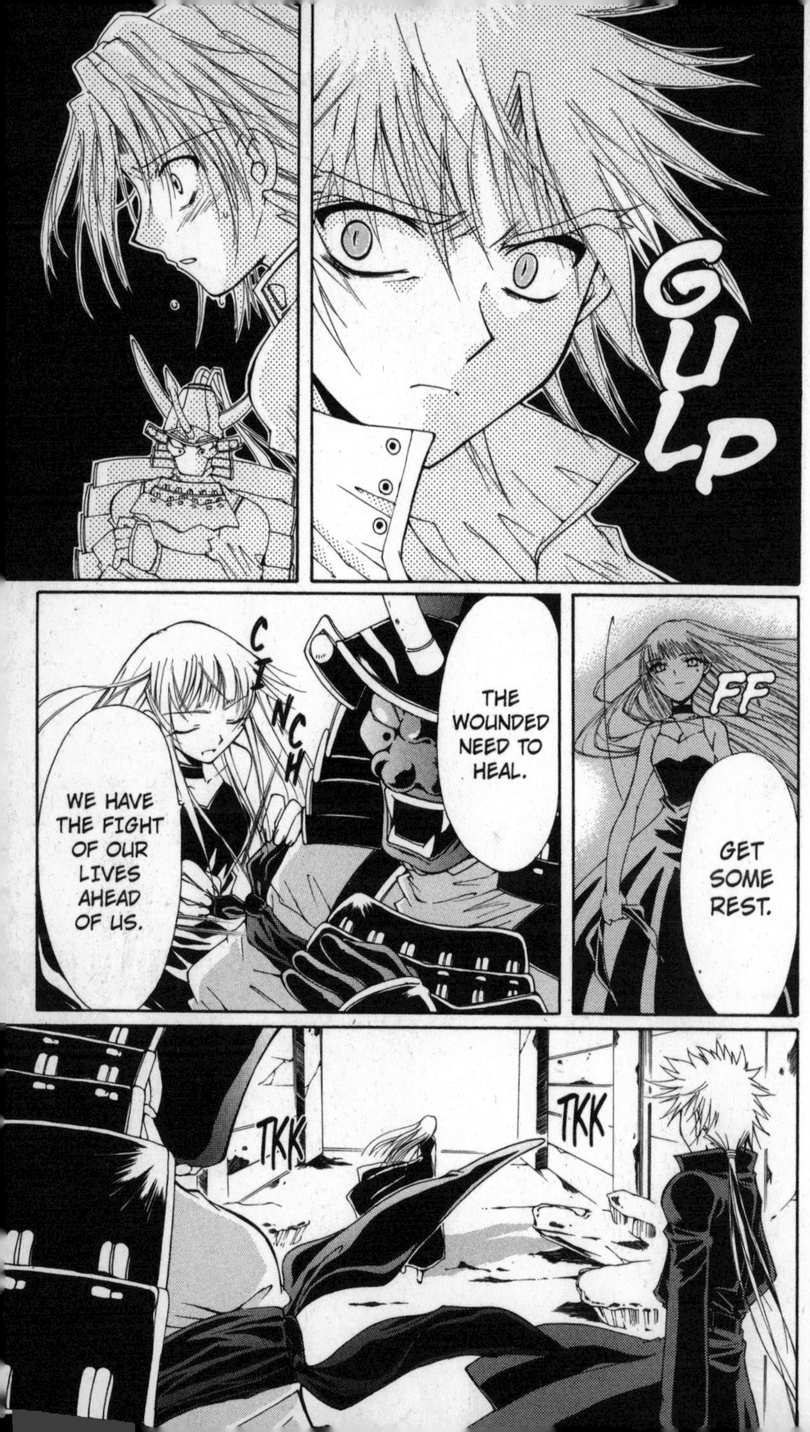
GULP
FF
GET SOME REST.
THE WOUNDED NEED TO HEAL.
CINCH
WE HAVE THE FIGHT OF OUR LIVES AHEAD OF US.
TKK
TKK

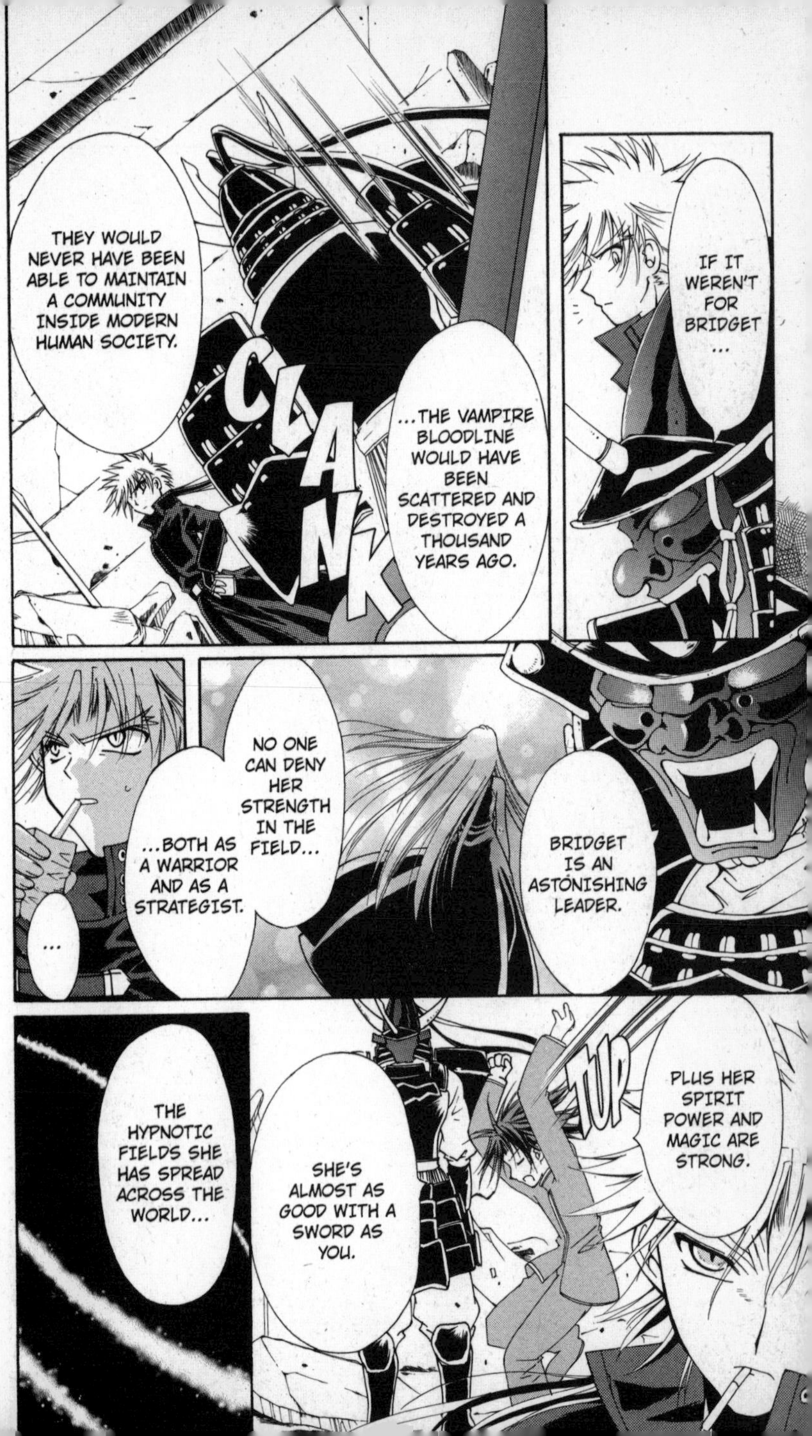
IF IT WEREN'T FOR BRIDGET ...
...THE VAMPIRE BLOODLINE WOULD HAVE BEEN SCATTERED AND DESTROYED A THOUSAND YEARS AGO.
CLANK
THEY WOULD NEVER HAVE BEEN ABLE TO MAINTAIN A COMMUNITY INSIDE MODERN HUMAN SOCIETY.
BRIDGET IS AN ASTONISHING LEADER.
NO ONE CAN DENY HER STRENGTH IN THE FIELD...
...BOTH AS A WARRIOR AND AS A STRATEGIST.
...
PLUS HER SPIRIT POWER AND MAGIC ARE STRONG.
TUP
SHE'S ALMOST AS GOOD WITH A SWORD AS YOU.
THE HYPNOTIC FIELDS SHE HAS SPREAD ACROSS THE WORLD...

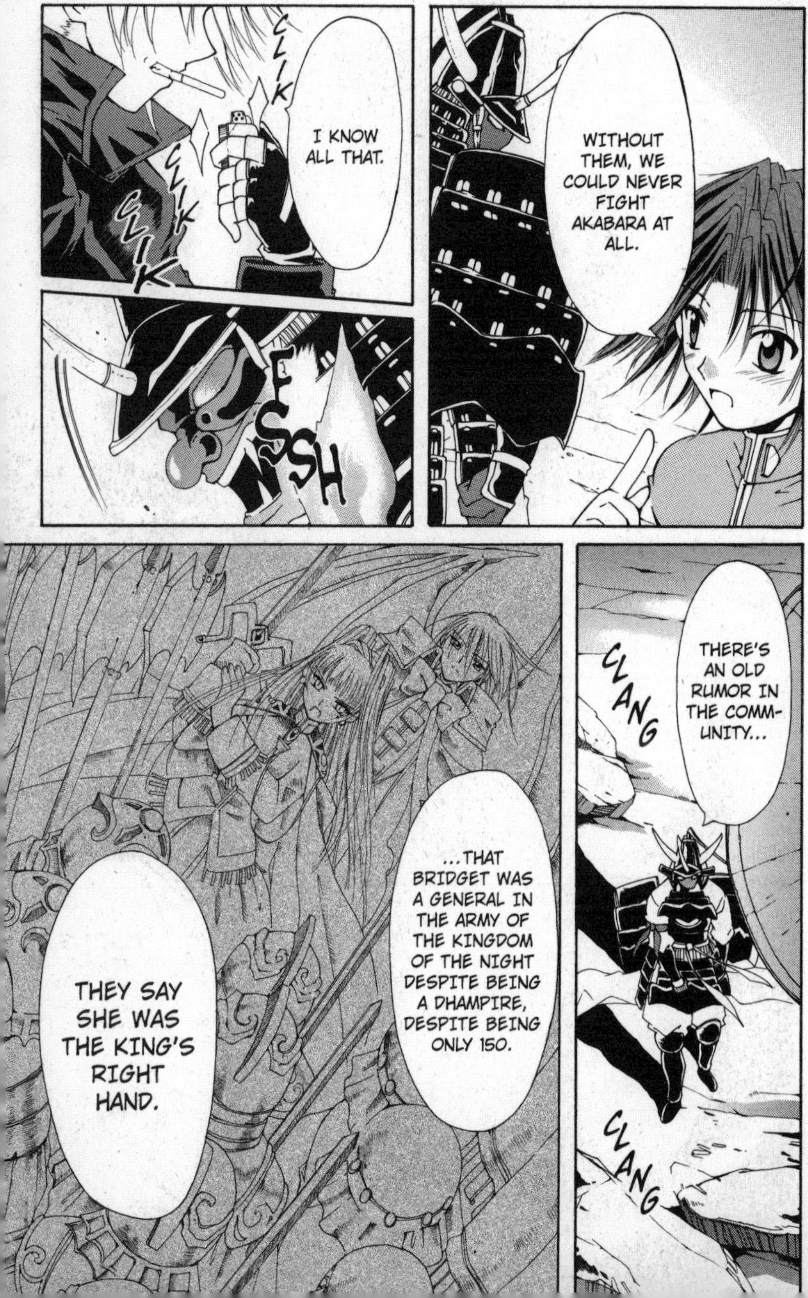
WITHOUT THEM, WE COULD NEVER FIGHT AKABARA AT ALL.
CLIK
CLIK
CLIK
I KNOW ALL THAT.
FSSH
CLANG
THERE'S AN OLD RUMOR IN THE COMMUNITY...
CLANG
...THAT BRIDGET WAS A GENERAL IN THE ARMY OF THE KINGDOM OF THE NIGHT DESPITE BEING A DHAMPIRE, DESPITE BEING ONLY 150.
THEY SAY SHE WAS THE KING'S RIGHT HAND.

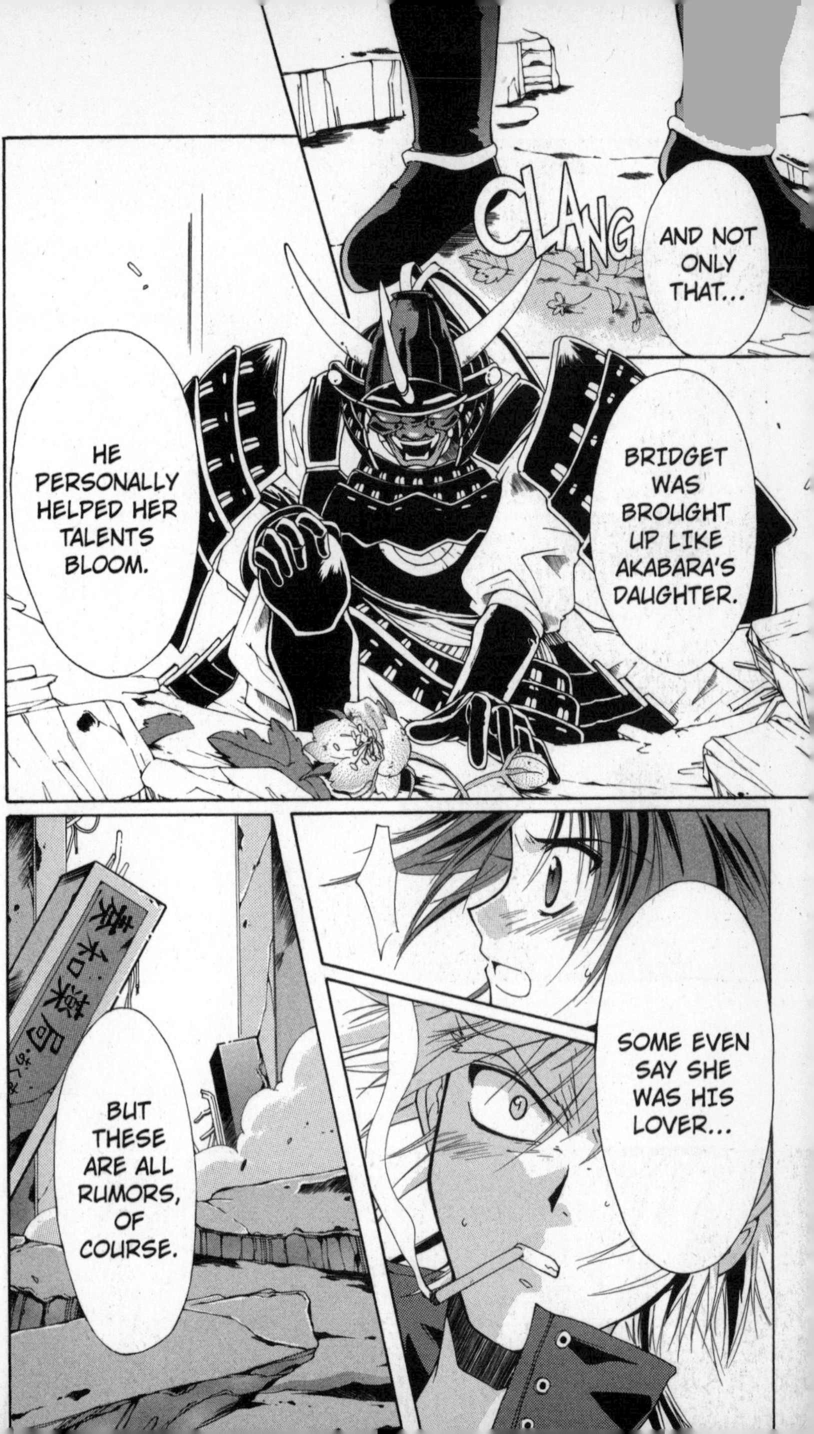
AND NOT ONLY THAT...
CLANG
BRIDGET WAS BROUGHT UP LIKE AKABARA'S DAUGHTER.
HE PERSONALLY HELPED HER TALENTS BLOOM.
SOME EVEN SAY SHE WAS HIS LOVER...
BUT THESE ARE ALL RUMORS, OF COURSE.

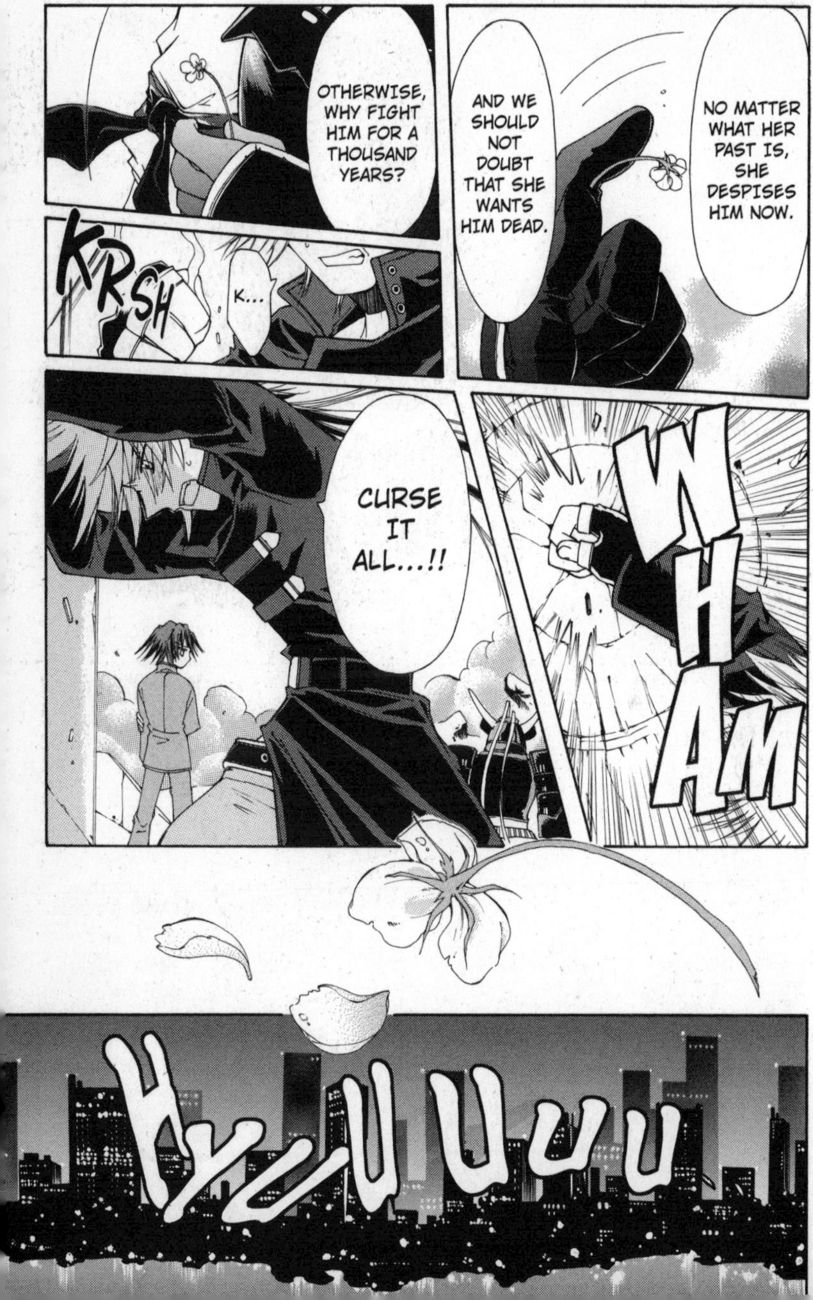
NO MATTER WHAT HER PAST IS, SHE DESPISES HIM NOW.
AND WE SHOULD NOT DOUBT THAT SHE WANTS HIM DEAD.
OTHERWISE, WHY FIGHT HIM FOR A THOUSAND YEARS?
KRSH
K...
WHAM
CURSE IT ALL...!!
HYUUUUUU

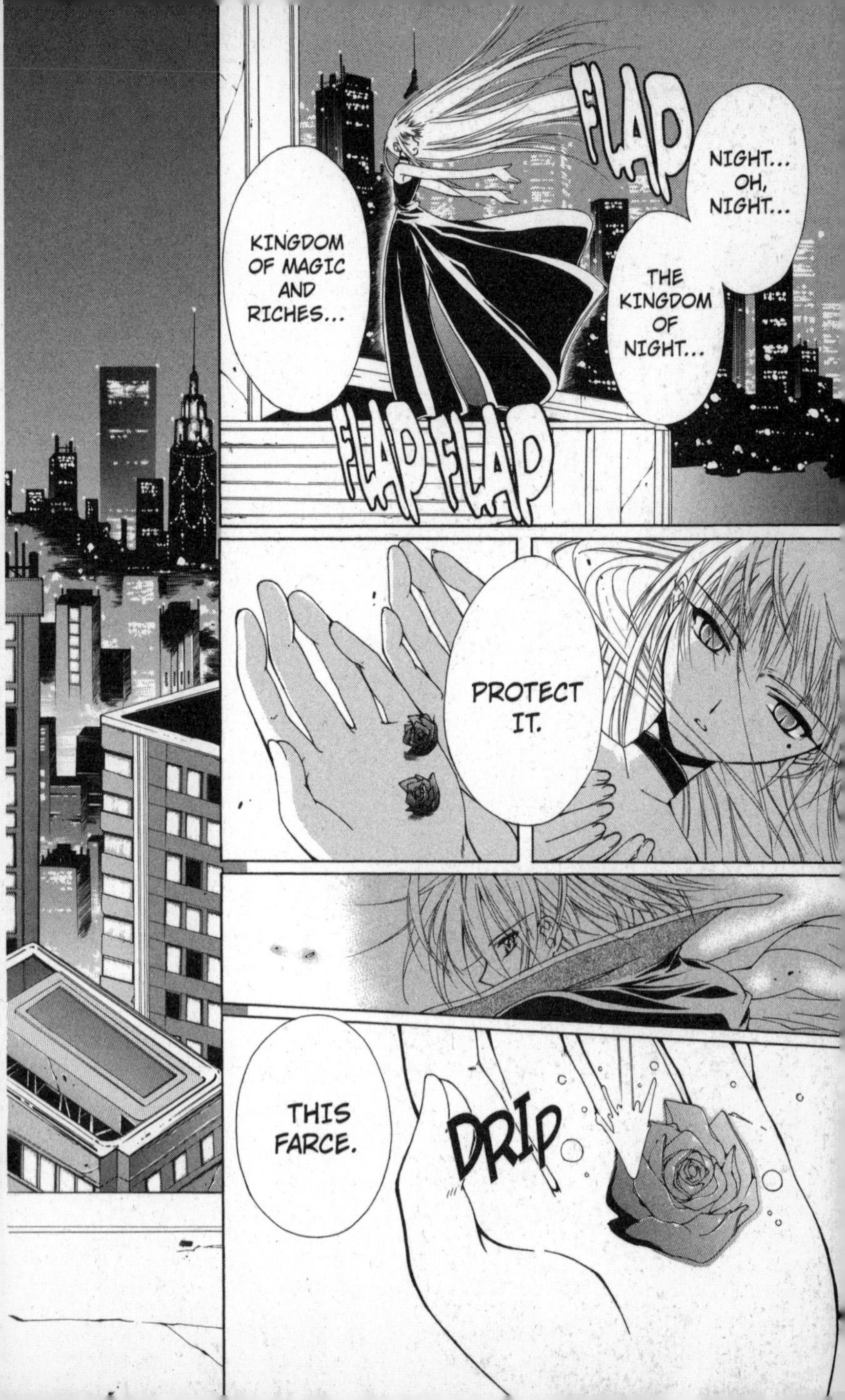
FLAP
NIGHT... OH, NIGHT...
THE KINGDOM OF NIGHT...
KINGDOM OF MAGIC AND RICHES...
FLAP FLAP
PROTECT IT.
DRIP
THIS FARCE.

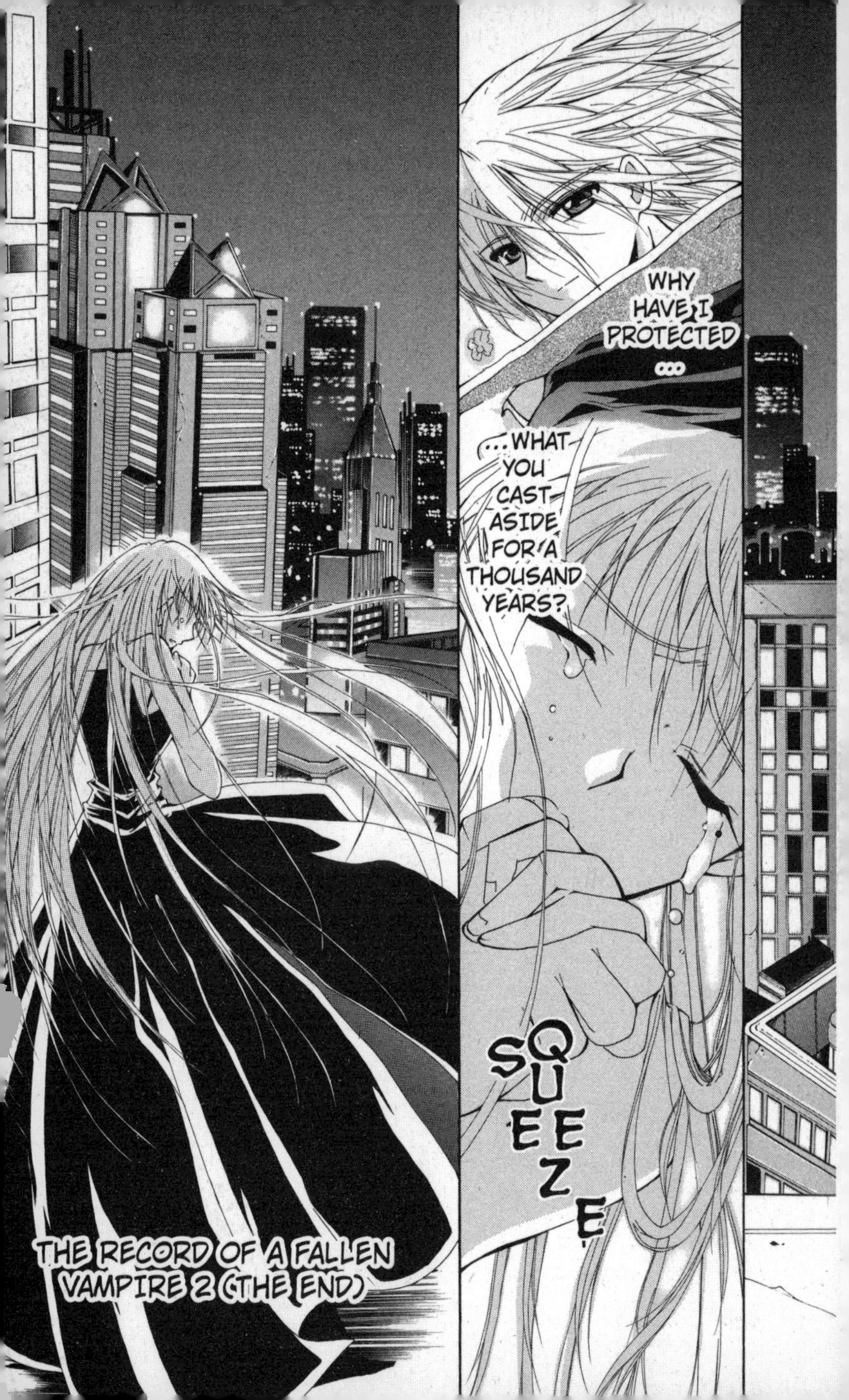
WHY HAVE I PROTECTED...
...WHAT YOU CAST ASIDE FOR A THOUSAND YEARS?
SQUEEZE
THE RECORD OF A FALLEN VAMPIRE 2 (THE END)

THE RECORD OF A FALLEN VAMPIRE, VOLUME 2!! AS THE STORY PROGRESSES, THE CHARACTERS' EMOTIONS ARE BECOMING CLEARER, MAKING THINGS MORE INTERESTING. AT THE SAME TIME, I'M STARTING TO WORRY ABOUT HOW TO MOVE THEM... LET ME DESCRIBE EACH OF THEM QUICKLY.

STRAUSS: HAVE TO DRAW HIM CAREFULLY. BEAUTY MAKES IT HARD.
KAYUKI: LOOKS LIKE SHE'S GOING TO RUIN HER LIFE.
LAETI: WORKS HARD AND EMBARRASSES HERSELF.
RENKA: TRY USING YOUR HEAD A LITTLE MORE. NEEDS A MODEL.
BRIDGET: LONG SUFFERING. HAIR IS A PAIN.
ETHEL: YOUR PERSONALITY IS JUST LIKE MINE.
FUHAKU: I TRY TO MAKE HIM LOOK RELIABLE. WHY IS HE IN ARMOR?
YUKI: SUCH A SHAME. *SNIFF.*
GM: ?
SEE YOU NEXT TIME!

ONCE AGAIN,
YURI KIMURA

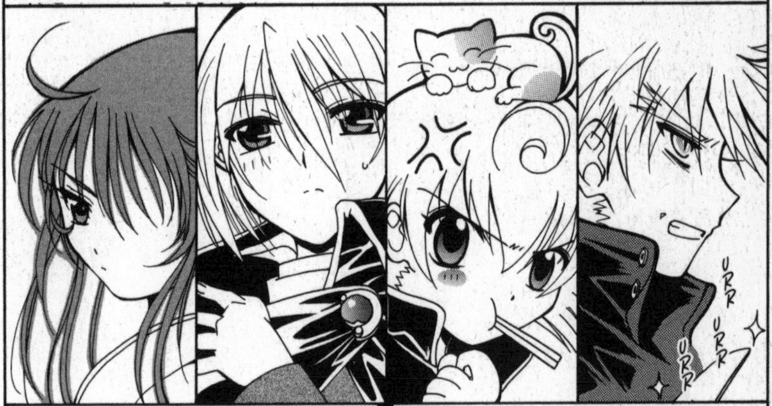
URR
URR
URR

THE RECORD OF A FALLEN VAMPIRE 2

SPECIAL THANKS

KASUMI AKIRA

EDITOR: NOBUAKI YUMURA

YUUKA NISHIOKA
SUDO

MARUKO ASAGATANI

AND ALL THE READERS!

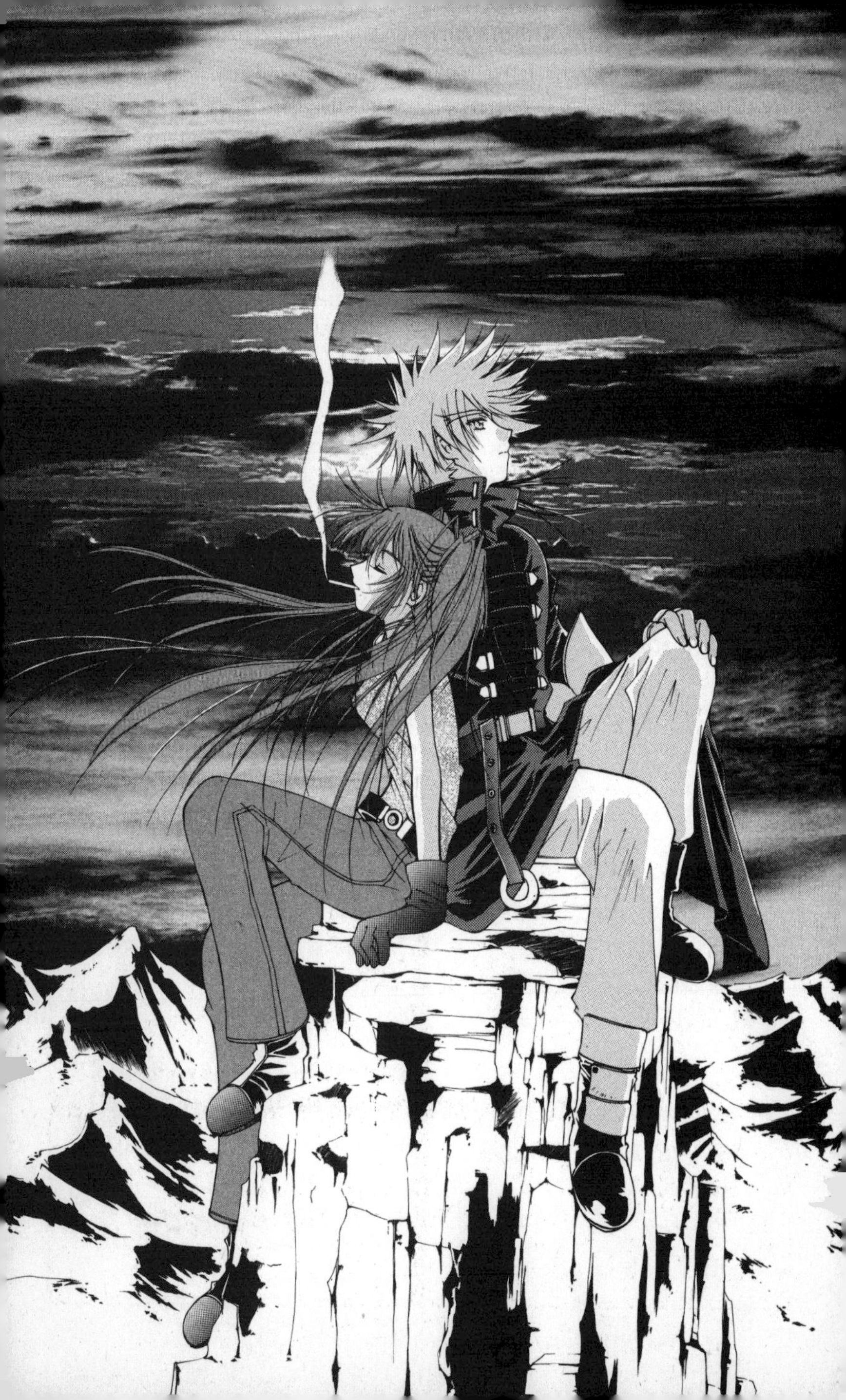

AUTHOR'S AFTERWORD

WHEN YOU HEAR THE WORDS "VAMPIRE STORY," WHAT SPRINGS TO MIND FIRST?

SINCE THIS STORY IS A MANGA, ODDS ARE YOU PROBABLY REACH OUT FROM THERE AND THINK OF OTHER MANGA, ANIME, GAMES, AND THE LIKE.

BUT WHAT ABOUT MOVIES? LIVE-ACTION MOVIES?

I'VE BEEN REFLECTING BACK ON THE MOVIES I WATCHED WITHOUT INTEREST BEFORE ACCEPTING THE JOB.

I'VE NEVER BEEN A BIG MOVIE BUFF, BUT THE FIRST MOVIE THAT SPRANG TO MIND WAS *KYUKETSUKI GOKEMIDORO.** I SNATCHED IT UP THE MOMENT THE DVD CAME OUT. I WATCHED IT AGAIN FROM THE BEGINNING THE MOMENT IT FINISHED.

OUT OF ALL THE POSSIBLE MOVIES I COULD HAVE THOUGHT OF, EVEN I THINK IT'S ODD THAT I THOUGHT OF THIS ONE, BUT IT HAS QUITE A REPUTATION AMONG THAT CROWD. IT COULD EVEN BE CALLED A HIT (BUT I DOUBT WE'LL EVER SEE IT BROADCAST IN PRIME TIME).

THERE'S A STRONG POSSIBILITY IT UNCONSCIOUSLY INFLUENCED ME WHEN I WAS CREATING THIS BOOK. ANYTHING I LIKE ENDS UP BEING A PART OF MY MIND.

IF YOU HAVE TIME, I RECOMMEND TRACKING DOWN A COPY. IT'S A REALLY GOOD MOVIE.

* *KYUKETSUKI GOKEMIDORO*, 1979: RELEASED IN THE U.S. AS *BODY SNATCHER FROM HELL* BUT IS ALSO KNOWN AS *GOKE THE VAMPIRE*.

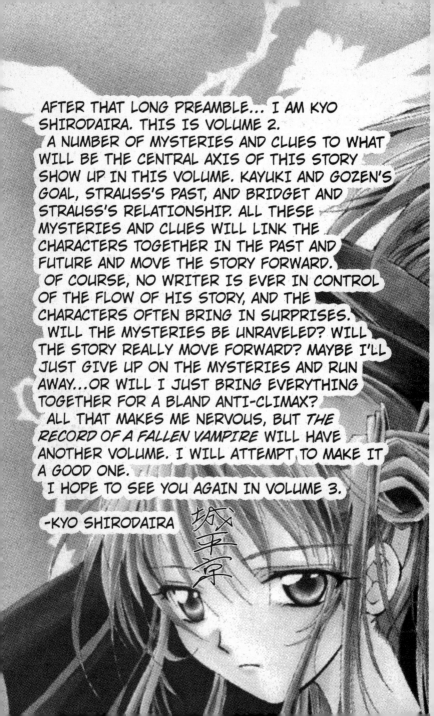

AFTER THAT LONG PREAMBLE... I AM KYO SHIRODAIRA. THIS IS VOLUME 2.

A NUMBER OF MYSTERIES AND CLUES TO WHAT WILL BE THE CENTRAL AXIS OF THIS STORY SHOW UP IN THIS VOLUME. KAYUKI AND GOZEN'S GOAL, STRAUSS'S PAST, AND BRIDGET AND STRAUSS'S RELATIONSHIP. ALL THESE MYSTERIES AND CLUES WILL LINK THE CHARACTERS TOGETHER IN THE PAST AND FUTURE AND MOVE THE STORY FORWARD.

OF COURSE, NO WRITER IS EVER IN CONTROL OF THE FLOW OF HIS STORY, AND THE CHARACTERS OFTEN BRING IN SURPRISES.

WILL THE MYSTERIES BE UNRAVELED? WILL THE STORY REALLY MOVE FORWARD? MAYBE I'LL JUST GIVE UP ON THE MYSTERIES AND RUN AWAY...OR WILL I JUST BRING EVERYTHING TOGETHER FOR A BLAND ANTI-CLIMAX?

ALL THAT MAKES ME NERVOUS, BUT *THE RECORD OF A FALLEN VAMPIRE* WILL HAVE ANOTHER VOLUME. I WILL ATTEMPT TO MAKE IT A GOOD ONE.

I HOPE TO SEE YOU AGAIN IN VOLUME 3.

-KYO SHIRODAIRA

THE RECORD OF A FALLEN VAMPIRE

VOL. 2
VIZ MEDIA EDITION

STORY BY: KYO SHIRODAIRA ART BY: YURI KIMURA

Translation & Adaptation...**Andrew Cunningham**
Touch-up Art & Lettering...**John Hunt**
Cover Design...**Courtney Utt**
Interior Design...**Izumi Hirayama**
Editor...**Amy Yu**

Editor in Chief, Books...**Alvin Lu**
Editor in Chief, Magazines...**Marc Weidenbaum**
VP of Publishing Licensing...**Rika Inouye**
VP of Sales...**Gonzalo Ferreyra**
Sr. VP of Marketing...**Liza Coppola**
Publisher...**Hyoe Narita**

Printed in the U.S.A.

Published by VIZ Media, LLC
P.O. Box 77010
San Francisco, CA 94107

10 9 8 7 6 5 4 3 2 1
First printing, August 2008

PARENTAL ADVISORY
THE RECORD OF A FALLEN VAMPIRE is rated T for Teen and is recommended for ages 13 and up. Contains strong language and fantasy violence.

RATED T FOR TEEN

ratings.viz.com